Interpersonal Grammar

This pioneering volume lays out a set of methodological principles to guide the description of interpersonal grammar in different languages. It compares interpersonal systems and structures across a range of world languages, showing how discourse, interpersonal relationships between the speakers and the purpose of their communication all play a role in shaping the grammatical structures used in interaction. Following an introduction setting out these principles, each chapter focuses on a particular language – Khorchin Mongolian, Mandarin, Tagalog, Pitjantjatjara, Spanish, Brazilian Portuguese, British Sign Language and Scottish Gaelic – and explores MOOD, POLARITY, TAGGING, VOCATION, ASSESSMENT and COMMENT systems. The book provides a model for functional grammatical description that can be used to inform work on system and structure across languages as a foundation for functional language typology.

J. R. MARTIN is Professor of Linguistics at the University of Sydney. His research interests include systemic functional theory, functional grammar, discourse semantics, register, genre and multimodality, focusing on English, Tagalog, Spanish and Korean. He was elected a fellow of the Australian Academy of the Humanities in 1998, and was head of its Linguistics Section from 2010 to 2012; he was awarded a Centenary Medal for his services to linguistics and philology in 2003. In April 2014 Shanghai Jiao Tong University opened its Martin Centre for Appliable Linguistics, appointing Professor Martin as director. From 2017 to 2019 he was Visiting Professor in the Department of Language Sciences at the Pontificia Universidad Católica de Chile.

BEATRIZ QUIROZ is Associate Professor in Language Sciences at the Pontificia Universidad Católica de Chile. Her current research, informed by systemic functional linguistics (SFL), focuses on an integrated description of clause systems in Chilean Spanish, with a special emphasis on system-structure relations. Her broader interests include language description, language typology and the various interactions between grammar and discourse.

GIACOMO FIGUEREDO is Associate Professor in Linguistics at the Federal University of Ouro Preto, Brazil, where he is an investigator in the Laboratory of Language Experimentation, carrying out empirical experimental research on language description, modelling and generation. His interests include language description, multilingual studies, language typology and translation.

Interpersonal Grammar

Systemic Functional Linguistic Theory and Description

Edited by

J. R. Martin
University of Sydney
Pontificia Universidad Católica de Chile

Beatriz Quiroz
Pontificia Universidad Católica de Chile

Giacomo Figueredo
Federal University of Ouro Preto, Brazil

CAMBRIDGE
UNIVERSITY PRESS

University Printing House, Cambridge CB2 8BS, United Kingdom

One Liberty Plaza, 20th Floor, New York, NY 10006, USA

477 Williamstown Road, Port Melbourne, VIC 3207, Australia

314–321, 3rd Floor, Plot 3, Splendor Forum, Jasola District Centre, New Delhi – 110025, India

79 Anson Road, #06–04/06, Singapore 079906

Cambridge University Press is part of the University of Cambridge.

It furthers the University's mission by disseminating knowledge in the pursuit of education, learning, and research at the highest international levels of excellence.

www.cambridge.org
Information on this title: www.cambridge.org/9781108493796
DOI: 10.1017/9781108663120

© Cambridge University Press 2021

This publication is in copyright. Subject to statutory exception and to the provisions of relevant collective licensing agreements, no reproduction of any part may take place without the written permission of Cambridge University Press.

First published 2021

A catalogue record for this publication is available from the British Library.

Library of Congress Cataloging-in-Publication Data
Names: Martin, J. R., 1950– editor. | Quiroz, Beatriz, 1976– editor. | Figueredo, Giacomo, editor.
Title: Interpersonal grammar : systemic functional linguistic theory and description / edited by J.R. Martin, University of Sydney, Pontificia Universidad Católica de Chile; Beatriz Quiroz, Pontificia Universidad Catolica de Chile; Giacomo Figueredo, Federal University of Ouro Preto, Brazil.
Description: Cambridge; New York, NY : Cambridge University Press, 2021. | Includes bibliographical references and index.
Identifiers: LCCN 2020046958 (print) | LCCN 2020046959 (ebook) | ISBN 9781108493796 (hardback) | ISBN 9781108663120 (ebook)
Subjects: LCSH: Functionalism (Linguistics) | Systemic grammar. | Grammar, Comparative and general. | Interpersonal communication.
Classification: LCC P147 .I58 2021 (print) | LCC P147 (ebook) | DDC 410.1/833–dc23
LC record available at https://lccn.loc.gov/2020046958
LC ebook record available at https://lccn.loc.gov/2020046959

ISBN 978-1-108-49379-6 Hardback

Cambridge University Press has no responsibility for the persistence or accuracy of URLs for external or third-party internet websites referred to in this publication and does not guarantee that any content on such websites is, or will remain, accurate or appropriate.

Contents

List of Figures		*page* vi
List of Tables		viii
List of Contributors		ix

1. Introduction: Theory and Description in Interpersonal Grammar across Languages — 1
   J. R. MARTIN, BEATRIZ QUIROZ AND GIACOMO FIGUEREDO

2. Interpersonal Grammar in Spanish — 34
   BEATRIZ QUIROZ

3. Interpersonal Grammar in Khorchin Mongolian — 64
   DONGBING ZHANG

4. Interpersonal Grammar in Mandarin — 96
   PIN WANG

5. Interpersonal Grammar in Tagalog: ASSESSMENT Systems — 130
   J. R. MARTIN AND PRISCILLA CRUZ

6. Interpersonal Grammar in Pitjantjatjara — 160
   DAVID ROSE

7. Interpersonal Grammar in Brazilian Portuguese — 191
   GIACOMO FIGUEREDO

8. Interpersonal Grammar in British Sign Language — 227
   LUKE A. RUDGE

9. Interpersonal Grammar in Scottish Gaelic — 257
   TOM BARTLETT

Index — 285

Figures

1.1	Some general English MOOD systems	page 5
1.2	General English MOOD and MODALITY systems	6
1.3	Further general English MOOD and MODALITY systems	8
1.4	Cross-classification of clauses by MOOD and TRANSITIVITY systems	12
1.5	Language strata	14
1.6	Basic NEGOTIATION systems (exchange rank)	16
1.7	ENGAGEMENT systems in English	20
1.8	Tenor relations (status and contact)	22
1.9	A stratified model of language in context	22
2.1	Basic SPEECH FUNCTION network in semantics	36
2.2	Propositions and proposals in relation to SPEECH FUNCTION choices	37
2.3	English MOOD network, with examples taken from Halliday	38
2.4	A MOOD system of Spanish	58
2.5	Basic negotiatory structures in three Romance languages	59
3.1	NEGOTIATION in Khorchin Mongolian	73
3.2	MOOD and verbal Predicator in Khorchin Mongolian	77
3.3	Types of indicative clause in Khorchin Mongolian	81
4.1	Trinocular perspective on interpersonal grammar	97
4.2	Primary contrast in MOOD	103
4.3	Imperative clauses in Mandarin	108
4.4	Interrogative clauses in Mandarin	121
4.5	Mandarin MOOD system (oriented to NEGOTIATION)	122
4.6	Complementary Mandarin MOOD system (oriented to NEGOTIATION and ENGAGEMENT)	123
5.1	Retrospective ASSESSMENT resources in Tagalog	146
5.2	Prospective ASSESSMENT resources in Tagalog	147
5.3	ENGAGEMENT systems in English (based on White, 2012, p. 56)	148
6.1	Tone contour graph of exchange pair (1)	161
6.2	Pitjantjatjara TONE system	163

6.3	IMPERATIVE MOOD system	170
6.4	INDICATIVE MOOD system	174
7.1	INTERLOCUTOR TYPE	195
7.2	Basic options for the system of NEGOTIATION in BP	195
7.3	The structure of exchange 3 from Text 1	198
7.4	Basic SPEECH FUNCTION options in BP	198
7.5	Initiating MOOD TYPE from above in BP with congruent realisations	204
7.6	The system of IMPERATIVE TYPE in BP	208
7.7	The system of INDICATIVE TYPE in BP	210
7.8	The system of MODAL RESPONSIBILITY in BP	215
7.9	MODAL RESPONSIBILITY, PRESUMPTION, PERSON and POLITENESS	217
7.10	System network of ASSESSMENT in BP	218
7.11	The system of MOOD in BP	223
8.1	Differences in manual parameters creating variation from GOOD (left) to BAD (a), BRIEF (b), COMPANY (c) and ELEVEN (d)	231
8.2	Two depicting constructions in BSL – DC:PAPERS-SIDE-BY-SIDE (left) and DC:PILE-OF-PAPER (right)	233
8.3	'The student is thinking hard' / STUDENT PT:PRO3SG CA: THINK-HARD	234
8.4	The system of SPEECH FUNCTION and congruent realisations	239
8.5	A system of MOOD in BSL	243
8.6	Interstratal relations and associated systems in BSL	244
8.7	The interpersonal networks of BSL	249
9.1	Provisional MOOD network for Gaelic, redounding with ENGAGEMENT	277
9.2	Rejected MOOD network for Gaelic, redounding with NEGOTIATION	278

Tables

1.1	Basic options for SPEECH FUNCTION	*page* 18
2.1	Resources 'at risk' in English negotiation	40
3.1	The typical discourse-semantic functions of Khorchin Mongolian indicative clauses	84
3.2	Types of imperative clause in Khorchin Mongolian	85
3.3	Imperative clauses in action exchanges	89
3.4	The typical discourse functions of Khorchin Mongolian imperative clauses	92
4.1	Classification of interrogatives in Mandarin	111
4.2	Three types of interrogative in Mandarin	121
5.1	Pronominal clitics in Tagalog	133
5.2	Assessment clitics in Tagalog	135
5.3	Clitic sequencing in Tagalog (tendencies)	135
5.4	Clitic sequencing in Tagalog: fuller proposal (tendencies)	145
6.1	TONE, MOOD, FORCE and ENGAGEMENT	165
6.2	SPEECH FUNCTION types and tones	166
6.3	Selections in IMPERATIVE MOOD PERSON	171
6.4	MODAL ASSESSMENT systems in Pitjantjatjara	185
6.5	Grammatical and phonological systems realising ENGAGEMENT	186
6.6	Lexicogrammatical and phonological resources for GRADUATION value	187
7.1	Exchange structure and NEGOTIATION functions in Text 1	196
7.2	NEGOTIATION, SPEECH FUNCTION and MOOD in Text 1	199
7.3	Congruent realisation of SPEECH FUNCTION in BP (full clauses)	201
7.4	Imperative verbal morphology for regular verbs	205
7.5	MOOD and TONE for imperative	207
7.6	Finite 'from below' in relation to tense and verbal modality	210
7.7	Cross-classification of MOOD and ASSESSMENT in PB	219
8.1	An example of the lexicogrammatical rank scale of BSL	234
8.2	Excerpt 1 analysed in interpersonal terms	250
8.3	Excerpt 2 analysed in interpersonal terms	251

Contributors

Tom Bartlett, University of Glasgow, Scotland
Priscilla Cruz, Ateneo de Manila University, Philippines
Giacomo Figueredo, Federal University of Ouro Preto, Brazil
J. R. Martin, University of Sydney, Australia; Pontificia Universidad Católica de Chile, Chile
Beatriz Quiroz, Pontificia Universidad Católica de Chile, Chile
David Rose, University of Sydney, Australia
Luke A. Rudge, Bristol Centre for Linguistics, University of the West of England, England
Pin Wang, Shanghai Jiao Tong University, China
Dongbing Zhang, University of International Business and Economics, China

1 Introduction: Theory and Description in Interpersonal Grammar across Languages

J. R. Martin, Beatriz Quiroz and Giacomo Figueredo

1.1 Interpersonal Grammar: Enacting Social Relations

This book focuses on the grammar of interpersonal systems in eight different languages (Khorchin Mongolian, Mandarin, Tagalog, Pitjantjatjara, Spanish, Brazilian Portuguese, British Sign Language and Scottish Gaelic) from the perspective of systemic functional linguistics (SFL) – with a focus on MOOD, MODALITY, POLARITY, TAGGING, VOCATION, ASSESSMENT and COMMENT systems. The chapters have been designed to illustrate the methodology whereby SFL grammatical descriptions are developed – including the concerns of data collection and criterial argumentation. The book accordingly provides a model for functional grammatical description and can thus be used to inform work on system and structure across languages as a foundation for functional language typology.

This is a book on description and methodology based on SFL theory. For an overview of interpersonal grammar in English, see Halliday and Matthiessen (2014). For the definitions and explanations of systems such as MOOD and MODALITY, see the book on SFL key terms (Matthiessen et al., 2010). For a detailed account of SFL language description, see Caffarel, Martin and Matthiessen (2004, chapter 1). And for an introduction to SFL theory, see Halliday and Matthiessen (2009), Martin, Wang and Zhu (2013) and Martin, Quiroz, Wang and Zhu (in press).

In this chapter we introduce our theoretical and methodological orientation. We begin in Section 1.2 with an overview of systemic functional linguistics, introducing its model of language and two descriptions of special relevance to this book. In Section 1.2.1 we focus on key theoretical dimensions – axis (system-and-structure relations), rank, metafunction and stratification. A particular concern of this book is the way in which interpersonal grammatical systems realise the discourse-semantic systems of NEGOTIATION and APPRAISAL. Accordingly, in Section 1.2.2 we present an outline of NEGOTIATION and APPRAISAL resources relevant to the interpretation of chapters in this volume. NEGOTIATION systems are responsible for a basic exchange structure of between one and five moves, plus dynamic tracking and challenging responses. APPRAISAL systems address the attitudes negotiated in exchanges, including the degree to which they are felt and the play of voices relevant to sharing feeling. At the end of this section, we introduce the understandings underpinning the model of context proposed by Martin (1992) for interpreting patterns of language use.

It is important to mention that the SFL notational conventions used in this chapter, and throughout this book, are basically those introduced in Matthiessen and Halliday (2009) and Martin, Wang and Zhu (2013). The morpheme-by-morpheme glossing of non-English examples is based on the Leipzig glossing rules. Further glossing is based in the dedicated SFL glossing conventions available at https://systemiclanguagemodelling.wordpress.com/glossing/.

In Section 1.3 we review the methodological implications of SFL's theoretical dimensions with respect to text-based data compilation, approaching grammar from above, axial reasoning and functional language typology. Our goal here is to establish the common ground on which functional descriptions informed by SFL can be constructed. In Section 1.4 we succinctly review key cross-linguistic research in SFL, including work centred on interpersonal grammar. Such work is an important background for the accounts presented in this volume. Finally, in Section 1.5 we introduce each chapter, highlighting the distinctive contribution of each to our understanding of interpersonal grammar.

1.2 Systemic Functional Linguistics

1.2.1 Theoretical Parameters

We begin with an overview of systemic functional linguistics, focusing on four key dimensions – axis (system-and-structure relations), rank, metafunction and stratification. Here we make special reference to the way in which SFL has informed grammatical descriptions across a range of languages, noting key contributions in the literature.

In SFL the fundamental dimension of analysis is **axis** – that is, system realised in structure. This entails modelling grammar as a system of paradigmatic oppositions, each with syntagmatic implications of some kind. The model privileges paradigmatic relations in the sense that structure is derived from system; but at the same time system and structure are bound together in the sense that without structuration, there is no system. Explaining and modelling this axial perspective on grammatical description is a crucial focus of each chapter in this book.

We should clarify here that in SFL axial reasoning is inspired by Whorf's recognition of both phenotypes and cryptotypes in language description. For Whorf (1945), phenotypes are classes we can recognise through overt marking, which we interpret here as including sequence of classes (i.e. a syntagm – with single segments as the limiting case), morphology (including affixation, agreement and government) and intonation. Modal verbal groups in English are a good example of this kind of category; this syntagm begins with a closed class of modal verbs, regularly followed by the base form of the following verb.

> Messi **must play** there.
> Messi **must be** playing there.
> Messi **must have** played there.

This modal syntagm however involves two cryptotypes: in SFL terms, modalised verbal groups versus modulated ones (a distinction akin to epistemic versus deontic modality in formal semantics). The distinction is clear if we reason from above and consider the kind of interpersonal move enacted by the clause – since exchanges negotiating information involving this syntagm are understood as modalised (negotiating probability) and exchanges negotiating goods-and-services involving this syntagm are understood as modulated (negotiating obligation).

modality type	
modalised (propositions)	*Messi must play there* (to have scored)
modulated (proposals)	*Messi must play there* (in order to score)

The distinction can also be made clear grammatically, by reasoning 'from round about' in terms of alternative realisations of modality. Modality in modalised clauses in English can be alternatively expressed with modal adverbs (but there are no verbal group complex alternatives):

> Messi must play there : Messi **certainly** plays there ::
> Messi would play there : Messi **probably** plays there ::
> Messi might play there : Messi **possibly** plays there

Conversely, modality in modulated clauses can be alternatively realised through verbal group complexes (but there are no adverbial alternatives):

> Messi must play there : Messi **is required to play** there ::
> Messi should play there : Messi **is supposed to play** there ::
> Messi could play there : Messi **is allowed to play** there

Whorf referred to emergent differentiation of this kind as a reactance and referred to classes motivated by evidence of this kind as cryptotypes. Note that Whorf's reasoning is based on relations among structures. Paradigmatic relations among modalised verbal groups are different from those for modulated ones; and since each set of verbal groups has a distinctive series of variations, we have the necessary motivation for recognition of a grammatical distinction (modalised versus modulated verbal groups and clauses).

Whorf's emphasis on the importance of reasoning from around has been further developed in SFL in relation to the concepts of enation and agnation (Gleason, 1965) – see Quiroz (2020) for an in-depth review of Whorf's and Gleason's contributions to SFL in general, and SFL language description in particular.

In simple terms enation refers to recurrent structural configurations with varying lexis, while agnation refers to systematic relations among structural configurations with comparable lexis. In the examples that follow, the first set of enate clauses enables us to see Subject ^ Finite ^ Predicator structure as a recurrent configuration in English grammar; and the second set confirms the Finite ^ Subject ^ Predicator structure.

enate **Subject ^ Finite ^ Predicator** structures
Messi has kicked the goal.
Federer has won the point.
Scott has made the shot.
Crosby has scored the goal.

enate **Finite ^ Subject ^ Predicator** structures
Has Messi kicked the goal?
Has Federer won the point?
Has Scott made the shot?
Has Crosby scored the goal?

The difference between these sets of structures, on the other hand, is a matter of agnation. The proportions among the clauses are set out below (a is to b, as c is to d etc.) and highlight the way in which English structures the difference between declarative and interrogative clauses (i.e. the sequence of the Subject and Finite functions).

Subject ^ Finite :	Finite ^ Subject ::
Messi has kicked the goal :	*Has Messi* kicked the goal ::
Federer has won the point :	*Has Federer* won the point ::
Scott has made the shot :	*Has Scott* made the shot ::
Crosby has scored the goal	*Has Crosby* scored the goal

1 Theory and Description in Interpersonal Grammar

From an SFL point of view, the exploration of reactances associated with a given cryptotype would be in fact the exploration of its associated agnation relations – proportionality, such as that illustrated in the tables above, is a critical feature of grammatical reasoning in SFL (cf. Halliday & Matthiessen, 2014, p. 68).

For some languages, reasoning 'from below', by bringing prosodic phonology into the picture, is an important consideration since basic MOOD options (such as declarative versus interrogative) may be distinguished by intonation rather than grammatical structure, and choices for rhythm and intonation play a crucial role in the realisation of moves in exchange structure. The extent to which rhythm and intonation are taken into account as far as lexicogrammar is concerned is a descriptive variable, explicitly addressed in relevant chapters of this volume.

Methodologically speaking, in SFL, axial reasoning about enation and agnation of the kind just illustrated is the foundation for modelling grammar as a system of paradigmatic oppositions, each with syntagmatic implications of some kind. In English, for example, the indicative clauses agnated above in relation to the sequence of their Subject and Finite functions contrast with imperative clauses which in the unmarked case lack these functions. We also need to take into account that Predicators in indicative clauses are realised by finite verbal groups and Predicators in imperative clauses by non-finite ones. These distinctions are formalised as a system network in Figure 1.1. The square brackets formalise options (e.g. if [indicative], then [declarative] or [interrogative]); and the realisation statements prefaced by downward slanting arrows specify the syntagmatic consequences of paradigmatic selections (e.g. if [indicative], insert a Subject function, insert a Finite function, and realise the Predicator function through a finite verbal group).

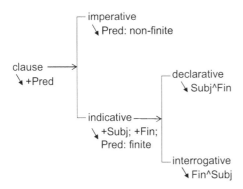

Figure 1.1 Some general English MOOD systems

Formalising these MOOD options allows us to specify the conditions under which an English clause can make choices for MODALITY – namely, that we choose indicative rather than imperative. This allows us to extend the network in Figure 1.1 to make room for the modalisation and modulation distinctions introduced in this chapter (Figure 1.2). The brace indicates that the declarative-or-interrogative and modal-or-non-modal systems cross-classify indicative clauses (i.e. [indicative] is an entry condition to both systems).

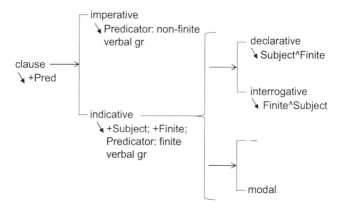

Figure 1.2 General English MOOD and MODALITY systems

In order to clarify the realisation statements involved in realising MODALITY it is necessary to review the structures we are proposing – and how they are organised by **rank**. Three agnate structures are presented in the following examples. In Example 1 modalisation is realised at clause rank through the function Modal (which is in turn realised at group rank through the adverbial group *certainly*). In SFL's rank-based model of constituency, a clause consists of one or more groups or phrases, a group of one of more words and a word of one or more morphemes (note that the adverbial group in the example might have been expanded as a multi-word adverbial group such as *almost certainly*). The Modal function can be realised in various positions in the clause (i.e. ***certainly*** *he has played there*; *he has **certainly** played there*; *he has played there,* ***certainly***). As the tables reveal, in SFL constituents are labelled for both class (what they are) and function (what they do); this class versus function complementarity (referred to as a category versus relation opposition in some models of language) enables grammatical descriptions that encode the crypto-grammatical agnation already introduced.

(1)

Messi	*certainly*	*has*	*played*	*there*
Subject	Modal	Finite	Predicator	Adjunct
nominal group	adverbial group	verbal group		adverbial group

1 Theory and Description in Interpersonal Grammar

In Example 2 the modality (realising either modalisation or modulation depending on the context) is realised at group rank through a verbal group which selects modality rather than tense to ground the clause (cf. the non-modalised verbal group in *Messi **does** play there*). Unlike the Modal function at clause rank in Example 1, the function we are calling Mod at group rank in Example 2 is fixed in position.

(2)

Messi	may	play	there
Subject	Finite	Predicator	Adjunct
nominal group	verbal group		adverbial group
...	Mod	Event	...

In Example 3 the modulation is realised at group rank through a verbal group complex, whose first verbal group selects an appropriate modulating verb or adjective as head (technically speaking its Event). Note that in SFL the Greek letter α is often used to represent the head of what is often referred to as an endocentric structure (cf. Pittman 1948 for a rich exploration of the concept of nuclearity).

(3)

Messi	is	allowed	to play	there
Subject	Finite	Predicator		Adjunct
nominal group	verbal group complex			adverbial group
...	$\alpha^{modulating}$		β	...
	verbal group		verbal group	
	Tense	Event^{modul}	Event	

Whatever the details of these analyses and possible alternative interpretations, what concerns us here is the way in which the realisation of modality has consequences at different ranks in English. For what Halliday and Matthiessen (2014) call explicit objective modalisation, we need a clause rank function, Modal, realised by an adverbial group (which will ultimately have a modal adverb as head): *Messi **certainly** has played there*. Their implicit subjective modality on the other hand has no effect on clause structure; it is the verbal group that makes the meaning (ultimately through a modal verb rather than one realising past, present or future tense): *Messi **may** have played there*. Their implicitly objective modulation similarly has no effect on clause structure; in this case, a verbal group complex is required, with a modulating verbal group as its head: *Messi **is allowed** to play there*. The clause rank paradigmatic interdependency among these distinctions, and their implications for English structure are outlined in Figure 1.3. We will not make space here to review the verbal group systems and structures noted in the realisation statements in this network (for details see Halliday and Matthiessen, 2014).

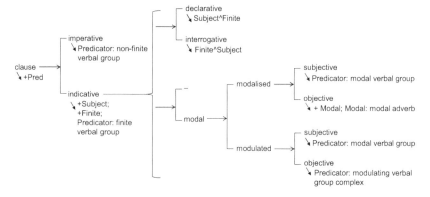

Figure 1.3 Further general English MOOD and MODALITY systems

It may be useful at this stage to provide a full analysis, organised by rank, of an English modalised clause (Example 4).

(4)

	he	certainly	didn't		play	there
Clause functions	Subject	Modal	Finite		Predicator	Adjunct
Group class	nominal group	adverbial group	verbal group			adverbial group
Group functions	Thing	Assessment	Tense		Event	Place
Word class	pronoun	adverb	aux verb		verb	adverb
Word functions	Head	Head	Suffix	Head	Suffix	Head	Head
Morpheme class	3SG.M	stem	adv	past	neg	stem	stem

In Korean, modality is also realised at clause and group rank, as shown in Example 5. At clause rank we find mobile Modality Marker functions such as *kkok* (without fail) (Shin, 2018). In the Korean examples here, where appropriate, we will use an *-er* suffix for clause rank functions, an *-ing* suffix for group/phrase rank functions and no suffix for word rank functions to help clarify the ranks across which the realisation of modality is distributed.

1 Theory and Description in Interpersonal Grammar

(5)

책을 꼭 읽어야 한다.								
chayg	*ul*	***kkok***		*ilk*	*-eya*	*ha*	*-n*	*-ta*
book	ACC	**without-PRES-DECL fail**		read	-LINK	must	-PRES	-DECL
		Modality Marker		Negotiator				
		adverbial group		verbal group				
		Assessment		Event		Modality Marking		
		adverb		verb		auxiliary verb		
				Head	Link	Head	Tense	EM
				stem	suffix	stem	suffix	suffix
'You must surely read books.'								

At group rank we find Event ^ Modality Marking structures such as the one involving the auxiliary verb *hata* 'must' in Example 6.

(6)

가야 한다				
ka	*-ya*	***ha***	*-n*	*-ta*
go	-LINK	**must**	-PRES	-DECL
verbal group				
Event		**Modality Marking**		
verb		**auxiliary verb**		
Head	Link	**Head**	Tense	Exchange Mark
stem	suffix	**stem**	suffix	suffix
'(You) must go.'				

Korean, in addition, deploys word rank realisations involving a Head ^ Modality Mark ^ Exchange Mark stem and suffix structure. An instance involving a modalisation of probability is presented in Example 7; the Modality Mark function is realised by the suffix *-keyss*.

(7)

사람이 많겠다.				
salam	*i*	*manh*	***-keyss***	*-ta*
people	NOM	there be many	**would**	-DECL
		verbal group		
		Event		
		verb		
		Head	**Modality Mark**	Exchange Mark
		stem	**suffix**	suffix
'There would be many people (there).'				

In Spanish, modality can also be realised at clause rank through Modal Adjuncts (through modalising adverbial groups such as *seguramente* and *probablemente*), at group rank by a Finite function (with modal verbs such as *deber* and *poder*), and at word rank through a modalising 'conditional' verb inflection (depending on the Spanish variety we are considering):

Messi **seguramente** juega ahí : Messi **debe** jugar ahí : Messi jugar-**ía** ahí
'Messi **probably** plays there' : 'Messi **must** play there' : 'Messi might play there'

Spanish modality can also be positioned as Head of a hypotactic structure (designated as α in Example 8 and linked by *que* to the rest of the clause).

(8)

Puede	*que*	Messi	jueg-ue	ahí
might	LK	Messi	play-3PS	there
(Modal) α	β			
		nominal group	verbal group	adverbial group
'Messi might play there.'				

This is in fact the main way of structuring the realisation of modality in Tagalog, for both modalisation and modulation (Martin and Cruz, 2018), as in Example 9.

(9)

dapat	*mo*	*-ng*	*lutu-in*	*ang*	*adobo*
should	2SG.NON-THEME	LK	cook-GOODS FOCUS	THEME MARKER	adobo
(Modal) α	β				
'You should cook the adobo.'					

Through hypotactic structures of this kind both languages, Spanish and Tagalog, are in effect making explicit the domain of the modality – namely, the clause as a whole. Such dependency structures have been interpreted as involving one kind of logical meaning in SFL (Halliday, 1994). So we might say that the interpersonal metafunction in Spanish and Tagalog is co-opting logical meaning in order to specify the prosodic scope of modal operators in structures like these (Martin, 1990, 1995; Martin & Cruz, 2018).

As observed in Halliday (1966) and Matthiessen (2004), the rank at which systems are realised – in clause structure, in group/phrase structure or in word structure, or in some combination of these – is an important typological variable. This is one motivation for preferring a model of constituency based on rank to one organised on a binary basis around immediate constituency (IC) analysis.

This brings us to the third key dimension of SFL theory we need to introduce here (alongside axis and rank) – namely, **metafunction**. By way of illustrating MOOD enation and agnation we chose examples involving sporting activity – material clauses in SFL terms (e.g. Halliday & Matthiessen, 2014). But the same proportionalities (based on the declarative versus interrogative opposition) are found for mental clauses construing affection, verbal clauses construing communication and relational clauses classifying phenomena. Examples of the way in which MOOD choices apply across agnate TRANSITIVITY structures are provided here.

TRANSITIVITY	MOOD (enate **Subject ^ Finite ^ Predicator** structures)
material	*Messi has kicked the goal.*
mental	*Federer has delighted the crowd.*
verbal	*Scott has reported his news.*
relational	*Crosby has been a hockey star for several years now.*

TRANSITIVITY	MOOD (enate **Finite ^ Subject ^ Predicator** structures)
material	*Has Messi kicked the goal?*
mental	*Has Federer delighted the crowd?*
verbal	*Has Scott reported his news?*
relational	*Has Crosby been a hockey star for several years now?*

In effect, what we are illustrating here is the way in which choices for MOOD cross-classify choices for TRANSITIVITY. This cross-classification in formalised in the network in Figure 1.4 – which comprises a simplified bundle of interdependent systems from Figure 1.3 alongside a simple system of clause types we might develop into a simultaneous bundle of interdependent systems if we were to pursue TRANSITIVITY analysis here. This kind of system bundling contrasts with that implicated by our discussion of rank above.[1] There we pointed out that modality can be realised at one or more ranks in a given language; choices for MODALITY, in other words, bundle as sets of options bearing on elements of structure organised along a hierarchy of constituency. Here we are looking at paradigmatic groupings of a different kind – organised not by rank but by what in SFL is referred to as metafunction. This dimension of SFL takes into account the organisation of language (and other semiotic systems) as resources for construing experience (ideational meaning), enacting social relations (interpersonal meaning) and composing information flow (textual meaning). The focus of this book, of course, is interpersonal meaning; but there will be points in the analyses of

---

[1] For a step by step introduction to system bundling (i.e. interdependency of systems) as the foundation of the theoretical concepts of rank, metafunction and stratification in SFL, see Martin et al. (2013).

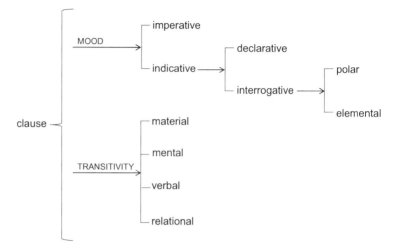

Figure 1.4 Cross-classification of clauses by MOOD and TRANSITIVITY systems

various languages where ideational and textual considerations can be usefully brought into the discussion.

The final key dimension of SFL we attend to in this introduction (alongside axis, rank and metafunction) is **stratification**. For this step let us return to the discussion of modality previously pursued in this section and take it a step further to include what Halliday and Matthiessen (2014) call explicit subjective modality. This involves setting up a present tense mental process of cognition (bold in the examples that follow) projecting what might happen (italic in the examples) – an α β dependency relation between clauses,[2] whose effect is comparable to the Spanish and Tagalog dependency relations we have previously reviewed. Declarative clauses are used to modalise a speaker's opinion and interrogative clauses to solicit a listener's one.

I reckon *Messi will kick the goal.*
I suppose *Federer will delight the crowd.*
I figure *Scott will report his news.*
I think *Crosby will be a hockey star.*

Do you reckon *Messi will kick the goal?*
Do you suppose *Federer will delight the crowd?*
Do you figure *Scott will report his news?*
Do you think *Crosby will be a hockey star?*

---

[2] This dependency relation is comparable to the Spanish and Tagalog dependency relations we reviewed in our discussion of logical structure and the scope of modality in Examples 8 and 9 (but the dependency relation is structured between clauses, not within clauses, in English).

Where speakers use this structure to modalise, the interpersonal tag (italics in the next examples) picks up the Subject and Finite (bold in the next examples) of the projected clause, not the projecting one – because that is the clause whose modality is being negotiated.

> I reckon **Messi will** kick the goal, *won't he*?
> I suppose **Federer will** delight the crowd, *won't he*?
> I figure **Scott will** report his news, *won't he*?
> I think **Crosby will** be a hockey star, *won't he*?

The first or second person present tense cognitive processes in these examples are each construing mental activity; but they are also symbolising modality – that is, the probability of the projected clause. Ideational grammatical resources are being used, metaphorically, to symbolise interpersonal discourse-semantic ones – an example of what SFL terms grammatical metaphor (Halliday & Matthiessen, 2014). So with examples like these the grammar is not simply realising discourse semantics (IDEATION, in particular); rather, it is symbolising meaning (ENGAGEMENT, in particular). Interstratal interactions of this kind are addressed in various chapters in this book, and in the following section.

This brings SFL's model of stratification into play – since however rich our grammar is, it cannot model grammatical metaphor on its own. Its interaction with a deeper level of abstraction is crucial. Levels of abstraction (i.e. strata) are generally modelled as cotangential circles in SFL, as in Figure 1.5. In models of stratification of this kind, discourse-semantic patterns are treated as patterns of lexicogrammatical patterns, which are in turn treated as patterns of phonological ones. Patterns on each stratum are modelled axially as groups of systems, organised by rank and metafunction.

This completes our tour of four key theoretical dimensions of SFL: axis, rank, metafunction and stratification. Of these, axis is fundamental, since it engenders the systems whose relative independence and interdependency is organised in descriptions with respect to rank (constituency), metafunction (type of meaning) and strata (level of abstraction).

1.2.2 NEGOTIATION *and* APPRAISAL

The two key interpersonal discourse-semantic systems underpinning the work on interpersonal grammar in chapters in this volume are NEGOTIATION (Martin, 1992) and APPRAISAL (Martin & White, 2005). NEGOTIATION systems are responsible for a basic exchange structure of between one and five moves in dialogue, plus dynamic tracking and challenging responses. APPRAISAL systems address the attitudes negotiated in exchanges, including the degree to which they are felt and the play of voices relevant to sharing feeling. The examples used in this section are adapted from the English translations of the

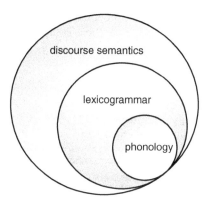

Figure 1.5 Language strata

Tagalog interaction considered in Chapter 5, Section 5.7 – an interaction between a dressmaker (DM) and her client (PC). They are exchanging text messages about a skirt with two layers (an outer gauze one with a pattern and an opaque solid-coloured inner layer). At issue is the length of the inner layer (referred to as the lining) in relation to the outer one.

One key NEGOTIATION system distinguishes between exchanges negotiating proposals (action exchanges involving an exchange of goods-and-services) and exchanges negotiating propositions (knowledge exchanges involving an exchange of information) – for the distinction between proposals and propositions, see Halliday (1984) and Halliday and Matthiessen (2014). Action exchanges have an obligatory move whereby goods are exchanged or a service undertaken by a primary actor (an A1 move), as in Example 10.

(10)   DM   A1   I'll look for the lining material at Maria's.

Information exchanges have a corresponding obligatory move whereby information is provided by a primary knower (a K1 move), as in 11.

(11)   DM   K1   I'm working at home today.

Alternatively, an exchange can be initiated by a secondary actor (an A2 move) or a secondary knower (a K2 move). In 12 the secondary actor requests service.

(12)   PC   A2   Can you look for the lining material, please?
        DM   A1   OK.

In 13 a secondary knower requests information about who is present.

(13)   PC   K2   Where are you working today?
        DM   K1   At home.

1 Theory and Description in Interpersonal Grammar   15

A third possibility is for an exchange to be initiated by a primary actor or knower (as in Examples 10 and 11), but this time checking first whether the goods-and-services are desired by the secondary actor (a delayed A1 move, Da1), or the information of interest to the secondary knower (a delayed K1 move). Note that what is referred to as an offer in Halliday's (e.g. 1984) SPEECH FUNCTION framework (his 'giving goods-and-services') would be interpreted here as realising either a Da1 or an A1 move; the lexicogrammatical realisations of the two types of offer are quite different (compare Examples 12 and 14), especially where the A1 type accompanies the actual provision of goods-and-services (rather than a promise to do so).

(14)   DM   Da1   Shall I look for the lining material at Maria's?
        PC   A2   OK.
        DM   A1   Alright.

(15)   DM   Dk1   I bet you're wondering where I'm working today?
        PC   K2   Where?
        DM   K1   At home!

In Examples 14 and 15, the obligatory A1 or K1 moves in the exchanges can be optionally followed up by the secondary actor or knower, and if present, the follow-up move can be optionally followed up by the primary actor or knower. The discourse function of follow-up moves (f) is to consolidate the successful negotiation of the nuclear A1 or K1 moves in an exchange. The exchanges in 16 and 17 are followed up along these lines.

(16)   DM   A1   I'll look for the lining material at Maria's.
        PC   A2f   Thanks.
        DM   A1f   You're welcome.

(17)   DM   K1   I'm working at home today.
        PC   K2f   Really?
        DM   K1f   Yup.

From a syntagmatic perspective, the structure for each exchange type can be expressed as a generalised structure potential (with optional moves in parentheses, and '^' specifying sequence):

>   Action exchanges: ((Da1)^A2)^A1^(A2f^(A1f))
>
>   Knowledge exchanges: ((Dk1)^K2)^K1^(K2f^(K1f))

From the perspective of axis (system/structure relations), the meaning potential at stake here can be formalised as a system network (including the relevant paradigmatic oppositions and their structural consequences). Martin and Rose's (2007) proposals for key NEGOTIATION systems and realisation statements are presented in Figure 1.6. In these abbreviated realisation statements '/'

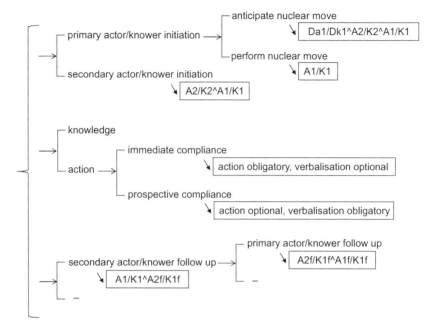

Figure 1.6 Basic NEGOTIATION systems (exchange rank)

between functions means 'one or the other' and '^' stands for sequence. Thus A2/K2^A1/K1 is a shorthand for specifying that A2 precedes A1 and K2 precedes K1.[3] For a comprehensive account of notation, see Halliday and Matthiessen (2009) and Martin et al. (2013).

Provision also needs to be made for what are referred to as tracking and challenging moves (Ventola 1987; Martin, 1992; Martin & Rose, 2007). Tracking moves clarify information that has not been confidently interpreted from a preceding move (sorting out ideational meaning before the conversation can move on); challenging moves resist the complaint positioning which a preceding move has presumed (subverting the interpersonal trajectory of the dialogue).

First, tracking. When an entire move needs to be replayed, triggers implicating a replay of the initiating move arrest the exchange. Non-compliant moves of this kind are referred to as confirmations in SFL, notated as 'cf' for

---

[3] In realisation statements '/' is typically used for conflated functions in SFL; that is not the meaning of the slash here – where it is used simply to stop the network from becoming too cluttered.

'confirmation request', and 'rcf' for 'response to confirmation request' in Example 18.

(18)   K1   I'm working at home today.
       cf   Sorry?
       rcf I'm working at home today.

When just part of the move needs to be replayed, an appropriate wh– word, spoken on a rising tone (a so-called 'wh–' echo question), can be used to query the relevant part of the move – for example, the location in 19.

(19)   K1   I'm working at home today.
       cf   You're working where?
       rcf At home.

When speakers simply want to check that they have heard correctly, the relevant part of the preceding move can be repeated, possibly on a rising tone, as in 20.

(20)   K1   I'm working at home today.
       cf   At home?
       rcf Yes.

The same tracking sequences are used for both information and goods-and-services exchanges, so examples involving Da1, A2 and A1 moves will not be canvassed here.

More significant disruptions may arise when the addressee is not comfortable with the way they have been positioned by a move in an exchange and challenge this positioning. In information exchanges, for example, the addressee may not know the answer to a K2 request for information and refuse the primary knower role which has been assigned to them. Non-compliant moves of this kind are referred to as challenges in SFL, notated as 'ch' in the analyses in Example 21.

(21)   K2   Will you be working at home today?
       ch   I don't know yet.

In goods-and-services exchanges, non-compliance involves an addressee's disinclination or inability to enable a nuclear A1 move. A typical challenge to an A2 move is illustrated in Example 22. The secondary actor responds to this challenge (notated as 'rch'), urging compliance, and is rewarded with the A1 move the exchange was initiated to enact.

(22)   A2   Can you look for the lining material at Maria's, please?
       ch   I probably can't this morning.
       rch Please.
       A1   Oh, OK, I'll do it.

One further type of exchange structure we need to consider is the possibility of a checking move (notated as 'check' in Examples 23 and 24). In knowledge exchanges these are realised on a separate tone group, following a pause in the rhythm (a silent beat); their function is to secure a verbal response from the addressee (as in 23). In terms of both this function and their realisation, they can be thought of as a delayed 'tag'.

(23)   K1   It's a little shorter than floor length.
        check   Isn't it?
        K2 f   Right.

In action exchanges (e.g. Example 24), checking moves promote a compliant verbal response from the addressee (typically a primary actor).

(24)   A2   Make it between knee and ankle length.
        check   OK?
        A1   OK.

Moves in exchange structure are realised by classes of move constituting the system of SPEECH FUNCTION. Halliday (1984) introduces a grammarian's perspective on these systems; this interpersonal clause semantics is consolidated in the various editions of his *Introduction to Functional Grammar* (initially 1985) – Table 1.1 is based on Table 4.2 of the fourth edition (Halliday & Matthiessen, 2014, p. 137). The key systems here deal with the commodity being negotiated (goods-and-services versus information), whether the interpersonal move is giving or demanding, whether it is initiating or responding, and whether the response is expected or discretionary. The model is by and large based on the resources available for distinguishing initiating moves grammatically, along with the substitution and ellipsis patterns characterising responses. What Halliday refers to as 'congruent' realisations of SPEECH FUNCTION (discourse semantics) in MOOD (lexicogrammar) are exemplified in Table 1.1. As we can see, Halliday's

Table 1.1 *Basic options for* SPEECH FUNCTION

		Initiation	Response	
			expected	discretionary
give	goods-and-services	offer	acceptance	rejection
		Shall I pour?	*– Please do.*	*– No, thanks.*
demand		command	undertaking	refusal
		Let's go.	*– OK.*	*– Let's not.*
give	information	statement	acknowledgement	contradiction
		He's left.	*– Yes, he has.*	*– No, he hasn't.*
demand		question	answer	disclaimer
		Did he go?	*– He did.*	*– I don't know.*

perspective is limited to initiation and response pairs in dialogue (comparable to the adjacency pair orientation of Conversation Analysis – aka CA).

NEGOTIATION and SPEECH FUNCTION systems afford an essential discourse-semantic perspective on the grammatical resources used to negotiate propositions and proposals across languages. Their relative generality (cf. Martin & Quiroz, 2020, in press) makes it possible to compare and contrast languages with respect to the grammatical and phonological realisation of comparable discourse moves – including the rank at which distinctions are made, and the way in which experiential and logical structures are brought into play as grammatical metaphors or to specify the scope of modality as illustrated above.

Turning to APPRAISAL (Martin & White, 2005), the central system is ATTITUDE, which allows speakers to propose three main types of feeling to be shared: AFFECT (emotional reactions), JUDGEMENT (of people's character and behaviour) and APPRECIATION (of the value of things). These are exemplified in turn below. The realisation of this system is mainly lexical, and so, with the exception of Comment Adjuncts (cf. Martin et al., 2013, pp. 96–7), ATTITUDE is not a central focus of this volume.

> AFFECT   I **like** that lining material.
> JUDGEMENT   You've done it **well**.
> APPRECIATION   It won't look **funny**.

The system of GRADUATION allows feelings to be graded, along a scale from high to low (as italicised here).

> AFFECT   I *really* **like** that lining material.
> JUDGEMENT   You've done it *rather* **well**.
> APPRECIATION   It won't look *a bit* **funny**.

Finally the system of ENGAGEMENT provides options for positioning opinions in relation to one another. The monogloss option admits no voices other than the speaker's own. Heteroglossic contraction closes down an alternative voice that is already in play – drawing on concession and polarity in the second example (in bold). And heteroglossic expansion acknowledges opinions other than the speaker's own – drawing on modalisation in the third example (in bold).

> monogloss   The skirt and the multiway are fine.
> heterogloss: contract **But** the lining is**n't** the right length.
> heterogloss: expand   **I reckon** the skirt and multiway are perfect.

Martin and White's (2005) proposals for the discourse semantics of ENGAGEMENT in English are networked in Figure 1.7. As indicated by exemplary realisations, a number of interpersonal grammatical resources are implicated – including CONCESSION, POLARITY, MODALITY and COMMENT.

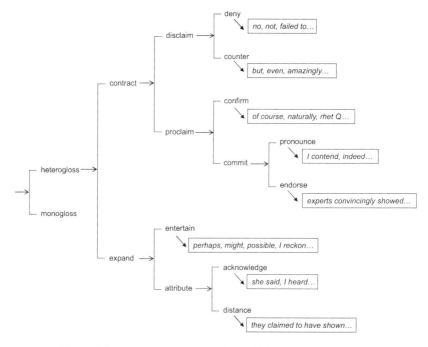

Figure 1.7 ENGAGEMENT systems in English

The APPRAISAL system offers a complementary perspective to NEGOTIATION as far as the semantics of interpersonal grammar is concerned. The ENGAGEMENT system in particular can be used to focus attention on the resources Matthiessen (2004) groups together as MODAL ASSESSMENT (including MODALITY and EVIDENTIALITY systems) alongside the use of Comment Adjuncts. In SFL work a focus on the grammatical realisation of SPEECH FUNCTION in clause structure has tended to background these resources, which may look marginal from the perspective of core MOOD options (declarative, interrogative, imperative etc.). But when it comes to negotiating feelings in discourse, they obviously play a central role.

In a functional theory of language, models of social context also have a critical role to play – since they encourage us to explore from a linguistic perspective the relationships between the intrinsic functionality of language (i.e. metafunctions) and the extrinsic functionality of context (i.e. register and genre). Models of context are also crucial to understanding language as comprised of probabilistic systems (Webster, 2005) – with choices inherently weighted as equiprobable or skew, and probabilities ongoingly re-weighted in relation to contextual choices as texts unfold. Conceived in this way models of context provide a deeper still perspective from which similarities and differences between languages can be interpreted – the effect of contextual relations of power and solidarity, for example, on choices for deference and honourification in some languages as opposed to a preference for grammatical metaphors of MOOD and MODALITY in others.

1.2.3   Register and Genre

In SFL, context is modelled as a higher stratum of meaning (Martin, 2016) – a pattern of linguistic patterns. Martin (1992) proposes a stratified model of context in which genre is realised by a pattern of register patterns – with register organised metafunctionally as field (construed by ideational meaning), tenor (enacted by interpersonal meaning) and mode (composed by textual meaning). In a model of this kind a culture is conceived as a system of genres – in practical terms a system of staged, goal-oriented social processes. The genre as a whole (and thus its stages) are realised through configurations of field, tenor and mode choices at the level of register. Genre families reviewed in Martin and Rose (2008) include stories, arguments, reports, explanations, procedures and protocol.

Field, as elaborated in Hao (2020) and Doran and Martin (in press), is a resource for construing phenomena – as activity or items and their attendant properties. Tenor is a resource for enacting social relations – with respect to contact (solidarity) and status (power). And mode is a resource for texturing discourse – along two clines, one extending from language in action through language as reflection and the other ranging from casual dialogue through turn-restricted interviews to monologic orations.

The most important of these register variables as far as interpersonal meaning is concerned is obviously tenor. A general topology of tenor relations is presented in Figure 1.8, along with exemplary social relations (drawing on academic life). A speaker's relative position in a topology of this kind affects the NEGOTIATION and APPRAISAL meaning potential available and its likelihood of being taken up. Close colleagues, for example, have more attitude options to negotiate than distant ones; and a professor is more likely to monogloss opinions than the research student being supervised.

All of these possibilities and probabilities are, of course, conditioned by genre and the stage being performed as discourse unfolds. And we need to keep in mind that linguistic resources are not simply prescribed by social relations. Speakers negotiate them too – as friendships, for example, wax and wane, and social status rises and falls. An overview of the model as a whole is presented in Figure 1.9. While the focus of this book is interpersonal grammar, the model encourages descriptions which reason from above (a higher stratum or rank), from below (a lower stratum or rank) and roundabout (across simultaneous systems and metafunctions). The key to a robust analysis is shunting (or 'switching' in US railway parlance) (Halliday, 1961, p. 254) – as systems

22 J. R. Martin, Beatriz Quiroz and Giacomo Figueredo

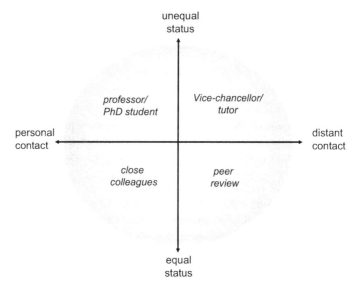

Figure 1.8 Tenor relations (status and contact)

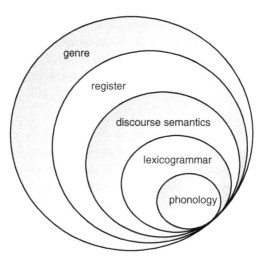

Figure 1.9 A stratified model of language in context

and structures are sorted into an account of the meaning potential of a particular stratum, rank and metafunction. The metaphor of trinocular vision is often used in SFL to characterise this shunting (e.g. Halliday 1996, p. 16) – as grammatical

1 Theory and Description in Interpersonal Grammar 23

resources, for example, are explored from above (in relation to a higher stratum or rank), from around in relation to simultaneous systems in the same or another metafunction) or from below (in relation to a lower rank or stratum).

1.3 Methodological Implications

Next we review the methodological implications of the theoretical dimensions introduced above with respect to text-based data compilation. There are four main factors to take into account – four dimensions of functionality, we might say:

i axis functionality
ii metafunctionality
iii co-textual functionality
iv contextual functionality

Axis functionality, as explained in Section 1.2.1, is fundamental, and encourages descriptions of interpersonal system/structure relations which are motivated by reasoning from above, from around and from below in relation to paradigms of enation and agnation (Halliday 1992, 1996). This argues for data that provides a rich range of enate and agnate clauses – rich enough to display the phenotypes and cryptotypes grounding interpersonal systems in structure. We will never, of course, assemble data that includes everything we need, particularly when looking for reactances. But we need enough to ensure that speaker 'intuitions' about what could or would be said do not lead us astray; and for many interpersonal systems (e.g. MODALITY and EVIDENTIALITY) it is very difficult for experienced linguists, let alone speakers, to bring the relevant 'proportionalities' – that is, enation and agnation relations – to consciousness and transparently 'gloss' the meaning of patterns involved (cf. Martin and Cruz, Chapter 5, and Figueredo, Chapter 7, in this volume).

Reasoning from round about means taking other systems into account, including systems from other metafunctions. This argues for data that provides a wide range of ideationally and textually agnate clauses – wide enough to show that interpersonal systems generalise across process types and adjustments to information flow. And wide enough to reveal where they do not so generalise – or tend not to. The combination of imperative clauses with relational processes would be a case in point, since instances are relatively rare (e.g. *matter to me, not him*) and sometimes take a moment of imagination to plausibly contextualise (e.g. *cost them 200 dollars an hour then*).

Reasoning from above implicates co-textual functionality. This is because discourse-semantic systems are realised through covariate structures of indefinite extent (Martin, 2015) – more often than not units larger than a clause (the exchange structures surveyed in Section 1.2.2, for example). This argues for data that provides a range of conversational structures which are diversified enough to reveal the many roles played by clauses as far as negotiating consensus is concerned. It is important here that the data includes compliantly negotiated exchanges as well as those that give way to resistance or misunderstanding. Repair and failure are as informative as consensus in this regard – as many chapters in this book demonstrate.

Reasoning from above additionally implicates contextual functionality. This argues for data that provides a varied range of tenor relations – varied enough to accommodate the clines of power and solidarity as they are enacted across a range of genres. Phases of discourse are important here, since tenor is enacted prosodically across clauses as well as indexed within – and it is important to allow scope for investigations of shifting and contested tenor relations as interlocutors struggle against expectations associated with their class, gender, ethnicity, dis/ability and generation.

All three types of reasoning bear on data compilation. The texts on which the grammatical descriptions are based need to be compiled from spontaneous language production and need to be compiled for a specific purpose. This purpose of course varies depending on research questions, problems and interests. Data can be compiled covering general social semiotic variables (as in the study of genre typology or the language of a social domain such as education, science, etc.), or it may be compiled to represent some specific grammar patterns of particular interest (as in the description of verbal group complexing in a given language). In this volume, our compilation draws on both perspectives in that chapters are concerned with explaining how language enacts exchanges, but also with documenting the recurrent grammar patterns involved. The descriptions are all based on spontaneous dialogic texts enacting interpersonal meaning in a range of registers.

A rich data set is also important because it informs the analysis of a recurrent grammar pattern relative to other recurrent patterns or any other variable of interest. Because language is a complex and powerful meaning-making resource, it is likely we can find many different kinds of patterns. The challenge is to determine which patterns are probable enough that they need to be accounted for as part of the description. In English, for example, a polar interrogative clause can be answered by polarity alone, or Subject and Finite, or polarity and Subject and Finite.

(25)   K2: Has Messi kicked the goal?
        K1: Yes. / He did. / Yes, he did.

Which of the three options in Example 24 should count, then, as the grammar structure realising the K2^K1 exchange? Clearly a full answer to this question is not only a matter of frequency; all three options are possible. Rather, we need to look the interaction between these patterns and other patterns (i.e. how MOOD is realised relative to how NEGOTIATION and ENGAGEMENT are realised) – and also make reference to the genre and the stage or phase in the text where the patterns were found.

The exemplifications deployed in Sections 1.2 and 1.3, constructed as they were for pedagogic purposes, were of course poor models of the kind of data characterised here. Fortunately contributors to this volume have been far more sensitive as far as co-textualised and contextualised data is concerned.

1.4 Functional Language Typology

Although best known for its groundbreaking work on English grammar (e.g. Halliday, 1985 and subsequent editions), SFL has evolved from its inception in relation to the description of a wide range of languages. Matthiessen and Halliday (2009), Martin, Wang and Zhu (2013) and Martin, Quiroz, Wang and Zhu (in press) offer an accessible and affordable trilogy of introductions to the theory, published as bilingual English/Chinese editions by the Higher Education Press, Beijing. Martin and Doran (2015a, 2015b, 2015c, 2015d, 2015e) bring together foundational papers, including one volume (2015b) dedicated to description across languages (Beja, French, Spanish, Chinese, Tagalog and Australian Sign Language). Full grammars based on SFL have been published for Gooniyandi (McGregor, 1990), Pitjantjatjara (Rose, 2001), Danish (Andersen et al., 2001), French (Caffarel 2006), Japanese (Teruya 2007) and Spanish (Lavid et al., 2010). And the chapters in Caffarel et al. (2004) profile the grammar of French, German, Japanese, Tagalog, Chinese, Vietnamese, Telegu and Pitjantjatjara. Mwinlaaru and Xuan (2016) provide a thorough survey of work in this tradition, which Martin, Doran and Figueredo (2020) extends in a volume featuring work on Khorchin Mongolian, Classical Tibetan, Brazilian Portuguese, Tagalog, Spanish, Chinese and Bahasa Indonesia.

Matthiessen (2004) draws on the first four decades of this tradition to propose a set of descriptive motifs and generalisations to guide future research. As far as interpersonal meaning is concerned, he generalises four grammatical systems, which he refers to as MOOD, POLARITY, MODAL ASSESSMENT and DISTANCE. The first two he takes as fundamental to the negotiation of the exchange of information (propositions) and of goods-and-services (proposals) as positive or negative indicative or imperative MOOD types. The latter two provide resources for fine-tuning this negotiation – through MODALITY and EVIDENTIALITY systems (generalised as MODAL ASSESSMENT) and HONOURIFICATION and POLITENESS systems (generalised as DISTANCE).[4] Taking

---

[4] The contrast drawn here is between participant deference (HONOURIFICATION) and addressee deference (POLITENESS) – that is, is a speaker deferring to someone they are talking about or someone they are talking to?

advantage of the focus on paradigmatic relations in SFL, he makes two important observations: (i) that languages differ more from one another with respect to the more specific options in system networks than the more general ones, and (ii) that languages differ more from one another with respect to the nature of the syntagmatic realisation of these options than with respect to the options themselves.

In later work (Matthiessen et al., 2008; Matthiessen, 2018), these observations are extended to include the generalisation that languages differ more from one another at lower strata than at higher ones. This point was first introduced in language typology work informed by SFL by Martin (1983), who compared participant identification in English, Tagalog and Kâte. It is further elaborated in Martin and Quiroz (2020), who draw on Martin's discourse semantics (Martin, 1992; Martin and Rose, 2003, 2007) to explore identification in English and Spanish (for a related comparative study focusing on these two languages' recursive TENSE systems, see Martin and Quiroz, in press).

Interpersonal grammar (MOOD systems in particular) is the focus of Teruya et al.'s (2007) survey of Danish, French, Spanish, Òkó, Thai and Japanese. They propose a typological cline ranging from languages with Mood-based structures (foregrounding distinct Subject and Finite functions) and Predicator-based structures (foregrounding the structure of verbal groups) – their Figure 27.3. This work is extended to Niger-Congo languages in Mwinlaaru et al. (2018). Martin (2018a) brings together a set of papers dealing with Korean, Tagalog, Pitjantjatjara and Spanish and encompassing a wide range of interpersonal phenomena (including POLARITY, MODAL ASSESSMENT and DISTANCE systems, grammatical metaphor and kinship relations). In his introduction to this special issue of *Functions of Language*, Martin (2018b) proposes a set of questions that need to be considered when exploring interpersonal resources in language description. We have adjusted these concerns here, dividing them into questions oriented to NEGOTIATION and questions oriented to APPRAISAL (including ENGAGEMENT systems). They reflect the top-down discourse-semantic perspective we would recommend by way of deepening our understanding of interpersonal meaning from the perspective of functional language typology (Martin & Quiroz, 2020) – as informed by SFL and affine functional theories:

NEGOTIATION

> How are congruent moves realised, in initiations and responses (first versus second pair parts as Conversation Analysis [CA] would phrase it)?
> What range of resources establish the arguability of an exchange (via TENSE/ASPECT, MODALITY, POLARITY, EVIDENTIALITY etc.)?
> Is the arguability of a clause mainly established at its beginning or end? And at what rank/s is it established?

1 Theory and Description in Interpersonal Grammar   27

> Are there prosodic patterns of realisation involved in engaging the clause in interaction and making it arguable (e.g. concord/agreement, inversion, contraction, repetition, discontinuous syntagms)?
> Are the entities most at risk in an exchange made explicit as a modally responsible 'Subject' – necessarily or as needed – via position, adposition, cliticisation or inflection, and with or without agreement?
> Which resources position the speaker in relation to the addressee (e.g. DEFERENCE, VOCATION) – necessarily or as needed? Are they mainly grammatical or lexical?
> Are there resources positioning the speaker in relation to non-addressees (e.g. HONOURIFICATION)? Are they mainly grammatical or lexical?
> What patterns of ellipsis characterise compliant negotiations of initiating moves (second pair parts in CA terms)?
> What patterns of minor and major clause characterise non-compliant negotiation (i.e. tracking and challenging moves, aka insertion sequences in CA terms)?
> What is the role of prosodic phonology (intonation and rhythm) in distinguishing interpersonal options?

APPRAISAL

> How are attitudes lexicalised? How suitable is their classification as systems of AFFECT, JUDGEMENT or APPRECIATION?
> What resources are deployed to grade attitude (e.g. submodification, repetition, inherently graded lexis, prosodic phonology)?
> How is attitude propagated 'prosodically' across phases of discourse (e.g. via the saturation, dominance or intensity motifs suggested in Martin [2008], Martin and White [2005])?
> What range of resources lexicogrammaticalise ATTITUDE (comment adverbs, manner adverbs, mental processes, mental state relational processes, epithets, diminutives)?
> How is attitude focalised (i.e. sourced via projection, circumstance of angle)?
> How are relevant voices acknowledged, sourced, affirmed or shut down (via projection, MODALITY, EVIDENTIALITY, negation, concession or comment particles or adverbials)?

We do not, of course, intend this as a closed list of concerns; it needs to be continually updated, as our range of descriptions and attendant understandings grows. And we need to take care that our focus on interpersonal meaning is not an excluding one. Ideational resources, after all, construe the meanings we negotiate, and textual resources compose them. We have to remember to look around, alongside shunting up and down among strata and ranks. As emphasised in Teruya et al. (2015), the full picture will always end up being a threefold one. Trinocular vision is key.

1.5 Chapters in This Volume

We close this introduction by briefly introducing the following chapters in this volume, highlighting their distinctive contributions to our understanding of interpersonal grammar.

Quiroz (Chapter 2) develops a carefully reasoned analysis of Spanish resources enacting the negotiability of propositions and proposals. Following a review of the ways in which English and French structure the arguability of moves in conversation, she turns to Spanish – demonstrating that it is the Predicator function, realised by verbal group resources, that manages negotiability (with respect to those resources 'most at risk' in the exchange). She shows that functions such as Subject or Finite have no place in the interpersonal grammar of a Spanish clause and closes with an overview of basic negotiatory structures in Romance languages, from the perspective of functional language typology.

Zhang (Chapter 3) provides a insightfully argued description of interpersonal grammar in Khorchin Mongolian. Following a basic introduction to Khorchin Mongolian clause types and their structure, he develops a distinctive NEGOTIATION system for the language. He then moves on to specify in detail how NEGOTIATION is related to MOOD options – including their realisation across clause, verbal group and verb structure. Beginning with the basic clause distinction between [indicative] and [imperative], he shows that the key functions in the interpersonal grammar of Khorchin Mongolian are Negotiator and Scope, with the Negotiator further specified as Predicator, Positioner and Interrogator – and either Scope or Negotiator including an Inquirer function in elemental interrogatives. The role played by this interpersonal grammar in realising NEGOTIATION is then carefully reviewed drawing on examples from conversations among family members, colleagues and interactions between peasants and government officials.

Wang (Chapter 4) builds on the rich tradition of systemic functional descriptions of Mandarin Chinese, revisiting its interpersonal grammar from the perspectives of NEGOTIATION and ENGAGEMENT – illustrated through data drawn from courtroom discourse. Wang clarifies the central role played by the Predicator in the grammar of MOOD, working alongside Modal Adjunct, Moderator and Inquirer functions. In addition to a well-reasoned discussion of types of interrogative, Wang develops complementary perspectives on indicative clauses in Mandarin – differentiated in terms of the weight given to reasoning from above or from below (NEGOTIATION versus ENGAGEMENT). As a contribution to functional language typology this underscores the importance of a trinocular orientation to language description (balancing reasoning from above, from round about and from below) and the need to take the systems of both NEGOTIATION and APPRAISAL (its ENGAGEMENT subsystem, in particular) into account when considering the grammatical resources enacting interpersonal meaning.

Martin and Cruz (Chapter 5) complement their work on Tagalog MOOD (Martin & Cruz, 2018) with a focus on what Matthiessen (2004) generalises across languages as MODAL ASSESSMENT. They focus on the enclitic particles realising the grammatical system they term ASSESSMENT. Like Wang (Chapter 4), they are concerned with the realisation of the discourse-semantic system of ENGAGEMENT in interpersonal grammar. Based on a close reading of two phases of dialogue, they classify ASSESSMENT clitics as either retrospectively contracting or prospectively expanding, as Tagalog speakers negotiate consensus around propositions and proposals. As a final step, they bring context into the picture, demonstrating that a full interpretation of interpersonal resources in Tagalog will have to make explicit reference to considerations of register (especially tenor) and genre.

Rose (Chapter 6) adopts a trinocular perspective on MOOD in Pitjantjatjara, stressing the importance bringing the phonological system of TONE into the picture. He prefers to interpret the relation between these two systems as neither a matter of delicacy (with tone choices subclassifying grammatical ones), nor of interstratal realisation. Instead, he adopts a 'coupling' perspective, treating MOOD and TONE selections as co-instantiating discourse-semantic systems. It follows from this perspective that Pitjantjatjara does not distinguish declarative from interrogative in Rose's description of the grammar of MOOD – cf. Quiroz (Chapter 2) who treats TONE as realising grammatical distinctions. Based on this modelling Rose develops a rich detailed description of the interaction among discourse-semantic (SPEECH FUNCTION, ENGAGEMENT and GRADUATION), lexicogrammatical (MOOD) and phonological (TONE) systems – explicitly specifying tone choice in all examples.

Figueredo (Chapter 7) draws on corpus evidence, working down from NEGOTIATION and SPEECH FUNCTION systems to compose a description of the interpersonal grammar of Brazilian Portuguese. He argues for the centrality of the Predicator as far as MOOD choice is concerned, bringing in Subject and Finite functions to specify more delicate options. At each step he takes care in building the analysis to relate grammatical categories upwards to the interpersonal discourse semantics they enact. Of particular value is his analysis of modal responsibility – as interlocutors negotiate consensus around both propositions and proposals. As a final challenging step he addresses in detail the contribution of modal particles realising ENGAGEMENT options to this negotiation.

Rudge (Chapter 8) makes a crucial contribution to functional language typology by engaging with the interpersonal grammar of a sign language – British Sign Language (BSL), in particular. Opening the discussion he stresses the significance of the visual-spatial modality through which BSL speakers communicate and outlines the three main dimensions of its expression plane (manual, non-manual and spatio-kinetic). He then shows how these resources as mobilised to realise SPEECH FUNCTION and MOOD systems. The main factors differentiating types of move and their polarity are changes in non-manual and/ or spatio-kinetic production (e.g. raised versus lowered eyebrows, head shake versus head nod), alongside the use of manual signs to specify the kind of information requested in elemental interrogatives and MODALITY. He closes with an insightful analysis of a phase of dialogue based on this analysis.

Bartlett (Chapter 9) describes the interpersonal grammar of Scottish Gaelic using a text-based approach. This enables him to move via the discourse-semantic systems of NEGOTIATION and ENGAGEMENT to an exploration of how distinctions in these systems are related to function structures in lexicogrammar. Bartlett identifies the Predicator and Finite as crucial functions realising MOOD features in Scottish Gaelic and describes in detail how different structures at lower ranks, clitics in particular, are organised to enact the different clause interpersonal types. Bartlett's approach offers a particularly important contribution to this volume – he argues that indicative MOOD in Scottish Gaelic, unlike other languages, does not involve a primary opposition between [declarative] and [interrogative] in relation to NEGOTIATION. Rather, indicative MOOD's primary agnation is between [assertive] and [non-assertive], which is related to the system of ENGAGEMENT in discourse semantics. Typologically, he reinforces the stance proposed by the other chapters in this volume – particularly those of Zhang, Wang, and Martin and Cruz – namely that organisation of MOOD needs to be accounted for in terms of how it realises both NEGOTIATION and ENGAGEMENT.

References

Andersen, T. H., Petersen, U. H. & Smedegaard, F. (2001). *Sproget Som Ressource: Dansk Systemisk Funktionel Lingvistik i Teori og Praksis*. Odense: Odense Universitetsforlag.
Caffarel, A. (2006). *A Systemic Functional Grammar of French*. London: Continuum.
Caffarel, A., Martin, J. R. & Matthiessen, C. M. I. M., eds., (2004). *Language Typology: A Functional Perspective*. Amsterdam: John Benjamins.
Doran, Y. J. & Martin J. R. (in press). Field Relations: Understanding Scientific Explanations. In K. Maton, J. R. Martin and Y. Doran, eds., *Teaching Science: New Insights into Knowledge and Language in Education*. London: Routledge.
Gleason, H. A. (1965). *Linguistics and English Grammar*. New York: Holt, Rinehart & Winston.

Halliday, M. A. K. (1961). Categories of the Theory of Grammar. *Word*, *17*, 241–92.
Halliday, M. A. K. (1966). The Concept of Rank: A Reply. *Journal of Linguistics*, *2*(1), 110–18.
Halliday, M. A. K. (1984). Language as Code and Language as Behaviour: A Systemic Functional Interpretation of the Nature and Ontogenesis of Dialogue. In R. Fawcett, M. A. K. Halliday, S. Lamb and A. Makkai, eds., *The Semiotics of Culture and Language*, Vol. 1 of *Language as Social Semiotic*. London: Frances Pinter, pp. 3–35.
Halliday, M. A. K. (1985). *An Introduction to Functional Grammar*, 1st ed., London: Edward Arnold.
Halliday, M. A. K. (1992). Systemic Grammar and the Concept of a 'Science of Language'. In J. J. Webster, ed., (2003), *On Language and Linguistics*, Vol. 3 of *The Collected Works of M. A. K. Halliday*. London: Continuum, pp. 199–212.
Halliday, M. A. K. (1996). On Grammar and Grammatics. In R. Hasan, C. Cloran and D. Butt, eds., *Functional Descriptions. Theory in Practice*. Amsterdam: John Benjamins, pp. 1–38.
Halliday, M. A. K. & Matthiessen, C. M. I. M. (2009). *Systemic Functional Grammar: A First Step into the Theory*. Beijing: Higher Education Press.
Halliday, M. A. K. & Matthiessen, C. M. I. M. (2014). *Halliday's Introduction to Functional Grammar*. London: Edward Arnold.
Hao, J. (2020). *Analysing Scientific Discourse from a Systemic Functional Linguistic Perspective: A Framework for Exploring Knowledge Building in Biology*. London: Routledge.
Lavid, J., Arús, J. & Zamorano-Mansilla, J. R. (2010). *Systemic Functional Grammar of Spanish: A Contrastive Study with English*. London: Continuum.
Martin, J. R. (1983). Participant Identification in English, Tagalog and Kâte. *Australian Journal of Linguistics*, 3 (1), 45–74. DOI: https://doi.org/10.1080/07268608308599299.
Martin, J. R. (1990). Interpersonal Grammatization: Mood and Modality in Tagalog. *Philippine Journal of Linguistics*, *21*(1), 2–50.
Martin, J. R. (1992). *English Text: System and Structure*. Amsterdam: John Benjamins.
Martin, J. R. (1995). Logical Meaning, Interdependency and the Linking Particle Na/Ng in Tagalog. *Functions of Language*, *2*(2), 189–228.
Martin, J. R. (1998). Participant Identification in English, Tagalog and Kâte. *Australian Journal of Linguistics*, *3*(1), 45–74.
Martin, J. R. (2008). What Kind of Structure? – Interpersonal Meaning and Prosodic Realisation across Strata. *Word*, *59*(2), 113–43.
Martin, J. R. (2015) Meaning beyond the Clause: Co-textual Relations. *Linguistics and the Human Sciences*, *11*(2–3), 203–35.
Martin, J. R. (2016). Meaning Matters: A Short History of Systemic Functional Linguistics. *Word*, *61*(2), 35–58.
Martin, J.R., ed., (2018a) *Interpersonal Meaning: Systemic Functional Linguistics Perspectives*. (Special issue of *Functions of Language*, *25*(1)).
Martin, J. R., ed., (2018b) Introduction: Interpersonal Meaning: Systemic Functional Linguistics Perspectives. (Special issue of *Functions of Language*, *25*(1)), 2–19.
Martin, J. R. & Cruz, P. (2018). Interpersonal Grammar of Tagalog: A Systemic Functional Linguistics Perspective. *Functions of Language*, *25*(1), 54–96.

Martin, J. R. & Doran, Y. J., eds., (2015a). *Grammatics*, Vol. I of *Systemic Functional Linguistics: Critical Concepts in Linguistics*. London: Routledge.

Martin, J. R. & Doran, Y. J., eds., (2015b). *Grammatical Descriptions*, Vol. 2 of *Systemic Functional Linguistics: Critical Concepts in Linguistics*. London: Routledge.

Martin, J. R. & Doran, Y. J., eds., (2015c). *Around Grammar: Phonology, Discourse Semantics and Multimodality*, Vol. 3 of *Systemic Functional Linguistics: Critical Concepts in Linguistics*. London: Routledge.

Martin, J. R. & Doran, Y. J., eds., (2015d). *Context, Register and Genre*, Vol. 4 of *Systemic Functional Linguistics: Critical Concepts in Linguistics*. London: Routledge.

Martin, J. R. & Doran, Y. J., eds., (2015e). *Language in Education*, Vol. 5 of *Systemic Functional Linguistics: Critical Concepts in Linguistics*. London: Routledge.

Martin, J. R., Doran, Y. J. & Figueredo, G., eds., (2020). *Systemic Functional Language Description: Making Meaning Matter*. London: Routledge.

Martin, J. R. & Quiroz, B. (2020). Functional Language Typology: A Discourse Semantic Perspective. In J. R. Martin, Y. J. Doran and G. Figueredo, eds., *Systemic Functional Language Description: Making Meaning Matter*. London: Routledge, pp. 189–237.

Martin, J. R. & Quiroz, B. (in press). Functional Language Typology: SFL Perspectives. In M. Kim, J. Munday, P. Wang and Z. Wang, eds., *Systemic Functional Linguistics and Translation Studies*. London: Bloomsbury.

Martin, J. R., Quiroz, B., Wang, P. & Zhu, Y. (in press). *Systemic Functional Grammar: Another Step into the Theory – Language Description*. Beijing: Higher Education Press.

Martin, J. R. & Rose, D. (2003). *Working with Discourse: Meaning beyond the Clause*, 1st ed., London: Continuum.

Martin, J. R. & Rose, D. (2007). *Working with Discourse: Meaning beyond the Clause*, 2nd ed., London: Continuum.

Martin, J. R. & Rose, D. (2008). *Genre Relations: Mapping Culture*. London: Equinox.

Martin, J. R., Wang, P. & Zhu, Y. (2013). *Systemic Functional Grammar: A Next Step into the Theory – Axial Relations*. Beijing: Higher Education Press.

Martin, J. R. & White, P. (2005). *The Language of Evaluation: Appraisal in English*. London: Palgrave.

Matthiessen, C. M. I. M. (2004). Descriptive Motifs and Generalizations. In A. Caffarel, J. R. Martin, and C. M. I. M. Matthiessen, eds., *Language Typology: A Functional Perspective*. Amsterdam: John Benjamins, pp. 537–673.

Matthiessen, C. M. I. M. (2018). The Notion of a Multi-lingual Meaning Potential: A Systemic Exploration. In A. Sellemi-Baklouti and L. Fontaine, eds., *Perspectives from Systemic Functional Linguistics*. London: Routledge, pp. 90–120.

Matthiessen, C. M. I. M. & Halliday, M. A. K. (2009). *Systemic Functional Grammar: A First Step into the Theory*. Beijing: Higher Education Press.

Matthiessen, C. M. I. M., Teruya, K. & Lam, M. (2010). *Key Terms in Systemic Functional Linguistics*. London/New York: Continuum.

Matthiessen, C. M. I. M., Teruya, K. & Wu, C. (2008). Multilingual Studies in a Multi-dimensional Space of Interconnected Language Studies. In J.J. Webster, ed., *Meaning in Context: Implementing Intelligent Applications of Language Studies*. London: Continuum, pp. 146–220.

McGregor, W. B. (1990). *A Functional Grammar of Gooniyandi*. Amsterdam: Benjamins.

Mwinlaaru, I. N., Matthiessen, C. M. I. M. & Akerajola, E. (2018). A System-Based Typology of MOOD in Niger-Congo Languages. In A. Agwuele and A. Bodomo, eds., *The Handbook of African Linguistics*. London: Routledge, pp. 93–117.

Mwinlaaru, I. N. & Xuan, W. W. (2016). A Survey of Studies in Systemic Functional Language Description and Typology. *Functional Linguistics*, 3(8).

Pittman, R. S. (1948) Nuclear Structures in Linguistics. *Language*, 24(3), 287–92.

Quiroz, B. (2020). Experiential Cryptotypes: Reasoning about PROCESS TYPE. In J. R. Martin, Y. J. Doran and G. Figueredo, eds, *Systemic Functional Language Description: Making Meaning Matter*. London: Routledge, pp. 102–28.

Rose, D. (2001). *The Western Desert Code: An Australian Cryptogrammar*. Canberra: Pacific Linguistics.

Shin, G-H. (2018) Interpersonal Grammar of Korean: A Systemic Functional Linguistics Perspective. *Functions of Language*, 25(1), 20–53.

Teruya, K. (2007). *A Systemic Functional Grammar of Japanese*. London: Continuum.

Teruya, K., Akerejola, E., Andersen, T. H., Caffarel, A., Lavid, J., Matthiessen, C. M. I. M., Petersen, U. H., Patpong, P. & Smedegaard, F. (2007). Typology of MOOD: A Text-Based and System-Based Functional View. In R. Hasan, C. M. I. M. Matthiessen and J. Webster, eds., *Continuing Discourse on Language: A Functional Perspective*, Vol. 2, London: Equinox Publishing, pp. 859–920.

Teruya, K. & Matthiessen, C. M. I. M. (2015). Halliday in Relation to Language Comparison and Typology. In J. J. Webster, ed., *The Bloomsbury Companion to M. A. K. Halliday*, London: Bloomsbury, pp. 427–52.

Ventola, E. (1987). *The Structure of Social Interaction: A Systemic Approach to the Semiotics of Service Encounters*. London: Frances Pinter.

Webster, J. J., ed., (2005). *Computational and Quantitative Studies*. Vol. 6 of *The Collected Works of M. A. K. Halliday*). London: Continuum.

Whorf, B. L. (1945). Grammatical Categories. *Language*, 21(1), 1–11.

2 Interpersonal Grammar in Spanish

Beatriz Quiroz

2.1 Introduction

Traditionally, descriptive work on Spanish has shown little interest in specifically addressing the grammatical resources available to enact interactive roles and negotiate meanings in dialogue. The approaches closest to this concern are arguably those inspired by Benveniste (1970), who proposed that a number of resources in *langue*, actualised and shaped by the 'act of enunciation', position interlocutors in the 'figurative framework' of dialogue. With respect to the linguistic resources 'actualised' in his figurative framework, Benveniste offers a new perspective on the so-called main syntactic functions in the continental European descriptive tradition. He claims that statements, questions and exhortations ('assertion', 'interrogation' and 'intimation', respectively) cannot be understood if not with respect to the act of enunciation, which necessarily positions the speaker in relation to an addressee (pp. 15–16). Thus, in the francophone linguistic tradition, Benveniste provides a new perspective on traditional sentence types, locating them within the dynamics of interlocution and coreference.

Beyond Benveniste's contributions, however, grammatical descriptive work on Spanish does not offer a systematic framework for the study of linguistic resources used by speakers to negotiate relationships and position themselves in a dialogic exchange (e.g. Bosque & Demonte, 1999; Di Tullio, 2014). One reason for this may be the fact that grammatical studies in the Hispanic tradition have not been particularly interested in resources used in interactive daily-life contexts. Moreover, the deployment of such resources in naturally occurring texts was until recently not taken too seriously as a source of empirical evidence in Spanish grammar studies.

Systemic functional linguistics (henceforth, SFL), on the other hand, has long been explicitly concerned with such resources within the framework of a general and integrated theory of language. Indeed, in his first comprehensive contextually oriented approach to interpersonal meaning, Halliday (1984) puts forward the idea that specific resources in the linguistic system have evolved out of the interactive needs that are intrinsic to semiosis as *behaviour* (pp. 7–8). These resources, in his view, have the same status as other resources which tend to be disproportionately focused on in descriptive work – especially in approaches heavily influenced by 'philosophical grammars', which privilege the 'representational' component at the expense of the interpersonal (as also argued in Poynton, 1990).

Taking English as the point of departure, Halliday shows that the structuring of dialogue shows regularity within the internal organisation of the linguistic system (Halliday, 1984, p. 33). As a form of 'linguistic behaviour', dialogue can be approached in terms of systems of choice across linguistic strata and linguistic units (p. 10). In this way, he offers a perspective on the interpersonal grammar of English in relation to strata and units 'from above', and that today is fully developed in comprehensive and well-known descriptions (Halliday, 1985, 1994; Halliday & Matthiessen, 2014).

This chapter aims at exploring the specificities of the interpersonal grammar of Spanish following a similar approach – that is, one which begins with functional motivations in order to understand the Spanish clause as an exchange 'from above'. The chapter is organised in three sections. To begin with, it focuses on the interpersonal metafunction in general, taking a look at the (discourse-)semantic motivations for addressing the clause as a resource to negotiate interactive roles and semiotic commodities; this is initially explored through an account of MOOD in English. These motivations will then be connected to the pioneering work by Caffarel (1995, 2006) on the French clause. Her work will be shown to lay the foundations for understanding typological differences that are key for the account of the interpersonal grammar of languages other than English, and of Romance languages in particular. Based on the discussion in previous sections, the chapter then moves on to a discourse-oriented account of interpersonal resources in Spanish, with a special focus on Chilean Spanish. The chapter closes with a discussion of the implications of the perspective adopted both for descriptive work in Spanish and for typological work that is sensitive to convergence and divergence across languages.

2.2 Interpersonal Grammar 'from Above'

2.2.1 SPEECH FUNCTION *Variables (English)*

In his exploration of the interpersonal grammar of English, Halliday (1984) proposes a top-down interstratal view of clause resources deployed in dialogue. He begins by considering systems at higher orders of semiotic organisation in social context, beyond language, and then turns to their relation to linguistic systems in semantics and lexicogrammar. In semantics, Halliday recognises

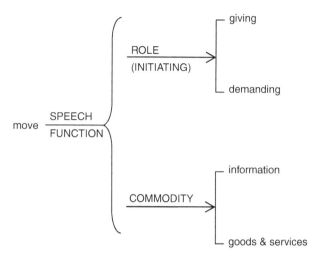

Figure 2.1 Basic SPEECH FUNCTION network in semantics (adapted from Halliday & Matthiessen 2014, p. 136)

a system organising two very general and fundamental resources at stake in dialogic moves: (i) those concerning the type of 'commodity' exchanged in the interaction, and (ii) those concerning the speech roles adopted and assigned by interlocutors (e.g. Halliday, 1994, p. 68; Halliday & Matthiessen, 2014, p. 136). As seen in Figure 2.1, these resources constitute the system of SPEECH FUNCTION, which includes the ROLE and COMMODITY subsystems.

The ROLE system accounts for very general choices concerning the interactive roles taken up by the speaker: giving or demanding. When speakers enact these roles in initiating dialogic moves they simultaneously assign complementary roles to the addressee(s), who may take them up or challenge them in subsequent, responding moves not represented in the network of Figure 2.1 (but considered in Halliday 1994, p. 69; Halliday & Matthiessen 2014, p. 136). The COMMODITY system accounts for either the exchange of non-linguistic goods-and-services (if the speaker requires or offers a course of action not coded linguistically) or the exchange of information (if the speaker demands or gives information that is *necessarily* coded linguistically – or semiotically).

The cross-classification of these primary choices in ROLE and COMMODITY in initiating moves defines, in turn, four general kinds of move in semantics: statements, questions, commands and offers. The system network in Figure 2.2 informally shows these functions as shorthand names for bundles of features chosen along the network from left to right (rather than features in the network itself). From a semantic point of view, Halliday (1985, 1994) would also argue that

2 Interpersonal Grammar in Spanish

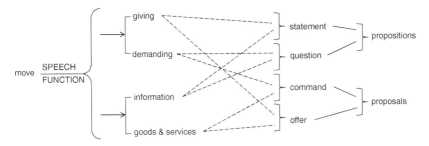

Figure 2.2 Propositions and proposals in relation to SPEECH FUNCTION choices

specific kinds of move have a distinctive potential for arguability depending on the commodity exchanged. SPEECH FUNCTION variables concerned with the exchange of information 'can be affirmed or denied, and also doubted, contradicted, insisted on, accepted with reservation, qualified, tempered, regretted, and so on' in the exchange (p. 70). That is, statements and questions share a basic type of negotiability defining them as **propositions**. In contrast, interpersonal moves involving the exchange of goods-and-services cannot be affirmed or denied: their negotiability does not depend on the validity of the information being given or demanded, but rather on the compliance, refusal, acceptance or rejection of courses of action. Accordingly, commands and offers are grouped together as **proposals** (1994, pp. 69, 71). As can be seen in the network of Figure 2.2, propositions and proposals are not, strictly speaking, systemic features, but shorthand labels grouping interpersonal moves concerning the negotiation of information or goods-and-services, respectively (for the motivation of features in system networks in SFL, see Martin et al., 2013).

Halliday (1984, 1985, 1994) proposes that general SPEECH FUNCTION variables in semantics are typically realised in English lexicogrammar by distinct clause types in the system of MOOD. In other words, statements, questions, commands and offers **congruently** correlate with basic clause types in the lexicogrammatical stratum: declarative, interrogative and imperative clauses.[1] In general terms, SFL typological research points to the cross-linguistic validity of this interstratal correspondence, since speakers of all languages negotiate roles and semiotic commodities in dialogue, which can be in turn related to basic clause types or **clause moods** in the lexicogrammar (Matthiessen et al., 2008; Teruya et al., 2007). According to this assumption, propositions,

---

[1] Non-congruent interactions between choices at different strata are modelled in SFL in terms of grammatical metaphor. Within the interpersonal metafunction, mood metaphors account for the fact that the same speech function may be realised by interpersonal clause types different from those congruently associated with them (e.g. Halliday, 1984, pp. 13–14; 1994, p. 363ff.).

including statements and questions, would tend to be realised in MOOD lexicogrammatical systems as indicative clauses, including declarative and interrogative clauses, respectively. The grammar of proposals, however, appears to be less elaborate than that of propositions (as Halliday suggests, based on his work on English); while commands tend to be congruently realised by imperative clauses, offers, in general, do not regularly correlate in the same way with distinct clause patterns (Halliday 1984, p. 20, Teruya et al., 2007, p. 868, Matthiessen et al., 2008, pp. 168–9).

2.2.2 The Negotiatory Structure of the Clause (English)

In English, the (congruent) lexicogrammatical realisation of interpersonal moves in primary MOOD choices at the lexicogrammatical stratum involves, 'from below', specific structural configurations for each clause type. Figure 2.3 shows these structural configurations by means of realisation statements preceded by a slanted arrow.

The English MOOD network thus shows that Subject and Finite are critical functions in the structure of the clause. Their presence (or absence), as well as their relative positioning in the sequence, constitute the key patterns motivating a number of clause contrasts along the network. From a structural point of view, then, Subject and Finite make up the interpersonal 'core' of the English clause, and this is one important reason why they are grouped together in what is known as the Mood element. There are, however, other reasons, semantic in nature, for grouping together the two functions in this way. Halliday argues that, when looked at 'from above', Subject and Finite are essential for the 'arguability status' assigned to the clause.

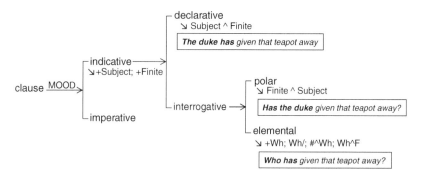

Figure 2.3 English MOOD network, with examples taken from Halliday (1994, p.74)

The arguability status of the clause, according to Halliday, depends, on the one hand, on the element assigned modal responsibility for the proposition or proposal. That is, the 'person' – interactant or non-interactant – held interpersonally responsible either for the various assessments of validity associated with the arguability of propositions or for the compliance associated with the arguability of proposals. In English, Halliday would argue that modal responsibility falls in fact on the Subject function in clause structure (for further discussion about modal responsibility, see Figueredo, Chapter 7).

The second aspect contributing to the arguability status of the clause concerns the structural element grounding the clause to the 'here and now' of the speech event. In Halliday's view, such an element in English is the Finite function, which grounds the clause to the speech event by means of temporal and modal distinctions (Halliday, 1994, pp. 75ff.; Halliday & Matthiessen, 2014, pp. 144ff.). Other elements which are not crucial for the interpersonal status of the clause are thus placed outside this interpersonal core, that is, within the Residue – including (i) the Predicator, the section of the verbal group that does not play any key interpersonal role in the English clause and is recognised as separate from the Finite; (ii) one or two Complements encoding elements that can *potentially* be held modally responsible (through voice alternation); and (iii) experiential (circumstantial) Adjuncts (Halliday, 1994, p. 78ff., Halliday & Matthiessen 2014, p. 151ff.).[2] In this way, Subject and Finite in the Mood element carry the interpersonal 'burden' of the English clause as an interactive event. In fact, Halliday claims that this interpersonal core tends to remain constant in the unfolding of the dialogic exchange – unless an active step is taken by interlocutors to modify this pattern (Halliday, 1985, p. 77).

Martin (1992) extends this account of the interpersonal structure of the English clause from a discourse-oriented perspective. Based on work by Berry (1981) and Ventola (1987), he proposes a more dynamic account of interstratal interactions within the interpersonal metafunction in an analysis intended to move beyond adjacency pairs to longer sequences of interactive moves in dialogue. Modelling the structuring of dialogue as a process oriented to the resolution of exchanges, he notes that in English the Mood element can be further characterised in terms of the structural meanings put forward by interlocutors in the interaction. The Mood element is thus treated as the central domain of interpersonal meanings most 'at risk' in English because interlocutors tend to make a number of choices for Subject and the Finite, in ways that are more or less collaborative, to facilitate the progression of dialogic exchanges towards their resolution – with a strong tendency to ellipse in

---

[2] For the sake of the discussion in this chapter, Modal Adjuncts, which are interpersonal in nature, have not been accounted for. However, mainstream English descriptions include them either within the Mood element as Mood Adjuncts or within the Residue as Comment Adjuncts (Halliday 1994, p. 83, Halliday & Matthiessen 2014, p. 184).

successive moves those resources that are interpersonally less central to the exchange (i.e. those grouped in the Residue [Martin, 1992, p. 461ff.]).

In Martin's detailed analysis, reviewed in Table 2.1, the Subject is a primary resource enabling interlocutors to assign and dynamically negotiate (e.g. confirm, challenge, etc.) the modal responsibility of propositions and proposals in English. The Finite function, for its part, enables interlocutors to replay and, if necessary, adjust or substitute choices in POLARITY (negative or positive), MODALITY and (primary) TENSE. Based on this analysis, Martin proposes that Subject and Finite make up the basic **negotiatory structure** within the domain of the English clause (1992, p. 464).

The first descriptive study adopting a comparable discourse-oriented point of view to the interpersonal grammar of a language other than English was

Table 2.1 *Resources 'at risk' in English negotiation (adapted from Martin 1992, pp. 464–5)*

	Subject	Finite
[replay Mood]		
If I argue with you,	I	do
I must take up a contrary position.	I	must
– Yes.	(you)	(must)
[adjust POLARITY]		
This isn't an argument.	This	isn't
– Yes, it is!	it	is
– No, it isn't.	it	isn't
[adjust MODALITY]		
– Well, an argument isn't just contradiction.	arg.	isn't
– It can be.	it	can
– No, it can't.	it	can't
[substitute Subject]		
– You were the last one to use it yesterday.	you	were
– No, I wasn't.	I	wasn't
Andrew was.	Andrew	was
[substitute part of Residue]		
– I came here for a good argument.	I	(did)
– No, you didn't.	you	didn't
You came here for an argument.	you	(did)
[replace proposition]		
You came here for an argument.	you	(did)
– Well, an argument isn't just contradiction.	argument	isn't

Caffarel (1995) in her description of the French clause, showing important differences from the patterns described for English (see Section 2.2.3). Likely inspired by her pioneering work, Teruya et al. (2007) review the interpersonal structure of a number of languages and suggest that the way in which core interpersonal clause resources are deployed and foregrounded in verbal exchanges shows clear cross-linguistic variation. A typological **cline** comparing the 'basic negotiatory structure' of the languages under analysis is then proposed (p. 913). Languages which tend to negotiate mainly by means of two discrete Subject and Finite structural functions, like English, are located near the 'Mood element–based' pole, whereas those which tend to negotiate by means of the Predicator function, realised through a verbal group, are located near the 'Predicator-based' pole. Teruya et al. suggest that along this cline, Romance languages such as French and Spanish occupy an intermediate position.

Before specifically proposing an alternative interpretation for Spanish, Caffarel's (1995, 2006) discourse-oriented perspective to the interpersonal grammar of French will be reviewed in more detail.

2.2.3 Interpersonal Resources in a Romance Language: The Descriptive Contribution of the French Clause

Caffarel's (1995, 2006) account of French lexicogrammar has provided important foundations for understanding the specific nature of interpersonal resources in Romance languages from a discourse-semantic point of view. First, from the viewpoint of the congruent realisation of choices in SPEECH FUNCTION, Caffarel shows that interpersonal clause types in French are structurally motivated by configurations different from English – admitting even more delicate possibilities in choices that are comparable in English (1995, p. 24). Thus, where English distinguishes between declarative and polar interrogative clauses through the relative sequence of Subject and Finite, polar interrogative clauses in French admit three more delicate choices with distinct realisations – including (i) changes in intonation (rising tone for polar interrogatives), (ii) the presence of the interrogative marker *est-ce que*, or (iii) the sequencing of Finite before Subject (as in English) (1995, pp. 6, 8). Examples provided by Caffarel (1995, p. 30; see Example 2) illustrate these possibilities for the more general feature [interrogative: polar] (see the system network in Caffarel, 1995, p. 28):

(1) *Tu aimes les gâteaux.*

(2) a *Tu aimes les gâteaux, hein?*
b *Est-ce que tu aimes les gâteaux?*
c *Aimes-tu les gâteaux?*

In this way Caffarel introduces an important principle – 'from above' the motivation of choices in MOOD in terms of basic interpersonal moves does seem to apply cross-linguistically. But crucial differences are to be found in the language-specific structural resources motivating systemic choices *within* lexicogrammar (1995, pp. 2, 23).

Secondly, from the viewpoint of the dynamics of verbal negotiation, Caffarel's analysis reveals that in French three elements of structure, Subject, Finite and the Predicator, constitute the interpersonal core of the French clause – since the three functions are the main resources that are put 'as risk' by interlocutors in the progression of the dialogic interaction (1995, pp. 3–6; 2006, pp. 121ff.). In other words, in French, the verbal group realising the Finite and Predicator, alongside the nominal group realising the Subject, are the resources routinely tossed back and forth in verbal exchanges. In light of this pattern, Caffarel proposes the term **Negotiator** to group together the functions making up the interpersonal core of the clause in French – as illustrated in Example 3, adapted from Caffarel (1995, p. 8):

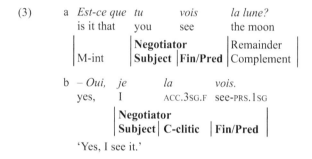

As seen in the example, Caffarel (1995, 2006) analyses other structural elements, including Complements (and Adjuncts), outside this basic negotiatory structure. The **Remainder** is thus the section of the French clause which is not central for the establishment of its negotiability status – neither in terms of the progression towards the resolution of verbal exchanges nor in terms of the realisation of propositions/proposals (cf. English in Halliday, 1985, 1994; Halliday & Matthiessen, 2014; Martin, 1992). Functions like Mood interrogator (M-int) in Example 3a are interpreted as peripheral to both the Negotiator and the Remainder in the French clause (2006, p. 125). However, as shown in Example 3b, other elements may be included in the French Negotiator when realised by **clitics** – that is, non-salient particles closely associated with the verbal group. French clitics include pronominal elements indexing recoverable or identifiable entities at group rank, and they become part of the negotiation in verbal exchanges (Caffarel 1995, pp. 9, 16).

Similar patterns have been described in Brazilian Portuguese by Figueredo (2011, p. 175) based on the analysis of resources deployed by speakers in dialogic exchanges. Figueredo also recognises a Negotiator grouping together Subject, Finite and Predicator. Other SFL descriptive proposals for Romance languages, such as the ones Gouveia (2010) offers for European Portuguese and Lavid et al. (2010) for (standard) Peninsular Spanish, do not, however, consider the role of the clause in the dynamics of interaction. Despite this divergence, such descriptive proposals do converge on the critical role the verbal group *as a whole* plays in the realisation of key interpersonal distinctions made in these languages.

2.3 The Clause as Exchange in Spanish

From the perspective of the interpersonal metafunction, lexicogrammatical resources have been shown to contribute in various ways to the status of the clause as a move in the exchange. First, structural configurations that differ across languages tend to congruently realise comparable semantic SPEECH FUNCTION variables, crucially contributing to their negotiability status as propositions and proposals. Secondly, key elements in clause structure are foregrounded and deployed by speakers when they negotiate meanings in the unfolding of the dialogic exchange, allowing a more dynamic view of the basic negotiatory structure of the clause. Along these lines, interstratal relations have been shown to hold for English and in French in specific ways. The organisation of clause resources in Spanish is explored in this section, starting once again 'from above'.

Spanish subtitles for the Monty Python sketch analysed by Martin (1992, pp. 464–5) are presented in Example 4.[3] Following Leipzig notational conventions, word-for-word glosses are provided in a first layer, with hyphenation ('-') used to single out the verb inflection from the verb lexical root, and the equal sign ('=') to indicate clitic elements. In a second layer, the analysis of constituents at group/phrase rank is provisionally shown without specifying yet the structural functions realised by each of them at clause rank. Finally, a semi-idiomatic English back-translation is offered for each clause:

(4) A: a ¡*Oiga!*   *esto*   *no es*   *una discusión*
         listen-SUBJ.3SG   this   not be-PRS.3SG   a discussion
                                     nominal gr   verbal gr   nominal gr

'Hey, this is not a discussion'

---

[3] These subtitles, provided by an anonymous YouTube user, were retrieved on 1 April 2010 from www.youtube.com/watch?v=4KzlLYsIPvE. See the transcription of the English original in Martin (1992, p. 465).

B: b – Sí lo=es
       | yes ACC.N=be-PRS.3SG |
       | verbal gr |
       'It is indeed it'

A: c Son   solo   contradicciones
      | be-PRS.3PL | | only | | contradictions |
      | verbal gr | | adv gr | | nominal gr |
      'They are only contradictions'

B: d – No lo=son
       | not ACC.N=be-PRS.3PL |
       | verbal gr |
       'They are not it'

A: e Sí son
       | yes be-PRS.3PL |
       | verbal gr |
       'They are indeed'

B: f – No lo=son
       | not ACC.N=be-PRS.3PL |
       | verbal gr |
       'They are not it'

A: g ¡Lo=son!
       | ACC.N=be-PRS.3SG |
       | verbal gr |
       'They are it!'

   h ¡Me=acab-a de contradecir!
       | ACC.1SG=finish-PRS.3SG LNK contradict.INF |
       | verbal gr (complex) |
       'You have just contradicted me!'

B: i – No lo=h-e hecho
       | not ACC.N=have-PRS.1SG have.PRTCP |
       | verbal gr |
       'I have not done it'

A: j ¡Lo=h-izo!
       | ACC.N=have-PST.3SG |
       | verbal gr |
       'You did it!'

2 Interpersonal Grammar in Spanish   45

B: k   – *No no no no no*
       'No no no no no'

A: l   *Lo=acab-a de hacer   de nuevo*
       | ACC.N=finish-PRS.3SG LNK have.INF | again |
       | verbal gr (complex) | adv gr |
       'You just did it again'

B: m   – *No no*
       'No no'

   n   *son   tonterías*
       | be-PRS.3PL | nonsense |
       | verbal gr | nom gr |
       'They are nonsense'

A: o   *Esto   es   basura*
       | this | be-PRS.3SG | rubbish |
       | nom gr | verbal gr | nom gr |
       'This is rubbish'

B: p   – *No lo=es*
       | not ACC.N=be-PRS.3SG |
       | verbal gr |
       'It is not it'

A: q   *Entonces d-e=me   un buen argumento*
       | then | give-SBJ.3SG=ACC.1SG | a good argument |
       | conj | verbal gr | nominal gr |
       'Then give me a good argument'

B: r   – *Usted no me=h-a dado   un buen argumento*
       | you | not DAT.1SG=have-PRS.3SG give.PRCTP | a good argument |
       | nom gr | verbal gr | nominal gr |
       'You haven't given me a good argument'

A: s   *[[Discutir y contradecir]]   no es   lo mismo*
       | [[discuss.INF and
         contradict.INF]] | not be-PRS.3SG | the same |
       | [[clause complex]] | verbal gr | nominal gr |
       'Discussing and contradicting is not the same'

B: t   – *Pued-e ser*
       | can-PRS.3SG be.INF |
       | verbal gr |
       'It can be'

A: u   ¡No!
        'No!'

    v   ¡no pued-e!
        | not can-PRS.3SG |
        | verbal gr |

        'it cannot!'

    w   [[Discutir]]   es   [[dar una serie de opiniones para
                                         llegar a una opinión común.]]
        | [[discuss.INF]] | be-PRS.3SG | [[give.INF a series of opinions to
        | | | arrive at a common opinion]] |
        | [[clause]] | verbal gr | [[clause complex]] |

        'Discussing is to give a series of opinions in order to reach
        a shared opinion'

B: x   – No lo=es
        | not be-PRS.3SG |
        | verbal gr |

        'It is not it'

A: y   Sí lo=es
        | yes be-PRS.3SG |
        | verbal gr |

        'It is it indeed'

    z   No es   nada más   [[contradecir]]
        | not be-PRS.3SG | | nothing more | | [[contradict.INF]] |
        | verbal gr | | adverbial gr | | [[clause: non-finite]] |

        'It is not only just contradicting'

B: aa – Mir-e,
        | look-SUBJ.3SG |
        | verbal gr |
        'Look'

    bb Si   discut-o   con usted,
        | if | | discuss-PRS.1SG | | with you |
        | conj | | verbal gr | | prep phrase |

        'If I discuss with you,'

2 Interpersonal Grammar in Spanish

cc *Teng-o que tomar*   *la posición contraria*

| have-PRS.1SG LNK take.INF | the position contrary |
| verbal gr (complex) | nominal gr |

'I have to take the contrary position'

A: dd *Pero*   *no es*   *solo*   *[[decir que no]]*

| but | not be-PRS.3SG | only | [[say.INF LNK no]] |
| conj | verbal gr | adv gr | [[clause complex]] |

'but it is not just saying no'

B: ee – *¡Que*   *sí!*
LNK   yes
'Yes (indeed)'

A: ff *¡Que*   *no!*
LNK   no
'No (indeed)'

gg *La discussión*   *es*   *un proceso intelectual*

| the discussion | be-PRS.3SG | a process intellectual |
| nominal gr | verbal gr | nominal gr |

'The discussion is an intellectual process'

hh *[[Contradecir]]*   *es*   *solo*   *[[decir lo contrario]]*

| [[contradict.INF]] | be-PRS.3SG | only | [[say.INF the contrary]] |
| nominal gr | verbal gr | adv gr | [[clause]] |

'Contradicting is just saying the contrary'

B: ii – *No lo=es*

| not ACC.N=be-PRS.3SG |
| verbal gr |

'It is not it'

A: jj *Sí lo=es*

| yes ACC.N=be-PRS.3SG |
| verbal gr |

'It is it indeed'

B: kk – *Para nada*
'Not at all'

A: ll *Ahora*   *mir-e ...*

| now | look-SUBJ.3SG |
| conj | verbal gr |

'Now, look ...'

In this dialogic text, the finite verbal group, mostly on its own, appears to be a key resource to put interpersonal meanings 'at risk' in Spanish. Such meanings are often replayed and adjusted in responding moves through choices in PERSON, TENSE and POLARITY within the domain of the verbal group alone. The pro-verb *hacer* ('to do') is frequently used to negotiate these meanings in responding moves, as in Examples 4i and 4j. However, responding moves may also replay the experiential ('lexical') meaning of the verbal group, as in Example 5, where some clauses from the subtitles have been revised to allow for this possibility:

(5) A: h *¡Me=acab-a de contradecir!*
ACC.1SG=finish-PRS.3SG LNK contradict.INF
'You have just contradicted me!'

B: i' *– No lo=h-e contradicho*
not ACC.3SG=have-PRS.1SG contradicted.PRTCP
– 'I haven't contradicted you'

A: j' *¡Me=contradij-o!*
ACC.1SG=contradict-PST.3SG
'You contradicted me!'

B: k *Me=acab-a de contradecir*   *de nuevo*
ACC.1SG=finish-PRS.3SG LNK contradict.INF   again
'You just contradicted me again'

As in Romance languages in general, the portmanteau inflectional verb morphology conflates a number of distinctions that are key to grounding the clause to the speech event. First, the exchange in Example 4 shows that, in Spanish, the modally responsible person (interactant or non-interactant) is necessarily part of the inherent negotiability of propositions and proposals – since the choice of person in the verb inflection is *obligatory* in any finite clause. Other 'persons' may be optionally included in the negotiation by means of pronominal clitics, either accusative or dative – as illustrated by clauses in Examples 4d and 4q, which deploy *lo* (accusative, neuter third person) and *me* (dative, first person singular), respectively. These non-salient elements are so closely associated with the verb(s) in the Spanish verbal group, that many scholars suggest that clitics are on their way to become inflectional morphemes (e.g. Belloro, 2007; Fernández Soriano, 1999; Vázquez Rozas & García Salido, 2012). Thus still within the verbal group, pronominal clitics in Spanish allow for choices in PERSON other than the modally responsible one replayed by the inflectional morphology.

The POLARITY of the clause, either positive or negative, is replayed within the domain of the verbal group as well, both by means of the negative particle *no* or the emphatic positive particle *sí* in the same tone group (Carbonero Cano, 1980; Dumitrescu, 1973) – as is illustrated in the clauses in Examples 4d and 4e.

Basic negotiatory resources centred in the finite verbal group also play an important role in the congruent realisation of different interpersonal moves in Spanish – as can be seen in the following exchange extracts taken from call centre service encounters (from data analysed by Castro, 2010).

(6)   a   *No camb-ia los canales*
            'It doesn't change the channels'

      b   *–¿No cambi-a los canales el control remoto?*
            – 'Does not the remote control change the channels?

(7)   a   *¿Cancel-ó el día de ayer?*
            'Did you pay yesterday?'

      b   – Correcto
            – 'Correct'

      c   *¿A qué hora cancel-ó?*
            'What time did you pay?'

      d   *– Doce cincuenta y cuatro minutos con doce segundos*
            – 'Twelve fifty-four and twelve seconds'

Example 6a shows the congruent realisation of a statement through a (non-elliptical) declarative clause; Examples 6b and 7a illustrate the congruent realisation of questions through polar interrogatives; and Example 7c shows the congruent realisation of a question by an elemental clause. Polar interrogative clauses are the resources typically used in question moves seeking for confirmation, while elemental clauses are regularly associated with question moves seeking information (Caffarel, 1995, p. 7). The examples show that the congruent realisation of statements and questions in Spanish mainly depends on two kinds of resources: (i) the choice in TONE, with falling tone in declarative clauses and rising tone in polar interrogatives;[4] and (ii) the presence of an interrogative marker, as is the case in elemental interrogatives, typically at initial position (Martínez Celdrán & Fernández Planas, 2013, pp. 214–13, 221).

---

[4] Phonological choices in TONE apply to the Tonic element in the tonic group (Halliday & Greaves, 2008). The Tonic element is analogous to the unit known as *tonema* in Spanish descriptive tradition (after Navarro Tomás, 1944); it is the section of the tone group where its major pitch movement takes place – in the unmarked case centring on its last salient syllable (Martínez Celdrán & Fernández Planas, 2013).

The relative sequence of clause constituents (nominal groups and verbal groups) does not bear on interpersonal distinctions. In the same way, the presence or absence of a nominal group showing syntagmatic agreement relations with the finite verbal group does not play any interpersonal role – since the person modally responsible for the negotiability of the propositions is realised by contrasts in PERSON in the verb inflection.

As for the realisation of commands, the following exchange in Example 8, taken from the same service encounter data, illustrates the main possibilities. In this example, a speaker is giving a series of instructions to his daughter on the phone (whose responses cannot be heard in the recording).

(8) S: a *Hija,   necesit-o   que prend-a   los dos deco*
            daughter need-PRS.1SG LNK switch.on-SUBJ.3SG the two decoders
            'Child, I need you to switch on the two set-top boxes'

      S: b *El de la pieza de mi ma ...*
            'The one in my mum's roo ... '

      S: c *Necesit-o   que   prend-as   los dos deco*
            need-PRS.1SG   LNK   switch.on-SUBJ.2SG the two decoders
            'I need you to switch on the two set-top boxes'

      S: d *Prend-e   el cable.*
            switch.on-IMP.2SG   the cable
            'Switch on the cable TV'

      S: e *Sí, los dos*
            'Yes, both'
            tanto el de arriba como el de la pieza mía
            'the one upstairs as well as the one in my room'

      S: f *Sí, los dos.*
            'Yes, both.'

      S: g *Prend-e   la tele y todo*
            switch.on-IMP.2SG   the telly and all
            'Switch on the telly and all'

      S: h *Ya, chao.*
            'OK, bye.'

In this exchange, the realisation of a series of commands ranges from non-congruent, by means of declarative clauses in Examples 8a and 8c, to congruent, by means of imperative clauses, in 8d and 8g. In imperative clauses, the verb inflection conflates choices in PERSON (second person singular) and 'verb mood' (in the examples, imperative morphology). The realisation of commands shows again that crucial interpersonal meanings are centred in the finite verbal group, in the case of imperative clauses, through a specific range of morphological contrasts at word rank. Once again, the presence or absence of a nominal group establishing agreement relations with the finite verbal group is immaterial to the identification of imperative clauses.

At this point, it is worthwhile noting that imperative clauses are not restricted to clauses selecting for imperative mood morphology (cf. Lavid et al. 2010). As shown by Quiroz (2017a, 2018), a key lexicogrammatical pattern featuring them as the congruent realisation of commands involves the position of clitic elements relative to the inflected verb. Imperative clauses selecting positive polarity in Spanish *obligatorily* require the postposition ('enclisis') of any clitic (pronominal or non-pronominal), as in *Deme un buen argumento* ('Give **me** a good argument') in the clause in Example 4q. This pattern clearly distinguishes imperative clauses from indicative clauses, where clitics generally *precede* the inflected verb ('enclisis'): obligatorily in those clauses including a simplex verbal group, as in Examples 4b, 4d and 4f–g; optionally if specific verbal group complexes are present, since clitics may be attached to the last verb in sequence if this takes an infinitive or gerundive form. This distinctive clitic patterning shows that, in the Spanish spoken in the Americas, imperative clauses allow for 'present subjunctive' morphology as well. The possibility of present subjunctive morphology allows in turn for further choices in PERSON in Spanish imperative clauses (though still restricted), and no further temporal and modal distinctions, as is the case in indicative clauses (Quiroz 2008, 2017a, 2018).

2.3.1 *The Negotiator in Spanish*

It has been shown so far that resources at stake both in the dynamics of dialogue and in the realisation of SPEECH FUNCTION variables in the Spanish clause are centred in the domain of the finite verbal group. The negotiability of the clause – insofar as it realises propositions or proposals in lexicogrammar – is largely established by means of intonation and/or resources in the verbal group. This is so regardless of the presence or absence of other constituents at clause rank, their positioning relative to the verbal group or any potential agreement relations.

Consequently, from the viewpoint of the basic structure of the clause, it is the finite verbal group as a whole that realises what is here identified as the **Predicator** function. Within the Negotiator, this is the minimal element required to establish the negotiability of a (non-elliptical) clause. The analysis of this basic structure is provided in Examples 9 and 10.

(9) a *Teng-o*   *dos decodificadores*   *en mi casa.*
      have-PRS.1SG   two set-top boxes   in my house
      Negotiator   **Remainder**
      Predicator
      verbal group   nominal group   prepositional phrase
      Finite/Event
      'I have two set-top boxes at home.'

   b *Los=teng-o.*
     ACC.3PL=have-PRS.1SG
     Negotiator
     Predicator
     verbal group
     P-clitic Finite/Event
     'I have them.'

(10) a *No cambi-a*   *los canales.*
       not change-PRS.3SG   the channels
       Negotiator   **Remainder**
       Predicator
       verbal group   nominal group
       Neg Finite/Event
       'It does not change the channels.'

   b *No los=cambi-a.*
     not ACC.3PL=change-PRS.3SG
     Negotiator
     Predicator
     verbal group
     Neg P-clitic Finite/Event
     'It doesn't change them.'

In the analysis provided, the finite verbal group is the central interpersonal resource in the Spanish clause. More specific distinctions admitted within the domain of this constituent are here interpreted as functions one rank below, that is, at group rank: Neg(ator), Finite and Event (for a systemic account of the Spanish verbal group, see Quiroz, 2013, 2017b; Martin et al., in press). In a way similar to French, examples show that other elements can be made part of the negotiation if they involve clitics (accusative and/or dative, if pronominal), which in the analysis here proposed realise P(articipant)-clitic, also within the internal structure of the verbal group (for the functions assigned to non-pronominal clitics in Spanish, see Quiroz, 2013, 2017b).

This interpretation of the interpersonal basic negotiatory structure of the Spanish clause is different from French (Caffarel, 1995, 2006) and from Portuguese (Figueredo, 2011; Gouveia, 2010) – not simply in the ways it factors out the contributions at clause and at group rank. Here, functions such as Subject and Finite are not proposed as part of the interpersonal structure of the clause. As already suggested, there is no evidence that the nominal group entering into 'agreement' relations with the finite verbal group in Spanish can be interpreted interpersonally. This agreeing constituent does not play any role in establishing the negotiability status of the clause, which is consistent with the fact that such a constituent is not generally put 'at risk' by interlocutors in dialogic exchanges, as shown in Examples 4 and 6–8. The person held modally responsible for the validity of the proposition or the compliance of the proposal is, instead, routinely replayed and adjusted by person contrasts in the portmanteau verb morphology, within the domain of the Predicator. This strongly suggests treating the so-called explicit Subject of Spanish reference grammars from a different angle (as it will be discussed in the conclusion, Section 2.4).

The recognition of a Finite element contributing to critical interpersonal contrasts 'from above' is not justified at clause rank either. Various structural probes used in English and French to recognise such a function can be reviewed in relation to Spanish. First, in question-answers adjacency pairs, Spanish does not isolate any element that is comparable to the English Finite. Replies to confirming questions in Examples 11 and 12 show that the proposition (or proposal) can be replayed either through a Polarity Adjunct, as in Examples 11a and 12a, or by means of the Predicator, as in 11b and 12b.

(11)   ¿No cambi-a   los canales?

   Predicator

   'Doesn't it change the channels?'
   a   – No.
   b   – No, no los=cambi-a.
        – 'No, it does not change them.'

(12)   ¿H-as prendido   el cable?

   Predicator

   'Have you switch on the cable TV?'
   a   – Sí.
        – 'Yes.'
   b   – Lo=h-e prendido.
        – 'I have switched it on.'

In other words, the examples show that responses to confirming questions in Spanish may replay or adjust the polarity of the proposition only by means of a polarity Modal Adjunct in elliptical clauses (cf. Halliday, 1994, p. 92; Halliday & Matthiessen, 2014, p. 175). Alternatively, responding moves may replay the proposition through the finite verbal group realising the Predicator,[5] needed *as a whole* for choices in (primary and secondary) TENSE, PERSON and

---

[5] Nonetheless, as seen in the clause in Example 4v, some canonical modal verbs such as *poder* and *deber* may be replayed on their own in responding moves. In some complex verbal groups (so-called verb periphrases), the alpha element (α) can also be picked out in a similar way (see Fernández de Castro, 2000).

MODALITY at the rank immediately below the clause (Quiroz, 2013, 2017b; Martin et al., in press).

Another probe used to single out the Finite in languages such as English as well as Brazilian Portuguese involves interpersonal tags ('Mood tags' in Halliday & Matthiessen, 2014, p. 148; Figueredo, 2011). Comparable elements used by speakers to elicit the confirmation in Spanish are irrelevant for the recognition of a Finite (or a Subject). At least in Chilean Spanish, there are several interpersonal tags available to speakers, which instead replay the polarity of the whole proposition or proposal. In the following examples, tags in Spanish (underlined) are specifically used to confirm statements (Example 13), commands (14) and offers (15).

(13) *No cambi-a los canales el control remoto, ¿cierto? / ¿verdad? / ¿no?*
'The remote control does not change the channels, right? / true? / no?'

(14) *Prend-e el decodificador, ¿ya?*
'Switch on the set-top box, OK?'

(15) *¿Prend-o el decodificador o no?*
'Should I switch on the set-top box or not?'

Another pattern often used to recognise a discrete Finite is its position relative to other elements in the structure. Caffarel (2006) shows that negative polarity markers and some Modal Adjuncts clearly 'mark off' Subject, Finite and Predicator as discrete structural functions in the French clause. She argues that the Subject is outside the scope of negation (as it precedes the polarity marker *ne*) and that both the polarity marker *pas* and Modal Adjuncts in general further contribute to the identification of a separate Finite function within the French Negotiator (2006, pp. 128, 134). In Spanish, however, structural possibilities differ from the French pattern, as shown in the comparison between Examples 16 and 17.

(16) | *Je* | *ne* | *le lui* | *ai* | *probablement* | *pas* | *donné.* |
|---|---|---|---|---|---|---|
| I | not | it him | have | probably | not | given |
| **Nego** ... | | | | **Remainder** | ..**tiator** | |
| Subject | A-neg | | Finite | Modal Adjunct | A-neg | Predicator |

'I probably didn't give it to him.'

(17) a *Probablemente*   *no se=lo=h-e dado.*
probably   not DAT.3SG=ACC.3SG have-PRS.1SG given.PRCTP
Remainder   **Negotiator**
Modal Adjunct   **Predicator**
adverbial group   verbal group
'Probably I haven't given it to him.'

b *No se=lo=h-e dado*   *probablemente.*
   not DAT.3SG=ACC.3SG have-PRS.1SG given.PRCTP   probably
   Negotiator   **Remainder**
   Predicator   **Modal Adjunct**
   verbal group   adverbial group
   'I haven't given it to him probably.'

In Spanish, where the positioning of clause rank constituents is very flexible (unlike in French), any element is structurally outside the scope of negation if it is preceding a negative Predicator (Quiroz, 2013). Unmarked polarity is thus realised within the Predicator, with particles *no* and *sí* always leading the sequence in the internal structure of the verbal group. At group rank, the positioning of elements relative to each other is, in fact, rather fixed. Between polarity particles and the inflected verb, the only elements that can be potentially inserted are clitics (not more than two and following a very strict order, e.g. Fernández Soriano, 1999). Alarcos (1980) notes that non-salient *no*, which is thus analysed here as part of the Predicator, is quite different from other resources classified as 'negation adverbs' in that it is necessarily attached to the 'verbal nucleus' (1980, p. 333) – thus clearly distinguishing it from stressed polarity Modal Adjuncts *no* or *sí* replaying polarity on their own as an elliptical clause, in a separate tone group (as in Examples 11a and 12a). Carbonero Cano (1980, p. 165) offers a similar treatment when he proposes the characterisation of non-salient *no* as a 'verb modifier'.

As for other Modal Adjuncts, their positioning further supports the interpretation of an interpersonal centre embodied by the Predicator, since they can only precede or follow this function – as Examples 17a and 17b show with *probablemente* (see Quiroz, 2013, for a basic systemic account of the verbal group in Chilean Spanish). Such a Modal Adjunct could never be interpolated between an arguably separate Finite and Predicator the way it is possible in French (or in English). Any alteration in the sequencing of elements that tries to force the delimitation of a separate Finite is either rarely found in highly spontaneous spoken language, as in Example 18a, or plainly ungrammatical, as illustrated by Examples 18b and 18c.

(18) a ? *No se=lo=h-e*   *probablemente*   *dado.*
        not DAT.3SG=ACC.3SG=have-PRS.1SG probably   give.PRTCP
        ? 'I haven't probably given it to him.'

     b * *No se=lo*   *probablemente*   *h-e dado.*
        not DAT.3SG=ACC.3SG probably   have-PRS.1SG give-PRTCP
        * 'I haven't probably given it to him.'

     c * *Se=lo=h-e*   *probablemente*   *no dado.*
        DAT.3SG=ACC.3SG=have-PRS.1SG probably   not give.PRTCP
        * 'I haven't probably given it to him.'

The account of the interpersonal core of English, French and Spanish 'from above' shows, therefore, a number of significant differences. In English, the resources establishing the negotiability of the clause and foregrounded in the dialogic exchange are interpreted in terms of the 'subjecthood' and 'finiteness' made manifest by two discrete elements in the structure of the clause – that is, Subject · Finite, grouped together as the Mood element (Halliday, 1994; Halliday & Matthiessen, 2014). In French, the resources on which the negotiability of the clause rest are centred in three functions, Subject · Finite · Predicator, grouped together as the Negotiator (Caffarel, 1995, 2006). In Spanish, the relevant interpersonal contrasts and the structural resources at stake are realised within the domain of the finite verbal group alone. Accordingly, from a structural point of view, the Predicator is the fundamental function grounding the Spanish clause to the speech event – being, at the same time, the core of the negotiatory structure at play in unfolding dialogue. This is not surprising if one considers that the sole presence of a Predicator is, all other things being equal, enough for the full realisation of a non-elliptical finite clause in Spanish (as seen in Examples 4h–j).

2.3.2 The Clause as Exchange: Implications for the Contrastive Analysis of Structure

The discourse-semantic orientation adopted here to address the interpersonal structure of the Spanish clause has a number of consequences when contrasted with the account of English clause structure taken as point of departure in early SFL accounts of Spanish (e.g. Ghio & Fernández, 2008; Menéndez et al., 1999).

In English, the Subject has been characterised 'from above' in terms of the constituent which is 'elevated interpersonally' as the element held modally responsible for the proposition or proposal (Teruya et al., 2007, p. 877). But in Spanish, a structural Subject function realised by a nominal group at clause rank is immaterial for the establishment of modal responsibility. The analysis of dialogic exchanges shows that portmanteau inflectional morphology in the verbal group indicates by itself the person modally responsible for the proposition or the proposal (i.e. the speaker, the addressee or a non-interactant). This explains why the so-called grammatical subject, strictly understood in terms of syntagmatic agreement relations with the verbal group, may be present or not – since it does not play a role in establishing the status of the clause as an exchange. In this sense, the account offered here diverges from the interpretation of Spanish offered by Lavid et al. (2010), who do assume the existence of a Subject in the interpersonal structure of the Spanish clause (2010, p. 237).

As for 'finiteness', SFL accounts of the English clause associate this notion with those contrasts (apart from modal responsibility) that confer on the clause its 'arguable' status (e.g. Halliday, 1994, p. 75). This interpretation in English is only applicable to proposals, not to propositions, since only propositions are grounded to the speech event by means of key (temporal or modal) contrasts mediated by the Finite. Secondly, the alternative discourse-semantic interpretation offered by Martin (2000) concerned with the dialogic exchange from a more dynamic perspective points to the English Subject as the 'nub' of the negotiation, while contrasts centred in the Finite are posited as the 'terms' around which the negotiation unfolds (p. 68). The interactive complementarity of these two functions and the crucial role they play in English dialogue comes out very clearly in his analysis of interactive data (e.g. the Monty Python *sketch* and the fight among siblings analysed in Martin, 1992, pp. 468ff.).

From neither point of view there is evidence in Spanish justifying a discrete Finite function. Lavid et al. (2010), in fact, agree on the irrelevance in a Finite function in Peninsular Spanish – pointing at the structural patterns already reviewed (i.e. the absence of interrogative tags picking up such a function, its irrelevance for mood type distinctions and the replay of the whole verbal group in elliptical clauses (2010, pp. 242–3). In other words, the 'grounding' of the clause in Spanish does not seem to be structurally dissociated from modal responsibility – at clause rank, at least. It is portmanteau morphology in the finite verbal group, that is the resource that substantially contributes to the negotiability of the clause 'from below', including all of the relevant conflated contrasts at lower ranks.[6] In this sense, it is worthwhile taking into account the traditional notion of 'finiteness' in Western linguistics, which can be traced back to Priscian's Latin grammar. In Priscian's view, finiteness is not restricted to word classes nor tense contrasts and additionally includes pronominal reference 'to define' (Lat. *finire*) the 'grounding of the utterance' from a *semantic* perspective (Maas, 2004, p. 362).

Based on the patterns reviewed in Spanish, the MOOD network in Figure 2.4 can be proposed (for an in-depth discussion of the axial motivation of the MOOD system in Spanish see Quiroz 2017a, 2018).

2.4 Conclusion

In this chapter, the starting point was the review of the (discourse-)semantic patterns motivating 'from above' the interpersonal grammar of Spanish. This involved looking at the clause as a resource for the basic negotiation of interactive roles (giving and demanding) and semiotic commodities (information and goods-and-services) in dialogue. This view on the negotiability (or

---

[6] Nonetheless, the identification of a Finite function in the internal structure of the verbal group is convenient to account for the (primary) tense distinctions contributing to ground the clause to the speech event (see Quiroz, 2013, and Martin et al., in press, for a systemic-functional outline of tense in Spanish).

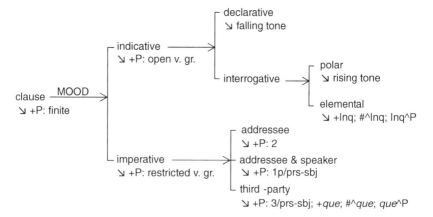

Figure 2.4 A MOOD system of Spanish (adapted from Quiroz, 2018)

'arguability') of the clause has been complemented with a more dynamic analysis of key clause resources speakers put 'at risk' in the process oriented to the resolution of exchanges. Drawing on the analysis offered by Caffarel (1995, 2006) for the basic negotiatory structure of French, the Negotiator function here has been proposed as the discourse-semantic function representing the interpersonal 'core' of the Spanish clause (in a way comparable to the Mood element in English). The Spanish Negotiator covers within its domain key contrasts routinely negotiated (replayed, adjusted or substituted) in dialogue. Specifically, the Predicator, through the finite verbal group, emerges as the function minimally required in the basic negotiatory structure of the Spanish clause.

Since the recognition of a Subject function cannot be justified from an interpersonal point of view in Spanish, the nominal group establishing agreement relations with the finite verbal group may be accounted for in terms of other metafunctional components (i.e. experiential and/or textual – see Martin et. al., in press; Quiroz, 2013). From a non-SFL perspective, discourse-oriented studies provide various explanations for why such an 'agreeing' nominal group (traditionally analysed as 'grammatical subject') may appear in spoken and written Spanish texts. Such explanations include the need to establish (information) contrasts – to recover the identity of discourse referents or introduce new ones, the need to specify the lexical meaning of a non-interactant referent or the need to assign a given element 'topical' status (Comajoan, 2006; Silva-Corvalán, 1984, 2003; Travis, 2007). From an SFL perspective, such patterns can be associated with systems of choice motivated by other metafunctions, both

2 Interpersonal Grammar in Spanish

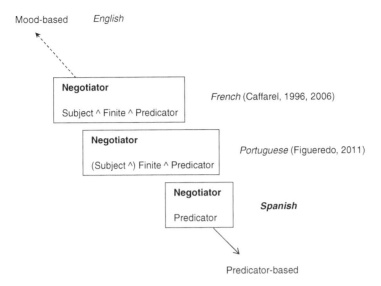

Figure 2.5 Basic negotiatory structures in three Romance languages

in the lexicogrammar and discourse semantics (e.g. by choices in IDENTIFICATION, IDEATION or PERIODICITY, comparable to those proposed by Hao, 2020; Martin, 1992; Martin & Rose, 2007).

In terms of cross-linguistic contrasts, Figure 2.5 proposes a cline of typological characterisation – drawing on comparable SFL accounts of the interpersonal grammar of English, French and Portuguese. Along this cline, English is located near the Mood-based pole, being a canonical (and rather typologically exotic) example of languages that negotiate by means of Subject and Finite functions. Romance languages, on the other hand, tend to occupy those positions near the Predicator-based pole – as languages negotiating through the verbal group. It is this constituent that emerges as a crucial resource both in Spanish and in other Romance languages.

The discourse-semantic approach proposed in this chapter has foregrounded the functional and interactive motivation of interpersonal lexicogrammatical resources, as deployed in situated texts (specifically in the context of dialogic negotiation). It is suggested that basic interpersonal clause types and their internal structure are motivated 'from above' by the interactive needs of Spanish speakers.

Space limitations have precluded the analysis of additional features that contribute to a full account of the interpersonal structure in the Spanish clause. This would involve (i) exploring the systemic organisation of MOOD in terms of the axial (system-structure) complementarity defining the paradigmatic environment of the clause 'from around' (for which see the detailed analysis in Quiroz, 2017a, 2018), as well as (ii) exploring those systems of choice *along the rank scale* contributing to interpersonal Spanish distinctions 'from below' – specially within the domain of the verbal group (but see Quiroz, 2013, 2017b). Certainly, the significance of a fully fledged 'trinocular' perspective – 'from above', 'from around' and 'from below' – resides in making possible the integrated and functional description of the lexicogrammar of any language (Halliday, 2003, p. 202ff.; 2002, p. 408ff.). Nonetheless, the specific value of the view 'from above' carefully explored in this chapter lies, as suggested by Martin (1983), in it being a crucial starting point for SFL typological work – preventing the imposition of descriptive categories developed for lexicogrammar of one language, such as English, onto another, such as Spanish.

References

Alarcos, E. (1980). *Estudios de Gramática Funcional del Español* [Studies in a Functional Grammar of Spanish], 3rd ed., Madrid: Gredos.
Belloro, V. (2007). *Spanish Clitic Doubling: A Study of the Syntax-Pragmatics Interface*. Unpublished PhD dissertation, State University of New York at Buffalo.
Benveniste, É. (1966). *Problèmes de Linguistique Générale* [Problems in General Linguistics], Vol. I. Paris: Éditions Gallimard.
Benveniste, É. (1970). L'appareil formel de l'enonciation [The Formal Apparatus of Enunciation]. *Langages*, 17, 12–18.
Berry, M. (1981). Systemic Linguistics and Discourse Analysis: A Multi-layered Approach to Exchange Structure. In M. Coulthard and M. Montgomery, eds., *Studies in Discourse Analysis*. London: Routledge & Kegan Paul, pp. 120–45
Bosque, I. & Demonte, V., eds., (1999). *Gramática Descriptiva de la Lengua Española* [Descriptive Grammar of the Spanish Language], 3 vols. Madrid: Espasa.
Caffarel, A. (1995). Approaching the French Clause as a Move in Dialogue: Interpersonal Organisation. In R. Hasan and P. Fries, eds., *On Subject and Theme: A Discourse Functional Perspective*. Amsterdam: John Benjamins, pp. 1–49.
Caffarel, A. (2006). *A Systemic Functional Grammar of French: From Grammar to Discourse*. London: Continuum.
Carbonero Cano, P. (1980). Afirmación, negación, duda [Assertion, Negation, Doubt]. *Revista Española de Lingüística*, 10, 161–76.
Castro, S. (2010). *Las Disfluencias en el Habla Espontánea de Santiago de Chile* [Disfluencies in Spontaneous Speech in Santiago, Chile]. Unpublished master's thesis, Pontificia Universidad Católica de Chile, Santiago, Chile.
Comajoan, L. (2006). Continuity and Episodic Structure in Spanish Subject Reference. In J. Clancy Clements and J. Yoon, eds., *Functional Approaches to Spanish Syntax: Lexical Semantics, Discourse and Transitivity*. Basingstoke: Palgrave Macmillan, pp. 53–79.
Di Tullio, Á. (2014). *Manual de Gramática del Español* [Manual of Spanish Grammar], 2nd ed., Buenos Aires: Waldhuter Editores.

Dumitrescu, D. (1973). Apuntes sobre el uso enfático de sí (adv.) en el español contemporáneo [Notes on the Emphatic Use of Sí (adv.) in Contemporary Spanish]. *Revue Roumaine de Linguistique*, 18(5),407–13.

Fernández de Castro, F. (2000). *Las Perífrasis Verbales en el Español Actual* [Verbal Periphrases in Current Spanish]. Madrid: Gredos.

Fernández Soriano, O. (1999). El pronombre personal. Formas y distribuciones. Pronombres átonos y tónicos [The Personal Pronoun: Forms and Distributions. Tonic and Atonic Pronouns]. In I. Bosque and V. Demonte, eds., *Sintaxis Básica de las Clases de Palabras*. Vol. 1 of *Gramática Descriptiva de la Lengua Española)*. Madrid: Espasa, pp. 1209–73.

Figueredo, G. (2011). *Introdução ao Perfil Metafuncional do Português Brasileiro: Contribuições para os Estudos Multilíngues* [Introduction to the Metafunctional Profile of Brazilian Portuguese: Contributions to Multilingual Studies]. Unpublished PhD dissertation, Universidade Federal de Minas Gerais, Belo Horizonte, Brazil.

Ghio, E. & Fernández, M. D. (2008). *Lingüística Sistémico Funcional: Aplicaciones a la Lengua Española* [Systemic Functional Linguistics: Applications to the Spanish Language]. Santa Fe: Universidad Nacional del Litoral.

Gouveia, C. (2010). Towards a Profile of the Interpersonal Organization of the Portuguese Clause. *Documentação de Estudios em Linguística Teorica e Aplicada*, 26(1), 1–24.

Halliday, M. A. K. (1984). Language as Code and Language as Behaviour: A Systemic Functional Interpretation of the Nature and Ontogenesis of Dialogue. In R. Fawcett, M. A. K. Halliday, S. Lamb and A. Makkai, eds., *Language as Social Semiotic*. Vol. 1 of *The Semiotics of Culture and Language*. London: Frances Pinter, pp. 3–35.

Halliday, M. A. K. (1985). *An Introduction to Functional Grammar*, 1st ed., London: Edward Arnold.

Halliday, M. A. K. (1994). *An Introduction to Functional Grammar*, 2nd ed., London: Edward Arnold.

Halliday, M. A. K. (2002). On Grammar and Grammatics. In J. Webster, ed., *On Grammar*. Vol 1 of *The Collected Works of M.A.K. Halliday*. London: Continuum, pp. 384–417.

Halliday, M. A. K. (2003). Systemic Grammar and the Concept of a 'Science of Language'. In J. Webster, ed., *On Language and Linguistics*. Vol. 2 of *The Collected Works of M.A.K. Halliday*. London: Continuum, pp. 199–212.

Halliday, M. A. K. & Greaves, W. S. (2008). *Intonation in the Grammar of English*. London: Equinox.

Halliday, M. A. K. & Matthiessen, C. M. I. M. (2014). *Halliday's Introduction to Functional Grammar*. London: Routledge.

Hao, J. (2020). *Analysing Scientific Discourse from a Systemic Functional Linguistic Perspective: A Framework for Exploring Knowledge Building in Biology*. London: Routledge.

Lavid, J., Arús, J. & Zamorano Mansilla, J. R. (2010). *Systemic Functional Description of Spanish: A Contrastive Study with English*. London: Continuum.

Maas, U. (2004). Finite and Non-finite from a Typological Perspective. *Linguistics*, 42 (2), 359–85.

Martin, J. R. (1983). Participant Identification in English, Tagalog and Kâte. *Australian Journal of Linguistics*, 3(1), 45–74. DOI: https://doi.org/10.1080/07268608308599299.

Martin, J. R. (1992). *English Text: System and Structure.* Amsterdam: John Benjamins. DOI: https://doi.org/10.1075/z.59.
Martin, J. R. (2000). Grammar Meets Genre: Reflections on the 'Sydney School'. *Arts: The Journal of the Sydney University Arts Association*, 22, 47–95.
Martin, J. R., Quiroz, B., Wang, P. & Zhu, Y. (in press). *Systemic Functional Grammar: Another Step into the Theory – Grammatical Description.* Beijing: Higher Education Press.
Martin, J. R. & Rose, D. (2007). *Working with Discourse: Meaning Beyond the Clause*, 2nd ed., London: Continuum.
Martin, J. R., Wang, P. & Zhu, Y. (2013). *Systemic Functional Grammar: A Next Step into the Theory – Axial Relations.* Beijing: Higher Education Press.
Martínez Celdrán, E. & Fernández Planas, A. M. (2013). *Manual de Fonética Española: Articulaciones y Sonidos del Español* [Manual of Spanish Phonetics: Spanish Articulations and Sounds], 2nd ed., Barcelona: Ariel Letras.
Matthiessen, C. M. I. M., Teruya, K. & Canzhong, W. (2008). Multilingual Studies as a Multi-dimensional Space of Interconnected Language Studies. In J. Webster, ed., *Meaning in Context: Implementing Intelligent Applications of Language Studies.* London: Continuum, pp. 146–220.
Menéndez, S. M., Gil, J. M. & Baltar, R. (1999). *La Gramática Sistémico-Funcional: Una Introducción* [Systemic Functional Grammar: An Introduction]. Buenos Aires: Facultad de Filosofía y Letras, UBA.
Navarro Tomás, T. (1944). *Manual de Entonación Española* [Manual of Spanish Intonation]. Madrid: Guadarrama.
Poynton, C. (1990). The Privileging of Representation and the Marginalising of the Interpersonal: A Metaphor (and More) for Contemporary Gender Relations. In T. Threadgold and A. Cranny-Francis, eds., *Feminine/Masculine and Representation.* Sydney: Allen & Unwin, pp. 231–55.
Quiroz, B. (2008). Towards a Systemic Profile of the Spanish MOOD. *Linguistics and the Human Sciences*, 4 (*1*), 31–65. DOI: https://doi.org/10.1558/lhs.v4i1.31.
Quiroz, B. (2013). *The Interpersonal and Experiential Grammar of Chilean Spanish: Towards a Principled Systemic-Functional Description Based on Axial Argumentation.* Unpublished PhD dissertation, University of Sydney, Sydney, Australia. www.isfla.org/Systemics/Print/Theses/BQuiroz_2013.pdf (last accessed 23 October 2020).
Quiroz, B. (2017a). Gramática interpersonal básica del español: una caracterización sistémico-funcional del sistema de MODO [Basic Interpersonal Grammar of Spanish: A Systemic-Functional Account of the MOOD System]. *Lenguas Modernas*, 49, 157–82.
Quiroz, B. (2017b). The Verbal Group. In T. Bartlett and G. O'Grady, eds., *The Routledge Handbook of Systemic Functional Linguistics.* London: Routledge, pp. 301–18. DOI: https://doi.org/10.4324/9781315413891.
Quiroz, B. (2018). Negotiating Interpersonal Meanings: Reasoning about MOOD. *Functions of Language*, 25(1), 135–63. DOI: https://doi.org/10.1075/fol.17013.qui.
Silva-Corvalán, C. (1984). Topicalización y pragmática en español [Topicalisation and Pragmatics in Spanish]. *Revista Española de Lingüística*, 14, 1–19.
Silva-Corvalán, C. (2003). Otra mirada a la expresión del sujeto como variable sintáctica [Another Look to the Expression of Subject as Syntactic Variable]. In

H. López Morales, F. Moreno Fernández and R. Barriga Villanueva, eds., *Lengua, Variación y Contexto: Estudios Dedicados a Humberto López Morales*. Madrid: Arco Libros, pp. 849–60

Teruya, K., Akerejola, E., Andersen, T. H., Caffarel, A., Lavid, J., Matthiessen, C. M. I. M., Petersen, U. H., Patpong, P. & Smedegaard, F. (2007). Typology of MOOD: A Text-Based and System-Based Functional View. In R. Hasan, C. M. I. M. Matthiessen and J. Webster, eds., *Continuing Discourse on Language: A Functional Perspective*, vol. 2. London: Equinox, pp. 859–920

Travis, C. (2007). Genre Effects on Subject Expression in Spanish: Priming in Narrative and Conversation. *Language Variation and Change*, *19*(2), 101–35.

Vázquez Rozas, V. & García Salido, M. (2012). A Discourse-Based Analysis of Object Clitic Doubling in Spanish. In K. Davidse, T. Breban, L. Brems and T. Mortelmans, eds., *Grammaticalization and Language Change: New Reflections*. Amsterdam: John Benjamins, pp. 271–97.

Ventola, E. (1987). *The Structure of Social Interaction: A Systemic Approach to the Semiotics of Service Encounters*. London: Frances Pinter.

3 Interpersonal Grammar in Khorchin Mongolian

Dongbing Zhang

3.1 Introduction

This chapter provides a description of the basic interpersonal clause system in Khorchin Mongolian – the system of MOOD.[1] The linguistic phenomena described in the MOOD system in this chapter constitute an important part of the description of the Khorchin Mongolian sentence in Mongolian Linguistics (e.g. Bayancogtu, 2002; Caganhada, 1995).[2] Considered from the perspective of systemic functional linguistics (hereafter SFL), the MOOD system is one of the three perspectives on the clause – that is, the interpersonal perspective in contrast to ideational and textual (Martin et al., Chapter 1, this volume). This chapter first reviews the traditional description of the Khorchin Mongolian clause with a focus on the reference grammar by Bayancogtu (2002). It will then provide an integrated description of the comparable phenomena from the perspective of SFL.

3.1.1 *'Sentence' Grammar of Khorchin Mongolian*

3.1.1.1 Types of Sentences Bayancogtu (2002, pp. 419–34) classifies Khorchin Mongolian sentences in five different ways:

I am grateful for the insightful suggestions I received from the editors on the earlier draft of this chapter. I am particularly grateful for the informants of this study, who generously allowed me to record their conversations.

[1] Following the conventions in SFL, system names are written in small caps, except when non-SFL work is reviewed.

[2] The term sentence is used in SFL to refer to the graphological unit between two full stops. It is typically coextensive with clause complex in grammar. The use of the term *ogüleberi* 'sentence' in Mongolian linguistics is preserved when descriptions in that tradition is reviewed. The classical Mongolian script (i.e. Modern Written Mongolian) is transliterated with the scheme provided in Nasunbayar et al. (1982, p. 37).

3 Interpersonal Grammar in Khorchin Mongolian

i In terms of the realisation of the predicate: descriptive and narrative. Bayancogtu (2002, p. 420) does not provide an explanation. The examples show that the predicates in descriptive and narrative sentences are realised by nominal and verbal elements, respectively.
ii In terms of MOOD: declarative, interrogative, imperative and exclamative.
iii In terms of the relationship between sentences: simple and combined; within combined: coordinating or subordinating. Coordinating sentences are comparable to clauses in paratactic relations in SFL, and subordinating ones are related in terms of embedding (Halliday, 1994). According to Bayancogtu (2002, pp. 425–7), coordinating sentences are relatively independent while a subordinate sentence in a subordinating relation functions as part of the main sentence. Therefore, his account does not include what SFL refers to as hypotactic dependent clauses (see Halliday, 1994, pp. 221–5).
iv In terms of constituency: unexpanded, expanded and elliptical. Unexpanded sentences comprise subject and predicate. Expanded sentences involve the additional elements of attribute, object, adverbial and so on.
v In terms of the flexibility of the constituents: free and bound. The constituents in a bound sentence cannot be substituted freely.

The classification shows different degrees of variability. For example, classifications (i) and (ii) are independently variable as shown in Example 1.[3]

(1) a descriptive and declarative   ɘn mɐn nɛ mɐl
                                        this 1PL GEN cattle
                                          'This (is) our cattle.'

    b descriptive and interrogative   ɘn mɐn nɛ mɐl uː
                                          this 1PL GEN cattle IP
                                          '(Is) this our cattle?'

    c narrative and declarative t^hɘr mɐːt^{h}ɘr jɐp-ɘn
                                          3SG tomorrow leave-NPST
                                          'She leaves tomorrow.'

    d narrative and interrogative t^hɘr mɐːt^{h}ɘr jɐp-ɘn uː
                                          3SG tomorrow leave-NPST IP
                                          'Does she leave tomorrow?'

In contrast, there are some restrictions between classifications (ii) and (iii), classifications (ii) and (iv) and classifications (ii) and (v). In relation to (ii) and (iii), embedded sentences cannot be interrogative. In relation to (ii) and (iv), the

---

[3] The examples are adapted from Bayancogtu (2002, pp. 420–1). The phonemic transcription is adapted to reflect the variety of Khorchin Mongolian examined in this chapter. The morpheme-by-morpheme glossing used in this chapter mainly follows the Leipzig Glossing Rules (2015); the additional abbreviations used are INTJ = interjection, IP = interrogative particle, MP = modal particle, NDEF = non-definite, TEMP = temporal.

elliptical elements of a sentence are restricted by the MOOD type – for example, the 'pro-words' in elemental interrogative sentences cannot be elided. In relation to (ii) and (v), idioms are more likely to be declarative than interrogative.

Pending further SFL research on the interdependencies between clause systems in Khorchin Mongolian, it seems that classification (i) is more oriented towards the ideational layer of meaning (i.e. the linguistic resources for construing experience as configurations of occurrence and entity and of entity and entity/quality), and classifications (ii) to (v) are more oriented towards the interpersonal layer of meaning (i.e. the linguistic resources for enacting social relations, casting the interlocutors into different roles and fine-tuning the arguability of a proposition). This chapter focuses on systems comparable to classification (ii) and sets aside its interaction with the other classifications for future research.

3.1.1.2 Sentence Structure Some of Bayancogtu's (2002) classifications depend on the structural analysis of a sentence. He identifies two 'main' constituents and three 'secondary' constituents. The main constituents are subject and predicate; the secondary constituents are attribute, object and adverbial. Bayancogtu (2002) does not provide specific criteria for identifying the different constituents except that they can be realised by various classes of words. The clauses in Examples 1a and 1c would be analysed as Examples 2a and 2b.

(2) a

ɘn	mɐn	nɛ	mɐl
this	1PL	GEN	cattle
subject	attribute		predicate

'This (is) our cattle.'

b

tʰɘr	mɐːtʰɘr	jɐp-ɘn
3SG	tomorrow	leave-NPST
subject	adverbial	predicate

'She leaves tomorrow.'

The structural analysis in Bayancogtu (2002) is only relevant to some types of sentences reviewed in the previous section. For example, in classification (iv), an unexpanded sentence comprises only subject and predicate. An expanded sentence involves one or more of attributes, objects and adverbials. No attempt has been made to relate the structural analysis with the classification of sentences in terms of MOOD. Reference grammars such as Tserenpil and Kullman (2008, pp. 360–6) even separate the classification in terms of MOOD from the other 'types of sentences' as 'kinds of sentences'. For them, 'kinds of sentences' include declarative, interrogative, imperative and exclamative.

3 Interpersonal Grammar in Khorchin Mongolian   67

They are not determined by the structure of the sentence. On the other hand, the 'types of sentences' are determined by the structure of the sentence – for example, unexpanded and expanded sentences.

This disjunction between sentence structure and MOOD-based sentence classification in (Khorchin) Mongolian is likely due to the fact that MOOD in (Khorchin) Mongolian is determined by verbal suffixes and clause final particles, none of which have been traditionally considered relevant to sentence structure. Note that even for the types of sentence relevant to structural analysis, they are simply determined by the presence or absence of the 'secondary' constituents (i.e. expanded versus unexpanded) and the number of 'main' constituents (i.e. one predicate for simple and more than one for combined).

This chapter provides a layer of structural analysis for the Khorchin Mongolian clause in relation to MOOD from the perspective of SFL. MOOD will be described as an interpersonal system for clause. The options in the system are realised by particular structural configurations. The basic principle is thus that categories in lexicogrammar should be established based on 'lexicogrammatical reflex' (Halliday, 1985, p. xx). As Martin, Wang and Zhu (2013, p. 19) puts it, 'if no structural consequence, then no system'.

3.1.2 Towards the Interpersonal Grammar in Khorchin Mongolian

3.1.2.1 Data and Methodology This description of Khorchin Mongolian interpersonal grammar is based on conversational data collected during December 2017 to February 2018 in Jalaid Banner, Hinggan League, Inner Mongolia Autonomous Region, People's Republic of China. The examples mainly come from three data sets: (i) conversations between family members at home, (ii) conversations between colleagues at their office and (iii) conversations between government officials and peasants during a routine visit to the peasants' home. Occasionally introspective data are used to show certain patterns. The data are transcribed using Elan/Praat with IPA phonemic symbols. The phonemes by and large confirm Tiemei's (2015) description, except that /tʃʰ/ and /ʃ/ are distinct phonemes in the variety under examination. The transcriptions in this chapter consider case marking as separate items instead of suffixes following Penglin Wang's (1983) arguments.

The interpersonal grammatical categories are reasoned about from a 'trinocular perspective' (Halliday, 2009). As will be seen in the remainder of this chapter, the options in MOOD are considered (i) 'from below' in terms of the group rank realisations of the relevant clause rank functions, (ii) 'from around' in terms of the interdependencies between systems and (iii) 'from above' in terms of the discourse-semantic functions they realise. They are relevant to the theoretical categories of rank, axis and stratification as they are explained in Martin et al. (Chapter 1). An accessible introduction to trinocular reasoning in relation to interpersonal grammar is provided in Quiroz (2018).

3.1.2.2 SPEECH FUNCTION *versus* NEGOTIATION   The reasoning of MOOD options from above involves the discourse-semantic systems associated most closely with interactions. Two models of interaction were developed separately in SFL in the 1980s. One was Halliday's SPEECH FUNCTION-based interpretation of the English MOOD options (Halliday, 1984, 1985). The other was Berry's multifunctional formulation of exchange structure (Berry, 1981a, 1981b, 1981c, 1981d), developing the exchange rank originally proposed for classroom interaction in Sinclair and Coulthard (1975). Berry's interpersonal layer of exchange structure and her proposed textual system was later developed by Martin (1992) and Ventola (1987, 1988). Exchange structure is considered realising options from the interpersonal discourse-semantic system of NEGOTIATION in its later development (Martin, 1992, 2018; Martin & Rose, 2007).

The SPEECH FUNCTION-based model of interaction handles the relationship between pairs of interacts in terms of two simultaneous systems. One system is concerned with the roles of the interlocutors – that is, [giving] or [demanding]. The other system is concerned with the commodity being exchanged – that is, [information] or [goods-and-services]. The interaction between the two systems provides a semantic characterisation of the basic MOOD options in English. In the unmarked case, declarative clauses realise [giving; information], interrogative clauses [demanding; information] and imperative clauses [demanding; goods-and-services]. The semantic selection [giving; goods-and-services] does not have an unmarked realisation in English (Halliday, 1984, p. 20). The relationship between the selections from SPEECH FUNCTION and that from MOOD in English is exemplified in Example 3. The examples are from Halliday (1994, p. 69).

(3) SPEECH FUNCTION   unmarked MOOD choice
     giving; information   declarative   *He's giving her the teapot.*
     demanding; information   interrogative   *What is he giving her?*
     giving; goods-and-services   various   *Would you like this teapot?*
     demanding; goods-and-services imperative   *Give me that teapot!*

The NEGOTIATION system, on the other hand, handles interactions comprising up to five interacts. It generalises proportionalities such as the one in Example 4. The single colon (:) reads 'is to' and the double colon (::) reads 'as' (Halliday, 1966). The examples are from Berry (1981a, pp. 126–7) and Martin (2018, pp. 9–10).

(4) a   b   c
     – *Salisbury is the English* : – *In England, which*   : – *In England, which* ::
       Cathedral with the tallest   *cathedral has the*   *cathedral has the*
       spire.   *tallest spire?*   *tallest spire?*
                                    – *Salisbury.*   – *Salisbury.*
                                                                – *Yes.*

| – Joseph's here now. | – Who's there?
– Joseph. | : | – Wow, you'll never guess
who's here!
– Who's there?
– Joseph. |

In Example 4a the speaker indicates that they know the information and have authority over the information. In Example 4b, the first speaker indicates that they do not know the information and positions the second speaker as knowing the information. In Example 4c, the first speaker indicates that they know the information and check whether the second speaker also knows the information. After the second speaker indicates their knowledge of the information, the first speaker indicates their authority of the information. The speaker who knows the information and has authority over the information is referred to as 'primary knower' and the speaker who does not have authority over the information 'secondary knower' (Berry, 1981a, 1981b).

Structurally speaking, Berry (1981a) argues that for exchanges as in Example 4 to be well-formed there has to be a slot in which the primary knower indicates their knowledge of the information and shows authority over the information. This slot is called K1 (K=knower; 1=primary). The slot in which the secondary knower indicates their knowledge is called K2 (2=secondary). The slot in which the primary knower checks the secondary knower's state of knowledge is called Dk1 (D=delayed). Therefore, for an exchange concerning knowledge (i.e. a knowledge exchange) to be well-formed, K1 is obligatory under all circumstances. K2 is obligatory when the exchange is initiated by the secondary knower or when Dk1 is present. Dk1 is obligatory when the exchange is initiated by the primary knower and the secondary knower's state of knowledge is checked first. The second set of exchanges in Example 4 is thus analysed as Example 5.

(5) a K1 – Joseph's here now.
    b K2 – Who's there?
       K1 – Joseph.
    c Dk1 – Wow, you'll never guess who's here!
       K2 – Who's there?
       K1 – Joseph.

Martin (2018) refers to the types of exchanges in Examples 5a to 5c as [primary knower initiation: perform nuclear move], [secondary knower initiation] and [primary knower initiation: anticipate nuclear move], respectively. K1 is conceived as nuclear because of its obligatoriness. The term 'move' refers to the rank below exchange in Martin (1992, 2018), which is realised by a clause selecting independently for MOOD.

Comparable patterns are observed for exchanges concerning action (i.e. action exchanges) – as in Example 6. The interlocutor role 'primary actor' refers to the interlocutor who is responsible for performing the action; 'secondary actor' refers to the interlocutor who requests the other person to perform the action. The relevant functional slots are A1, A2, Da1. At Da1, the speaker checks the acceptability of the action before performing it at A1. A1 can be realised either verbally or non-verbally. The examples are from Martin (2018, pp. 9–10).

(6) a [primary actor initiation: perform nuclear move]

    A1 – Your Coke, sir. (while serving the Coke.)

   b [secondary actor initiation]

    A2 – Could I have a Coke instead (please)?
    A1 – OK.

   c [primary actor initiation: anticipate nuclear move]

    Da1 – Would you like a Coke, sir?
    A2 – OK.
    A1 – OK, sir.

The knowledge exchanges and action exchanges can potentially be followed up by the secondary knower/actor and then by the primary knower/actor as in – *Joseph's here now. – Really? – The very one!* (knowledge exchange) and – *Your Coke, sir – Thanks. – You're welcome.* (action exchange). This chapter only focuses on the non-follow-up interacts.

Halliday's (1984) SPEECH FUNCTION has been used extensively in the SFL descriptions of languages other than English (e.g. Caffarel et al. 2004; Mwinlaaru et al., 2018; Quiroz, 2013, 2018; Teruya et al., 2007). On the other hand, recent developments in SFL descriptive work informed by discourse semantics have productively engaged with Martin's (1992) NEGOTIATION system (e.g. Martin & Cruz, 2018; Martin et al., in press; Rose, 2018; Wang, 2020; Zhang, 2020b). The NEGOTIATION system enables us to see the various functions played by clauses at different points in an exchange. It is to this second enterprise that the current description of Khorchin Mongolian contributes.

3.2 NEGOTIATION in Khorchin Mongolian

Speakers of Khorchin Mongolian negotiate their knowledge of information through resources available for knowledge exchanges; and they negotiate the responsibility for carrying out an action through resources available for action exchanges. Exchanges may be initiated by the primary knower or secondary knower. They comprise recognisable structures with obligatory and optional elements in relation to the well-formedness of the exchange under examination.

3 Interpersonal Grammar in Khorchin Mongolian

The exchange in Example 7 exemplifies [secondary knower initiation]. The government official (O) takes up the secondary knower role; and the peasant (P) is cast in the role of primary knower.

(7) O = government official, P = peasant
    a O: K2   xən   ir-s   i:
                who   come-PST.PTCP   IP
                'Who came?'

    b P: K1   wutʃoɐŋpu   nɛ   xun   ir-tʃ
                Armed Forces Department   GEN   people   come-PST
                'People from the Armed Forces Department came.'

Instead of <u>accepting</u> the casted primary knower role as in [secondary knower initiation], one may <u>adopt</u> the primary knower role and cast the addressee in the secondary knower role (i.e. [primary knower initiation]). Two patterns emerge when this happens: (i) the speaker claims primary knower authority right away – as in Example 8; (ii) the speaker elicits information from the addressee and delays the stamping of primary knower authority until after this information is provided – as in Example 9. The exchange in 8 is from a workplace interaction between teachers (T = teacher); the exchange in 9 is adjusted from an interaction between a four-year-old girl (niece = N) and her uncle (U).

(8) T = teacher
    T1: K1   pi   pɔl   urlə   ir-tʃ   jɔl-x   uɛ
               1SG   TOP   morning   come-CVB   be.able.to-NPST.PTCP   NEG
               'I am not able to come in the morning.'

(9) N = niece, U = uncle
    a N: Dk1   ən   ju   kər   xiː-sən   tɐ
                 this   what   INS   make-PST.PTCP   IP
                 'What was this made from?'

    b U: K2   kʊjər
                flour
                'Flour.'

    c N: K1   tʰɐːr-tʃʰ
                correct-PRF
                '(It) is correct.'

The exchanges in Examples 8 and 9 show that K1 is obligatory under all circumstances for an exchange to be well-formed. As Martin (1992, p. 462) puts it, 'interlocutors work around an obligatory K1 ... which will resolve the exchange'. K2 is obligatory when an exchange is initiated by the secondary knower or when an exchange is initiated by the primary knower but the stamping of primary knower authority over the information is delayed. In the latter case, Dk1 is also obligatory.

Similar to the patterns observed for knowledge exchanges where the elements are organised with respect to an obligatory K1, elements in a Khorchin Mongolian action exchange configure relative to an obligatory A1. At A1 the primary actor carries out the action or provides a verbal promise. The exchange in Example 10 is a [primary actor initiation]. The daughter (D) is preparing for making a cake with her mother.

(10)   D = daughter
        D: A1   *ʃixir*   *kɐr-kɐ-ji*
                  sugar   out-CAUS-IMP.1
               'Let me take out some sugar.'

Alternatively, in [primary actor initiation] the primary actor may first check the acceptability of the action, hence delaying the performance – as in Example 11. The exchange occurred after the daughter had instructed her mother (M) to add yogurt into the bowl.

(11)   M = mother, D = daughter
      a   M: Da1   *xutəl-kə-ø*   *mɛ*
                       move-CAUS-NPST.PTCP   IP
                   '(Do I) move (= blend)?'

      b   D: A2   *xutəl-kə-ø*
                      move-CAUS-IMP.2
                   'Move (= blend).'

      c   M: A1   NV (= non-verbal)   (Mother starts the blender.)

The secondary actor may also initiate the exchange by requesting the action from the primary actor – as in Example 12 (i.e. [secondary actor initiation]).

(12)   D = daughter, M = mother
      a   D: A2   *ən*   *tɔtʰɔr*   *xi-ø*
                      PROX   inside   put-IMP.2
                  'Put (=separate) (the yolk) inside this (=the bowl).' (while pointing at the bowl)

      b   M: A1   NV   (Mother separates the yolk inside the bowl.)

Like K1 in a knowledge exchange, the examples so far show that A1 is obligatory under all circumstances for an action exchange to be well-formed. A2 is obligatory when an action exchange is initiated by the secondary actor or when an action exchange is initiated by the primary actor but the acceptability of the action is checked with the secondary actor first. In the latter case, Da1 is also obligatory. However, unlike the nuclear K1 in a knowledge exchange, A1 in an action exchange is not necessarily realised verbally – as in Examples 11 and 12. Alternatively, A1 may be realised as a verbal promise – as in Example 13 (introspective data).

3 Interpersonal Grammar in Khorchin Mongolian

(13) a A: A2   kɐr-ɔx   ui   lɛ   kɐn   liɛ   gi   gə-ø
                  out-NPST.PTCP time TEMP POSS garbage ACC throw-IMP.2
                  'When (you) go (out), throw out the garbage.'

    b B: A1   ɛi
                  INTJ
                  'Okay.'…
              NV   (B throws out the garbage when he leaves.)

Martin (2018, p. 11) uses the systemic opposition [immediate compliance] and [prospective compliance] in his NEGOTIATION system to account for the patterns observed in Examples 12 and 13 (for [immediate compliance] action is obligatory and verbalisation is optional; for [prospective compliance] action is optional and verbalisation is obligatory (Ventola, 1987, p. 101; also see Martin, 1992, pp. 48–9). The resources for knowledge exchange and action exchange are summarised as a system network in Figure 3.1. It shows that when information or action is unnegotiated, the information is directly imparted (at K1) or the action directly performed (at A1).

Note that the agnation pattern captured in Figure 3.1 is in contrast with Martin's (1992, 2018) networks. Therein the initiation of an exchange is privileged; thus the distinction in [perform nuclear move] and [anticipate

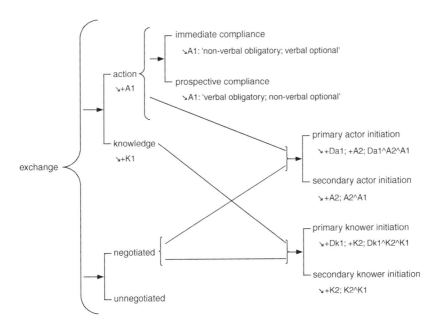

Figure 3.1 NEGOTIATION in Khorchin Mongolian

nuclear move] (the [unnegotiated] versus [negotiated] options in Figure 3.1) is considered more delicate.

One pending issue for action exchange has to do with the characterisation of the primary and secondary actor roles. The current characterisation is insufficient when both the speaker and the addressee are positioned as responsible for the carrying out of the action – as in Example 14 (introspective data).

(14) a A: A2 pɛtən ortɐr ʃirə ki ʃiltʃ-ul-jə
　　　　　　 1PL　　first　table　ACC　move-CAUS-IMP.1
　　　　'Let's move the table first.'

　　b B: A1 ɛi
　　　　　　 INTJ
　　　　'OK.'

　　B: NV (A and B moves the table together.)

At Example 14a both interlocutors are positioned as responsible for moving the table. The structural analysis – that the second move is obligatory for this exchange to be well-formed – shows that the first speaker adopts the secondary actor role and casts the addressee in the primary actor role, even though the first speaker is also responsible for carrying out the action. The second speaker accepts the casted primary actor role. To capture interlocutor roles assigned in action exchanges of this kind, we need to expand our characterisation of the primary actor and the secondary actor roles:

i Primary actor: the role assigned to the interlocutor who is responsible for carrying out the action when the action is expected to be accomplished by an individual interlocutor; or the role assigned to the interlocutor who consents to collectively carrying out the action.

ii Secondary actor: the role assigned to the interlocutor who carries out the action through the primary actor when the action is expected to be accomplished by an individual interlocutor; or the role assigned to the interlocutor who proposes a collective action.

In the remainder of this chapter, the MOOD options will be motivated in terms of their structural realisations. They are then characterised in relation to their functions in exchange structure.

3.3　Mood in Khorchin Mongolian: Indicative versus Imperative

The most basic grammatical distinction in the Khorchin Mongolian MOOD system is between [indicative] and [imperative]. The distinction is related to the verbal component of the clause. Indicative clauses may or may not contain a verbal component in their syntagm. Imperative clauses, on the other hand, require a verbal component. The exchanges in Examples 15 and 16 show the way indicative and imperative clauses work. The exchange in Example 15 is concerned with knowledge about a piece of information and Example 16 with performing an action. In Example 15, the K2 and K1 are realised by indicative clauses. While the clause in Example 15a does not involve a verbal component, the one in Example 15b does. In Example 16, the Da1 and A2 are realised by an indicative clause and an imperative clause respectively. They both involve verbal components. The MOOD types and the verbal components are highlighted in bold. By convention, clause boundaries are marked by a double slash (||). The glossing of the modal particle in Example 15b is provided in the square bracket in the translation line.

(15) F = father, D = daughter
    a F: K2 **indicative** *tʰɔr ɔn mɐpu mu* || *ɛltʃʰur mu*
        that TOP cleaning.towel IP hand.towel IP
        '(Is) that a cleaning towel or a hand towel?'

    b D: K1 **indicative** *ju tʃʰɐlɛ* **pɔl-ɔn** *ʃitɔ*
        what NDEF **become**-NPST MP
        '[You should have known that]
        (it) can be whatever (you want it to be).'

(16) M = mother, D = daughter
    a M: Da1 **indicative** *xutɔl-kə-ɵ mɛ*
        move-CAUS-NPST.PTCP IP
        '(Do I) move (= blend)?'

    b D: A2 **imperative** *xutɔl-kə-ɵ*
        move-CAUS-IMP.2
        'Move (= blend).'

    c M: A1 NV   (Mother starts the blender.)

When there is a verbal component in an indicative clause, it is marked for TENSE – as in Examples 15b and 16a, both of which are marked for the non-past tense. In contrast, the verbal component in an imperative clause is marked for PERSON – as in Example 16b, which is marked for [second person]. The verbal component in an indicative clause can be expanded by co-selecting from POLARITY, MODALITY and RELATIVE TENSE. These systems are not available to the verbal component in an imperative clause. The verbal components in both indicative clauses and imperative clauses select from ASPECT. Consequently, a verbal component functioning in an indicative clause is termed an elaborated verbal group and that in an imperative clause a restricted verbal group – with respect to their potential for selecting from the verbal group systems. The verbal group selections from the above mentioned systems are exemplified in Example 17. The term [restricted] is borrowed from Quiroz's (2013) description of the Chilean Spanish verbal group. For a detailed argumentation of the verbal group systems in Khorchin Mongolian, see Zhang (2020a).

(17) [verbal group: elaborated]
available systems: POLARITY, MODALITY, TENSE, RELATIVE TENSE, ASPECT

a
xutəl-kə-tʃ	jɔl-tʃ	ɛː-sən	kuɛ
move-CAUS-CVB	be.able.to-PROG	COP-PST.PTCP	NEG
	MODALITY and ASPECT	TENSE	POLARITY

'was not being able to move'

b
xutəl-kə-tʃ	jɔl-ntʃ	ɛː-sən	kuɛ
move-CAUS-CVB	be.able.to-FUT	COP-PST.PTCP	NEG
	MODALITY and RELATIVE TENSE	TENSE	POLARITY

'was not going to be able to move'

[verbal group: restricted]
available systems: PERSON and ASPECT

c
xutəl-kə-tʃ	ɛː-∅
move-CAUS-PROG	COP-IMP.2
ASPECT	PERSON

'stay moving'

The function of the verbal group in the interpersonal organisation of the Khorchin Mongolian clause will be referred to as Predicator. The Predicator in an indicative clause is realised by an elaborated verbal group if there is one; the Predicator in an imperative clause is realised by a restricted verbal group. The interpersonal structure of the clauses in Examples 15b, 16a and 16b can be analysed as Example 18 (verb.gp = verbal group).[4]

(18) a [indicative]

ju	tʃʰɐlɛ	**pɔl-ən**	ʃitə
what	NDEF	**become-NPST**	MP
		Predicator	
		verb.gp: elaborated	

'[You should have known that] (it) can be whatever (you want it to be).'

b [indicative]

xutəl-kə-∅	mɛ
move-CAUS-NPST.PTCP	IP
Predicator	
verb.gp: elaborated	

'(Do I) move (= blend)?'

---

[4] Note that the function is called Predicator, rather than Predicate, to be distinguished from the widely used terms 'subject' and 'predicate' in the analysis of Khorchin Mongolian sentence (Bayancogtu, 2002, pp. 453–6). The function Predicator is systemically motivated as the component that distinguishes [indicative] from [imperative].

3 Interpersonal Grammar in Khorchin Mongolian

c [imperative]

xutəl-kə-ɵ move-CAUS-IMP.2
Predicator
verb.gp: restricted

'Move (= blend).'

The preselecting relationship between [indicative] and [imperative] at clause rank and [elaborated] and [restricted] at group rank is formalised in Figure 3.2. As mentioned earlier, there is not necessarily a verbal Predicator in an indicative clause. The options other than [verbal predication] are indicated by the dotted line in the system network. Non-verbal realisation of Predicator is set aside in this chapter due to the constraints of space. For a detailed description of the various realisations of Predicator in Khorchin Mongolian, see Zhang (2020b, chapter 4). The fact that imperative clauses require a verbal Predicator and that the verbal group selects [restricted] is sufficient to establish the systemic distinction between [indicative] and [imperative] in Khorchin Mongolian.

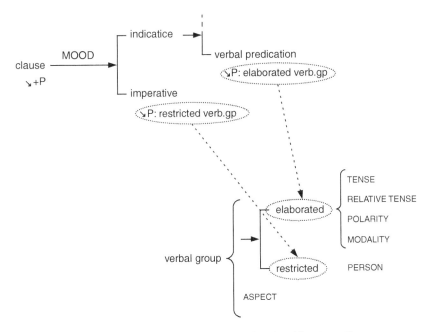

Figure 3.2 MOOD and verbal Predicator in Khorchin Mongolian

3.4 Types of Indicative and Their Functions in Exchange

3.4.1 Types of Indicative: Interrogative versus Declarative

The primary distinction in the Khorchin Mongolian indicative clause is between that of [interrogative] and [declarative]. While an interrogative clause typically involves an interrogative particle, a declarative clause does not. It is possible, however, for a declarative clause to end with a modal particle negotiating the positioning of the interlocutors. They position interlocutors as either knowing or not knowing the information under negotiation.

The clauses in Examples 15b and 16a (analysed as Example 19) are instances of [declarative] and [interrogative]. We will refer to the functions of the interrogative particles and the modal particles in the Khorchin Mongolian clause as Interrogator and Positioner, respectively. The term Interrogator is borrowed from Pin Wang's (2020) description of the Tibetan interrogative clause. In Example 19, the Positioner and the Interrogator are highlighted in bold.

(19) a declarative

ju what	tʃʰɐlɛ NDEF	pɔl-ən become-NPST	**ʃitə** MP
		Predicator	Positioner
		verbal group	modal particle

'[You should have known that] (it) can be whatever (you want it to be).'

b interrogative

xutəl-kə-ø move-CAUS-NPST.PTCP	**mɛ** IP
Predicator	Interrogator
verbal group	interrogative particle

'(Do I) move (= blend)?'

The Positioner in a declarative clause is optional. The declarative clause in Example 19a can be adapted as Example 20 without affecting its grammaticality.

(20)

ju what	tʃʰɐlɛ NDEF	pɔl-ən work-NPST
		Predicator
		verbal group

'Whatever works (≈ whatever is fine).'

3.4.2 Interrogative Clauses: Polar versus Elemental

There are two general types of interrogative clause: [polar] and [elemental]. They are exemplified in Examples 21 and 22, respectively. Unlike polar

3 Interpersonal Grammar in Khorchin Mongolian

interrogative clauses, an elemental interrogative clause requires an Inquirer function along with the Interrogator. Inquirer is realised by units involving nondefinite 'pro-words' – for example, *ju* 'what' in Example 22. The position of Inquirer is determined experientially, rather than interpersonally – that is, the missing experiential element is filled in by an Inquirer in situ. The term Inquirer is borrowed from Wang (Chapter 4, this volume). He uses the term to account for a comparable phenomenon in Mandarin. The unit involving the 'pro-word' can be a nominal group or verbal group, depending on what is being sought.

(21) interrogative: polar

ən	u:lpər	tʰɐ:r-ø	mɛ
PROX	sentence	correct-NPST.PTCP	IP
Predicator		Interrogator
verbal group		int. particle

'Is this sentence correct?'

(22) interrogative: elemental

ən	ju	kər	xi:-sən	tɐ
this	what	INS	make-PST.PTCP	IP
Inquirer		Predicator	Interrogator
nominal group		verbal group	int. particle

'What was this made from?'

In Khorchin Mongolian, the Inquirer can be used to seek information about entities, occurrences and qualities. The elemental interrogative clause in Example 22 solicits an entity. The Inquirer is realised by an instrumental nominal group (marked with the postposition *kər*), which realises a Circumstance in the experiential organisation of the clause. In Example 23a, the elemental interrogative clause also solicits an entity; but the Inquirer is conflated with a Participant.

(23) O = government official, P = peasant
a O: K2 interrogative: elemental

xən	ir-s	i:
who	come-PST.PTCP	IP
Inquirer/Participant	Predicator	Interrogator
nominal group	verbal group	int. particle

'Who came?'

b P: K1 declarative

wutʃoʋŋpu	nɛ	xun	ir-tʃ
Armed Forces Department	GEN	people	come-PST
			Predicator
			verbal group

'People from the Armed Forces Department came.'

In Example 24a, the clause solicits an occurrence; the Inquirer is conflated with the Process. Note that when the Inquirer conflates with the Process (an experiential function), it also conflates with the Predicator (an interpersonal function). The reverse is not necessarily true – the Predicator in Khorchin Mongolian may conflate with a participant (Zhang, 2020b, chapter 4). In Example 24b, the speaker used Mandarin Chinese, which is why there is no TENSE marker.

(24)   N = nephew, A = aunt
a N: K2   interrogative: elemental

xɔni	it-tʃ	pɐr-x	uɛ	pɔl ‖
all	eat-CVB	finish-NPST.PTCP	NEG	COND
	Predicator			
	verbal group			

   N: K2   int: el

jɐ:-n	tɐ
what-NPST	IP
Inquirer/Predicator/Process	Interrogator
verbal group	int. particle

'What happens if I don't finish them all?'

b A: K1   declarative

fakuan
fine
Predicator
verbal group

'(I) will fine (you).'

In an exchange with K2 ^ K1 structure, when the K2 is realised by a polar interrogative clause, the Predicator is typically replayed in the K1 – as in Example 25. On the other hand, when the K2 is realised by an elemental interrogative clause and the Inquirer is not conflated with the Predicator, it is typically the sought element that is provided in the K1 – as in Example 23. The Predicator is optionally replayed.

(25)   T = teacher
a T1:   K2   interrogative

ən	u:lpər	tʰɐ:r-ø	mɛ
PROX	sentence	**correct**-NPST.PTCP	IP
		Predicator	Interrogator
		verbal group	int. particle

'Is this sentence correct?'

b T2:   K1   declarative

tʰɐ:r-nɐ
correct-NPST
Predicator
verbal group

'(It) is correct.'

3 Interpersonal Grammar in Khorchin Mongolian   81

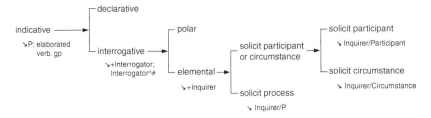

Figure 3.3 Types of indicative clause in Khorchin Mongolian

The common realisations of Inquirer in Khorchin Mongolian are:[5]
xən 'who'
ju 'what'
ɛl 'which'
ɛl nək 'which one'
jɐmər/ jɐmərti 'what like'
jɐmər tʃirək 'how'
xət/ xətən/ xəti 'how many/ how much'
xɐː/ xɐːkur/ ɛltəkur 'where'
xətʃə 'when'
jɐːkɐt 'why'
jɐː-n what-NPST 'to what/ what happen(s)' (a 'wh– verb')
The general types of indicative clause introduced so far are summarised as a system network in Figure 3.3.

In contrast to Figure 3.3 the more delicate options for [elemental] could have included three features in one system – [solicit participant], [solicit process] and [solicit circumstance]. They would be realised by the conflation of the Inquirer and the respective experiential clause functions – Participant, Process and Circumstance. In contrast, the formalisation in Figure 3.3 privileges the conflation of functions in the same metafunction (Inquirer/Predicator) and contrasts it with the conflation of functions from different metafunctions (the interpersonal function Inquirer is conflated with the experiential functions Participant and Circumstance).

3.4.3 Indicative Clauses and Exchange Structure

The distinction between [interrogative] and [declarative] is also justifiable in terms of their discourse-semantic functions. Broadly speaking, interrogative

---
[5] Some of the question words listed in Bayancogtu (2002, p. 237–40, 252–4) are not included here, either because they are groups containing question words, e.g. xəti tʃʰinə 'how much extent', or they are not commonly used in the Khorchin Mongolian variety spoken in Hinggan League (or more specifically Jalaid Banner), e.g. jutʰər 'what'.

clauses may function in both knowledge and action exchanges; declarative clauses function typically in knowledge exchanges.

As far as knowledge exchanges are concerned, interrogative clauses typically realise Dk1 and K2. The interrogative clauses in Examples 26, 27 and 28 realise Dk1, non-initiating K2 and initiating K2, respectively. Declarative clauses, on the other hand, typically realise K1. The declarative clauses in Examples 26c, 27c and 28b realise non-initiating K1. It is also possible for a declarative clause to realise non-initiating K2 – as in Examples 26b, which is an elliptical declarative clause. Declarative clauses realising K2 position the speaker as knowing the information but without primary knower authority.

(26) N = niece, U = uncle

a N: **Dk1 interrogative**

ɔn ju kər	xiː-sɔn	te
this what INS	make-PST.PTCP	IP
	Predicator	Interrogator
	verbal group	int. particle

'What was this made from?'

b U: **K2 declarative**

kojɔr
flour

'Flour.'

c N: **K1 declarative**

tʰeːr-tʃʰ
correct-PRF
Predicator
verbal group

'(It) is correct.'

(27) N = niece, U = uncle

a N: **Dk1 interrogative**

ɔn ju kər	xiː-sɔn	te
this what INS	make-PST.PTCP	IP
	Predicator	Interrogator
	verbal group	int. particle

'What was this made from?'

b U: **K2 interrogative**

kojɔr	mɛ
flour	IP
	Interrogator
	int. particle

'Is it flour?'

c N: **K1 declarative**

tʰeːr-tʃʰ
correct-PRF
Predicator
verbal group

'(It) is correct.'

3 Interpersonal Grammar in Khorchin Mongolian

(28) T = teacher
a T1: **K2 interrogative**

ən u:lpər	tʰɛ:r-ø	mɛ
PROX sentence	correct-NPST.PTCP	IP
Predicator		Interrogator
verbal group		int. particle

'Is this sentence correct?'

b T2: **K1 declarative**

tʰɛ:r-nɛ
correct-NPST
Predicator
verbal group

'(It) is correct.'

A declarative clause may also realise initiating K1 and initiating K2 – as in Examples 29 and 30, respectively. Like non-initiating K2 realised by declarative clauses, initiating K2 realised by a declarative clause positions the speaker as knowing the information but lacks primary knower authority; this means the addressee is positioned as knowing the information and having primary knower authority.

(29) T = teacher
a T1: **K1 declarative**

tʰər	ixin	ən	ortʰɛ	sɛnlo	kər
DIST	daughter	3POSS	before	trike	INS

'[You know] her daughter was commuting'

T1: **K1 declarative**

jɛp-tʃ	ɛ:-tʃ	fɛ
commute-PROG	COP-PST	MP
Predicator		Positioner
verbal group		modal particle

'(to school) by motorised trike before.'

b T2: **K2f**

ŋ:
INTJ

'Yes (≈ She was).'

(30) T = teacher
T1: **K2 declarative**

ən u:lpər	tʰɛ:r-ən	pɛ
PROX sentence	correct-NPST	MP
Predicator		Positioner
verbal group		modal particle

'This sentence [may] be correct, [right?]'

T2: **K1 declarative**

tʰɛ:r-nɛ
correct-NPST
Predicator
verbal group

'(It) is correct.'

Unlike declarative clauses, interrogative clauses also realise Da1 in action exchanges. Different from Dk1, where the addressee's knowledge is checked, at Da1 it is the acceptability of the action that is being checked. This is exemplified in Example 31.

(31) M = mother, D = daughter

a M: **Da1 interrogative**

xutəl-kə-ø	mɛ
move-CAUS-NPST.PTCP	IP
Predicator	Interrogator
verbal group	int. particle

'(Do I) move (= blend)?'

b D: A2 imperative

xutəl-kə-ø
move-CAUS-IMP.2
Predicator
verbal group

'Move (= blend).'

c M: A1 NV (Mother starts the blender.)

The discourse-semantic systems of NEGOTIATION thus enable us to see the typical discourse functions that declarative and interrogative clauses serve. This typical association between clause and exchange functions are summarised in Table 3.1.

3.5 Types of Imperative and Their Functions in Exchange

3.5.1 Types of Imperative: Interactant versus Non-Interactant

This section turns to the discussion of imperative clauses. Unlike the Predicator in an indicative clause, the Predicator in an imperative clause is realised by a restricted verbal group. The Predicator in an imperative clause is related to the interlocutor

Table 3.1 *The typical discourse-semantic functions of Khorchin Mongolian indicative clauses*

grammar		discourse semantics
indicative in MOOD	NEGOTIATION	Primary knower authority
declarative	K1	yes
	non-initiating K2	no
	initiating K2	no
interrogative	Dk1*	yes
	non-initiating K2	no
	initiating K2	no
	Da1*	not applicable

*Dk1 and Da1 are unlikely to be realised by [interrogative: elemental]

3 Interpersonal Grammar in Khorchin Mongolian

Table 3.2 *Types of imperative clause in Khorchin Mongolian*

	clause: MOOD (imperative)	group choice realising the Predicator: PERSON	suffixes in the head of the verbal group
interactant	speaker inclusive	first person	-j (~ -jɐ, -jə, -ji, -jɔ)
	speaker exclusive	second person	-ø
non-interactant		third person	-k (~ -kɐ, -kə, -kɔ, -ək)

who is positioned as responsible for carrying out an action – discussed in SFL as the 'modally responsible participant' (see Halliday, 1994, pp. 76–8). The modally responsible participants as they are encoded in the Predicator of a Khorchin Mongolian imperative clause can be interactants (the speaker, the addressee or both the speaker and the addressee) or non-interactants. This is achieved mainly through the PERSON system in the verbal group. The selection of PERSON in the Predicator is realised at word rank through verbal suffixes on the head verb. The relationship among the types of [imperative] in MOOD at clause rank, options in PERSON at group rank and the realisations of PERSON at word rank is summarised in Table 3.2.

3.5.2 Types of Interactant Imperative: Speaker Inclusive versus Speaker Exclusive

Two types of interactant imperative clause are marked morphologically: [speaker inclusive] and [speaker exclusive]. A speaker inclusive imperative clause either positions the speaker as modally responsible or positions both the speaker and the addressee as modally responsible. A speaker-exclusive imperative clause, on the other hand, only positions the addressee as modally responsible. In the interaction in Example 32, 32a is realised by a speaker-exclusive imperative clause, and 32b is realised by a speaker-inclusive imperative clause. In 32a, the addressee (Hairhan) is positioned as modally responsible for eating the oranges. In 32b, the speaker (the grandmother) is positioned as modally responsible for offering the oranges (imp: [imperative]; excl = [imperative: speaker exclusive], incl = [imperative: speaker inclusive]).

(32) G = grandmother; the grandmother is offering Hairhan (the granddaughter) some oranges
Exchange 1

a G: A2 **imp: excl**

xɛːrxɐn	itə-ø
Hairhan	eat-IMP.2
	Predicator
	verb.gp: 2nd person

'Hairhan, eat.'

***

Exchange 2

b G: A1 **imp: incl**

tʃʰɐmɐ	t	ʃiɔ	ʃiɔ	nɛ	***uk-jə***
2SG	DAT	small	small	GEN	**give**-IMP.1
					Predicator
					verb.gp: 1st person

'Let (me) give you the smaller ones.'

It is possible for the verbal group that selects [first person] to realise a speaker inclusive imperative clause that positions both the speaker and the addressee as modally responsible. This may be distinguished from the speaker-inclusive imperative clause that only positions the speaker as modally responsible through context or through an explicit first person plural pronominal realisation of the participant as in Example 33 (adjusting Example 32a).

(33) **speaker inclusive**

pɛtən	***it-jə***
1PL	eat-IMP.1
	Predicator
	verb.gp: 1st person

'Let's eat.'

As with Example 33, the pronominal realisation of the modally responsible participant is also possible in a speaker-inclusive imperative clause that does not position the addressee as sharing the modal responsibility – as in Example 34 – and in a speaker-exclusive imperative clause – as in Example 35. Note that in Example 34b, the first person plural pronoun *pɛtən* denotes an 'exclusive we'. This is disambiguated through the second person pronominal realisation of the recipient of the orange *tʃʰɐmɐ t* 'to you'.

(34) speaker inclusive: exclude addressee

a

pi	tʃʰɐmɐ	t	ʃiɔ	ʃiɔ	nɛ	***uk-jə***
1SG	2SG	DAT	small	small	GEN	give-IMP.1
						Predicator
						verb.gp: 1st person

'Let me give you the smaller ones.'

b

pɛtən	tʃʰɐmɐ	t	ʃiɔ	ʃiɔ	nɛ	***uk-jə***
1PL	2SG	DAT	small	small	GEN	give-IMP.1
						Predicator
						verb.gp: 1st person

'Let us give you the smaller ones.'

3 Interpersonal Grammar in Khorchin Mongolian   87

(35)   speaker exclusive (addressee)

a
tʃʰi	itə-ø
2SG	eat-IMP.2
Predicator	
verb.gp: 2nd person	

'You eat.'

b
tʃʰɛtən	itə-ø
2PL	eat-IMP.2
Predicator	
verb.gp: 2nd person	

'You eat.'

3.5.3   Non-interactant Imperative Clauses

When the verbal group realising the Predicator in a Khorchin Mongolian imperative clause is marked for [third person], the interlocutor positioned as modally responsible is not directly apparent from the clause itself. This type of imperative clause is used when the speaker intends an action to be continued without interruption. It can be the addressee who is positioned as responsible for not interfering with the action construed. Alternatively, it can be both the speaker and the addressee who are positioned as responsible for not interfering with the action. There is usually evidence from the co-text that can be used to disambiguate the positioning. This type of imperative clause is referred to as a non-interactant imperative clause. The 'actor' encoded in the clause is a non-interactant (i.e. it can only be replaced with a third person pronoun).

The clause in Example 36a exemplifies a non-interactant imperative clause that positions the addressee as modally responsible for not interfering with the boiling of the pot. The sister (S) informs her brother (B) that she is going to feed the pigs and the brother should leave the pot boiling. There are two exchanges in Example 36. The first exchange is initiated by the secondary actor (A2). The second exchange is initiated by the primary actor (A1). Example 36c is double coded as A1/A2f because it can be interpreted as a response to either A2 in Exchange 1 or A1 in Exchange 2 (n-int = [imperative: non-interactant]).

(36)   S = sister, B = brother
Exchange 1
a S: A2 **imp: n-int**
tʰɔkɔ	pæʃəl-tʃ	ɛ:-kɐ
pot	boil-PROG	COP-IMP.3
Predicator		
verb.gp: 3rd person		

'Let the pot boil.
(≈You leave the pot alone)'

***

Exchange 2

b S: A1 imp: incl

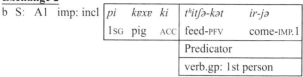

'I will feed the pigs and come back.'

c B: A1/A2 f *m:*
        INTJ
        'OK.'

In Example 36a, the addressee positioning of the non-interactant imperative clause is apparent from the co-text given that the speaker is positioned as responsible for other tasks as realised by the speaker-inclusive imperative clause in Example 36b. (Contextually, the sister walks out of the room while uttering 36b, which is another indication that she is not positioning herself as responsible in 36a).

Similarly, a non-interactant imperative clause may position both the speaker and the addressee as modally responsible for not interfering with an action. In Example 37 (adjusting Example 36), both the speaker and the addressee are positioned as being responsible for not interfering with the boiling of the pot. This is again disambiguated in the co-text. Both the interlocutors are positioned as responsible for other actions in Example 37b – drinking alcohol.

(37) **Exchange 1**
a A2 **imp: n-int**

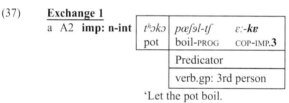

'Let the pot boil.'
(≈Let's leave the pot alone)'

***

Exchange 2

b A2 imp: incl | *pɛtən ʊrtɛ:r ɛrɔx* | *ʊ:-tʃ   ɛ:-jɐ*
                  | 1PL   first   alcohol | drink-PROG COP-IMP.1
                  | | Predicator
                  | | verb.gp: 3rd person

'Let's drink alcohol first.'

Examples 36 and 37 show that when A2 is realised by a non-interactant imperative clause, and when the addressee is positioned as modally responsible for not interfering with an action, the speaker typically proposes another action that they will engage in. When both the speaker and the addressee are positioned as modally responsible for not interfering with an action, the speaker typically proposes another action that both the interlocutors will engage in. If alternative actions are not proposed, the context is usually sufficient to disambiguate the modally responsible participant.

3.5.4 Imperative Clauses and Exchange Structure

The examples so far show that imperative clauses typically realise functions in action exchanges. The realisation of functions in action exchanges through [imperative] is summarised in Table 3.3.

Imperative clauses in Khorchin Mongolian may also realise functions in knowledge exchanges. The exchange in Example 38 follows T2's request for swapping session with T1. The non-initiating K1 at Example 38c is realised by a speaker-inclusive imperative clause.

(38) T = teacher
Exchange 1
a T1: K2 interrogative

jɐ-ø	i:
what-NPST.PTCP	IP
Inquirer/Predicator	Interrogator
verbal group	int. particle

'What is going on? (≈Why?)'

***

Exchange 2
b T1: K2 interrogative

pɐs	kɔtiɛ-ntʃ	ɛː-ø	mɛ
Again	escape-FUT	COP-NPST.PTCP	IP
	Predicator	Interrogator	
	verbal group	int. particle	

'Are you escaping again?'

Table 3.3 *Imperative clauses in action exchanges*

grammar	discourse semantics	Examples
imperative in MOOD	NEGOTIATION	
speaker inclusive	initiating A1	(32b)
	initiating A2	(37b)
speaker exclusive	initiating A2	(32a)
	non-initiating A2	(11b)
non-interactant	initiating A2	(36a)

c T2: **K1 imp: incl**

kɔtiɛ-ji
escape-IMP.1
Predicator
verb.gp: 1st person

'Let me escape.
(≈ I will escape)'

It is also possible for a speaker-exclusive imperative clause to realise non-initiating K1 in a knowledge exchange. This is typically the case when the speaker is allocating different tasks to the addressees. In Example 39 (introspective data), A is asking about his duty after all his other colleagues have been assigned different tasks.

(39) a A: K2 interrogative

ŋət pi	ju	xiː-ø	iː
if.so 1SG	what	do-NPST.PTCP	IP
	Inquirer	Predicator	Interrogator
	nom.gp	verbal group	int. particle

'What do I do then?
(now that all the tasks seem to have been allocated)'

b B: **K1 imp: excl**

tʰi nɔm iː	tɔkʃəl-ø
2SG book ACC	tidy-IMP.2
	Predicator
	verb.gp: 2nd person

'You tidy the books.'

Similar patterns are observed for non-interactant imperative clauses. They can realise non-initiating K1. The exchanges in Example 40 (adjusting Example 36) show this pattern. The K1 at 40c is realised by a non-interactant imperative clause.

(40) S = sister, B = brother
Exchange 1
a S: A1 imp: incl

pi	kɛxɐ	ki	tʰitʃə-kət	ir-jə
1SG	pig	ACC	feed-PFV	come-IMP.1
			Predicator	
			verbal group complex	

'I will feed the pigs and come back.'

***

Exchange 2
b B: K2 interrogative

ŋət tʰɔkɔ ki	jɐ-ø	iː
if.so pot ACC	what-NPST.PTCP	IP
	Inquirer/Predicator	Interrogator
	verbal group	int. particle

'Then what do (I) do with the pot?'

3 Interpersonal Grammar in Khorchin Mongolian   91

c S: **K1** **imp: n-int**

tʰɔkɔ	pæʃəl-tʃ	ɛː-kʊ
pot	boil-PROG	COP-IMP.3
	Predicator	
	verb.gp: 3rd person	

'Let the pot boil.
(≈ You leave the pot alone)'

B: K2f ɔː
          INTJ
       'I see.'

A non-interactant imperative clause may also realise an initiating K1 – as in Example 41c (an elliptical non-interactant imperative clause). The interaction in Example 41 is an excerpt from a negotiation of morning shifts between teachers. The two teachers are dividing the shifts among the three of them (the interlocutors and another teacher). Note that in 41d the K2f is also realised by a non-interactant imperative clause. As K2f is not the nuclear function in a knowledge exchange, further consideration is not pursued here.

(41) T = teacher
Exchange 1
a T1: K2 interrogative

mɛːtʰər urlə	xən	pɔs-ø	iː
tomorrow morning	who	get.up-NPST.PTCP	IP
	Inquirer	Predicator	Interrogator
	nom.gp	verbal group	int. particle

'Who will get up (early) tomorrow morning?'

b T2: K1 imp: incl

pi	pɔs-jɔ
1SG	get.up-IMP.1
	Predicator
	verbal group

'Let me get up (early). (≈ I will get up early)'

***

Exchange 2
c T1: **K1** **imp: n-int**

nukətur	urlə	nʊrʊ
day.after.tomorrow	morning	Nara

'Let Nara (get up early) the morning of the day after tomorrow.'

d T2: K2f imp: n-int

nʊrʊ	pɔs-kɔ
Nara	get.up-IMP.3
	Predicator
	verbal group

'Let Nara get up (early).'

92 Dongbing Zhang

The non-elliptical version of Example 41c is provided in Example 42.

(42) imp: n-int

nukətur	urlə	nerɐ	pɔs-kɔ
day.after.tomorrow	morning	Nara	get.up-IMP.3
			Predicator
			verbal group

'Let Nara (get up early) the morning of the day after tomorrow.'

The typical discourse-semantic functions of imperative clauses surveyed so far are summarised in Table 3.4 (expanding Table 3.3).

3.6 Conclusions

This chapter has sketched the basic systems and structures of the Khorchin Mongolian interpersonal grammar at clause rank. Systemically, a Khorchin Mongolian clause is either [indicative] or [imperative]; and if [indicative], it is either [declarative] or [interrogative]. Structurally, the elements Predicator, Positioner, Interrogator and Inquirer realise the options in the MOOD system. The Predicator and optionally the Positioner, Interrogator and Inquirer constitute the negotiatory structure of the clause. The negotiatory elements tend to be realised towards the end of the clause, featuring what Matthiessen (2018) calls an 'interpersonal finale'. The negotiatory meaning they establish scopes over the remainder of the clause. In discourse-semantic terms, the speaker hands over the turn by casting the addressee in various interlocutor roles.

The significance of this description is twofold. First, the description provides a unified account of the types of clause and their corresponding structures in Khorchin Mongolian, complementing the notionally defined clause categories

Table 3.4 *The typical discourse functions of Khorchin Mongolian imperative clauses*

grammar	discourse semantics		
imperative in MOOD	NEGOTIATION		Examples
speaker-inclusive	initiating A1		(32b)
	initiating A2		(37b)
	non-initiating K1		(38c)
speaker-exclusive	initiating A2		(32a)
	non-initiating A2		(11b)
	non-initiating K1		(39b)
non-interactant	initiating A2		(36a)
	initiating K1		(41c)
	non-initiating K1		(40c)

in the traditional descriptions of Khorchin Mongolian. For example, the distinction between [indicative] and [imperative] lies in the different realisations of the Predicator; and the distinction between [declarative] and [interrogative] is recognised by the possibility of declarative clauses to include a Positioner and interrogative ones as an Interrogator.

Secondly, the description provides a discourse-semantic interpretation of the options in the Khorchin Mongolian MOOD system. To this end, the chapter has described the structure of Khorchin Mongolian interactions in relation to the ways the interlocutors position one another in terms of their knowledge of the information and their responsibility for carrying out the action under negotiation. This structural view of interaction has made it possible to characterise the discourse functions of the Khorchin Mongolian clauses in a systematic way.

The approach taken in this chapter – motivating the grammatical systems in terms of language-specific grammatical structures and characterising the grammatical systems with respect to the structure of interaction – is potentially relevant to the exploration of interpersonal grammars in other languages.

References

Bayancogtu (2002). [*Horcin aman ayalgun u sudulul*, A Study of Khorchin Dialect]. Hohhot: Inner Mongolia University Press.

Berry, M. (1981a). Systemic Linguistics and Discourse Analysis: A Multi-Layered Approach to Exchange Structure. In M. Coulthard and M. Montgomery, eds., *Studies in Discourse Analysis*. London: Routledge & Kegan Paul, pp. 120–45.

Berry, M. (1981b). Systemic Linguistics and Discourse analysis: A Multi-Layered Approach to Exchange Structure. Mimeo (a longer version of Berry, 1981a).

Berry, M. (1981c). Polarity, Ellipticity and Propositional Development, Their Relevance to the Well-Formedness of an Exchange (A Discussion of Coulthard and Brazil's Classes of Move). *The Nottingham Linguistic Circular*, *10*(1), 36–63.

Berry, M. (1981d). Towards Layers of Exchange Structure for Directive Exchanges. *Network*, 2, 23–31.

Caffarel, A., Martin, J. R. & Matthiessen, C. M. I. M., eds., (2004). *Language Typology: A Functional Perspective*. Amsterdam/Philadelphia: John Benjamins.

Caganhada (1995). 蒙古语科尔沁土语研究 [*Menggu yu keerqin tuyu yanjiu*, A Study of Khorchin Mongolian Dialect]. Beijing: Social Sciences Academic Press.

Cenggeltei (1999). [*Odo üye in monggol helen u jui (nemen zasagsan heblel*, A Grammar of Modern Mongolian (A Revised Edition)]. Hohhot: Inner Mongolia People Publishing House.

Halliday, M. A. K. (1966). Some Notes on 'Deep' Grammar. *Journal of Linguistics*, 2 (1),57–67.

Halliday, M. A. K. (1984). Language as Code and Language as Behaviour: A Systemic-Functional Interpretation of the Nature and Ontogenesis of Dialogue. In Fawcett, R., Halliday, M.A.K., Lamb, S. and Makkai, A., eds., *The Semiotics of Culture and Language*. Vol. 1 of *Language as Social Semiotic*. London: Frances Pinter, pp. 3–35.

Halliday, M. A. K. (1985). *An Introduction to Functional Grammar*. London: Arnold.
Halliday, M. A. K. (1994). *An Introduction to Functional Grammar*, 2nd ed., London: Arnold.
Halliday, M. A. K. (2009). Methods – Techniques – Problems. In M. A. K. Halliday and J. Webster, eds., *Continuum Companion to Systemic Functional Linguistics*. London: Continuum, pp. 59–86.
Halliday, M. A. K. & Matthiessen, C. M. I. M. (1999). *Construing Experience through Meaning: A Language-Based Approach to Cognition*. London/New York: Continuum.
Hao, J. (2020). *Analysing Scientific Discourse from a Systemic Functional Perspective: A Framework for Exploring Knowledge Building in Biology*. London: Routledge.
Martin, J. R. (1992). *English Text: System and Structure*. Amsterdam/Philadelphia: John Benjamins.
Martin, J. R., Wang, P. & Zhu, Y. (2013). *Systemic Functional Grammar: A Next Step into the Theory – Axial Relations*. Beijing: Higher Education Press.
Martin, J. R. (2018). Introduction – Interpersonal Meaning: Systemic Functional Linguistics Perspectives. *Functions of Language*, 25(1), 2–19.
Martin, J. R. & Cruz, P. (2018). Interpersonal Grammar of Tagalog: A Systemic Functional Linguistic Perspective. *Functions of Language*, 25(1), 54–96.
Martin, J. R. & Rose, D. (2007). *Working with Discourse*, 2nd ed., London/New York: Continuum.
Martin, J. R., Quiroz, B., Wang, Pin & Zhu, Y. (in press). *Systemic Functional Grammar: Another Step into the Theory – Grammatical Description*. Beijing: Higher Education Press.
Matthiessen, C. M. I. M. (2018). The Notion of Multilingual Meaning Potential: A Systemic Exploration. In A. Sellami-Baklouti and L. Fontaine, eds., *Perspectives from Systemic Functional Linguistics*. New York/London: Routledge, pp. 90–120.
Mwinlaaru, I.N., Matthiessen, C. M. I. M. & Akerejola, E. S. (2018). A System-Based Typology of MOOD in Niger-Congo Languages. In A. Agwuele and A. Bodomo, eds., *The Routledge Handbook of African Linguistics*. London/New York: Routledge, pp. 93–117.
Na-Gancigsurung, Gardi, Wa-Secin & Cinggeltu, eds., (2005). [*Helen u šinzilel un nere tomiya*, Terms in Linguistics]. Hohhot: Inner Mongolia Education Press.
Nasunbayar, Haserdeni, Turgen, Cogtu, Tawadagba, Naranbatu & Secen. (1982). [*Orcin cag un monggul hele*, Modern Mongolian]. Hohhot: Inner Mongolia Education Press.
Quiroz, B. (2013). *The Interpersonal and Experiential Grammar of Chilean Spanish: Towards a Principled Systemic-Functional Description Based on Axial Argumentation*. Unpublished PhD thesis, University of Sydney, Sydney, Australia.
Quiroz, B. (2018). Negotiating Interpersonal Meanings: Reasoning about MOOD. *Functions of Language*, 25(1), 135–63.
Rose, D. (2018). Sister, Shall I Tell You? Enacting Social Relations in a Kinship Community. *Functions of Language*, 25(1), 97–134.
Sinclair, J. M. & Coulthard, M. (1975). *Towards an Analysis of Discourse: The English Used by Teachers and Pupils*. Oxford: Oxford University Press.

Teruya, K., Akerejola, E., Andersen, T., Caffarel, A., Lavid, J., Matthiessen, C. M. I. M., Petersen, U., Patpong, P., & Smedegaard, F. (2007). Typology of MOOD: A Text-Based and System-Based Functional View. In R. Hasan, C. M. I. M. Matthiessen and J. Webster, eds., *Continuing Discourse on Language: A Functional Perspective*. London: Equinox Publishing, pp. 859–920.

Tiemei (2015). [*Monggol helen u horcin aman ayalgun u abiyan u dagun uhagan u zadalulta*, Acoustic Phonetics of Khorchin Mongolian]. Unpublished PhD thesis, Inner Mongolia University.

Tserenpil, D. & Kullman, R. (2008). *Mongolian Grammar*, 4th revised ed., Ulaanbaater: Admon.

Ventola, E. (1987). *The Structure of Social Interaction: A Systemic Approach to the Semiotics of Service Encounters*. London: Frances Pinter.

Ventola, E. (1988). The Logical Relations in Exchanges. In J. D. Benson and W. S. Greaves, eds., *Systemic Functional Approaches to Discourse*. Norwood, NJ: Ablex, pp. 51–72.

Wang, Penglin. (1983). 关于蒙古语族"格附加成分"的问 [*Guanyu menggu yuzu "ge fujia chengfen" de wenti*, On case marking in Mongolic languages]. *Minority Languages of China 1*, 41–64. Weblink: https://caod.oriprobe.com/articles/34292030/guan_yu_meng_gu_yu_zu__ge_fu_jia_cheng_fen__de_wen.htm.

Wang, Pin. (2020). Axial Argumentation and Cryptogrammar in Interpersonal Grammar: A Case Study of Classical Tibetan MOOD. In J. R. Martin, Y. Doran and G. Figueredo, eds., *Systemic Functional Language Description: Making Meaning Matter*. New York/London: Routledge, 73–101.

Zhang, D. (2020a). Axial Argumentation below the Clause: The Verbal Group in Khorchin Mongolian. In J. R. Martin, Y. Doran and G. Figueredo, eds., *Systemic Functional Language Description: Making Meaning Matter*. New York/London: Routledge, pp. 35–72.

Zhang, D. (2020b). *Negotiating Interpersonal Meaning in Khorchin Mongolian: Discourse and Grammar*. Unpublished PhD thesis, University of Sydney, Sydney, Australia. https://hdl.handle.net/2123/22835

4 Interpersonal Grammar in Mandarin

Pin Wang

4.1 Interpersonal Clause Grammar: A Trinocular Perspective

This chapter presents a text-based study of the enactment of interpersonal meaning in Mandarin, with particular focus on the system and structure of MOOD – the part of interpersonal grammar that serves as a resource for negotiating meaning in a clause in a dialogic exchange (Martin, 1992, p. 31). In systemic functional linguistics (SFL), grammatical studies adopt a 'trinocular orientation', taking into account three complementary perspectives on linguistic phenomena. These are 'from above', relevant meaning from the stratum of semantics; 'from round about', related choices at the level of lexicogrammar and agnation in systems; and 'from below', realisation at lower ranks of lexicogrammar or the stratum of phonology (Halliday, 1978, pp. 130–1, 1996; Matthiessen & Halliday, 2009, pp. 36–7). This principle of trinocularity in grammatical description is promoted by Halliday as a critical methodological feature of argumentation in functional grammars (Halliday, 1992, p. 3).

Semantics is referred to as discourse semantics in this study since our grammatical description and analysis are based on text-scale meanings – meaning beyond the clause (Martin, 1992, pp. 1, 14; Martin, 2002, p. 54; Martin, 2015; Martin & Rose, 2007). Taking discourse semantics as the point of departure means that we give considerable weight to the perspective 'from above' – since lexicogrammar is positioned in the model as responsible for realising discourse-semantic functions. Therefore, this study is an attempt to complement previous studies on MOOD in Mandarin (e.g. Halliday & McDonald, 2004; Li, 2007; Zhang, 2009) – by approaching grammar from discourse semantics.

Dialogic exchanges are enacted through the interpersonal discourse-semantic systems of NEGOTIATION and APPRAISAL; and within APPRAISAL, the subsystem ENGAGEMENT is especially relevant (Martin & Rose, 2007; Martin & White, 2005). Despite the fact that these discourse-semantic systems of NEGOTIATION and APPRAISAL are modelled for English, the description of

4 Interpersonal Grammar in Mandarin   97

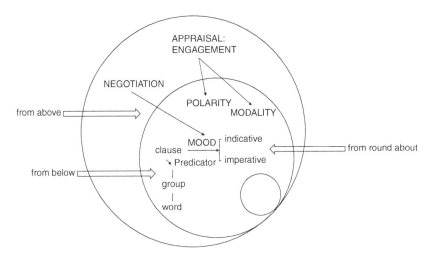

Figure 4.1 Trinocular perspective on interpersonal grammar

Mandarin follows the same theoretical principles and takes advantage of the trend for systemic features at a low level of delicacy to be shared across languages (Martin & Quiroz, 2020).

The system of NEGOTIATION is realised in Mandarin by the grammatical system of MOOD, the central focus of this chapter; ENGAGEMENT is realised in MODALITY and POLARITY systems that co-select with MOOD, as will be shown in following sections. The systemic contrasts at the level of grammar at clause rank, such as imperative versus indicative MOOD type, are in turn realised through structural configurations within the clause or at ranks below. Figure 4.1 aggregates the trinocular perspective on interpersonal discourse semantics and lexicogrammar introduced in this section.

4.2 Contextually Driven Data Compilation

The grammatical description developed in this chapter is based on a corpus compiled from authentic Mandarin texts produced in a courtroom in China. Courtroom discourse is of special significance to this study because it involves substantial proportions of spontaneous dialogue among various parties at the trial. For the focus text in this study, the courtroom parties include the judge, two prosecutors, two defendants and their respective defence lawyers and a court police officer.

Here is a very brief introduction to the court case that produces the focus text for analysis: the two defendants, each in an expensive car, raced against each other at a speed substantially exceeding the legal limit. The two vehicles lost control, caused damage to the vehicles and crashed into barriers along the road; the passenger in one defendant's car was injured and hospitalised. Both defendants were convicted of reckless driving and they admitted to the crime they had committed.

In terms of a stratified perspective on context (Martin, 2014; Martin & Rose, 2008), courtroom trial discourse is a macro-genre involving a series of staged, goal-oriented social processes realised by configurations of field, tenor and mode register variables. Among these variables, tenor is concerned with the 'socially meaningful participant relationships' (Halliday, 1978, p. 143) in which the text is positioned. The interlocutors in the discourse, their professional traits and their statuses and roles in the situation provide the interpersonal frame in relation to which the interlocutors negotiate their social position through language.

In our case the status relations among the interlocutors are unequal in that the judge and prosecutors are more powerful than defendants and defence lawyers. This is reflected in the lack of reciprocity of language choices that can be detected, especially during the interrogation stage, as the judge and prosecutors mainly raise questions and the defendants are required to answer them. The court police officer assumes a position of control over all other parties in the courtroom, which is enacted through announcements of courtroom procedures that everybody present is expected to follow.

4.3 From Above: Discourse Semantics of Interpersonal Meaning

The grammatical system of MOOD is responsible for realising the discourse-semantic system of NEGOTIATION; the latter is concerned with linguistic resources for exchanging goods-and-services and information in dialogic discourse. Halliday (1984) introduces his clause semantic system of SPEECH FUNCTION from a grammarian's perspective, with options for giving and demanding goods-and-services and information. Martin (1992) develops his discourse-semantic system of NEGOTIATION, drawing on earlier work by Sinclair and Coulthard (1975), Berry (1981) and Ventola (1987). While SPEECH FUNCTION focuses on what are generally termed (following Conversation Analysis) adjacency pairs in dialogue, NEGOTIATION allows for up to five basic moves in an exchange, along with additional tracking and challenging options. NEGOTIATION is realised by SPEECH FUNCTION in terms of rank (Martin, 2018, p. 8).

In the model of NEGOTIATION introduced in Martin (1992) and Martin and Rose (2007), action exchanges involve an exchange of goods-and-services; in such exchanges the provider of the goods or services is known as the primary actor, and the move involving the primary actor providing goods or services is labelled A1. The demander of the goods or service is known as the secondary actor, whose move is labelled A2. The A1 move may consist of simply the provision of the goods or enactment of the service demanded – without being accompanied by language. These two moves are exemplified by the following excerpt in our data:

Court police officer	A2	*quanti*	*qili*
		all	rise
		'All rise.'	
People in court	A1	[those present stand up]	

By contrast, knowledge exchanges involve an exchange of information. In such exchanges the person who has authority over the information provided is known as the primary knower, whose move is labelled K1; the person who requests the information is known as the secondary knower and enacts the K2 move. These two moves are exemplified in the following dialogue:

Judge	K2	*cici*	*shexian*	*shenme*	*zuiming*
		this time	suspected	what	crime
		'What crime are you suspected of this time?'			
Defendant	K1	*weixian*	*jiashi*		
		danger	drive		
		'Reckless driving.'			

An exchange can also be initiated by the primary actor or knower, in moves that delay the provision of goods-and-services or information and check whether they are in fact required by the secondary actor or knower. These moves are labelled Da1 and Dk1, respectively. Moves that optionally follow the delivery of goods or services or information and are performed by the secondary actor or knower are labelled A2f and K2f, respectively. These moves can be further followed up by the primary actor or knower in culminative moves labelled A1f and K1f.

Alongside the ten moves presented above, there are confirming, challenging and checking moves, and responses to these moves – which are enacted to clarify or resist what is proposed in a preceding move, or secure a response from the addressee in the following move (Martin, 2018, pp. 9–11).

The grammatical system of MOOD in Mandarin also interacts with other interpersonal grammatical systems such as MODALITY and POLARITY, which are relevant to the other interpersonal discourse-semantic system, APPRAISAL – specifically its subsystem ENGAGEMENT, which is concerned with sourcing evaluation and how the speaker engages with and acknowledges related voices (Martin & White, 2005, p. 93). The ENGAGEMENT system first distinguishes between monoglossic moves (in which the speaker presents no dialogic alternatives and makes reference to no voices other than the speaker's own), and heteroglossic moves (which do recognise dialogic alternatives). Heteroglossic resources can either contract dialogic space by restricting or invalidating alternative voices, or expand dialogic space by allowing for alternative positions. Contraction often involves negation or concession, and expansion is commonly realised through modality or projection (Martin, 2018, p. 12).

Taking the discourse-semantic system of NEGOTIATION as the point of departure, this chapter analyses our focus text compiled from the courtroom discourse introduced in Section 4.2, and illustrates our analysis using the following text excerpts, with each move in the exchanges functionally labelled (using CP for court police officer, DL for defence lawyer, PR for prosecutor, JU for judge and DE for defendant). We offer just a free translation in English at this stage; more detailed glossing will be provided when moves are analysed in detail below.

CP	A2	*qing bianhuren he gongsuren ru ting* 'Defence lawyers and prosecutors, please enter the courtroom.'
DL, PR	A1	[entering courtroom]

***

CP	A2	*quanti qili* 'All rise.'
All	A1	[those present stand up]

***

CP	A2	*qing shenpanyuan ru ting* 'Judge, please enter the courtroom.'
JU	A1	[judge enters courtroom]

***

JU	A2	*qing zuoxia* 'Please sit down.'
All	A1	[those present sit down]

***

CP	K1	*kai ting qian zhunbei gongzuo yijing jiuxu* 'Preparatory work before the opening of court session is done.'
	=K1	*keyi kai ting* 'The court session can be started.'

***

JU	K2	*beigaoren, ni de chusheng riqi* 'Defendant, your date of birth?'
DE1	K1	*yijiujiusi nian ba yue shiliu hao* '16 August 1994.'

***

4 Interpersonal Grammar in Mandarin   101

JU	A2	*shuohua shengyin da yidian*
		'May (your) voice rise a little.'
DE1	A1/K1[1]	[Raising voice] *yijiujiusi nian*
		'The year 1994.'

***

JU	K2	*tong qisushu suo zaiming de xinxi yizhi ma*
		'Is it consistent with the information recorded in the indictment?'
DE1	K1	*yizhi*
		'(It is) consistent.'

***

JU	K2	*ni yiqian shifou shou guo falü chufen*
		'Have you received any legal punishment before?'
DE1	K1	*meiyou*
		'(I) haven't.'

***

JU	K2	*cici shexian shenme zuiming*
		'What crime are (you) suspected of this time?'
DE1	K1	*weixian jiashi*
		'Reckless driving.'

***

JU	K2	*heshi bei jiya*
		'When were (you) detained?'
DE1	K1	*si yue shier hao*
		'12 April.'
JU	cf	*erlingyiwu nian*
		'The year 2015.'
DE1	rcf	*erlingyiwu nian si yue shier hao*
		'12 April 2015.'

***

JU	K2	*heshi bei xingshi juliu*
		'When were (you) placed in criminal detention?'
DE1	K1	*en ... shi xiawu san dian zuoyou*
		'Er ... around 3 p.m.'
JU	cf	*shi erlingyiwu nian si yue shier ri de ...*
		'It is ... 12 April 2015.'
DE1	rcf	*... de xiawu san dian zuoyou*
		'Around 3 p.m.'

***

---

[1] This move represents an A1/K1 linguistic service (Ventola, 1987; Martin & Zappavigna, 2016), involving a coupling of two exchange roles: an A1 compliant response to the proposal (raising voice) and a K1 proposition (responding to the K2 request of knowledge).

JU	K2	*heshi bei qubaohoushen*
		'When were (you) released on bail?'
DE1	K1	*erlingyiwu nian wu yue shier hao xiawu liu dian*
		'Six p.m. on 12 May 2015.'

***

JU	K2	*jianchayuan de qisushu fuben ni shoudao le ma*
		'Have (you) received a copy of indictment of the procuratorate?'
DE1	K1	*shoudao le*
		'(I) have received it.'

***

JU	K2	*beigaoren bianhuren shifou dou ting qingchu le*
		'The defendants and defence lawyers have all heard clearly, yes or no?'
DE, DL	K1	*ting qingchu le*
		'(We) heard clearly.'

***

PR2	K2	*ni ji bu jide xianchang de shenme weizhi ... xieshang de*
		'Do you remember at what location of the site you negotiated?'
DE2	K1	*youdian ji bu qing le*
		'Somehow (I) do not remember clearly.'

***

PR2	K2	*ni qu yiyuan de shijian shi shenme shihou*
		'What was the time you went to the hospital?'
DE1	K1	*xiawu liang dian zuoyou ba*
		'Should be around 2 p.m.'

***

JU	K2	*beigaoren ... ni you mei you yijian*
		'Do you have any objection?'
DE1	K1	*meiyou*
		'(I) don't have (any).'

***

JU	K2	*dou meiyou yijian shi ba liang wei bianhuren*
		'Defence lawyers, you don't have (any objection), do you?'
DL	K1	*meiyou*
		'(I) don't have (any).'

***

JU	K2	*xuyao xunwen shi bu shi*
		'(You) need to interrogate (the defendants), don't you?'
PR1	K1	*xuyao*
		'(I) need to.'

4.4 From Round About and Below: Paradigmatic Choices and Realisations in MOOD

The primary contrast in dialogic exchanges is between an exchange of action and an exchange of knowledge. This is realised in the stratum of lexicogrammar through the grammatical system of MOOD, by distinguishing between MOOD options responsible for action and knowledge exchanges. Major moves involving action exchanges – that is, A1 and A2 – behave differently in their grammatical realisations in that A2 moves are congruently realised by the imperative MOOD type, while A1 moves are typically performed non-linguistically or occasionally realised by minor clauses promising delivery of goods or services (e.g. *Hao(de)* in Mandarin, equivalent to *OK, Yes* in English). Knowledge exchanges on the other hand are congruently realised in grammar through the indicative MOOD type. This primary contrast in the grammatical system of MOOD is represented in Figure 4.2. The MOOD system is applicable to major clauses, hence the entry condition 'major'.

At this level of delicacy the systemic layout of MOOD choices is similar across many languages (Matthiessen, 2004; Matthiessen et al., 2008; Teruya et al., 2007) – for example, English (Halliday & Matthiessen, 2014, p. 24), German (Steiner & Teich, 2004, p. 145), French (Caffarel, 2006, p. 139), and Tagalog (Martin, 2004, p. 287 – and is widely recognised (Quiroz, 2008, p. 54). Structural realisations, however, are varied, and in order to motivate the systemic distinction we must determine how elements in clause structure engage the clause in different types of negotiation (including how they make the clause arguable).

In English, for example, the structural motivation of the distinction between the indicative and imperative clauses rests on the presence or absence of clause functions Subject and Finite (Halliday & Matthiessen, 2014, p. 140). The indicative MOOD type requires the insertion of Subject and Finite while the imperative does not. It is this Mood element comprising Subject and Finite that is essential for realising interpersonal meaning in dialogic negotiations in English. Subject is treated as an interpersonal function which encodes modal responsibility (Martin, 1992, p. 461), and Finite is an interpersonal function in the English MOOD structure establishing the arguability of the clause negotiation in relation to POLARITY, MODALITY and TENSE. In addition, the

Figure 4.2 Primary contrast in MOOD

sequencing of Subject and Finite plays a significant part in motivating and realising indicative MOOD choices at further levels of delicacy.

How specific choices are motivated by structural patterns is a language-specific empirical question, and the reasoning linking the functional motivations and structural consequences of systemic choices should be always made explicit for a specific language (Quiroz, 2018, p. 136). It will be proposed here that in Mandarin the Predicator plays an essential role and serves as the functionally motivated locus in the realisation of MOOD systems; other important functions include the Inquirer and the Moderator. Next, we will explore how the distinction between the imperative and indicative MOOD types is motivated through structural configurations, overtly and covertly, in relation to the Predicator of a Mandarin clause.

4.4.1 Imperative Clauses

As the congruent realisation of the A2 move in an exchange of goods or services, imperative clauses typically feature a Predicator realised by a word group without any aspectual marking by 'clitics' (a class label used for a dependent element at the group rank) on its head word. If the primary actor is the addressee (i.e. a second person imperative), it is often left implicit. Optionally, a Modal Adjunct *qing* 'please' can precede the Predicator. Examples 1 and 2 are from the courtroom data examined here, with functions and classes of relevant elements labelled below the word-for-word glossing line – with annotation for clause-rank functions (e.g. Predicator), group-rank classes (e.g. word group), group-rank functions (e.g. Event) and word-rank classes (e.g. verb) – and finally a free translation on the bottom line of each example.[2] Note that elements which are not relevant to the MOOD structure are not labelled for either function or class.

(1)   CP   A2 | *quanti* | *qili* |
               |----------|--------|
               | all | stand up |
               | | Predicator |
               | | word group |
               | | Event |
               | | verb |
               | 'All rise.' |

---

[2] The numbered examples in this chapter follow the interlinear glossing rules developed by Systemic Language Modelling (SLaM) Network. The glossing conventions can be found via this website link: https://systemiclanguagemodelling.wordpress.com/glossing.

4 Interpersonal Grammar in Mandarin

(2)   JU   A2

qing	*zuoxia*
please	sit down
Modal Adjunct	Predicator
	word group
	Event
	verb
'Please sit down.'	

A third person imperative requires that the entity which is responsible for the provision of goods or services (the primary actor) is made lexico-grammatically explicit and positioned before the Predicator as in Examples 3–5.

(3)   CP   A2

qing	*bianhuren*	*he*	*gongsuren*	*ru*	*ting*
please	defence lawyer	and	prosecutor	enter	court
Modal Adjunct				Predicator	
				word group	
				Event	
				verb	
'Defence lawyers and prosecutors, please enter the courtroom.'					

(4)   CP   A2

qing	*shenpanyuan*	*ru*	*ting*
please	judge	enter	court
Modal Adjunct		Predicator	
		word group	
		Event	
		verb	
'Judge, please enter the courtroom.'			

(5) JU A2

shuohua	shengyin	da	yidian
speak	sound	big	a little
		Predicator	
		word group	
		Event	
		adjective	
'May (your) voice rise a little.'			

Note that in Mandarin an adjective or a verb can realise the group-rank function Event – as the head word of a word group that realises the Predicator. For this reason we only label the class that realises the function Predicator as 'word group' instead of specifying whether it is a verbal or adjectival group. The difference is captured at word rank where Event is specified as realised either through a verb or an adjective. Some reactances can serve to distinguish between a verb and an adjective. For example, an adjective can function as Epithet in a nominal group whereas a verb cannot; and an adjective is gradable whereas a verb is not. The glossing was illustrated in Examples 3–5.

In order to capture the aspectual dimension of the word group in the Predicator, we need to take into account the agnation and enation patterns given here – whereby the clitic *le*, typically following the Event, is the perfective aspect marker used in the indicative MOOD type:

imperative (no aspect)　　　　　indicative (perfective aspect)
quanti qili :　　　　　　　　　　*quanti qili=le* ::
'All rise.'　　　　　　　　　　　　'All rose.'

zuoxia :　　　　　　　　　　　　*zuoxia=le* ::
'Sit down.'　　　　　　　　　　　'(Someone) sat down.'

ru ting :　　　　　　　　　　　　*ru=le ting* ::
'Enter court.'　　　　　　　　　　'(Someone) entered court.'

shuohua shengyin da yidian :　　*shuohua shengyin da=le yidian*
'May (your) voice rise a little.'　'(Someone's) voice rose a little.'

It needs to be pointed out that the Predicator in indicative clauses has no explicit aspect marker to indicate the 'neutral', 'general' or 'habitual' aspect (i.e. imperfective). So indicative clauses with imperfective aspect do not look any different from imperative clauses. To see the difference between MOOD types we need to consider perfective aspect, noting that this is possible for

4 Interpersonal Grammar in Mandarin

indicative clauses but not for imperatives. This is where the notion of cryptogrammar comes into play.

The idea of a cryptogrammar is based on a concept of 'cryptotype' or 'covert category' formulated by Whorf in opposition to the concept of 'phenotype' or 'overt category'. It accounts for lexicogrammatical features that do not have an explicit syntactic, morphological or phonological manifestation in a given structure but are crucial for a language's meaning making. Since a covert grammatical category cannot be immediately recognised through an explicit marking, it is the grammarian's task to discover the 'reactance' of that category (see Whorf, circa 1936, 1937 in Whorf, 1956). Halliday and Matthiessen (1999, p. 569) suggest that 'many aspects of clause grammar, and of the grammar of clause complexes, are essentially cryptotypic'.

One cryptogrammatical characteristic of imperative clauses in Mandarin can be found out by subjecting the clause to a negation probe. The negation marker used for imperatives is *buyao* or *bie* (considered the abbreviated form of *buyao* [Zhu, 1982, p. 206]), whereas the indicatives require *bu* for the imperfective aspect or *mei(you)* for the perfective aspect. Compare the patterns below. Here the probe for the imperative MOOD type interacts with the ideational system of ASPECT, and interpersonal systems of POLARITY and MODALITY.

positive imperative	negative imperative
ru ting	***bie** ru ting* / ***buyao** ru ting*
'Enter court.'	'Don't enter court.'
positive indicative (imperfective aspect)	negative indicative (imperfective aspect)
shenpanyuan ru ting	*shenpanyuan **bu** ru ting*
'Judges enter court.'	'Judges do not enter court.'
positive indicative (perfective aspect)	negative indicative (perfective aspect)
shenpanyuan ru=le ting	*shenpanyuan **mei(you)** ru ting*
'Judges entered court.'	'Judges did not enter court.'

Sometimes an imperative clause takes a particle *ba* in final position to express a tentative suggestion or wish (an optative MOOD type), as shown in Example 6. The particle *ba* is given the function label Moderator;[3] it solicits agreement from the addressee. In this case, one of the defendants suggests to the other that they should call the police, but leaves this suggestion open to negotiation by way of attaching the clause final Moderator to tone down the proposal.

---

[3] The function Moderator is partially comparable to 'Positioner' in Khorchin Mongolian (Zhang, Chapter 3, this volume) and Brazilian Portuguese (Figueredo, Chapter 7, this volume) in that both adjust choice in ENGAGEMENT and are realised by a particle; the Positioner, however, closely interacts with the Predicator and they constitute the Negotiator where the Predicator is realised verbally.

(6) DE1 A2

zanmen	bao	jing	ba
we (inclusive)	report	police	MOD[4]
	Predicator		Moderator
	verbal group		particle
'Let's call the police.'				

Imperative MOOD type and the structural motivation for differentiating it from the indicative type is outlined in the system network in Figure 4.3. The feature [imperative] is realised by having a Predicator without aspect cliticisation, and is further split into two options – [jussive] expressing a direct command and [optative] indicating a desire or wish. For the optative imperative to be realised, the clause function Moderator must be inserted, realised by a word class item – particle, which is lexicalised as *ba*. This particle is placed at the clause final position. These realisation statements are displayed using structural building rules for system networks listed in Martin et al. (2013, pp. 41, 48). In Figure 4.3, the realisation statements for features [indicative] and [imperative] are shorthand ones since ASPECT is a word group system rather than a clause-rank system. However, clause-rank function Predicator is always realised by a word group which selects from the ASPECT system.

4.4.2 Declarative Clauses

Clauses choosing declarative MOOD type are the congruent realisation of K1 moves – imparting knowledge. Declarative clauses are recognised as the unmarked option in the MOOD system, because it is the option that combines

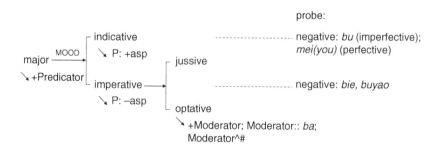

Figure 4.3 Imperative clauses in Mandarin

---

[4] The abbreviation MOD stands for modal particle, following Halliday and McDonald (2004).

the most freely with other clausal systems (Halliday & McDonald, 2004, p. 331), lacks a specific structural marker and has relatively high frequency in discourse (Li, 2007, p. 127; Huang & Liao, 2002, p. 110).

As Halliday and McDonald (2004, p. 332) point out, in Mandarin the function Subject plays no part in signalling the declarative MOOD type. A declarative clause in Mandarin requires only the Predicator as the obligatory function. Examples 7 and 8 are taken from our data.

(7) CP K1

kai	ting	qian	zhunbei	gongzuo	yijing	jiuxu
open	court	before	prepare	work	already	ready
						Predicator
						word group
						Event
						adjective

'The preparatory work before the opening of court session is done.'

(8) CP K1

keyi	kai	ting
can	open	court
Predicator		
word group		
	Event	
	verb	

'The court session can be started.'

Note that in Example 7, the nominal group *kai ting qian zhunbei gongzuo* 'preparatory work before the opening of court session' plays no part in the realisation of the declarative MOOD type, but serves textually as the Theme of the clause, and serves ideationally to specify the Participant that is involved in the Process of getting ready.

The clause final particle *ba*, functioning as Moderator in the imperative MOOD type introduced in the previous section, can also be attached to the end of a declarative clause – in which case it marks the speaker's uncertainty with respect to the knowledge they provide. In our data there is an exchange where the K1 move is realised by an elliptical clause that ends with the particle *ba*. *Should be* is used in the free translation to capture the meaning of *ba*.

PR2　K2　*ni qu yiyuan de shijian shi shenme shihou*
　　　　　'When did you go to the hospital?'
DE1　K1　*xiawu liang dian zuoyou* **ba**
　　　　　'**Should be** around 2 p.m.'

We can expand the elliptical clause in K1 into a full major clause as shown in Example 9.

(9)　DE1　K1

shijian	*shi*	*xiawu*	*liang*	*dian*	*zuoyou*	*ba*
time	be	afternoon	two	o'clock	around	MOD
	Predicator					Moderator
	word group					particle
	Event					
	verb					
'The time should be around 2 p.m.'							

At this stage we can see that the particle *ba* in itself is not a differentiating structural factor for either the imperative or the declarative MOOD type. The crucial function that distinguishes between imperative and declarative is the Predicator – which is realised through the word groups where negation and aspect are realised. Example 10 is modified from Example 9, adding a Neg function to the verbal group; the particle *ba* once again gives the proposition a touch of uncertainty.

(10)　DE1　K1

bu	*shi*	*xiawu*	*liang*	*dian*	*zuoyou*	*ba*
NEG	be	afternoon	two	o'clock	around	MOD
Predicator						Moderator
word group						particle
Neg	Event					
	verb					
'It may not be around 2 p.m.'						

4.4.3　*Interrogative Clauses*

As the congruent realisation of a K2 move in an exchange of knowledge, a clause in the interrogative MOOD type raises a question and seeks information – thereby inviting a declarative clause that realises a K1 move in a dialogue. A question can solicit knowledge of various kinds: it can seek a piece of unknown or missing information in a proposition that the addressee is expected to provide; it can comprise a complete proposition asking the addressee only to confirm whether the proposition is true or false; and it can provide two or more alternatives for the addressee to select from in their response.

Given the variety of interrogatives and their structural configurations in Mandarin, several classifications have been suggested. In traditional terms it is generally agreed that there are four kinds of questions (e.g. Huang, 1984; Huang & Liao, 2002):

 i *tezhi* 'refer in particular' question;
 ii *shifei* 'right–wrong' question;
 iii *zhengfan* 'face–reverse' question;
 iv *xuanze* 'select' question.

Note that these four types are called 'questions' rather than 'interrogatives' because not all of them are treated as features in the system of interrogative MOOD in this chapter. This will be further pursued in Section 4.4.3.4. Here they only serve as the point of departure, based on traditional grammar, for the description of interrogative MOOD type in Mandarin.

Mandarin interrogatives are also classified from a functional perspective, by Li and Thompson (1981), Halliday and McDonald (2004) and Li (2007). Table 4.1 presents a comparison of these classifications.

From the table we can see that the *shifei* 'right–wrong' and *zhengfan* 'face–reverse' interrogatives are grouped together as polar interrogatives by Halliday and McDonald (2004) and Li (2007), subdivided into biased and unbiased; whereas Li and Thompson (1981), on the other hand, group *zhengfan* 'face–reverse' and *xuanze* 'select' interrogatives together as disjunctive questions. Li and Thompson (1981, p. 546) have another type of question besides those mentioned: tag questions. However, their tag question always involves two

Table 4.1 *Classification of interrogatives in Mandarin*

	Li and Thompson (1981)	Halliday and McDonald (2004); Li (2007)
tezhi 'refer in particular'	question-word question	elemental
shifei 'right–wrong'	particle question	polar: biased
zhengfan 'face–reverse'	disjunctive question: A-not-A type	polar: unbiased
xuanze 'select'	disjunctive question: constituents connected by *haishi*	

clauses, the first of which is a declarative, and the second, realising the 'tag', is an 'A-not-A'–type disjunctive question, using their terminology. We shall examine the congruent realisations of K2 moves, together with their responses, in our data and explore their paradigmatic contrasts and structural realisations from below.

4.4.3.1 Elemental Interrogative Among the various types of interrogatives in Mandarin, the elemental type is the one that causes the least controversy. It is known as a *tezhi* question in traditional Mandarin grammar, meaning 'refer to something in particular', equivalent to a wh– question in English and soliciting the missing ideational information.

In Mandarin an elemental interrogative also features the insertion of an interrogative function realised by lexical items such as *shenme* 'what', *nali* 'where', *shui* 'who', *zenme* 'how' and so on. For this study the interrogative word group realising the enquiring element in a clause is functionally labelled Inquirer rather than Wh (since Mandarin interrogative word groups are not characterised by *wh* in their graphological form). A number of Inquirers are realised by word groups that share the common word *shenme* 'what' – such as *shenme shihou* 'what time, when', *shenme difang* 'what place, where', *wei shenme* 'for what, why'. In fact, the interrogative word *shenme* 'what' can combine with any noun to form a nominal group realising the Inquirer function (e.g. Example 11).

(11) JU K2

cici	shexian	shenme	zuiming
this time	suspected	what	crime
		Inquirer	
		nominal group	
'What crime are you suspected of this time?'			

In Mandarin, the Inquirer is positioned where the missing piece of information would be in a declarative clause. This is illustrated in Example 12, which is based on the response to Example 11 – but expanded to its full clause form.

(12) DE1 K1

(cici)	shexian)	weixian	jiashi	(zuiming)
(this time)	suspected)	danger	drive	(crime)
	(Predicator)			
	(word group)	nominal group		
'(I am suspected of the crime of) reckless driving.'				

Examples 13 and 14 also illustrate an elemental interrogative and its response. In Example 13 the Inquirer is realised by the nominal group *he shi* 'what time, when', *he* being a more literary version of *shenme* 'what' and *shi* is the shortened form of *shijian* 'time', which also sounds more refined. Such literary and cultured wording is appropriate in the courtroom context where the formal, polished speech favoured by people with higher social status is preferred.

(13) JU K2

he	shi	bei	jiya
what	time	PASS	detain
Inquirer			
nominal group			
'When were you detained?'			

(14) DE K1

si	yue	shier	hao	(bei	jiya)
4	month	12	number	(PASS	detain)
				(Predicator)	
nominal group				(verbal group)[5]	
'(I was detained on) 12 April.'					

Note as well that in Examples 11–14 the textual and ideational functions conflated with the Inquirer in the interrogative clauses have not been labelled, as they are not relevant to the realisation of MOOD in Mandarin. It is sufficient at this stage simply to recognise that the position of the Inquirer depends on these ideational functions.

4.4.3.2 Addressee-Oriented Interrogatives An addressee-oriented interrogative in Mandarin is structurally formed by adding a clause-rank particle at the end of a declarative clause. This has the function of checking whether the knowledge proposed in the K2 move is correct or not. In traditional Mandarin grammar this type of interrogative is known as a *shifei* question, with *shifei* literally meaning 'right–wrong'. Halliday and McDonald (2004) and Li (2007) term this type of interrogative 'biased polar'. It is regarded as 'biased' because only one polarity choice, either positive or negative, is provided in the question; this does not imply that all such interrogatives presuppose or expect an answer that is either positive or negative.

---

[5] The Predicator is realised by verbal group here, not a word group with a verb as head word, because adjectives cannot be passivised.

The function realised by the clausal final particle is labelled Moderator. The most frequently used particle realising this Moderator is *ma*, a non-salient syllable spoken on a neutral tone. The *ma* interrogative does not assume either a positive or a negative answer. Consider the following two exchanges in the data, each with a *ma* interrogative clause realising the K2 move and a declarative realising the K1 move in response – numbered as Examples 15–18.

(15) JU K2

tong	*qisushu*	*zaiming*	*de*	*xinxi*	*yizhi*	*ma*
with	indictment	record	LK	information	consistent	Q
					Predicator	Moderator
					word group	particle
					Event	
					adjective	

'(Is it) consistent with the information recorded in the indictment?'

(16) DE1 K1

yizhi
consistent
Predicator
word group
Event
adjective

'(It is) consistent.'

(17) JU K2

jianchayuan	*de*	*qisushu*	*fuben*	*ni*	*shoudao*	=*le*	*ma*
procuratorate	LK	indictment	copy	you	receive	PERF	Q
					Predicator		Moderator
					word group		particle
					Event	Asp	
					verb	clitic	

'Have (you) received a copy of the indictment of the procuratorate?'

(18) DE1 K1

shoudao	=*le*
received	PERF
Predicator	
verbal group	
Event	Asp
verb	clitic

'(I) have received (it).'

4 Interpersonal Grammar in Mandarin

In Examples 15 and 17, the Moderator appears immediately after the Predicator in both examples, because in Example 15 the standard of comparison must precede the word group *yizhi* 'consistent' and in Example 17 *jianchayuan de qisushu fuben* 'a copy of the indictment of the procuratorate' is thematised textually. An alternative thematic organisation is presented in Example 19.

(19) JU K2

ni	*shoudao*	*=le*	*jianchayuan*	*de*	*qisushu*	*fuben*	*ma*
you	receive	PERF	procuratorate	LK	indictment	copy	Q
	Predicator						Moderator
	word group						particle
'Have (you) received a copy of the indictment of the procuratorate?'							

In Examples 16 and 18, both K1 response moves repeat the Predicator to affirm the proposition in the K2 moves, highlighting once again that in Mandarin the Predicator is the key interpersonal function in a declarative clause. The response moves might also include a Polarity Adjunct *shide* 'yes, correct', affirming the proposition, or *bu* 'no', contradicting the proposition. Note again that the negation markers differ between the imperfective aspect (*bu*) and the perfective (*mei[you]*).

    imperfective *tong qisushu zaiming de xinxi yizhi ma*
                        '(Is it) consistent with the information recorded in the indictment?'
                        ***shide**, yizhi*   ***bu**, bu yizhi*
                        'Yes, (it is) consistent.'   'No, (it is) not consistent.'

    perfective   *jianchayuan de qisushu fuben ni shoudao=le ma*
                        'Have (you) received a copy of the indictment of the procuratorate?'
                        ***shide**, shoudao=le*   ***bu**, mei(you) shoudao*
                        'Yes, (I) have received (it).' 'No, (I) have not received (it).'

It is also worth observing that in Mandarin if the interrogative move is negative, the Polarity Adjuncts *shide* and *bu* in response moves work differently from *yes* and *no* in English. Example 20 (modified from Example 17) and its responses in Examples 21 and 22 exemplify the use of *shide* and *bu* in affirming and denying a proposition.

(20) K2

qisushu	*fuben*	*ni*	***mei(you)***	*shoudao*	*ma*
indictment	copy	you	NEG.PERF	receive	Q
			Predicator		Moderator
			word group		particle
'Haven't (you) received a copy of the indictment?'					

(21) K1

shide,		*mei(you)*	*shoudao*
yes		NEG.PERF	receive
Polarity Adjunct		Predicator	
		word group	
'Right, (I) haven't received (it).'			

(22) K1

bu,	shoudao	=le
no	receive	PERF
Polarity Adjunct	Predicator	
	word group	
'No. (I) have received (it).'		

In English if one wants to agree to the proposition that a copy of the indictment has not been received, the Polarity Adjunct in the response would be *no*, as in *No, I haven't received it*. If one wants to contradict that proposition, the Polarity Adjunct in the response would be *yes*, as in *Yes, I have received it*.

Note that we are treating negation as realised inside the word group realising the Predicator in Mandarin, since the form of its realisation is conditioned by aspect (see Section 4.4.1). We can contrast this analysis with the realisation of negation in English as a Mood Adjunct – Example 23.

(23) K2

Have	you	not	received	a copy of the indictment
Finite	Subject	Mood Adjunct	Predicator	Complement

Taking this into account we can reason that the Polarity Adjuncts *shide* 'yes' and *bu* 'no' in Mandarin affirm or deny the Predicator, while in English they affirm or deny the proposition as a whole. It would also be interesting to compare this to other languages such as German and French, where an additional Modal Adjunct, *doch* and *si*, respectively, is used to contradict a negative proposition.

In an addressee-oriented interrogative clause, the clause final particle can also be *ba*. Unlike *ma*, the particle *ba* marks an interrogative that involves the speaker's high expectation that the proposition being negotiated is true and that the addressee will confirm the proposition. See Example 24 where the particle *ba* sits at the end of an interrogative clause in a K2 move (in an example slightly modified from our data), along with its response in Example 25.

(24) JU K2

dou	mei	you	yijian	ba
all	NEG	have	objection	MOD
	Predicator			Moderator
	word group			particle
'You do not have any objection, do you?'				

(25) DL K1

mei	you
NEG	have
Predicator	
word group	
'(We) do not have (any objection).'	

4 Interpersonal Grammar in Mandarin

Here the clause with the particle *ba* is treated as interrogative rather than declarative in function, mainly because it congruently realises a K2 move soliciting a response (and expecting an affirmative one). The K1 move can either affirm or contradict the proposition, using a clause centring on the Predicator, with or without the Polarity Adjunct *shide* or *bu* – like the responses elicited by an interrogative clause with the particle *ma*:

    K2 *dou meiyou yijian **ba***
          'You don't have any objection, do you?'
    K1 ***shide**, meiyou yijian*   ***bu**, you yijian*
          'We don't have any objection.' 'We do have some objection.'

4.4.3.3 Proposition-Oriented Interrogative The proposition-oriented type of interrogative is traditionally described in Mandarin grammar as a *zhengfan* question, in which *zheng* literally means the 'face side' and *fan* the 'reverse side' of something flat. In a 'face–reverse' interrogative both the positive and the negative sides of the proposition are provided, and the addressee needs to give either a positive or a negative version of that proposition. Hence its name, proposition-oriented, here. It may be because the response is either positive or negative that Halliday and McDonald (2004) and Li (2007) treat such interrogatives as 'polar'; and they appear to treat such interrogatives as 'unbiased' because both sides of the proposition are made explicit in the question.

The proposition-oriented interrogative features a Predicator that is realised by a word group complex, in which a word group first appears in the positive, paratactically followed by a word group in the negative containing the same Event (either a verb or an adjective). Example 26 is a proposition-oriented interrogative, where two word groups *you* 'have' and *mei you* 'not have' are juxtaposed to realise the interrogative MOOD type, with the second word group extending the first one. Example 27 is the response to this interrogative (a negative one).

(26)   JU K2

ni	*you*	*mei*	*you*	*yijian*
you	have	NEG	have	objection
	Predicator			
	word group complex			
	1	+2		
'Do you have any objection?'				

(27)   DE1 K1

mei	*you*
NEG	have
Predicator	
word group	
'(I) do not have (any objection).'	

The proposition-oriented interrogative allows for the word group complex realising the Predicator to be discontinuous. Adjusting Example 26 we arrive at Example 28, where the second component of the word group complex is placed after *yijian* 'objection', the object of the verb *you* 'have'.

(28) JU K2

ni	*you*	*yijian*	*mei*	*you*
you	have	objection	NEG	have
	Predi ...			... cator
	word ...			... group complex
	1			+2
'Do you have any objection?'				

It is worth noting that there is a phonological conditioning in relation to the structure of Predicator in the proposition-oriented interrogative in Mandarin. If the word group in the positive polarity is comprised of two or more syllables, the Event of the first word group may be reduced to its first syllable (rendering the word phonologically incomplete). There is one such instance in our data, Example 29. Here the verb *jide* 'remember' is realised through its first syllable *ji* in the first word group of the complex. This reduction in phonological form is only a tendency, rather than a rule, since it is equally grammatical to use the full phonological form, as in *jide bu jide* (literally 'remember not remember').

(29) JU K2

ni	*ji*	*bu*	*jide*	...
you	remember	NEG	remember	
	Predicator			
	word group complex			
	1		+2	
'Do you remember ... '				

In contrast to addressee-oriented interrogatives, proposition-oriented interrogatives cannot be responded to through a move with the Polarity Adjuncts *shide* 'yes' or *bu* 'no'; the response move can only be realised by a declarative clause with either a positive or negative Predicator (as in Example 27).

A special kind of proposition-oriented interrogative uses the verb *shi* 'be right, correct', forming the verbal group complex *shi bu shi* 'be right or not be right'. In formal contexts *shi bu shi* can be alternatively replaced by *shi fou*, where *fou* is a literary, refined form of *bu shi*. The interrogative clause comprising the verbal group complex *shi bu shi* or *shi fou* is followed by another clause containing the proposition that the addressee is asked to affirm or contradict. Example 30 is a question involving an interrogative of this type. We treat it here as a clause complex consisting of two clauses; the *shi fou* clause realises the interrogative MOOD type of the move, whereas the other clause

4 Interpersonal Grammar in Mandarin

(a declarative) establishes the proposition. That is to say, a *shi bu shi* (or *shifou*) question splits the ideational and interpersonal components into two clauses in a paratactic relationship. Only the interpersonal component is responsible for the interrogative MOOD type (e.g. clause 2 in Example 30).

(30) JU K2

beigaoren	bianhuren	shi	fou	dou	ting	qingchu	=le
defendant	defence lawyer	be right	not be right	all	hear	clear	PERF
1 ...		≪=2≫		... 1			
		Predicator		Predicator			
		verbal group complex		word group			
		1	+2				
'The defendants and defence lawyers have all heard clearly, yes or no?'								

The addressee can choose to respond either using the Predicator in the declarative clause, as in Example 31 (the actual response in our data), or choosing between the positive or negative in the proposition-oriented interrogative.

(31) DE, DL K1

ting	qingchu	=le
hear	clear	PERF
Predicator		
word group		
'(We) heard clearly.'		

Some Chinese scholars treat this *shi bu shi* interrogative as another type of interrogative, distinct from other proposition-oriented interrogatives (Tao, 1998; Ding, 1999). Their arguments are largely based on the practice in traditional Mandarin grammar of analysing MOOD at the level of sentence (clause complex in SFL terms), rather than clause. Example 32 from our data better demonstrates that a *shi bu shi* interrogative comprises two clauses forming a paratactic clause complex since *shi bu shi* can also be positioned after the declarative presenting the proposition being negotiated. The response addresses the declarative clause in the clause complex, as in Example 33.

(32) JU K2

xuyao	xunwen	shi	bu	shi
need	interrogate	be right	NEG	be right
1		=2		
Predicator		Predicator		
word group complex		verbal group complex	
1	+2	1	+2
'(You) need to interrogate the defendants, yes or no?'				

(33) PR1 K1

xuyao
need
Predicator
word group
'(I) need to.'

4.4.3.4 'Select' Question The title of this subsection is worded 'question' rather than 'interrogative' because such questions are not treated as realising the MOOD system in Mandarin in this chapter. But they are worth accounting for since a majority of traditional Mandarin grammars list them as a type of interrogative (e.g. Zhu, 1982; Zhang, 1997; Huang & Liao, 2002; Hu, 2011, to name just a few).

A *xuanze* 'select' question, as it is called in traditional Mandarin grammar, is actually realised by a clause complex (Huang & Liao, 2002, p. 113), not a clause. Such a question offers two or more alternatives for the addressee to select from – with the last two alternatives connected by the conjunction *haishi* 'or'. Example 34 is a 'select' question realised by a clause complex, with two clauses in an extending paratactic relationship. Note that the proposition-oriented interrogative with *shi bu shi* (*shi fou*) in the previous section also features clause complexing, but it is the '=2' paratactic clause alone that realises the interrogative MOOD type. Here in a 'select' question, neither of the clauses in the clause complex can realise the interrogative MOOD type independently.

(34)

ni	chi	fan	haishi	chi	mian
you	eat	rice	or	eat	noodle
1			+2		
'Do you eat rice or noodle?'					

Thus far, the clause-level interrogatives in Mandarin that congruently realise K2 moves are of three types: elemental interrogatives, addressee-oriented interrogatives and proposition-oriented interrogatives. Halliday and McDonald (2004) and Li (2007) group addressee-oriented and proposition-oriented interrogatives together as polar interrogatives for the obvious reason that they both solicit either a positive or a negative response to the proposition in question, as opposed to elemental interrogatives which demand missing ideational information from the addressee.

From below, the structure of mood elements of the three types of interrogatives are all distinct from one another. The clause-rank functions that realise MOOD for elemental, addressee-oriented and proposition-oriented interrogatives are Inquirer, Moderator and Predicator, respectively. The Predicator in

4 Interpersonal Grammar in Mandarin

proposition-oriented interrogatives has to be realised by a word group complex, whose positive and negative components are allowed to be discontinuous. The response to an addressee-oriented interrogative or a proposition-oriented interrogative typically features picking up the Predicator from the interrogative and giving it either positive or negative polarity. Since both positive and negative are realised in the Predicator of a proposition-oriented interrogative, the response is actually selecting between the two given alternatives. Polarity Adjunct *shide* 'yes' or *bu* 'no' can be used in response to addressee-oriented interrogatives. These features are summarised in Table 4.2.

Based on the above discussion, a system network for interrogative MOOD type in Mandarin can be devised as shown in Figure 4.4. The elemental interrogative is set apart from the others because the addressee-oriented and proposition-oriented interrogatives are cryptogrammatically based on the Predicator – since they solicit a response replaying the Predicator in the interrogative. The elemental interrogative requires an insertion of the function Inquirer and conflation with whatever ideational function it enquires about. The addressee-oriented interrogative has the function Moderator inserted and

Table 4.2 *Three types of interrogative in Mandarin*

	elemental	addressee-oriented	proposition-oriented
Clause-rank function realising MOOD	Inquirer	Moderator	Predicator
Predicator realised by word group complex			+
Response using Predicator from interrogative		+	+
Response using Polarity Adjunct *shide* or *bu*		+	
Response choosing between polar alternatives given in interrogative			+

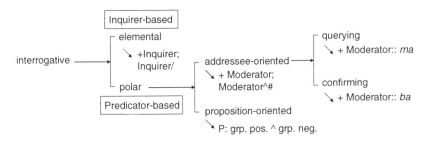

Figure 4.4 Interrogative clauses in Mandarin

placed at the end of the clause, and the Moderator can be lexically realised by either *ma* (which queries the truthfulness of proposition) or *ba* (which tentatively confirms the proposition and seeks agreement from the addressee) – thus realising features [querying] and [confirming], respectively. The proposition-oriented interrogative requires the Predicator to be realised by word group complexing with the positive preceding the negative.

4.5 Mood in Mandarin: A Synopsis from a Complementary Perspective

From the analysis in Section 4.4, we can consolidate the MOOD system in Mandarin as outlined in Figure 4.5. This system is oriented to the realisation of the discourse-semantic system of NEGOTIATION. The main problem with this classification is that if we reason from round about and below it is impossible to find phenotypical or cryptotypical evidence for the feature [interrogative] which justifies its opposition to [declarative].

Therefore this calls for a complementary perspective, in which the discourse-semantic system of ENGAGEMENT can be accorded greater relevance as far as the mood choices in Mandarin are concerned. Particularly relevant is the dialogically expanding resource 'entertain' (Martin & White, 2005, p. 104), which allows for individual subjectivity to be expressed when presenting a proposition or proposal for negotiation. In Mandarin, this can be foregrounded by setting up a simultaneous system alongside the primary mood distinction between [indicative] and [imperative]; both indicative and imperative clauses would select from this system, as shown in Figure 4.6.

This system, oriented as it is to the realisation of the discourse-semantic system of ENGAGEMENT, has two options: [pose] and [tender]. The feature [pose] indicates that we table a proposition or proposal for assessment, opening up the dialogic space; [tender] on the other hand means that we proffer the

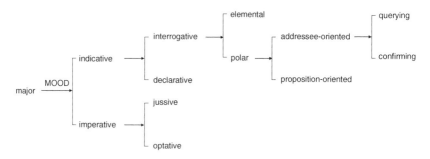

Figure 4.5 Mandarin MOOD system (oriented to NEGOTIATION)

4 Interpersonal Grammar in Mandarin

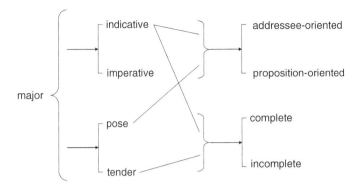

Figure 4.6 Complementary Mandarin MOOD system (oriented to NEGOTIATION and ENGAGEMENT)

proposition or proposal as not negotiable. The [pose] option is realised by a modal element at the end of a clause (e.g. *ma*, *ba*).

For imperative clauses, the tender type is jussive, and tables a direct demand for goods or services, as shown in Examples 1–5. The pose type is optative, which opens up negotiating space around the obligation – structurally realised by insertion of a clause final Moderator, as in Example 6. Below we reproduce and modify Example 6 as Examples 35 and 36 to illustrate this point.

(35)

[imperative; pose]			
zanmen	*bao*	*jing*	*ba*
we (inclusive)	report	police	MOD
	Predicator		Moderator
	verbal group		particle
'Shall we call the police.'			

(36)

[imperative; tender]		
zanmen	*bao*	*jing*
we (inclusive)	report	police
	Predicator	
	verbal group	
'Let's call the police!'		

The indicative can also select from [pose] and [tender], and either selection will lead to further MOOD choices. For the posing indicative, Mandarin has a fairly broad range of resources for assessment of probability of propositions. On the one hand, a Moderator can be placed at the end of an indicative clause, realised by a variety of particles fine-tuning modal assessment. In the previous section we have analysed Moderators realised by the particle *ma* in the [addressee-oriented interrogative] (Examples 15, 17, 19 and 20), and Moderators realised by *ba* in both [addressee-oriented interrogative] (Example 24) and [declarative] (Examples 9 and 10). From the perspective of ENGAGEMENT, the distinction between interrogative and declarative featuring the particle *ba* can both be viewed as posing the probability of the proposition for negotiation with the addressee. At this stage, we can group the indicative clauses with a Moderator together with the feature [addressee-oriented]. Apart from *ma* and *ba*, there are in Mandarin other clause rank particles such as *a, ne, la*, each modifying the dialogic space in its own manner. This, however, is beyond the scope of the present study.

In addition, for the posing indicative, the Predicator of a clause can be realised by a word group complex, juxtaposing the positive and negative alternatives of the same Event, and thus choices for both affirming and dismissing the proposition are presented in the clause. This was analysed as proposition-oriented interrogative clause in the previous section, as in Examples 26, 28–30 and 32. We continue to use the name [proposition-oriented] for the feature in this alternative perspective. Examples 37 and 38 are reproduced from Examples 24 and 26, respectively. Taken out of context, an indicative clause with the Moderator *ba* (e.g. Example 37) can realise either a K2 or a K1 move in a dialogic exchange.

(37)

\[indicative; pose: addressee-oriented\]					
dou	*mei*	*you*	*yijian*	*ba*	
all	NEG	have	objection	MOD	
	Predicator			Moderator	
	word group			particle	
'You do not have any objection, do you?'				

(38)

\[indicative; pose: proposition-oriented\]				
ni	*you*	*mei*	*you*	*yijian*
you	have	NEG	have	objection
	Predicator			
	word group complex			
	1	+2		
'Do you have any objection?'				

For the tendering indicative, the clause is more oriented toward the ideational dimension of the proposition. A further choice is made between [complete] and [incomplete] in accordance with whether the ideational meaning in the clause is complete. The complete clauses are analysed as declaratives (as in Examples 7 and 8), and the incomplete ones as elemental interrogatives (as in Examples 11 and 13) in the previous section. Examples 39 and 40, reproduced from Examples 12 and 11, respectively, capture this distinction. In Example 40, an Inquirer is deployed to sort out the incomplete experiential meaning that is complete in Example 39.

(39)

[indicative; tender: complete]				
cici	shexian	weixian	jiashi	zuiming
this time	suspected	danger	drive	crime
'I am suspected of the crime of reckless driving this time.'				

(40)

[indicative; tender: incomplete]			
cici	shexian	shenme	zuiming
this time	suspected	what	crime
		Inquirer	
		nominal group	
'What crime are you suspected of this time?'			

Cross-linguistically, enquiries about missing information have different realisation pattern in grammar. They either share a realisation pattern with interrogatives, as with English wh– interrogatives which adopt the Finite ^ Subject sequence like polar interrogatives,[6] and in Khorchin Mongolian (Zhang, Chapter 3, this volume). Alternatively, the realisation bears no structural similarity to interrogatives but resembles that of declaratives, with the missing ideation filled in by an Inquirer in situ – as in Mandarin, Classical Tibetan (Wang, 2020) and Vietnamese (Thai, 2004).

Thus, the congruent grammatical realisations of various moves in the system of NEGOTIATION are scattered across the systems shown in Figure 4.6 once ENGAGEMENT is brought into the picture at a lower delicacy. Taking ENGAGEMENT into account in the description of MOOD in Mandarin is mainly motivated by structural considerations, and ENGAGEMENT can serve as an augmentation to NEGOTIATION, since the agnation patterns of Mandarin MOOD structure cannot be directly derived from NEGOTIATION alone.

4.6 Conclusion

In this chapter we explored interpersonal grammar in Mandarin, focusing on MOOD system and structure from an axis-oriented trinocular perspective. The

---

[6] There is one exception to this rule: in an English wh– interrogative, when the function Wh conflates with Subject, then Subject comes before Finite, e.g. *Who will sing this song?* See Martin et al. (2013, p. 45) for discussion.

analysis shows that MOOD in Mandarin is not only responsible for negotiating knowledge and action exchanges between moves in dialogue, but it also closely interacts with MODALITY and POLARITY systems that are associated with the subsystem ENGAGEMENT of the discourse-semantic system APPRAISAL. According to Teruya et al. (2007, p. 913), MOOD in Mandarin is largely Predicator-based. McDonald (1998, p. 252) also suggests that the Predicator can be identified as the element which tends to remain constant in dialogic exchanges. This chapter supports these viewpoints and identifies the Predicator as a clause-rank function that is realised by a word group – without specifying the type of the word group since the Event can be either a verb or an adjective. Apart from Predicator, MOOD in Mandarin also involves the clause final function of Moderator, and the Inquirer function in case of elemental interrogative (where it fills in certain gaps of ideational meaning of the clause).

In this chapter we first approached MOOD in Mandarin from the discourse-semantic system of NEGOTIATION, and then complemented the description with a perspective oriented towards both NEGOTIATION and ENGAGEMENT. This complementary perspective gives more consideration to structural realisations from below, and arrives at a different model, reflected in a different set of system network relations. This consolidated descriptive model points to the fact that MOOD in Mandarin does not only negotiate the exchange of knowledge or action, but also engages with the speaker's assessment of probability of a proposition or obligation of a proposal.

References

Berry, M. (1981). Systemic Linguistics and Discourse Analysis: A Multi-Layered Approach to Exchange Structure. In M. Coulthard and M. Montgomery, eds., *Studies in Discourse Analysis*. London: Routledge & Kegan Paul, pp. 120–45.
Caffarel, A. (2006). *A Systemic Functional Grammar of French*. London/New York: Continuum.
Caffarel, A., Martin, J. R. & Matthiessen, C. M. I. M., eds., (2004). *Language Typology: A Functional Perspective*. Amsterdam: John Benjamins.
Ding, L. (1999). 从问句系统看"是不是"问句 [*Cong wenju xitong kan 'shi bu shi' wenju*, A Study of 'Shi Bu Shi' Questions from the Perspective of Question System]. 中国语文 [*Zhongguo Yuwen*, Studies of the Chinese Language], 6, 415–20.
Halliday, M. A. K. (1978). *Language as Social Semiotic: The Social Interpretation of Language and Meaning*. London: Edward Arnold.
Halliday, M. A. K. (1984). Language as Code and Language as Behaviour: A Systemic-Functional Interpretation of the Nature and Ontogenesis of Dialogue. In R. P. Fawcett, M. A. K. Halliday, S. M. Lamb and A. Makkai, eds., *Language as Social Semiotic*. Vol I. of *The Semiotics of Language and Culture*. London: Pinter, pp. 3–35.
Halliday, M. A. K. (1992). Systemic Grammar and the Concept of a 'Science of Language'. *Waiguoyu* (*Journal of Foreign Languages*), 2, 1–9.

Halliday, M. A. K. (1994). *An Introduction to Functional Grammar*, 2nd ed. London: Arnold.
Halliday, M. A. K. (1996). On Grammar and Grammatics. In R. Hasan, C. Cloran and D. Butt, eds., *Functional Descriptions: Language Form and Linguistic Theory*. Amsterdam/Philadelphia: John Benjamins, pp. 1–38.
Halliday, M. A. K. & Matthiessen, C. M. I. M. (1999). *Construing Experience Through Meaning: A Language-based Approach to Cognition*. London/New York: Continuum.
Halliday, M. A. K. & Matthiessen, C. M. I. M. (2014). *Halliday's Introduction to Functional Grammar*, 4th ed. London: Routledge.
Halliday, M. A. K. & McDonald, E. (2004). Metafunctional Profile of the Grammar of Chinese. In A. Caffarel, J. R. Martin and C. M. I. M. Matthiessen, eds., *Language Typology: A Functional Perspective*. Amsterdam: John Benjamins, pp. 305–96.
Hu, Y. (2011). 现代汉语 [*Xiandai Hanyu*, Modern Chinese]. Shanghai: Shanghai Education Press.
Huang, B. (1984). 陈述句，疑问句，祈使句，感叹句 [*Chenshu Ju, Yiwen Ju, Qishi Ju, Gantan Ju*, Declaratives, Interrogatives, Imperatives, Exclamatives]. Shanghai: Shanghai Education Publishing House.
Huang, B. & Liao, X. (2002). 现代汉语 [*Xiandai Hanyu*, Modern Chinese] II. Beijing: Higher Education Press.
Li, E. S. (2007). *A Systemic Functional Grammar of Chinese: A Text-based Analysis*. London/New York: Continuum.
Li, C. N. & Thompson, S. A. (1981). *Mandarin Chinese: A Functional Reference Grammar*. Berkeley/Los Angeles/London: University of California Press.
Martin, J. R. (1992). *English Text: System and Structure*. Amsterdam: John Benjamins.
Martin, J. R. (2002). Meaning Beyond the Clause: SFL Perspectives. *Annual Review of Applied Linguistics*, 22, 52–74.
Martin, J. R. (2004). Metafunctional Profile of the Grammar of Tagalog. In A. Caffarel, J. R. Martin and C. M. I. M. Matthiessen, eds., *Language Typology: A Functional Perspective*. Amsterdam: John Benjamins, pp. 255–304.
Martin, J. R. (2014). Evolving Systemic Functional Linguistics: Beyond the Clause. *Functional Linguistics*, *1* (3).
Martin, J. R. (2015). Meaning beyond the Clause: Co-Textual Relations. *Linguistics and the Human Sciences*, *11* (2–3), 203–35.
Martin, J. R. (2018). Interpersonal Meaning: Systemic Functional Linguistics Perspective. *Functions of Language*, 25(1), 2–19.
Martin, J. R. & Quiroz, B. (2020). Functional Language Typology: A Discourse Semantic Perspective. In J. R. Martin, Y. J. Doran and G. Figueredo, eds., *Systemic Functional Language Description: Making Meaning Matter*. New York and London: Routledge, pp. 189–237.
Martin, J. R. & Rose, D. (2007). *Working with Discourse: Meaning beyond the Clause*, 2nd ed., London/New York: Continuum.
Martin, J. R. & Rose, D. (2008). *Genre Relations: Mapping Culture*. London/Oakville: Equinox.
Martin, J. R. & White, P. (2005). *The Language of Evaluation: Appraisal in English*. London: Palgrave.
Martin, J. R. & Zappavigna, M. (2016). Rites of Passion: Remorse, Apology and Forgiveness in Youth Justice Conferencing. *Linguistics and the Human Sciences*, *12* (2–3),101–21.

Martin, J. R., Wang, P. & Zhu, Y. (2013). *Systemic Functional Grammar: A Next Step into the Theory – Axial Relations*. Beijing: Higher Education Press.

Matthiessen, C. M. I. M. (2004). Descriptive Motifs and Generalisations. In A. Caffarel, J. R. Martin and C. M. I. M. Matthiessen, eds., *Language Typology: A Functional Perspective*. Amsterdam: John Benjamins, pp. 537–673.

Matthiessen, C. M. I. M. & Halliday, M. A. K. (2009). *Systemic Functional Grammar: A First Step into the Theory*. Beijing: Higher Education Press.

Matthiessen, C. M. I. M., Teruya, K. & Wu, C. (2008). Multilingual Studies as Multi-Dimensional Space of Interconnected Language Studies. In J. Webster, ed., *Meaning in Context: Implementing Intelligent Applications*. London/New York: Continuum, pp. 146–220.

McDonald, E. (1998). *Clause and Verbal Group Systems in Chinese: A Text-based Functional Approach*. Unpublished PhD dissertation, Macquarie University, Sydney, Australia.

Quiroz, B. (2008). Towards a Systemic Profile of the Spanish MOOD. *Linguistics and the Human Sciences*, 4(1), 31–65.

Quiroz, B. (2018). Negotiating Interpersonal Meaning: Reasoning about MOOD. *Functions of Language*, 25(1), 135–63.

Sinclair, J. M. & Coulthard, R. M. (1975). *Towards an Analysis of Discourse: The English Used by Teachers and Pupils*. London: Oxford University Press.

Steiner, E. & Teich, E. (2004). Metafunctional Profile of the Grammar of German. In A. Caffarel, J. R. Martin and C. M. I. M. Matthiessen, eds., *Language Typology: A Functional Perspective*. Amsterdam: John Benjamins, pp. 139–84.

Tao, L. (1998). "是不是" 问句说略 ['*Shi bu shi' wenju shu*olue, A Brief Account of 'Shi Bu Shi' Questions]. 中国语文 [*Zhongguo Yuwen*, Studies of the Chinese Language], 2, 105–7.

Teruya, K., Akerejola, E., Andersen, T. H., Caffarel, A., Lavid, J., Matthiessen, C. M. I. M., Petersen, U. H., Patpong, P. & Smedegaard, F. (2007). Typology of MOOD: A Text-Based and System-Based Functional View. In R. Hasan, C. M. I. M. Matthiessen and J. Webster, eds., *Continuing Discourse on Language: Functional Perspective*, vol. II. London: Equinox, pp. 859–920.

Thai, M. D. (2004). Metafunctional Profile of the Grammar of Vietnamese. In A. Caffarel, J. R. Martin and C. M. I. M. Matthiessen, eds., *Language Typology: A Functional Perspective*. Amsterdam: John Benjamins, pp. 397–431.

Ventola, E. (1987). *The Structure of Social Interaction: A Systemic Approach to the Semiotics of Service Encounters*. London: Pinter.

Wang, P. (2020). Axial Argumentation and Cryptogrammar in Interpersonal Grammar: A Case Study of Classical Tibetan MOOD. In J. R. Martin, Y. Doran and G. Figueredo, eds., *Systemic Functional Language Description: Making Meaning Matter*. London: Routledge, 73–101.

Whorf, B. L. (circa 1936). A Linguistic Consideration of Thinking in Primitive Communities. In B. L. Whorf (1956), *Language, Thought, and Reality: Selected Writings of Benjamin Lee Whorf*. (Edited and with an introduction by J. B. Carroll). Cambridge, MA: The MIT Press, pp. 65–86.

Whorf, B. L. (1937). Grammatical Categories. In B. L. Whorf (1956), *Language, Thought, and Reality: Selected Writings of Benjamin Lee Whorf*. (Edited and with an introduction by J. B. Carroll). Cambridge, MA: The MIT Press, pp. 87–101.

Whorf, B. L. (1956). *Language, Thought, and Reality: Selected Writings of Benjamin Lee Whorf*. Edited and with an introduction by J. B. Carroll. Cambridge, MA: The MIT Press.

Zhang, B. (1997). 疑问句功能琐议 [*Yiwenju gongneng suoyi*, Trivial Comments on the Functions of Questions]. 中国语文 [Zhongguo Yuwen, Studies of the Chinese Language], *2*, 104–10.

Zhang, D. (2009). 汉语语气系统的特点 [*Hanyu yuqi xitong de tedian*, Some Characteristics of Chinese MOOD System]. 外国语文 [*Waiguo Yuwen*, Foreign Language and Literature], *25* (5), 1–7.

Zhu, D. (1982). 语法讲义 [*Yufa Jiangyi*, Lectures on Chinese Grammar]. Beijing: Commercial Press.

5 Interpersonal Grammar in Tagalog: ASSESSMENT Systems

J. R. Martin and Priscilla Cruz

5.1 Interpersonal Grammar in Tagalog

Tagalog grammar has been explored from the perspective of systemic functional linguistics (hereafter SFL) in a series of papers, beginning with Buenaventura-Naylor (1975). Work on clause grammar (see Martin 1981, 1983, 1988, 1993, 1995, 1996; Martin & Cruz, 2019) is consolidated in Martin's (2004) metafunctional profile; interpersonal grammar in particular is addressed in Martin (1990) and Martin and Cruz (2018). As with much SFL work on interpersonal grammar (cf. Martin, 2018; Mwinlaaru et al., 2018; Teruya et al., 2007), the point of departure from a discourse-semantic perspective has been the exchange of goods-and-services and information in dialogue – with a focus on MOOD, MODALITY, POLARITY and TAGGING systems. As surveyed in Matthiessen (2004), these resources are complemented across languages by what he refers to as MODAL ASSESSMENT systems (including resources for modality and/or evidentiality, among others). In this paper, we extend work on the interpersonal grammar of Tagalog by focusing on these resources, specifically addressing a grammatical system which we will refer to as ASSESSMENT. From a discourse-semantic perspective (Martin & Rose, 2007; Martin & White, 2005), ASSESSMENT is particularly involved in the realisation of ENGAGEMENT, as interlocutors negotiate consensus around propositions and proposals, and the attitudes they inscribe or invoke. We begin with a brief introduction to what Schachter and Otanes (1972) refer to as 'enclitic particles' (which we will refer to simply as 'clitics' for short), and then zero in on those clitics which enact a play of voices around the negotiation of a move in Tagalog dialogue. Schachter and Otanes's term, enclitic particles, captures the fact that these words are elements of clause structure (and so perhaps best treated as particles in SFL terminology) but are dependent on another element of clause structure (as clitics are in the structure of groups and phrases) – so they are 'embryonic clitics', from the perspective of grammaticalisation, we might say. Sensitive positioning of these voices is an essential dimension of conversation if interlocutors are to successfully align around shared knowledge and values. ASSESSMENT is a crucial interpersonal resource for meaning in this respect.

5.2 Tagalog Clitics

Tagalog clitics are elements of clause structure which depend on a preceding clause segment containing a salient syllable. This 'pre-enclitic' segment may be verbal, nominal or adverbial (or a part of one of these) and encode ideational or interpersonal meaning. This range of dependency means that Tagalog clitics are clause-rank segments and cannot be generalised as part of the structure of a particular class of group or phrase (cf. verbal group clitics in French or Spanish; Caffarel, 2006; Quiroz, 2010). Although an optional resource, most moves in a Tagalog conversation employ one or more clitics.

By way of illustrating this patterning, we consider the following phase of dialogue (Text 1) – simplified at this stage, in ways we will clarify later. This recorded text has been adapted to hide the identity of those involved, in ways that do not affect the analysis of clitics in this paper; it is used with the permission of interlocutors. The point of departure for our analysis is co-textualised contextualised clitics. The text is taken from a conversation in which Dan is discussing his son's wedding plans with his sisters. Dan's aunt and uncle have agreed to be godparents (in Tagalog *ninong at ninang sa kasal* translates to 'godfather and godmother at the wedding') for Dan's son and his bride at their wedding; they would be expected to parade down the aisle in their finery in the opening phase of a traditional ceremony. Dan's aunt, however, is refusing to play her part in this tradition – something which offends Dan.

The dialogue is presented, clause by clause. Column 1 marks the speaker (sisters Ange and Pam, and brother Dan). Row 1 includes a word-by-word rendering of the Tagalog interaction, with standardised spelling. Pronoun clitics are marked in bold, prefaced by '='. Row 2 provides a word-for-word glossing, and Row 3, a 'free' translation. For glossing conventions specific to this paper see the Appendix; otherwise, Leipzig glossing has been deployed.

1.1	Ange	*Huwag*	*=mo*	*-ng*	*pa-lakar-in*	*si*	*Tita*
		NEG[1]	NT.2SG	LK	NFIN.CAUS-walk-P2F	T	auntie
		\multicolumn{6}{l}{'don't make Auntie walk'}		

---

[1] Following Leipzig glossing conventions, glosses for closed system items on this row will be formatted in small caps; this formatting is not to be confused with the use of small caps in SFL to name systems.

1.2

Ange	Kung	ayaw	=niya.
	if	refuse	NT.3SG
	'if she doesn't want to.'		

1.3

Ange	S<in>abi	=niya	sa	iyo	noon-ng	umpisa,	e.
	<PERF.P2F>say	NT.3SG	CIR	OBL.2SG	back.at-LK	start	eh
	'She told you back at the start, you know.'						

1.4

Dan	Bakit?
	why
	'Why?'

1.5

Pam	Hindi	=siya	nag-la~lakad	sa	kasal
	NEG	T.3SG	IMPERF.P lF~walk	CIR	wedding
	'She doesn't walk at weddings'				

1.6

Pam	S<in>abi	=niya	sa	iyo	iyon	dati,	di	ba?
	<PERF.P2F>say	NT.3SG	CIR	OBL.3SG	yon	previously	NEG	?
	'she told you that previously, didn't she?'							

1.7

Dan	Oo ...
	yes
	'Yes ...'

1.8

Dan	pero	bakit	hindi?
	but	why	NEG
	'but why not?'		

Five of the clauses in this phase of dialogue include pronominal clitics. Two (both *niya* 'she') depend on verbs (*sinabi* 'told' in clauses 1.3 and 1.6); two depend on negative adverbials (*mo* 'you' on the negative imperative marker *huwag* in 1.1 and *siya* 'she' on the negative indicative marker *hindi* in 1.5), and one, *niya* 'she', depends on the negative modulation marker *ayaw* 'doesn't want' in 1.2.

Tagalog's paradigm of pronominal clitics is outlined in Table 5.1. As we can see from Text 1 they construe participants in transitivity structure. Along with person and number, the system distinguishes clitic pronouns which function as Theme from those which do not.

5 Interpersonal Grammar in Tagalog: ASSESSMENT Systems

Table 5.1 *Pronominal clitics in Tagalog*

	'Thematicity'	only	+ other/s
speaker	Theme	*ako* 'I'	*kami* 'we' exclusive
	Non-Theme	*ko* 'I'	*namin* 'we' exclusive
speaker/addressee	Theme	*tayo* 'you SG or PL and me' inclusive	
	Non-Theme	*natin* 'you SG or PL and me' inclusive	
addressee	Theme	*ka* 'you SG'	*kayo* 'you PL'
	Non-Theme	*mo* 'you SG'	*ninyo* 'you PL'
non-interlocutor	Theme	*siya* 's/he'	*sila* 'they'
	Non-Theme	*niya*	*nila*

Text 1 is, in fact, a simplified rendering of the conversation that took place. The actual dialogue unfolded as Text 1', which now includes both pronominal and non-pronominal clitics (the latter marked in bold). It is these non-pronominal clitics which realise the system we are referring to as ASSESSMENT in this paper. A word-by-word glossing for assessment clitics has not been provided at this stage. However, a second row of translation has been offered, to suggest the kind of contribution the assessment clitics make in conversation. Since a comparable set of ASSESSMENT resources has not yet been described for English, it is not possible to capture precisely what is going on – a matter we pursue in the remainder of the paper.

1'.1

Ange	*Huwag*	=*mo*	-*ng*	*pa-lakar-in*	*si*	*Tita*
	NEG	NT.2SG	LK	NFIN.CAUS-walk-P2F	T	auntie
	'Don't make Auntie walk'					

1'.2

Ange	*kung*	*ayaw*	=*niya*.
	if	refuse	NT.3SG
	'if she doesn't want to.'		

1'.3

Ange	*S<in>abi*	=***naman***	=*niya*	*sa*	*iyo*	*noon-ng*	*umpisa*	=*pa*	=***lang***,	*e.*
	<PERF.P2F>say		NT.3SG	CIR	OBL.2SG	back.at-LK	start			eh
	'she told you back at the start, you know.'									
	'She *told*[2] you way back at just the start, you know.'									

---

[2] We use italics here and in 1'.6 to indicate that this word would carry the major pitch movement in the tone group in which it is spoken – the Tonic segment in Halliday and Greaves' (2008) terms.

1'.4

Dan	Bakit?
	why
	'Why?'

1'.5

Pam	Hindi	=**nga**	=siya	nag-la~lakad	sa	kasal
	NEG		T.3SG	IMPERF.P1F~walk	CIR	wedding
	'she doesn't walk at weddings'					
	'She simply doesn't walk at weddings'					

1'.6

Pam	S<in>abi	=**naman**	=niya	sa	iyo	iyon	dati	=**pa**,	di	ba?
	<PERF.P2F>say		NT.3SG	CIR	OBL.3SG	yon	previously		NEG	?
	'she told you that previously, didn't she'									
	'she *told* you that ages ago, didn't she?'									

1'.7

Dan	Oo ...
	yes
	'Yes ...'

1'.8

Dan	pero	bakit	hindi?
	but	why	NEG
	'but why not?'		

Tagalog's paradigm of assessment clitics is outlined in Table 5.2. Following Schachter and Otanes (1972) and Schachter (1973) we have not included *muli/ uli/ulit* 'again' in this table. It is far less attracted than the clitics in Table 5.2 to interpersonal pre-enclitic segments realising negation (*hindi* 'doesn't/didn't' etc., *huwag* 'don't'), modalisation (e.g. *baka* 'maybe', *siyempre* 'always') or modulation (e.g. *gusto* 'want', *ayaw* 'not want') – focusing as it does on repetition of ideational meaning. If included to account for its sequencing potential in relation to other clitics, it could be added to Column 2. Morphophonemic alternations are marked with a slash (for *din/rin* 'too' and *daw/raw* 'reportative'). The clitic *lang* 'just' has a less common, more formal two-syllable variant, *lamang*. The clitics have been divided into one-syllable and two-syllable groups, a distinction which is relevant to clitic sequencing (see Table 5.2). Their additional alignment into Columns 2–5 will be explained in Section 5.5. For each clitic an attempt has been made to provide a general characterisation of the meaning in play, along with a potential English gloss (in single quotes).

5 Interpersonal Grammar in Tagalog: ASSESSMENT Systems

Table 5.2 *Assessment clitics in Tagalog*

One-syllable	na	culminative 'already'	nga	intensity 'indeed'
	pa	extending 'still'	daw/raw	reportative 'was said'
	man	counter-expectancy 'even'	ho	deference 'sir/ma'am'
	din/rin	match 'too'	po	(greater) deference
	lang	downplay 'just'	ba	interrogative[3] '?'
Two-syllable	lamang	downplay 'just'	kaya	speculate 'possibly'
	muna	precedence 'first'	pala	surprise '!'
	naman	difference 'but'	sana	optative 'hopefully'
	kasi	cause 'because'	yata	uncertainty 'perhaps'
	tuloy	effect 'as a result'		

As illustrated in Text 1', a clause may involve one or more clitics; and when two or more clitics depend on the same element of clause structure, they have to be sequenced in relation to one another. Drawing on Schachter and Otanes (1972) and Schachter (1973), Martin (1990) suggests the sequencing outlined in Table 5.3 – for a formal perspective on clitics and Tagalog clause structure, see Kroeger (1998). This table reflects the very strong tendency for one-syllable pronominal clitics to precede two-syllable clitics, along with the very strong tendency for one-syllable pronominal clitics to precede one-syllable assessment ones and for two-syllable pronominal clitics to follow two-syllable assessment ones. As far as we are aware, to date there is no corpus research confirming these patterns. And we need to stress that we are dealing with tendencies here, not absolute rules.

Table 5.3 *Clitic sequencing in Tagalog (tendencies)*

1 syllable		^2 syllable	
pronominal ^	assessment	assessment	^ pronominal
ka	na	muna	ako
ka	pa	naman	kami, naming
mo	man	kasi	tayo, natin
	din/rin	tuloy	kayo, ninyo
	lang	lamang	siya, niya
	nga	kaya	sila, nila
	daw/raw	yata	
	ho	pala	
	po	sana	

---

[3] The clitic *ba* behaves structurally as part of this paradigm but in fact realises the MOOD feature interrogative (Martin & Cruz, 2018); this draws attention to the interdependency of MOOD and ASSESSMENT systems, which we are not formalising explicitly in this paper.

5.3 Exchanging Goods-and-Services and Information

At this point we return to Text 1, which we explore as an exchange of goods-and-services and information. We do this to make explicit the relevant interpersonal co-textual relations – that is, moves enacted in exchange structure (as outlined in Chapter 1 of this volume) and their grammatical realisation through MOOD, MODALITY and TAGGING systems (based on Martin & Cruz, 2018). Text 1 is repeated, with an added column (Column 2) annotated for exchange structure following Martin and Cruz's (2018) adoption of the analysis proposed in Ventola (1987), Martin (1992) and Martin and Rose (2007).

This phase of dialogue opens with an A2 'command' move realised by a negative imperative clause (1.1). To simplify the discussion we will not analyse the dialogue for both NEGOTIATION and SPEECH FUNCTION, but simply supplement moves in exchange structure with Halliday's (e.g. 1984, 1994) SPEECH FUNCTION categories (e.g. K1 'statement', A2 'command' etc.). Ange's directive to Dan is expanded by a dependent conditioning clause incorporating Auntie's disinclination into the prohibition (1.2).

1.1	Ange	A2 ...	*Huwag*	=*mo*	-*ng*	*pa-lakar-in*		*si*	*Tita*
			NEG	NT.2SG	LK	NFIN.CAUS-walk-P2F		T	auntie
			'don't make Auntie walk'						

1.2	Ange	... A2	*kung*	*ayaw*	=*niya.*
			if	refuse	NT.3SG
			'if she doesn't want to.'		

Ange further justifies her advice in a K1 'statement' move realised through a declarative clause which reminds Dan that Auntie had told him she would not walk back when wedding plans were getting under way (1.3). This move ends with the clause final particle *e*, which reinforces the contrariness of Ange's position in relation to Dan's. Clause final particles (*a, e, ha, o*) are not addressed in this paper and are not included as part of the ASSESSMENT system proposed here; this needs to be reconsidered from a discourse-semantic perspective in future research, including their interaction with MOOD and prosodic phonology.

1.3	Ange	K1	*S<in>abi*	=*niya*	*sa*	*iyo*	*noon-ng*	*umpisa,*	*e.*
			<PERF.P2F>say	NT.3SG	CIR	OBL.2SG	back.at-LK	start	eh
			'She told you back at the start, you know.'						

Unhappy with this advice, Dan then challenges with a K2 'question' move realised by an elliptical elemental interrogative clause (1.4).

5 Interpersonal Grammar in Tagalog: ASSESSMENT Systems

1.4	Dan	K2	Bakit?
			why
			'Why?'

Ange's sister Pam replies on her behalf with a K1 'answer' move realised by a negative declarative clause – explaining that Auntie does not walk down the aisle at weddings (1.5).

1.5	Pam	K1	Hindi	=siya	nag-la~lakad		sa	kasal
			NEG	T.3SG	IMPERF.P1F~walk		CIR	wedding
			'She doesn't walk at weddings'					

Pam then reinforces the fact that Dan has known about this from the start with a K1 'statement' move realised by a declarative clause, which is tagged to explicitly encourage a consensual response from Dan (1.6).

1.6	Pam	K1	S<in>abi	=niya	sa	iyo	iyon	dati,	di	ba?
			<PERF.P2F>say	NT.3SG	CIR	OBL.3SG	yon	previously	NEG	?
			'she told you that previously, didn't she?'							

Dan in fact agrees, through a K2 f 'acknowledgement' move realised by an elliptical declarative clause (1.7).

1.7	Dan	K2f	Oo ...
			yes
			'Yes ...'

But he immediately withdraws cooperation through a challenging K2 'question' move realised by an elliptical negative elemental interrogative clause (1.8).

1.8	Dan	K2	pero	bakit	hindi?
			but	why	NEG
			'but why not?'		

And so the debate goes on (Auntie did not in the event walk down the aisle).

5.4 Negotiating Proposals and Propositions

The analysis of exchange structure presented in Section 5.3 provides us with the co-textual perspective we need to interpret the assessment clitics included in Text 1' (discussed move by move). As Ange's prohibitive A2 move makes clear, we are dropping in on a debate; Ange is arguing against Dan's inclination to try and persuade Auntie to walk down the aisle (1'.1 and 1'.2).

1'.1

Ange	A2 ...	Huwag	=mo	-ng	pa-lakar-in	si	Tita
		NEG	NT.2SG	LK	NFIN.CAUS-walk-P2F	T	auntie
		'Don't make Auntie walk'					

1'.2

Ange	... A2	kung	ayaw	=niya.
		if	refuse	NT.3SG
		'if she doesn't want to.'		

Ange's next move, her supporting K1 statement, includes three assessment clitics. The first is *naman*, which we gloss here, abbreviating the Table 5.2 term 'difference', as DIFFER; it positions Ange's move in opposition to Dan's opinion, which she wants to foreclose. The second line of translation in 1'.3 uses English intonation (marked tonicity, signalled by italics on *told*) to reflect this opposition.

The other two assessment clitics, *pa* and *lang*, come late in the clause – since they bear directly on when Auntie made her opinion known, at the beginning of wedding plans. The clitic *pa* is glossed as EXTENDING, and it here positions the start of wedding plans as temporally distant in relation to the current discussion – as ancient history, one might say. The second line of 'free' translation reflects this distancing by intensifying how far back in time plans began (i.e. *way back*).

The clitic *lang* is glossed as DOWNPLAY, which can be interpreted here as positioning the wedding plans as not then in full swing, but just getting under way. English *just* in the translation reflects this diminution fairly well.

Taken together the three assessments nuance Ange's K1 move as an attempt to shut down debate on the grounds that everyone knew about Auntie's position from the beginning of wedding plans and so the issue should not be debated again now.

1'.3

Ange	K1	S<*in*>abi	=***naman***	=niya	sa	iyo	noon-ng	umpisa	=***pa***	=***lang***,	e.
		<PERF.P2F>say	DIFFER	NT.3SG	CIR	OBL.2SG	back.at-LK	start	EXTENDING	DOWNPLAY	eh
		'She told you back at the start, you know.'								
		'**She *told* you way back at just the start, you know.**'								

Dan is undeterred and asks why (1'.4).

1'.4

Dan	K2	*Bakit?*
		why
		'Why?'

5 Interpersonal Grammar in Tagalog: ASSESSMENT Systems

This prompts Pam to generalise Auntie's position as a rule, a K1 move she reinforces with the intensifying assessment clitic *nga* (glossed through the intensifying adverb *simply* in the translation – 1'.5).

1'.5	Pam	K1	*Hindi*	*=nga*	*=siya*	*nag-la~lakad*	*sa*	*kasal*
			NEG	INTENSITY	T.3SG	IMPERF.P1F ~walk	CIR	wedding
			'she doesn't walk at weddings'						
			'She simply doesn't walk at weddings'						

And Pam then reiterates Ange's 'ancient history' move, using the same countering assessment clitic *naman*, and the same distancing clitic *pa* to position Auntie's opinion as beyond debate (1'.6). The clitic *pa* again appears late in the clause since it bears directly on when Auntie made her feelings known. The translation uses marked tonicity again to reflect *naman*, and lexicalised intensification (*ages ago*) with respect to *pa*.

1'.6	Pam	K1	*S<in>abi*	*=naman*	*=niya*	*sa*	*iyo*	*iyon*	*dati*	*=pa,*	*di*	*ba?*
			<PERF.P2F>say	DIFFER	NT.3SG	CIR	OBL.3SG	yon	previously	EXTENDING	NEG	?
			'she told you that previously, didn't she'										
			'she *told* you that ages ago, didn't she?'										

Dan acknowledges Pam's position (1'.7).

1'.7	Dan	K2f	*Oo* ...
			yes
			'Yes ...'

But insists on continuing the debate (1'.8).

1'.8	Dan	K2	*pero*	*bakit*	*hindi?*
			but	why	NEG
			'but why not?'		

5.5 ASSESSMENT Systems

In Section 5.4, we have indicated something of the challenge of interpreting the contribution of assessment clitics to discourse for general readers. English grammar lacks a system with comparable value (*valeur*), and this compromises both our metalinguistic glossing and our translations. The co-textualisation provided by the exchange structure analysis in Section 5.3 helps with our interpretation; but it cannot on its own provide the full picture. For this we need to look more carefully at the metalanguage and glossing suggested in Table 5.2. We will deal first with the clitics in Column 2.

The contribution of some of these assessment clitics can be usefully explored in pairs, which we will illustrate for pedagogic purposes with constructed examples formulated in relation to wedding plans.

Later on in the dialogue Ange comments that Auntie has a rule about not walking down the aisle at weddings. The meaning of *tuloy* (effect) and *kasi* (cause) in relation to a comment of this kind is illustrated in Texts 2 and 3. In Text 2, Auntie not walking (2.2) is positioned by *tuloy* as the effect of her rule (2.1).

2.1

Rule	niya	iyon;
rule	POSS.3SG	T.that
'That's her rule;'		

2.2

hindi	=*tuloy*	mag-la~lakad.
NEG	EFFECT	CONT.P1F~walk
'so she won't walk.'		

In Text 3, Auntie not wanting to walk (3.1) is positioned by *kasi* as caused by her rule (3.2).

3.1

Hindi	nag-la~lakad	si	Tita;
NEG	IMPERF.P1F~walk	T	Auntie
'Aunt doesn't walk;'			

3.2

rule	=*kasi*[4]	niya	iyon.
	CAUSE	POSS.3SG	T.that
'because that's her rule.'			

For our next pairing, *naman* and *din/rin*, let us imagine that Ange not only reminds Dan that Auntie has informed him she would not walk down the aisle but that she has told him too. In Text 4.1, *naman* plays the same countering role illustrated in 1'.3; in 4.2, *rin* marks the parallel between the two tellings (4.1 and 4.2).

4.1

S<in>abi	=*naman*	niya	sa	iyo;
<PERF.P2F>	DIFFER	NT.3SG	CIR	OBL.2SG
'She *told* you;'				

4.2

s<in>abi	=ko	=*rin*	iyon.
<PERF.P2F>	NT.1SG	MATCH	T.that
'I said it too.'			

---

[4] Note that *kasi* interrupts the nominal group *rule niya* 'her rule', enclitic as it is to the first word in the clause with a salient syllable.

5 Interpersonal Grammar in Tagalog: ASSESSMENT Systems

Next we compare *na* and *pa*, which we can think of in general terms as a perfective versus imperfective opposition. In Text 5.1, *na* marks the accomplishment of the telling and contrasts with *pa* in 5.2 which marks continuation of the quarrelling.

5.1

S<in>abi	=na	niya	ito	sa	iyo;
PERF.P2F>	CULMINATIVE	NT.3G	T.3SG	CIR	OBL.2SG
'She's already told you;'					

5.2

bakit	=pa	kayo	nag-a~away?
why	EXTENDING	T.2PL	IMPERF.1PF~quarrel
'why do you keep quarrelling?'			

Other assessment clitics do not enter into oppositions of this kind. The clitic *lang*, and its less common, more formal variant *lamang*, are used to downplay a proposition or proposal. In Text 6, it isolates Auntie as the only one who does not want to walk.

6

Si	Tita	=lang	ang	ayaw	mag-lakad.
T	auntie	DOWNPLAY	T	REFUSE	NFIN-walk
'Auntie is the only one who doesn't want to walk.'					

The clitic *muna* has the general meaning of precedence. This might involve positioning one proposition (Text 7.2) before an ensuing one (7.1).

7.1

Bago	siya	p<um>asok
before	T.2SG	<PERF.P1F>leave
'Before he went to work'		

7.2

nag-pa-hinga	=siya	=muna.
PERF.1PF-CAUS-rest	T.2SG	PRECEDENCE
'he rested first.'		

Muna can also be used in proposals to forestall an anticipated event (Text 8).

8.1

Huwag	=ka	=muna-ng	um-alis.
NEG	T.2SG	PRECEDENCE-lk	PREF.P1F-leave
'Don't leave yet;'			

8.2

Mag-pa-hinga	ka	=muna.
NFIN.1PF -CAUS-rest	T.2SG	PRECEDENCE
'Rest a while (before ...).'		

The clitic *man* is associated with counter-expectancy, as exemplified in the concessive clause complex (Texts 9.3–4).

9.1

Sorry.
'Sorry.'

9.2

Hindi	=ako	ma-ka~ka-punta	sa	wedding	mo.
NEG	T.1SG	ABLE-CONT-go	CIR		POSS.2SG
'I couldn't go to your wedding.'					

9.3

Gustuh-in	ko	=man,
want-P2f	NT.2SG	COUNTER-EXPECTANCY
'Though I wanted to,'		

9.4

di	puwede	=kasi	sa	trabaho.
NEG	can	CAUSE	CIR	WORK
'I couldn't because of work.'				

In negative indicative clauses it combines with *lang* to ramp up the counter-expectancy of the non-occurrence of a state or event. We have not glossed either *man* or *lang* in Text 10 since it is their combination in a negative indicative clause that makes meaning – a meaning which cannot be inferred directly from their stand-alone meaning in other contexts.

10

Hindi	=man	=lang	=siya	b<um>ili	ng	damit.
NEG			T	<PERF.P1F>buy	NT	dress
'She didn't even buy a dress.'						

There are several interactions of this kind, with for example MOOD, POLARITY and ASPECT, to be considered in a full account of assessment clitics; and there are a few clitic sequences which enact meanings that cannot be predicted from the sum of their respective parts (*na naman*, interpretable as 'again', for example). Martin (1990) provides more examples. A full account of these factors is well beyond the scope of this paper. Schachter and Otanes (1972) provide the most comprehensive list of usages; but what is really needed is corpus-based research. Our brief tour of Column 2 assessment clitics has offered just an indication of the range of meanings contributed by these resources to the negotiation of proposals and propositions. Our main purpose here has been to suggest that the Column 2 assessment clitics are by and large

5 Interpersonal Grammar in Tagalog: ASSESSMENT Systems

concerned with managing perspectives in discourse – justifying, countering, matching, terminating, extending and/or undercutting points of view. There is much more than a simple exchange of goods-and-services and information going on.

We now turn to the assessment clitics in Column 4 of Table 5.2. The clitic *ba* marks a proposition as interrogative (and formed part of the tag *hindi ba* in Text 1'.6); it is optional in elemental interrogatives (compare Text 12 with 1'.8). We will not analyse *ba* as a clitic when it is realised as part of the tag *hindi ba* (abbreviated as *di ba*); it realises TAGGING, not MOOD, in this structure (Text 11).

11
Ayaw	**=ba**	=*niya?*
refuse	?	NT.3SG
'Doesn't she want to?'		

12
Pero	*bakit*	**=ba**	*hindi?*
but	why	?	NEG
'But why not?'			

The clitics *ho* and *po* mark deference (Text 13). *Po* is used more commonly in social formulas. Schachter and Otanes (1972), whose grammar was completed by the early 1960s, suggest that *ho* is less respectful than *po* and more frequently used by younger speakers. We are not aware of contemporary data on these patterns of usage, which may have changed.

13
Good morning,	**=po**	ma'am.
	POL	
'Good morning, ma'am.'		

The clitic *daw/raw* indicates that the move in question needs to be ultimately sourced to someone other than the speaker (Text 14).

14
Greetings	**=daw**	sa	iyo.
	REPORTATIVE	CIR	OBL.2sg
'Passing on greetings to you.'			

The clitic *nga* adds intensity to proposals and propositions. A forceful A2 command move is exemplified in Text 15.

15
Huwag	=ka	**=nga**	um-alis.
NEG	T.2SG	INTENSITY	NFIN.P1F-LEAVE
'Don't you leave.'			

A strong affirming K1 statement move (cf. 1'.5) is illustrated in 16.

16

Ayaw	=*nga*	=*niya.*
refuse	INTENSITY	NT.3SG
'She really doesn't want to.'		

Turning to two-syllable clitics in Column 4 of Table 5.3, *kaya* enacts speculation in requesting moves (e.g. the speculative K2 question in 17 and the speculative A2 suggestion in 18).

17

La~lakad	=***kaya***	=*siya?*
CONT.P1F~walk	SPECULATE	T.3SG
'Do you suppose she'll walk?'		

18

Mag-lakad	=*ka*	=***kaya***	sa	kasal.
NFIN.1PF-walk	T.2SG	SPECULATE	CIR	wedding
'Perhaps you should walk at the wedding.'				

The clitic *yata* also signals uncertainty, but in information-giving K1 moves (19).

19

Hindi	***yata***	la~lakad	si	Tito.
NEG	UNCERTAINTY	CONT.P1F~walk	T	Uncle
'Uncle may not walk.'				

The clitic *sana* is optative. An example referring to a past event is presented in Text 20, with indicative MOOD type. For future events, imperative MOOD type is deployed (21).

20

Nag-pa-hinga	=***sana***	=*siya.*
PERF.P1F-CAUS-rest	OPTATIVE	T.3SG
'I hope she rested.'		

21

Mag-pa-hinga	=***sana***	=*siya.*
NFIN.P1F-CAUS-rest	OPTATIVE	T.3SG
'I hope she'll rest.'		

Our final assessment clitic, *pala*, registers mild surprise (22).

22

L<um>akad	=***pala***	si	Tita!
<PERF.1PF>walk	SURPRISE	T	auntie
'Auntie walked, after all.'			

5 Interpersonal Grammar in Tagalog: ASSESSMENT Systems   145

The meaning of the members of this set of clitics is easier to pin down, relatively speaking, than for the Table 5.3 Column 2 clitics presented previously. They are less affected by MOOD, POLARITY and ASPECT, and sequences have no special meaning beyond the sum of the parts. Martin (1981) explores the Column 2 group (*na, pa, man, din/rin, lang/lamang, muna, naman, kasi* and *tuloy*) in relation to Tagalog's system of conjunctive relations, showing that in many cases, particularly in dialogue, they can function as an alternative resource for connecting figures (via additive, comparative, temporal or consequential conjunctive relations). Martin (1990) comments that the second group (*ba, ho, po, daw/raw, nga, yata, kaya, sana,* and *pala*), on the other hand, find alternative expression through a diverse range of interpersonal resources, including PROJECTION, VOCATION, MODALITY and INTERJECTION. The complementarity of the two groups allows him to suggest a further sequencing tendency for Tagalog clitics – namely, the tendency for the Column 2 group in Table 5.4 to precede the Column 3 group and the Column 4 group to precede the Column 5 group (note that the table respects the one-syllable/two-syllable and pronominal/non-pronominal parameters established in Table 5.3). This fuller proposal is presented in Table 5.4.

Table 5.4 *Clitic sequencing in Tagalog: fuller proposal (tendencies)*

1 syllable			^2 syllable		
	retrospective	prospective	retrospective	prospective	
pronoun	^	^	^	^	pronoun
ko	na	nga	muna	yata	ako
ka	pa	daw/raw	naman	kaya	kami, namin
mo	man	ho	kasi	sana	tayo, natin
	lang	po	tuloy	pala	kayo, ninyo
	din/rin	ba	lamang		siya, niya
					sila, nila

As included in Table 5.4, from this point in our discussion we will label the first group (*na, pa, man, din/rin, lang/lamang, muna, naman, kasi,* and *tuloy*) 'retrospective' assessment clitics. By this term we are suggesting that their main function in discourse is to relate the move in which they are realised to an alternative perspective in discourse – a perspective which may be realised in an adjacent move (Texts 1–10), or a move from earlier on in the co-text, or a perspective which interlocutors are aware of through participation in one or another shared context of culture. And we will provisionally label the second group (*ba, ho, po, daw/raw, nga, yata, kaya, sana,* and *pala*) 'prospective'

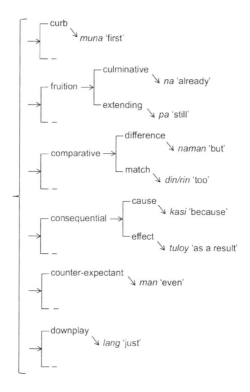

Figure 5.1 Retrospective ASSESSMENT resources in Tagalog

assessment clitics. By this term we are suggesting that their main function in discourse is to entertain the possibility of an alternative perspective – a perspective which may or may not be realised in an ensuing move but the potential for which the interlocutors are well aware of. An attempt to formalise these two resources as systems is offered as Figures 5.1 and 5.2. The entry condition for these ASSESSMENT systems is the clause. We will not attempt to formalise their interaction with MOOD, POLARITY and MODALITY systems presented in Martin (1990) and Martin and Cruz (2018) in this paper.

5.6 ASSESSMENT and ENGAGEMENT

We turn our attention now to the discourse semantics of Matthiessen's MODAL ASSESSMENT systems (Matthiessen, 2004). As noted by Figueredo (2015) in his work on Modal Particles in Brazilian Portuguese (cf. Zhang, Chapter 3, in this volume), the relevant interpersonal system is ENGAGEMENT, introduced as part

5 Interpersonal Grammar in Tagalog: ASSESSMENT Systems   147

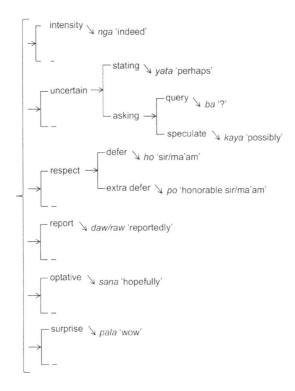

Figure 5.2 Prospective ASSESSMENT resources in Tagalog

of Martin and White's (2005) APPRAISAL framework. As Martin and White (2005) comment, ENGAGEMENT resources 'invite others to endorse and to share with them the feelings, tastes or normative assessments they are announcing' (p. 95). White (2012) characterises engagement as comprising a wide range of resources 'by which the speaker/writer engages dialogically with prior utterances on the same topic and potential responses' (p. 61). For White (2012), English realisations include 'attribution and evidentials, modals of probability, negation, certain types of meta discourse, concession, counter-expectationals, consequentiality and factives' (p. 61). Work on ENGAGEMENT was developed from Bakhtin/Voloshinov's concepts of heteroglossia and dialogism (Bakhtin, 1981; Voloshinov, 1995),[5] and brings together 'all those locutions which provide some means for the authorial voice to position itself with respect to, and hence to

---

[5] We concur with Bronckart and Bota (2011) who argue convincingly that work generally credited to Bakhtin should in fact be attributed to Voloshinov (cf. Voloshinov, 1995).

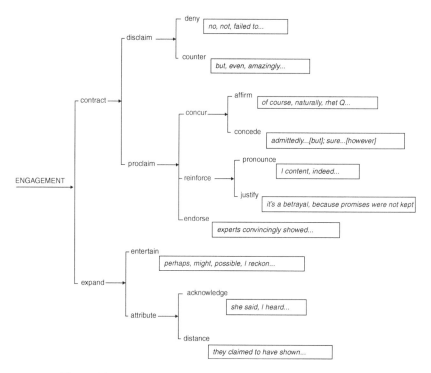

Figure 5.3 ENGAGEMENT systems in English (based on White, 2012, p. 56)

"engage" with, the other voices and alternative positions construed as being in play in the current communicative context' (White, 2012, p. 61).

The initial option in Martin and White's ENGAGEMENT system for English is heterogloss versus monogloss – that is, the choice of positioning a move or not (Martin & White, 2005). White's extension of Martin and White's heterogloss options is presented in Figure 5.3, along with illustrative realisations. As we can see, English uses a wide range of grammatical resources to realise dialogism. Comparable resources are available in Tagalog (as surveyed in Martin, 1981, 1990; Martin & Cruz, 2018). But as we have previously outlined, Tagalog has an important interpersonal resource, ASSESSMENT, which needs to be brought into play as its discourse-semantic ENGAGEMENT system is developed.

Developing a language specific ENGAGEMENT system for Tagalog is beyond the scope of this paper. We would suggest, however, that since Tagalog has a grammaticalised ASSESSMENT system, this might be a useful place to start in reconsidering less delicate ENGAGEMENT options. As part of this we need to ask whether the English [expand] versus [contract] opposition is an apt characterisation of the retrospective/prospective Tagalog complementarity previously introduced. Martin and White's notion of expanding the play of voices around a move (realised through MODALITY and PROJECTION) is perhaps not unreasonable as a characterisation of the discourse function of the prospective assessment clitics (*ba* 'interrogative', *ho* 'deference', *po* 'deference', *daw/raw* 'reportative', *nga* 'intensity', *yata* 'uncertainty', *kaya* 'speculate', *sana* 'optative' and *pala* 'surprise') – all of which acknowledge the interpersonal relevance of a voice other than the speaker's. But contracting the play of voices seems limiting as far as the retrospective assessment clitics are concerned (*na* 'culminative', *pa* 'extending', *man* 'counter-expectant', *din/rin* 'match', *lang/lamang* 'downplay', *muna* 'precedence', *naman* 'differ', *kasi* 'cause' and *tuloy* 'effect') – which overall position voices in relation to one another, without necessarily shutting one voice down. Perhaps an [acknowledge] versus [position] system would be a useful system to open up Tagalog ENGAGEMENT options.

The key point to keep in mind as this work proceeds is that interpersonal discourse-semantic resources have evolved to negotiate consensus – to get people on the same page, as it were. There is more going on than exchanging goods-and-services and information; interlocutors are sharing feelings, whether explicitly inscribed or implicitly invoked. And achieving consensus depends on more than POLARITY, MODALITY and MOOD. There are more subtle adjustments that need to be made, moment by moment, as discourse unfolds – which take into account a range of expectations as perspectives are accommodated and shared. Tagalog's ASSESSMENT system is a critical move-nuancing resource in this respect.

5.7   Context and ASSESSMENT

Although not specifically commented on previously, interpreting the contribution of assessment clitics to the negotiation of propositions and proposals in discourse depends on more than co-text – context (i.e. register and genre) also has to be taken into account. To foreground this we will focus now on three phases of an interaction between a dressmaker (DM) and her client (PC), taking into account relevant aspects of the text's field and tenor. The dressmaker and her client are exchanging text messages about a skirt with two layers (an outer gauze one with a pattern, and an opaque solid-coloured inner layer). At issue is the length of the inner layer (referred to as the lining, below) in relation to the outer one. Text 23 features the code switching (Bautista, 1979) characterising discourse in urban Manila, commonly referred to as 'Taglish'. Spelling and punctuation have been standardised.

The opening phase of the text introduces the dressmaker's proposal that the lining be shorter than the outer layer. The dressmaker sends greetings (Text 23.1), including the deference clitic *po* (and the corresponding polite Taglish address term *ma'am*). The tenor relations at stake here (i.e. unequal status) are thus made immediately clear. And she sends along some photos of the lining material (which turn out to present the kind and colour of the lining to be used, but not the actual lining itself).

23.1

DM	Gr	Good morning	=**po,**	ma'am.
			DEFER	
		'Good morning, ma'am.'		

The dressmaker announces that she is working at home (23.2), deferring as she did in 23.1 (via *po* and *ma'am*).

23.2

	K1	Work	at home	=**po**	=ako,	ma'am.
				DEFER	T.1sg	
		'I'm working at home, ma'am.'				

She then checks to see if it would be OK for her client if the lining of the skirt is a little short. In addition to the two deference clitics (*po, po*), she softens her suggestion with the down-toning clitic *lang* (23.3).

23.3

	K2 ...	OK	=**lang**	=**po**
			DOWNPLAY	DEFER
		'Would it be OK, ma'am,'		

23.4

	... K2	kung	iyon	lining	ng	palda	medyo	ma-iksi	=**po?**
		if	T.that		POSS	skirt	somewhat	ADJ-short	DEFER
		'if the lining of the skirt is a little short, ma'am?'							

In 23.4 (and 23.7 and 24.20), *po* appears later in the clause than it might have. This reflects the fact that the position of clitics after the first salient syllable in a clause is a strong tendency, not a rule; that some pre-enclitic clause segments attract clitics more strongly than others; and that *po*, in particular, seems comfortable in a culminative position – signalling deference at the point in a move where a higher-status speaker might be expected to take a turn (a 'transition relevance' position in conversation analysis terms; Sidnell & Sirens, 2013).

Her client, checks that the lining is, in fact, shorter, flagging her concern with the intensifying clitic *nga* (23.5).

23.5

PC	K2	Di	ba	mas	ma-iksi	=**nga**	iyon-ng	lining?
		NEG	?	more	ADJ-short	INTENISTY	T.that-LK	
		'The lining really is shorter, is it?'						

The dressmaker replies that it is, explaining that the skirt was floor length when she measured it in relation to the multiway dress she was making as well (23.6–23.9).

5 Interpersonal Grammar in Tagalog: ASSESSMENT Systems   151

23.6 | DM | K1 ... | Yes, | ma'am, |

23.7

... K1	kasi	=po	iyon-ng	length	ng	skirt	ay	40/Floor length	=po	=siya
	because	DEFER	T.that-LK		POSS		INV	skirt	DEFER	T.3sg
	'because the length of the skirt was 40/Floor length, ma'am'										

23.8

... K1	noon-ng	s-in-ukat	=ko	para	Multiway.[6]
	when-LK	<PERF.P2F> measure	NT.1SG	for	
	'when I measured it in terms of the multiway.'				

23.9 | PC | K2f | OK. |

Of note here is the way the *po* clitics enact a prosody of deference, both within a move (23.7) and across moves (23.1–4 and 23.7) – a prosody additionally propagated through the respectful vocative *ma'am*.

We pick up the discussion again as it returns to the question of the length of the skirt and its lining. The client checks that the multiway dress and skirt are the same length; the dressmaker confirms (*po* has been lexicalised as part of the polite agreement marker *opo* – from *oo po* 'yes DEFER', which does not occur) and the client acknowledges her confirmation (23.10–23.12).

23.10

PC	K1	Pareho	iyon-ng	haba	ng	multiway	at	palda.
		same	T.that-LK	length	POSS		and	skirt
		'The length of the multiway and skirt are the same.'							

23.11

DM	K2f ...	Opo,	ma'am.
		POL.yes	
		'Yes, ma'am.'	

23.12

PC	K1f	Sige.
		OK
		'OK.'

At this point, the dressmaker makes a move designed to establish the shorter length of the skirt's lining as a general principle (23.13). The clitics *lang* and *po* continue to enact the unequal status relations in play, while *kasi* positions the move as motivation for the suggestion that the lining be shorter than the outer layer of the skirt introduced in 23.3–4. This use of the assessment clitic *kasi* to position a move in relation to something established several moves earlier on in

---

[6] A multiway is a dress that can be worn in a number of different ways (also referred to as a convertible dress); for examples, see www.modelchic.com.au/multiway-dresses.

the discourse contrasts with the use of *kasi* as a clause initial conjunction (Martin, 1981), relating adjacent moves (e.g. *mas maiksi ang lining **kasi** laging mas maiski* 'the lining is shorter because they're always shorter').

23.13

DM	K1	Sa	lining	=lang	=po	=kasi	medyo	ma-iksi.
		CIR		DOWNPLAY	DEFER	CAUSE	somewhat	ADJ-short
		'Cos with lining it's just a little short, ma'am.'						

The dressmaker then checks again to see if her client will agree to the shorter lining (23.14). This move involves a saturating tenor prosody, involving *lang, po* and *ma'am* as in previous moves and also the plural second person pronoun *inyo* (in place of singular *iyo*).

23.14

K2	OK	=lang	=po	=ba	sa	inyo,	ma'am?
		DOWNPLAY	DEFER	?	CIR	OBL.2PL	
		'Would it be OK for you, ma'am?'					

This phase of the discussion continues with the dressmaker clarifying in 23.15 and 23.16 that the lining will be 'leg length' (as opposed to floor length), suggesting that floor length might be too long (23.17) and soliciting agreement from her client (23.18).

23.15

K1	Hanggang	binti	=po	iyon	length.
	as.far.as	leg	DEFER	T.that	
	'The length is as long as your leg, ma'am.'				

23.16

PC	K1	Mas	kaunti-ng	iksi	sa	floor length.
		more	little-LK	short	CIR	
		'It's a little shorter than floor length.'				

23.17

K1	Baka	masyado-ng	ma-haba	pag	floor length.
	maybe	too-LK	ADJ-long	if	
	'It would perhaps be too long if it were floor length.'				

23.18

K2	Di	ba?
	NEG	?
	'Wouldn't it?'	

After reassuring her client that the shorter lining will not look funny, the dressmaker continues stating that she will put the skirt on hold for a while as she looks for the material at Maria's house. The clitic *muna* in 23.19 positions its move as pre-empting completion of the lining; it is complemented here by

5 Interpersonal Grammar in Tagalog: ASSESSMENT Systems   153

the clitic *pa* in 23.20 which positions its move as the move that has to be done before the lining is completed.

23.19

	K1	Hold	=ko	=**muna**	ito-ng	palda.
			NT.1SG	PRECEDENCE	T.this-LK	SKIRT
	'I'll first put this skirt on hold for a while.'					

23.20

	K1	Hanap	=**pa**	=ako	ng	pang-lining	doon	kay	Ma'am	Maria ...	po
		search	EXTENDING	T.1SG	NT	for.purpose.of-	yonder	CIR			DEFER
	'And I'll look for the lining material over there at Ma'am Maria's later on.'											

This surprises the client (23.21) since she thought they had the lining material already (*na*) based on the pictures sent at the beginning of the exchange (which, in fact, only represented samples).

23.21

PC	K1	Di	ba	mayroon	=**na**	=tayo	pang-lining?
		NEG	?	EXIST	CULMINATIVE	T.INCL	for.purpose.of-
	'We already have the lining material, don't we?'							

The client then advises that she thinks the lining should be between knee and ankle length (23.22–24) so it will not look funny, a move the dressmaker politely defers to (*po*) in 23.25.

23.22

	K1 ...	In-i-isip	=ko
		IMPF~THINK	NT.1SG
	'I think'		

23.23

	... K1	iyon-ng	lining	sa	gitna	ng	tuhod	at	ankle.
		T.that-LK		CIR	middle	POSS	knee	and	
	'the lining should be between the knee and the ankle.'								

23.24

	K1	Para	di	na-ka~ka-tawa.
		so.that	NEG	CAUS-laugh
	'So that it won't look funny.'			

23.25

DM	K2f	Sige	=**po.**
		OK	DEFER
	'OK, ma'am.'		

The dressmaker then agrees to do her best to get that length; and dressmaker and client subsequently bond around their positive appreciation of the colour chosen for the lining over several moves.

The negotiation closes with the client suggesting that the two of them keep thinking about the length of the lining (23.26), to which the dressmaker agrees (23.27). The assessment clitics in 23.26 interrupt the nominal group *iyong haba iyon* 'that length that', with *na lang* downplaying this issue as the final matter to be sorted out. Tagalog allows for 'sandwich' deixis in nominal groups, in first and final position.

23.26	A2	Iyon-ng	haba	=na	=lang	iyon	isip-in	natin.
		T.that-LK	length	CULMINATIVE	DOWNPLAY	T.that	think-NFIN.P2F	NT.INCL
		'Let's just think about that length.'						

23.27	DM	A1	Sige,	ma'am.
			OK	
			'OK, ma'am.'	

The dressmaker then draws matters to a close by offering to find a way to comply (23.28), an offer gratefully accepted by the client (23.29 and 23.30). The dressmaker's follow-up move (23.31) matches the client's one (*din*), adding deference (*po* and *ma'am*).

23.28		A1 ...	Gawa-an	=ko	ng	paraan.
			do-NFIN.P3F	NT.1sg	NT	way
			'I'll find a way to do it.'			

23.29	PC	A2f ...	Sige.
			OK
			'OK.'

23.30		... A2f	Salamat.
			thanks
			'Thanks.'

23.31	DM	A1f	Thank-you	=din	=po,	ma'am.
				MATCH	DEFER	
			'Thanks again, ma'am.'			

Leave-takings are then exchanged. Notable here is the complementarity of the dressmaker's deference clitics (*po* in 23.32 and 23.34) and the client's use of the second person singular pronoun in 23.33 (cf. the dressmaker's use of plural *inyo* in 23.14).

23.32		Gr	God bless	=po.
				DEFER
			'God bless you, ma'am.'	

23.33

PC	RGr	Sa	iyo	=din.
		CIR	OBL.2sg	MATCH
		'You too.'		

23.34

DM	Gr	Bye	=po,	ma'am.
			DEFER	
		'Bye, ma'am.'		

We have not formalised our analysis of register (field, tenor, and mode) and genre in this section to any degree. Our goal was simply to establish that field (dressmaking), tenor (unequal status), mode (text message dialogue) and genre (service resolution) are all implicated in our interpretation of assessment clitics in discourse. Bringing context into the picture helps account for choices that cannot be explained simply in terms of adjacent co-text and the lexicogrammatical characterisations of the meaning of assessment clitics offered in Section 5.4. To replay just one example (23.13) from Text 23 by way of illustration, note that *lang* makes sense in terms of the tenor (unequal status), not in terms of undercutting something that has been said before; and interpreting *kasi* depends on shared knowledge of the field – specifically expectancies about the relative lining of the inner and outer layers of the skirt at stake here (which the dressmaker wants shared). And this nuancing of the move as a whole does not make sense without taking into account the need to make decisions in relation to a successful resolution of the phase of the service encounter unfolding as Text 23.

23.13

DM	K1	Sa	lining	=lang	=po	=kasi	medyo	ma-iksi.
		CIR		DOWNPLAY	DEFER	CAUSE	somewhat	ADJ-short
		'Cos with lining it's just a little short, ma'am.'						

5.8 Realisation and Instantiation

Figueredo (2015) notes a number of issues challenging the description of ASSESSMENT systems in Brazilian Portuguese – including the problem of clearly categorising subtypes, the interdependency of ASSESSMENT and other interpersonal systems, their distribution across registers and genres and their role in enacting dialogue. All of these challenges arose in one way or another in this paper. As a closing note we would like to push these issues a little deeper in relation to the hierarchies of realisation and instantiation in SFL (for an introduction to these dimensions, see Halliday and Matthiessen, 1999; Martin, 2010). Conceived in SFL terms, realisation is a hierarchy of abstraction involving metaredundancy – with higher strata interpreted as patterns of lower-strata ones (e.g. discourse semantics as a pattern of lexicogrammatical patterns and lexicogrammar as a pattern of phonological ones). Instantiation on the other hand is a hierarchy of generalisation – for Halliday and Matthiessen, a cline relating a system of meanings as a whole to the specific choices unfolding in a particular text (i.e. the sub-potentialisation of the system of language as a whole into specific registers, then more specific text types and ultimately a specific text).

Over the past few decades, SFL has relied heavily on realisation as far as language description is concerned. Foundational for these descriptions is SFL's approach to axial relations – bundled by stratum, metafunction and rank (Martin, Wang & Zhu, 2013; Matthiessen & Halliday, 2009). As far as Tagalog ASSESSMENT systems are concerned, this approach has serious limitations. For one thing, there is very little to work on in terms of structure, since most assessments are realised by single segments. Clitics, of course, have to be sequenced – in relation to the units they depend on and in relation to one another. But these sequences are not organised as function structures realising interpersonal grammatical systems. This is not to say that the sequencing cannot be interpreted functionally in very general terms. The sequencing of pronominal clitics, for example, places the two-syllable pronouns which function as Theme of a clause last, in a suitable late position in a clause as unmarked Theme; and the sequencing of retrospective clitics before prospective ones makes sense in terms of the role the retrospective group often plays in positioning a move in relation to a preceding one and the room the prospective group makes for an ensuing one. In general clitic makes an independent contribution to the meaning of a clause; and where a pair is involved (e.g. *na naman* 'again') the sequence as a whole makes meaning, not the configuration of its parts.

For another thing, the systems in Figures 5.1 and 5.2 do not offer very much by way of valeur. Each network includes a large number of simultaneous possibilities, and for the meaning of these choices we are by and large dependent on the names of the features involved. But naming categories in this region of meaning is a very problematic exercise (cf. Halliday, 1988, on the ineffability of grammatical categories). Martin (1990) adjusts Martin (1981) in an attempt to gloss the general meaning of the clitics involved, and Martin and Cruz (2018) adjust some of these terms again. We adjusted terms once more here. Scrutiny of these terms in relation to Schachter and Otanes (1972) quickly reveals that the range of uses they canvas cannot all be predicted from the names of the terms deployed. Some improvements could perhaps be made by treating ASSESSMENT systems as delicate MOOD options, and wiring in their interdependency with MODALITY and POLARITY systems – but this would involve treating many clitics as realising several systems and so fragment the complementarity of their contribution to discourse in relation to other interpersonal systems. And it would utterly disrespect their syntagmatic patterning as a cluster of enclitic particles, all contributing to what Martin and Cruz (2018) refer to as the Terms of a clause. Talk about ineffability (Halliday, 1988)! Time to give up? Or push on?

As we tend to forget, descriptions are afforded by theory. And it seems that with assessment clitics we have reached the limits of what SFL's realisation hierarchy has to offer. Good old reliable axis, strata, rank and metafunction are not going to do the job. Instantiation is the obvious place to turn, and it is for this reason that we spent a considerable part of this paper guiding readers move by move through Text 1, Text 1' and several phases of Text 23. By taking co-text and context into account, we can see what is going on; and our attempts to gloss the meaning of each move are revealing as far as the different realisation strategies deployed by Tagalog and English are concerned. Unfortunately, to date, development of the robust theory of instantiation we would ideally like to draw on has barely got off the ground. We sit, daunted by this challenge, in much the same way that Saussure, Mathesius and Bloomfield probed in awe, confounded by the realisation hierarchy it took the remainder of twentieth century to scaffold. Perhaps more and more text analysis can move us forward. And the meanings marginalised by realisation hierarchies will ultimately find a home in functional grammars we cannot yet devise.

Appendix Specific Glossing Conventions

PERF	perfective aspect (completed occurrence)
IMPERF	imperfective aspect (occurrence begun, not completed)
CONT	contemplated aspect (occurrence not begun)
NFIN	non-finite verb (no aspect)
P1F	Actor, Senser, Sayer Theme
P2F	Goal, Phenomenon, Verbiage Theme
P3F	Recipient, Receiver Theme
LK	linker
T	Theme participant
NT	non-Theme participant
CIR	Circumstance

References

Bakhtin, M. (1981). *The Dialogic Imagination*. Austin: University of Texas Press.

Bautista, M. L. (1979). *Patterns of Speaking in Filipino Radio Dramas: Sociolinguistic Analysis*. Tokyo: Institute for the Study of Languages and Cultures of Asia and Africa, Tokyo University of Foreign Studies.

Bronckart, J.-P. & Bota, C. (2011). *Bakhtine Démasqué: Histoire d'un Menteur, d'une Escroquerie et d'un Délire Collectif*. Paris: Droz.

Buenaventura-Naylor, P. (1975). Topic, Focus and Emphasis in the Tagalog Verbal Clause. *Oceanic Linguistics*, *14*, 12–79.
Caffarel, A. (2006). *A Systemic Functional Grammar of French: From Grammar to Discourse*. London: Continuum.
Figueredo, G. (2015). A Systemic Functional Description of Modal Particles in Brazilian Portuguese: The System of Assessment. *Alfa*, *59*(2), 275–302. DOI: http://dx.doi.org/10.1590/1981-5794-1504-3.
Halliday, M. A. K. (1984). Language as Code and Language as Behaviour: A Systemic Functional Interpretation of the Nature and Ontogenesis of Dialogue. In R. Fawcett, M. A. K. Halliday, S. Lamb and A. Makkai, eds., *The Semiotics of Culture and Language*. Vol. 1 of *Language as Social Semiotic*. London: Frances Pinter, pp. 3–35.
Halliday, M. A. K. (1988). On the Ineffability of Grammatical Categories. In J. D. Benson, M. J. Cummings and W. S. Greaves, eds., *Linguistics in a Systemic Perspective*, Vol. 1. Amsterdam: John Benjamins, pp. 27–51.
Halliday, M. A. K. (1994). *An Introduction to Functional Grammar*, 2nd ed., London: Edward Arnold.
Halliday, M. A. K. & Greaves, W. S. (2008). *Intonation in the Grammar of English*. London: Equinox.
Halliday, M. A. K. & Matthiessen, C. M. I. M. (1999). *Construing Experience Through Meaning: A Language-Based Approach to Cognition*. London: Continuum.
Kroeger, P. (1998). Clitics and Clause Structure in Tagalog. In M. L. Bautista, ed., *Pagtanaw: Essays on Language in Honor of Teodoro A. Llamzon*. Manila: Linguistic Society of the Philippines, pp. 53–72.
Martin, J. R. (1981). Conjunction and Continuity in Tagalog. In M. A. K. Halliday and J. R. Martin, eds., *Readings in Systemic Linguistics*. London: Batsford, pp. 310–36.
Martin, J. R. (1983). Participant Identification in English, Tagalog and Kâte. *Australian Journal of Linguistics*, *3*(1), 45–74. DOI: https://doi.org/10.1080/07268608308599299.
Martin, J. R. (1988). Grammatical Conspiracies in Tagalog: Family, Face and Fate – with Regard to Benjamin Lee Whorf. In J. D. Benson, M. J. Cummings and W. S. Greaves, eds., *Linguistics in a Systemic Perspective*. Amsterdam: John Benjamins, pp. 243–300.
Martin, J. R. (1990). Interpersonal Grammatization: Mood and Modality in Tagalog. *Philippine Journal of Linguistics*, *21*(1), 2–50.
Martin, J. R. (1992). *English Text: System and Structure*. Amsterdam: John Benjamins.
Martin, J. R. (1993). Clitics. In A. Gonzalez, ed., *Philippine Encyclopedia of the Social Sciences*. Quezon City: Philippine Social Science Council, pp. 237–40.
Martin, J. R. (1995). Logical Meaning, Interdependency and the Linking Particle na/ng in Tagalog. *Functions of Language*, *2*(2), 189–228.
Martin, J. R. (1996). Transitivity in Tagalog: A Functional Interpretation of Case. In M. Berry, C. Butler, R. Fawcett and G. Huang, eds., *Meaning and Form: Systemic Functional Interpretations*. New Jersey: Ablex, pp. 229–96.
Martin, J. R. (2004). Metafunctional Profile of the Grammar of Tagalog. In A. Caffarel, J. R. Martin and C. M. I. M. Matthiessen, eds., *Language Typology: A Functional Perspective*. Amsterdam: John Benjamins, pp. 255–304.
Martin, J. R. (2010). Semantic Variation: Modelling Realization, Instantiation and Individuation in Social Semiosis. In M. Bednarek and J. R. Martin, eds., *New Discourse on Language: Functional Perspectives on Multimodality, Identity, and Affiliation*. London: Continuum, pp. 1–34.

Martin, J. R. (2018). Interpersonal Meaning: Systemic Functional Linguistics Perspectives. *Functions of Language*, 25(1), 2–19.
Martin, J. R. & Cruz, P. (2018). Interpersonal Grammar of Tagalog: A Systemic Functional Perspective. *Functions of Language*, 25(1), 54–96.
Martin, J. R. & Cruz, P. (2019). Relational Processes in Tagalog: A Systemic Functional Perspective. In K. Rajandran and S. A. Manan, eds., *Discourses of southeast Asia: A Social Semiotic Perspective*. Singapore: Springer, pp. 225–251.
Martin, J. R. & Rose, D. (2007). *Working with Discourse: Meaning Beyond the Clause*, 2nd ed., London: Continuum.
Martin, J. R., Wang, P. & Zhu, Y. (2013). *Systemic Functional Grammar: A Next Step Into the Theory – Axial Relations*. Beijing: Higher Education Press.
Martin, J. R. & White, P. (2005). *The Language of Evaluation: Appraisal in English*. Basingstoke: Palgrave Macmillan.
Matthiessen, C. M. I. M. (2004). Descriptive Motifs and Generalizations. In A. Caffarel, J. R. Martin and C. M. I. M. Matthiessen, eds., *Language Typology: A Functional Perspective*. Amsterdam: John Benjamins, pp. 537–664.
Matthiessen, C. M. I. M. & Halliday, M. A. K. (2009). *Systemic Functional Grammar: A First Step into the Theory*. Beijing: Higher Education Press.
Mwinlaaru, I. N., Matthiessen, C. M. I. M. & Akerejola, E. (2018). A System-Based Typology of MOOD in Niger-Congo Languages. In A. Agwuele and A. Bodomo, eds., *The Handbook of African Linguistics*. London: Routledge, pp. 93–117.
Quiroz, B. (2010). *The Negotiation of Interpersonal Meanings Through the Spanish Verbal Group*. Paper presented at the 37th International Systemic Functional Congress, University of British Columbia, Vancouver, Canada.
Schachter, P. (1973). Constraints on Clitic Order in Tagalog. In A. Gonzalez, ed., *Parangal kay Cecilio Lopez: Essays in Honor of Cecilio Lopez on his Seventy-Fifth Birthday*. Manila: Linguistic Society of the Philippines, pp. 214–31.
Schachter, P. & Otanes, F. (1972). *Tagalog Reference Grammar*. Berkeley: University of California Press.
Sidnell, J. & Sirens, T., eds., (2013). *The Handbook of Conversation Analysis*. London: Blackwell.
Teruya, K., Akerejola, E., Andersen, T. H., Caffarel, A., Lavid, J., Matthiessen, C. M. I. M., Petersen, U. H., Patpong, P. & Smedegaard, F. (2007). Typology of MOOD: A Text-Based and System-Based Functional View. In R. Hasan, C. M. I. M. Matthiessen and J. Webster, eds., *Continuing Discourse on Language: A Functional Perspective*, Vol. 2. London: Equinox, pp. 859–920.
Ventola, E. (1987). *The Structure of Social Interaction: A Systemic Approach to the Semiotics of Service Encounters*. London: Frances Pinter.
Voloshinov, V. (1995). *Marxism and the Philosophy of Language*. Massachusetts: Harvard University Press.
White, P. R. R. (2012). Exploring the Axiological Workings of 'Reporter Voice' News Stories – Attribution and Attitudinal Positioning. *Discourse, Context and Media*, 1, 57–67.

6 Interpersonal Grammar of Pitjantjatjara

David Rose

6.1 Introduction

Pitjantjatjara is one of around sixteen language varieties spoken by people of Australia's Western Desert – who number some 7,000 speakers across 2 million square kilometres of arid lands. Western Desert peoples were hunter-gatherers until settling in small serviced communities between the 1930s and 1960s. Data for this study is taken from Rose (2001), which presents a description of an Australian Indigenous language in relation to the parameters of the social system that the language enacts. All the data is derived from sound recordings of spontaneous conversations and monologues.[1]

This chapter focuses on the grammatical system of MOOD in Pitjantjatjara, in relation to its discourse-semantic functions. The chapter begins by illustrating the coupling of features in MOOD and TONE to realise discourse-semantic SPEECH FUNCTION types. It then outlines options in APPRAISAL that are realised by such couplings, and illustrates the roles of MOOD and TONE in the structuring of exchanges. The systems of IMPERATIVE and INDICATIVE MOOD are then described in detail. The chapter concludes by outlining options for the appraisal systems of ENGAGEMENT and GRADUATION that are realised by couplings of MOOD, TONE and MODAL ASSESSMENT, and illustrates their functioning in an extended dialogue.

6.2 Intonation

Pitjantjatjara is a spoken language. As it has not evolved written modes of meaning (except in texts transcribing speech or translated from other languages), its phonology is an essential component of meaning making, particularly of interpersonal meanings. A multinocular perspective (Martin & Cruz, 2018) on interpersonal resources in Pitjantjatjara must therefore take into

---

[1] I am indebted to Nganyintja, Ilyatjari, Mutju, Tjulkiwa, Ivan Baker, Sammy and Cecily Lyons for the texts quoted here.

account not only discourse-semantic and lexicogrammatical systems but also phonological systems, together with relations between systems across and within these strata.

From a discourse-semantic perspective, interpersonal meanings are resources for social exchange between interactants, enacted prosodically. At the level of phonology, this prosody is carried on a wave of tonicity that rises and falls in pitch to realise delicate features of interpersonal meaning. This is illustrated in the exchange in Example 1 – in which a seeker of information, or secondary knower (K2), asks whether a third party found a particular food plant on a food gathering trip, and the primary knower (K1) affirms that they saw it and brought it back for the group.

(1) K1 uti   =ya   nyanga-ngi
         clearly   3PL   see-PST.CONT
         'Clearly they could see it?' (i.e. 'did they find it?')

     K2 uwa   nyaku-la   ura-ra   kati-ngu
         yes   see-IPFV   gather-IPFV   bring-PST
         'Yes, seeing it and gathering it, they brought it back'

One kind of meaning negotiated in this exchange is polarity, as the K1 question expects either an affirmative or negative response. At the level of grammar, the MOOD type of both clauses is indicative, realised by the presence of tense suffixes on the final verbs. But at the level of discourse semantics, their SPEECH FUNCTION types are distinguished as question and response statement by a contrast in pitch (i.e. tone contours). As in many languages, an inquiry about polarity is realised by a rising tone, while affirmation is realised by a falling tone.

This tone movement is graphed in Figure 6.1 – which images the frequency of the tones on which these two clauses were spoken (produced by the speech analysis software CECIL). Syllables are positioned approximately below the location on the tone contour on which they were articulated. There is a slash '/' between each rhythmic foot (which typically corresponds to a word plus affixes and enclitics in Pitjantjatjara), and a double slash '//' between the two tone groups. The prosody shown in Figure 6.1, of rising and falling pitch, is produced interactively between speakers.

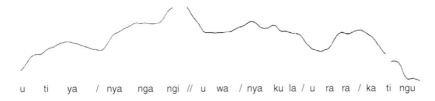

Figure 6.1 Tone contour graph of exchange pair (1)

The description of Pitjantjatjara phonology in Rose (2001) adopts the terminology introduced in Halliday (1967), which offers a general functional framework for particular descriptions of phonological systems. The basic semantic resource in TONE is the fall-rise pitch contrast, which can be broadly glossed as 'certain/uncertain'; but this resource is enriched by variations in the pitch and sequence of tones. Structurally, each move in Example 1 is realised by a tone group, consisting of obligatory Tonic and optional Pretonic feet. The Tonic foot carries the major pitch movement in a tone group. In this sequence, the major pitch movements are the high rise on *nya-ngangi*, initiating with an enquiry of polarity, and the high to low fall on *kati-ngu*, affirming in response. Significantly, these are the finite verbs in each move, that are inflected for tense; the inflections function interpersonally to realise INDICATIVE MOOD systems.

The preceding feet in each tone group here are Pretonic. In this instance, the Pretonics also carry pitch movements, up on the modal Adjunct *uti*, and down on affirming Adjunct *uwa* – with a slight fall-rise on the non-finite verbs, *nyaku-la ura-ra*. The phonological prosody of tone groups redounds with the grammatical prosody of clauses, from interpersonal Adjuncts to finite Processes, to realise an interpersonal prosody at the level of discourse semantics.

Halliday (1967) and Halliday and Greaves (2008) distinguish seven primary tones and two sets of secondary tones in English phonology. One set of secondary tones are Pretonic tones, while the others are delicate distinctions of primary Tonic tones. The description of Pitjantjatjara here, following Rose (2001), identifies five primary tones, with seven more delicate distinctions, and sets aside considerations of Pretonic tones. This degree of delicacy was found sufficient to describe the functions of tones in the data.

These options in the system of TONE are set out in Figure 6.2. The numbering system follows the conventions in Halliday (1967). The rise-fall pitch contrast distinguishes Tones 1 and 2. Tone 3 is approximately level, neutralising the contrast. Tone 4 embodies counter-expectancy, as 'apparently certain but actually uncertain'. Pitjantjatjara Tone 5 commences with a mid-high rise followed by a high-low fall (in contrast to English rise-fall). In the description here, Tones 2 and 4 have only one option each. Tones 1, 3 and 5 have neutral (.), augmented (+) and diminished (–) variants. Symbols are also shown for each option, that graphically illustrate pitch movements. These symbols have been used for text examples in Rose (2001, 2008), but the description here will use tone numbering.

6 Interpersonal Grammar of Pitjantjatjara 163

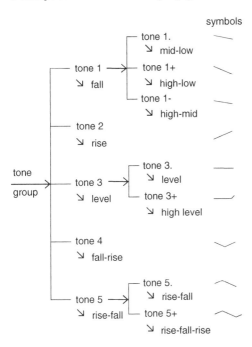

Figure 6.2 Pitjantjatjara TONE system

6.3 Discourse Semantics, Lexicogrammar and Phonology

The system of NEGOTIATION is described by Martin (1992, 2018) and Martin and Rose (2007) at two ranks – exchange and move. At exchange rank, the options are for speaker roles: obligatory primary roles and optional secondary roles. Three sets of simultaneous options in exchange structure are: INITIATION: primary/secondary role; EXCHANGE TYPE: action/knowledge; and optional FOLLOW-UP roles. More delicate options afford sequences of up to five roles in each exchange type. Exchange roles are realised by one or more moves. At move rank, the relevant system is SPEECH FUNCTION, following Halliday (1984) who also describes three sets of options – that is, COMMODITY: goods-and-services/inforormation; ROLE: giving/demanding; and MOVE: initiating/responding. These options give rise to four initiating SPEECH FUNCTION types: offer/command/question/statement, alongside compliant responses to each. These options are extended by Martin (1992) and Martin and Rose (2007) to include exclamations, calls and greetings. Moves concerned with goods-and-services are termed proposals, and those concerned with information are termed propositions.

In Pitjantjatjara, as in many other languages (Caffarel et. al., 2004), the primary proposal/proposition contrast in SPEECH FUNCTION is realised in lexicogrammar as the general opposition between imperative and indicative MOOD types. The entry condition for these MOOD options is a major clause. Responses, exclamations, calls and greetings are frequently realised by minor or elliptical clauses. However, all these options in SPEECH FUNCTION are also realised by selections in TONE, along with their grammatical realisations. In this regard, Rose (2001, 2008) followed Halliday (1967, 1994) to treat options in the Pitjantjatjara phonological system of TONE as realising delicate features in grammatical systems of MOOD and VOCATION. Halliday and Matthiessen (2014, p. 170) argue for this approach as follows:

Because a systemic account of grammar takes paradigmatic organization as fundamental, there is no problem with incorporating considerations of tone (or intonation, in general) into the account since terms in systems may [be] realised by different syntagmatic patterns such as fragments of constituency-like structure, e.g. 'declarative' Subject ^ Finite or prosodic patterns, e.g. 'reserved statement' tone 4.

However, paradigmatic organisation is only one fundamental dimension of language. Language systems are related to each other by stratum, metafunction and rank. Entry conditions for each paradigmatic system are dependent on these criteria. Hence [declarative] *Subject ^ Finite* and [reserved statement] *Tone 4* are not equivalent, as [declarative] is a feature in MOOD, and [statement] is a feature in SPEECH FUNCTION. A problem with this treatment is that it conflates features in semantic systems with delicate options in grammatical systems realised by features in phonological systems.

Nevertheless, as Halliday (1967) shows for English, and Rose (2001) shows for Pitjantjatjara, semantic functions of features in TONE are conditioned by grammatical selections in MOOD. This complex set of relations produces a rich variety of options for interpersonal meaning. Its complexity cannot be accounted for simply by realisation between strata, as Halliday and Greaves (2008, p. 64) acknowledge.

... rather than saying that 'the falling tone realizes a lexicogrammatical category of declarative which in turn realizes a semantic category of "statement"' we would say something like 'the falling tone realizes a complex feature consisting of declarative realizing "statement"'.

This 'bottom-up' perspective could be restated from a discourse-semantic perspective as '"statement" is realised by a complex relation of declarative and falling tone'. An alternative to grammatical delicacy, with these interstratal contradictions, is to treat this set of relations between features in multiple systems as co-instantiation or *coupling* of features in MOOD and TONE. Coupling is defined by Martin et al. (2013, p. 469) as 'the co-selection of linguistic resources across ranks, metafunctions, strata and modalities which are not specified by system/structure cycles'. In terms of the cline of instantiation proposed by Martin (2008), instantial couplings are a step down in meaning potential from the systemic features they combine. Like delicacy, steps along instantiation clines are relations of generality, sub-potentials of general systemic features. In fact, instantial relations of TONE, MOOD and SPEECH FUNCTION are continually emphasised by Halliday (1967) and Halliday and Greaves (2008) in terms of probabilities of co-selection. They describe sets of typical couplings of TONE and MOOD in terms of primary interpersonal moves, such as Tone 1 with declarative MOOD type to realise 'statement', and less frequent alternatives that realise subtypes of interpersonal moves, such as Tone 4 with declarative to realise 'reserved statement'. Such labels describe variations, not in MOOD, but in SPEECH FUNCTION types, realised by co-selections of features in MOOD and TONE.

In Pitjantjatjara, there is no grammatical distinction in indicative MOOD type between declarative and polar interrogative. However, indicative is most frequently coupled with Tone 1 to realise statements. Less frequently, indicative is coupled with Tone 2 to realise yes/no questions. Imperative is most frequently coupled with Tone 5 to realise commands. Tone 5 is also the unmarked option with elemental interrogatives, and with minor clauses realising exclamations, calls and greetings. A general semantic contrast could be drawn from these unmarked associations, between Tones 1, 3 and 4, which give information, and Tones 2 and 5, which demand information, action or attention.

Variations from these typical TONE/MOOD couplings afford a multiplicity of more delicate semantic functions for less frequent couplings. These are delicate options in APPRAISAL, the system of discourse-semantic resources concerned with evaluation (Martin & Rose, 2007; Martin & White, 2005), particularly the subsystems of FORCE and ENGAGEMENT. Table 6.1 sets out variants found in Rose (2001), for each coupling of TONE and MOOD. Options in FORCE are neutral, mild, strong or insistent. ENGAGEMENT is concerned with 'other voices' in a discourse. Options here are neutral, committed, uncommitted, reserved, inquiring or solidary.

Table 6.1 TONE, MOOD, FORCE *and* ENGAGEMENT

	MOOD			
tone	polar indicative	element interrogative	imperative	minor
1	neutral	mild	mild	mild
1+	strong	strong	strong	strong
1−	committed			committed
2	inquiring		inquiring	inquiring
3	uncommitted			
3+				solidary
4	reserved			
5		neutral	neutral	neutral
5+		interested	insistent	

These variations in FORCE and ENGAGEMENT are co-selected with options for types of interpersonal move, as well as types of Vocatives, which are also frequently spoken on a separate tone group. Table 6.2 shows common functions of choices in TONE in the contexts of propositions, proposals, exclamations, calls, greetings and Vocatives. Here, values in FORCE and ENGAGEMENT cross-classify SPEECH FUNCTION types and VOCATION types. For example, an inquiring proposition is a yes/no question, while an inquiring proposal is a request.

Table 6.2 SPEECH FUNCTION types and tones

	SPEECH FUNCTION			
tone	proposition	proposal	exclam., call, greeting	Vocative
1	neutral statement, mild element question	mild proposal	mild	mild
1+	strong statement, strong element question	strong proposal		
1–	committed statement		committed	
2	yes/no question	request	inquiry	
3	uncommitted statement			
3+			solidary	solidary
4	incomplete or reserved statement			deferent
5	neutral element question	neutral proposal	neutral	dominating
5+	interested element question	insistent proposal		

6.4 Exchange Structure

General options in the system of NEGOTIATION in Pitjantjatjara are similar to those described for other languages in this volume, following the general framework offered in Martin (1992) and Martin and Rose (2007). The primary choice in NEGOTIATION between exchanges of knowledge or action is realised grammatically as a primary choice between indicative and imperative MOOD types. The choice of initiating role is reflected in SPEECH FUNCTION options for statement or question in knowledge exchanges and command or offer in action exchanges. The option of follow-up roles tends to be realised by minor or elliptical clauses. The potential of exchange structures is summarised as follows, as sequenced formulae, with brackets indicating optionality:

((Da1) ^A2) ^A1 (^A2 f (^A1 f))

((Dk1) ^K2) ^K1 (^K2 f (^K1 f))

Example 2 illustrates an action exchange, initiated with a Da1 role, followed by a challenging move and A2 role. This is an exchange between a younger brother (YB) and elder brother (EB), whose contact is close but status is markedly unequal. The brothers are preparing to camp for the night, and the younger brother asks to sleep close to his elder (Da1). The elder brother refuses his request ('ch' for challenge), and commands him to sleep away from him (A2). Double slashes mark tone group boundaries. Tonic feet are indicated by bold font. SPEECH FUNCTION types and their APPRAISAL values are labelled to the right.

(2)

YB	Da1	// 1 kuta // 2 ngayulu nyanga-ngka **ngari** //	request
		elder.brother 1SG here-LOC lie :IMP	
		'Elder brother, may I sleep here?'	
EB	ch	// wiya	refusal
		no	
	A2	// 1+ ngura **nyara**-tja // 5+ tjitji **ma-ngari** // strong, insistent command	
		place yonder child apart-lie:IMP	
		'No! Over there, child, sleep apart!'	
	A1	[YB sleeps apart]	compliance

Both clauses in this exchange are in imperative MOOD type, realised by the uninflected verb stem *ngari*. However, the same MOOD choice in the grammar realises different SPEECH FUNCTION types and exchange roles at the level of discourse semantics. YB prefaces his request with the deferential vocative *kuta* 'elder brother', spoken on a deferential Tone 1. This is followed with a clause in imperative MOOD type, realising a proposal. As it is spoken on a rising Tone 2, the proposal is a request. As it is in first person, it is a request for the speaker to act, a delayed Da1 move, glossed as 'may I lie here?' As in yes/no questions, this rising tone expects a 'yes' or 'no' response.

EB challenges with a direct *wiya* 'no', followed on the same tone group by a contradictory command, including the dominating vocative *tjitji* 'child'. The command is stressed, first with an insistent Tone 1+ on the location *nyara-tja* 'yonder', emphasising the contrast with YB's *nyanga-ngka* 'here'. This stress is amplified with a 5+ tone on *ma-ngari* 'lie apart', realising an insistent command. The implicit A1 role in this exchange is YB's non-verbal complying response to obey his brother.

Example 3 illustrates a knowledge exchange, initiated with a Dk1 role, followed by a K2 role, and completed with a K1 role. This is a dialogue between younger and elder adult sisters (YS and ES), which illustrates their close but unequal relationship. The exchange begins as the younger sister has just run back to her elder sister after discovering a large python *kuniya* in a burrow *piti*. She breathlessly asks her elder sister *kangkuru* 'shall I tell you?' (Dk1). The elder sister responds with a K2 move complex, demanding to know what she has seen and what she is talking about, and the younger sister describes with awe what she has seen (K1).

(3) YS Dk1 // 1 **kangkuru** // 2 watja-lku =**na** =**nta** // yes/no question
              elder.sister   tell-FUT =1SG =2SG.ACC
              'Elder sister, shall I tell you?'

     ES K2   // 5 **nyaa** =n nya-ngu // 1+ **nyaa** // 1+ **nyaa** // strong and neutral
              what=2SG see-PST   what   what   element questions
              'What did you see? What? What?'
         =K2 // 5 **wala**-ngku watja-la //   neutral command
              quickly   tell-IMP
              'Tell me quickly!'
         =K2 //+ **nyaa** =n   wangka-nyi //   strong element question
              what =2SG say-PRS
              'What are you saying?'

     YS K1   // 1+ kuniya **pulk' alatjitu** tjarpa-ngu //   committed statement
              python   huge utterly enter-PST
              'An absolutely huge python has crawled into a burrow!'

The younger sister opens the exchange with a Dk1 move, including the deferential vocative *kangkuru*, on a mild 1– tone, and an interpersonal grammatical metaphor. She is proposing to give information to ES, but this is realised as a question on Tone 2 'shall I tell you?'.[2] The elder sister responds with a series of K2 moves, realised as element questions on neutral Tone 5 and strong Tone 1+, and a command also on strong Tone 1+. YS responds with a statement that is strongly committed on Tone 1+.

Example 4 illustrates a K2^K1^K2 f sequence. It is between two brothers-in-law (or 'wife's brothers' WB). WB1 is visiting the country of WB2 and they are planning a hunting trip. In Western Desert culture, brothers-in-law are careful to avoid any suggestion of unequal status, or of social distance. They address each other with the solidary *tju* 'mate'. Each move is heavily modalised in various ways, and avoids pronominal reference to the other.

WB1 first asks where they will go hunting in a K2 move complex. WB2 responds with a K1 suggestion, followed by a series of enthusiastic boasts about how much game he will spear. WB1 follows up with a series of appreciative exclamations as K2 f. Although the exchange is negotiating an activity, it is coded metaphorically as a knowledge exchange realised by indicative MOOD type. In particular, WB1's first K1 move is an indicative clause that realises an implicit suggestion, *(let's) give hunting a go over yonder*. Alternatively, this could be interpreted as an A1 move.

---

[2] As nominative is the unmarked case of pronouns, this is not specified in the glosses, in order to reduce their complexity, whereas marked cases such as accusative are specified, e.g. =1SG =2SG.ACC.

6 Interpersonal Grammar of Pitjantjatjara

(4)

WB1 K2	// 3+ **tju** // 5+ **yaaltji**-kutu //		interested
	mate where-ALLATIVE		element question
	'Mate, where to?'		
=K2	// 1 **yaaltji**-kutu-ngku // 5 **ngurilkati**-ku // 5+ **nyakukati**-ku //		mild and interested
	where-ALL-REFL search.out-FUT look.out-FUT		element questions
	'Where shall (we) go hunting?'		
WB2 K1	// 3+ **tju** // 1 nyara ungku-la **nyakukati**-nyi //		mild suggestion
	mate yonder give-IPF look.out-PRES		
	'Mate, (let's) give hunting a go over yonder.'		
=K1	// 1+ ka =na-tja **rungkal**-ku //		committed statement
	and=1SG-REFL spear-FUT		
	'So I myself will spear (so much game)'		
=K1	// 4 ngayulu **manti** // 1 tjinguru-mpa ngapul **putu** //		reserved statement
	1SG PROB:LOW PROB:LOW-PROB:MED eat unable		
	'I possibly, probably won't be able to eat it,'		
=K1	// 1 nguwan–tu **tjala** nguwan //		neutral statement
	nearly-PROB:HIGH burst nearly		
	'almost certainly burst, nearly.'		
WB1 K2 f	// 1+ **ngangkar** // 5 **alau** // 5 **alau** // 5 **palya** //		committed and neutral
	wow! oh oh alright		exclamations
	'Wow! Oh, oh! OK!'		

6.5 IMPERATIVE MOOD

Imperative MOOD type congruently realises the general interpersonal move of proposal – that is, a verbal move in an action exchange, obligating the addressee, speaker or a non-interlocutor to perform an action. Imperative clauses co-select from three systems, ORIENTATION, IMPERATIVE MOOD PERSON and MODULATION (Figure 6.3). Options in ORIENTATION express the obligation either directly or obliquely. These options are realised by endings of the finite verb instantiating the Process in a clause. For this reason, relational clauses without a Process cannot select for imperative MOOD type. Hence the entry condition to the imperative system is a free clause with a Process. Options in IMPERATIVE MOOD PERSON identify the obligated entity, realised by co-selections of identities in the exchange (addressee, speaker, non-interlocutor) with the participant functioning as Medium in the Process.[3] Finally, two marked options in MODULATION grade the obligation as high or low.

---

[3] Unlike some other languages, such as English, there is no structural distinction in Pitjantjatjara between experiential functions Medium and Process and interpersonal functions such as Subject and Predicator. For this reason, the function labels Medium and Process are retained here for the description of mood options. Rose (2001, p. 10) explains, 'a constituent analysis of mood structures in Western Desert has not been necessary, enabling an analytical focus on the prosodic patterns in which interpersonal meanings tend to be realised'.

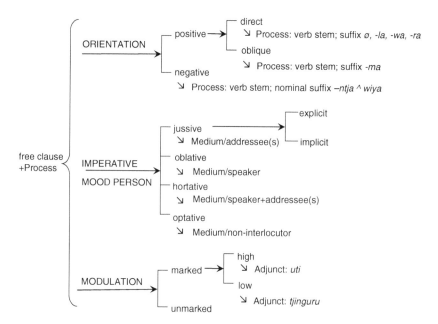

Figure 6.3 IMPERATIVE MOOD system

6.5.1 Orientation

Two types of imperative verb endings realise direct or oblique orientation. Direct forms depend on the syllabic form of the verb stem, or 'conjugation' in traditional terms, of which there are four verb classes, the verb stem without suffix or with the suffixes *–la, –wa, –ra*. The oblique suffix *–ma* may also realise continuous aspect, 'keep doing'.

6.5.1.1 Direct Direct orientation is by far the most frequent type. This is illustrated with the verb stem in Example 5, and with the suffix *–la* (6).

(5) // 5 **ma-pitja** //   neutral command
     away-move:IMP
     'Go away!'

(6) // 5 nyangatja   **urin**-tjinga-la //   neutral command
     this   turn-CAUSE-IMP
     'Turn this thing!'

From an experiential perspective, Examples 5 and 6 demand material actions. Example 7 illustrates an imperative inceptive relation 'become!', with suffix *–wa*.

(7)   // 1+ **pilun**-ari-wa //　　　　　　　　　strong command
　　　 quiet-become-IMP
　　　 'Be quiet!'

6.5.1.2 Oblique   The oblique type is realised by the suffix *-(n)ma*. Oblique orientation is exemplified in Example 8, translated as 'should do', and continuous aspect in Example 9, translated as 'keep doing'.

(8)   // 1 nyura   uti   **kulin**-ma //　　　　　mild command
　　　 2PL   clearly   listen-IMP:OBL
　　　 'You ought to listen!'

(9)   // 5 **rawa**   ana-ma //　　　　　　　　neutral command
　　　 continuously   go-IMP:OBL
　　　 'Keep on going!'

In negative imperative clauses, the distinction between direct and oblique imperative is neutralised, since the negative item *wiya* is appended to the verb with nominal suffix, as in Example 10.

(10) // 5 ngayulu   tjinguru   anku-ntja   **wiya** //   neutral offer
　　　 1S   maybe   go-NOMINAL   no
　　　 'Maybe I won't go.'

6.5.2   IMPERATIVE MOOD PERSON

Selections in the system of IMPERATIVE MOOD PERSON assign modal responsibility for an action to addressee, speaker, speaker + addressee or non-interlocutor. In other words, the entity obligated to carry out a proposal may be the addressee, speaker, both or neither. In Pitjantjatjara, the Medium is the active participant in a process, that acts, senses, says, attributes or identifies, so the modally responsible identity in a proposal is also the Medium. This contrasts with languages such as English, in which modally responsible Subject may conflate with other participant roles. Selections in IMPERATIVE MOOD PERSON give the imperative subtypes of jussive 'you do!', oblative 'I/we do!', hortative 'let's do!' and optative 's/he/they do!' The four options are set out in Table 6.3 and exemplified.

Table 6.3 *Selections in* IMPERATIVE MOOD PERSON

PERSON	MOOD type	Example
addressee	jussive	*ma-pitja* '(you) go!'
speaker	oblative	*ma-pitja = na* 'I'll go!'
speaker + addressee	hortative	*ma-pitja = la* 'let's go!'
non-interlocutor	optative	*paluru ma-pitja* 's/he'll go!'

6.5.2.1 Jussive
Jussive MOOD type congruently realises a command. As jussive is the most frequent option for imperative clauses, the addressee identity is typically left implicit.[4] However, it can also be explicitly realised by a pronoun, name or other resource realising VOCATION. The clause in Example 11 exemplifies implicit addressee, as the clause in Example 12 does explicit.

(11) // 5 **wala**-ngku   watja-la //   neutral command
         quickly   tell-IMP
      'Tell me quick!'

(12) // 1 **wiya** // 5 **wanti**   =ya   kunyu //   neutral command
         no   leave.it:IMP   2PL   it's said
      'No, you mob leave it, they said.'

The reportative item *kunyu* deflects responsibility for the command away from the speaker.

6.5.2.2 Oblative
Oblative MOOD type congruently realises an offer. Example 13 exemplifies oblative MOOD type in the context of a 'proposal complex', that is a command followed by an offer.

(13) 1   // 3 uwa   **ngalya**-pitja //   neutral command
              yes   come hither:IMP
           'All right, you come here,'

      +2 // 5 ka   ngayulu   paka-ra   **ma-pitja** //   neutral offer
              and   1s   arise-IPV   away-go:IMP
           'and I'll get up and go away.'

6.5.2.3 Hortative
Hortative MOOD type realises the proposal subtype 'suggestion' (Example 14). It includes speaker with addressee in a call to common action.

(14) // 1+ **a-ra**   =la   // 1 uru-kutu //   strong suggestion
           go-IMP   1PL   waterhole- ALLATIVE
      'Let's go to the waterhole!'

6.5.2.4 Optative
Optative mood (Example 15) realises a proposal whose modally responsible person may not be immediately present.

(15) // 1 paluru   uti   **wangka**-ma //   indirect proposal
           s/he   clearly   speak-IMP
      'She should speak!'

---

[4] Traditionally, implicit identities are referred to as ellipsis. Rose (2001) argues that zero realisation is one option in the system of clitic pronouns that function to background identities in discourse.

The optative configuration, of imperative MOOD type with modally responsible non-interlocutor, can only be translated as a modulated declarative in English. This translation fails to capture the precise meaning of the Pitjantjatjara indirect command. Indirect commands are realised by imperative clauses, the same as those with interlocutor MOOD PERSON types, so their grammar construes them as a type of proposal.

6.5.3 Modulation

In addition to options in TONE and the form of the verbal suffix, the obligation expressed in imperative clauses can also be modulated with the modal items *uti* and *tjinguru*. In this environment, these items realise high and low obviousness, respectively – that is, the force of the obligation is more or less obvious. Both items combine freely with either direct or oblique orientations.

6.5.3.1 High The item *uti* generally means 'obvious/open to view', and is used to amplify obligation (as the same metaphor is used in English), translated as 'clearly' in Examples 16 and 17.

(16) // 5 uti   =n   **ma-pitja** //   neutral command
         clearly 2S   move away:IMP
      'You ought to go.'

(17) // 1 nyura   uti   **kulin**-ma //   mild command
         2PL   clearly listen-IMP:OBL
      'You people ought to listen.'

6.5.3.2 Low The item *tjinguru* 'maybe' contrasts with *uti* to realise low obligation in imperative clauses (Examples 18 and 19).

(18) // 5 ngayulu tjinguru **a-ra** //   neutral offer
         1s   maybe   go-IMP
      'Maybe I'll go.'

(19) // 1 **paluru** tjinguru mantjin-ma //   mild command
         3s   maybe   get-IMP:OBL
      'Maybe she should get it.'

These options in modulation expand the negotiability of an imperative clause: by appealing to objective evidence, *uti* allows the potential for negotiation, while *tjinguru* expands it further.

174 *David Rose*

6.6 INDICATIVE MOOD

Indicative MOOD type congruently realises the general interpersonal move of proposition – that is, a move in a knowledge exchange. Indicative clauses co-select in five systems, INDICATIVE MOOD PERSON, INDICATIVE TYPE, POLARITY, PROBABILITY and ABILITY (Figure 6.4). The entry condition to these systems is a free clause. Where the clause includes a Process realised by a verb, indicative MOOD type is realised by a tense suffix on the verb stem. Where the clause expresses a relation, the MOOD type is inherently indicative and time is construed as persistent.

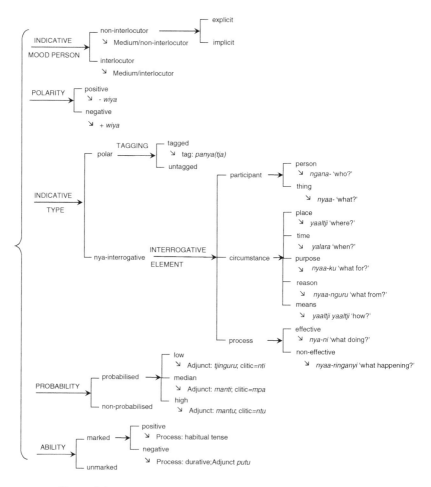

Figure 6.4 INDICATIVE MOOD system

6 Interpersonal Grammar of Pitjantjatjara

Options in INDICATIVE MOOD PERSON are realised by co-selections of identities in the exchange (interlocutor/non-interlocutor) with the participant functioning as Medium. The primary choice in INDICATIVE TYPE is between polar indicative and element interrogative. There is no lexicogrammatical distinction between statements and yes/no questions, which are distinguished by tone and exchange role. The feature [polar indicative] affords this choice in discourse semantics. Element interrogatives are termed *nya-interrogatives*, after their articulatory similarity (as in English wh– interrogatives). Interrogative elements include options for processes, along with participants and circumstance. Polarity is realised by presence or absence of the negative Adjunct *wiya*. Indicative clauses may take three options in probability, realised by modal Adjuncts or clitics. Ability may be marked positively by habitual tense or negatively by the Adjunct *putu* 'unable'.

6.6.1 INDICATIVE MOOD PERSON

In indicative clauses, there is a different assignation of modal responsibility to persons from that in imperative clauses. The unmarked option for Medium in an indicative clause is non-interlocutor, so that where the Medium identity is not present in the clause structure, it is presumably a non-interlocutor. Hence interlocutor identities must be realised explicitly, whereas there is a choice of explicit or implicit realisation for non-interlocutor.

Example 20 exemplifies explicit (clause 1) and implicit (clauses 2 and 3) realisations of the non-interlocutor *kuniya pulka alatjitu* in indicative clauses. The element referred to is underlined in the clause rank translation.

(20)
1 // 1+ kuniya **pulk'alatjitu**	tjarpa-ngu //			committed statement
python big utterly	enter-PST			
'A huge python entered a burrow.'				

2 // 1+ piti-ngka	=ni	**nguwanpa**	tjarpatju-nu //	committed statement
burrow-LOC	1S:ACC	nearly	put.in-PST	
'It nearly dragged me in.'				

3 // 1+ pulka	**mulapa** //			committed statement
big	really			
'It's really huge.'				

6.6.2 POLARITY

In positive process clauses, verbs are inflected for tense, while positive state clauses consist of Medium and Range, without a Process. In negative process clauses, verbs are inflected with the nominal suffix followed by *wiya*, as in negative imperative clauses (Example 10), and exemplified for negative indicative in Example 43. In negative state clauses, the Range is followed by *wiya* (Example 21).

(21)   // 1 paluru   mayitja   **wiya**   // 2 pany'tj' //
            he   boss   not   tag?
       'He's not the boss, is he?'

6.6.2.1 Polar Indicative As discussed previously, there is no grammatical distinction between statements and yes/no questions in Pitjantjatjara; rather the semantic distinction is realised by a coupling of indicative MOOD type with tone and exchange role. This is illustrated with the exchange in Example 1', in which both clauses are indicative, but the K2 question is spoken on rising Tone 2 and the K1 statement in response on a falling Tone 1.

(1')   K2   // 2 uti   =ya   **nyanga**-ngi //   yes/no question
              clearly   3PL   see-PST DUR
            'Could they see it clearly?'

       K1   // 1 uwa   nyaku-la   ura-ra   **kati**-ngu //   neutral statement
              yes   seeing   collecting   bring-PST
            'Yes, having seen it and collected it, they brought it back.'

6.6.2.2 Tagging Polar indicative clauses may be tagged, demanding confirmation of the proposition from the addressee. Tag questions consist of the anaphoric reference item *panyatja*, or the modal adverb *mulapa* 'really', spoken on Tone 2. In statements these items are often spoken with the final vowels ellipsed, sounding as *pany'tj'* (Example 21') or *mulap'* (22), while in questions they are complete (23).

(21') // 1 paluru mayitja **wiya** // 2 **pany'tj'** //   tagged neutral statement
             he   boss   not   tag?
       'He's not the boss, is he?'

(22)   // 1 tjinguru ngura iriti **an-u**   // 2 **mulap'** //   tagged neutral statement
             maybe   already   go-PST   true?
       'Maybe they've already gone, true?'

(23)   // 2 nyuntu   pitjantjatjara **wangka**-pai // **mulapa** //   tagged yes/no question
             2s   Pitjantjatjara speak-HAB   true?
       'Can you speak Pitjantjatjara, really?'

6.6.2.3 NY*a-Interrogative* Nya-interrogatives demand that information be supplied about one element of a clause, 'who, what, when, where, how, why, what happened or what x did' – that is, the identity of a participant, circumstance or process. The options for nya-elements correspond closely to the options for the TRANSITIVITY system as a whole – a metagrammatical microcosm within the grammatical system. Nya-interrogatives enact the TRANSITIVITY system as information exchange, mirroring the way that verbal and mental processes represent the MOOD system as configurations and sequences. Nya-elements are inflected for the transitivity roles in which they function, including types of Process, Medium and Range, and circumstances of Time, Place, Accompaniment, Means, Reason and Purpose. There is also a formal distinction between classes of entities, realised as *nyaa–,* and named entities, including people and places, realised as *ngana–*. There are four options for nya-processes, depending on process type and effectivity. The unmarked choice in TONE for nya-interrogatives is rise-fall Tone 5, as in imperatives, and this will be assumed in the examples of transitivity roles, unless otherwise specified.

6.6.2.4 Nya-Participants   Nya-participants may be people or things. The form of nya-element used for people is *ngana–* 'who?', inflected as for proper nouns. For things the nya-element is *nyaa–* 'what?', inflected as for proper nouns. Inflections vary according to the transitivity role of the nya-element, exemplified below for *ngana–* (Examples 24 and 25), and *nyaa–* (Examples 26 and 27).

(24)   ngana-lu   =nta   u-ngu
       who-ERG? [Actor] 2s:ACC [Goal]   give-PST
       'Who gave it to you?'

(25)   nyuntu ini   ngana-nya
       you name [Value]   who-ACC? [Token]
       'What's your name?'

(26)   punu   nyaa   nyaratja
       plant [Carrier]   what? [Attribute] yonder
       'What plant is that over there?'

(27)   nyaa-ngku   nyangatja   katanta-nu
       what-ERG? [Actor]   this [Goal]   break-PST
       'What broke this thing?'

6.6.2.5 Nya-Circumstances   Nya-circumstances   include   Locations, Purpose, Reason, Quality and Means. They are realised by variations on the nya-item stems, *nyaa–, ngana–* and *yaal–* with a circumstantial suffix. In circumstances of Place (Examples 28–30), the three nya-item stems have the following meanings:

   ngana-la   at what place/with whom? [4:64]
   nyaa-ngka   at/in/on what? [4:65]
   yaaltji   where? [4:66–7]

(28) nyuntu   ngura ngana-languru   pitja-nyi
      you   place what?-from   come-PRES
      'Where have you come from?'

(29) paluru panya   nyaa-ngka   ngara-nyi
      that one   what-LOC?   stand-PRES
      'What is that one standing on?'

(30) nyura   yaaltji-kutu   a-nanyi
      you-3   to where?   are going
      'Where are you all going to?'

Purpose is realised by *nyaa-ku* 'what for/why?' (31).

(31) nyaaku   piranma-ngku   ini panya   tju-nu   Council nyangatja
      why?   white-ERG   name ANAPH   put-PST   Council this
      'Why have the whites put this name on this Council?'

Reason is realised by *nyaa-nguru* 'from what (cause)?' (32).

(32) paluru   nyaa-nguru   pikatjarari-ngu
      he   from what?   did become sick
      'What did he get sick from?'

Quality is realised by *yaaltji yaaltji* 'how?' (33).

(33) yaalti yaaltji   nyangatja
      how?   this
      'How did this come to be?'

Means is realised by *nyaa-ngka* 'with what?' (34).

(34) paluru   nyaa-ngka   palya-nu
      he   with what?   did make
      'What did he make it with?'

6.6.2.6 Nya-Process There are four types of nya-process that demand information about different types of processes:

   nyaa-ri-nganyi   what's happening? (35)
   nyaa-ni   what's the Actor doing? (effective clauses) (36)
   yaaltji-ri-nyi   what's the Actor doing? (non-effective clauses) (37)
   yaaltji-nga-ra   how is the Actor doing something? (38)

(35) nyaa-ri-nganyi   // awai
      what-INCEPT-PRES?   hey
      'What's happening, ey?'

(36) nyuntu   palu-nya   nyaa-nu
      you   3s-ACC   what-PST?
      'What did you do to him?'

6 Interpersonal Grammar of Pitjantjatjara   179

(37)   mungartji   paluru   yaaltji-ri-ngangi
        yesterday   3S   how-INCEPT-PRES:CONT?
        'What was he doing yesterday?'

The verb asking 'manner of doing' *yaaltjinga-ra* typically occurs as a dependent process in a hypotactic verb complex (38).

(38)   ngayulu   yaaltjinga-ra   anku-ku
        β 1s   how-IPV?   α go-FUT
        'How will I go?'

6.6.3   Probability

Options in probability enable speakers to modalise propositions with three degrees of likelihood – low, median or high. These values are realised by the modal adjuncts *tjinguru*, *manti* and *mantu* respectively, or the clitic particles – *mpa*, *–nti* or *–tu*, respectively.

6.6.3.1 Low   The following clauses exemplify the low probability value realised by the modal adjunct *tjinguru* 'maybe'. Note the variations in TONE associated with low probability. In Example 39, the choice in TONE is the 'reserved' Tone 4, mirroring the uncertainty of the wording. In Example 40, the MOOD type is imperative realising an offer on neutral Tone 5, focused on *ngayulu* – that is, 'I rather than you may go.'

(39)   // 4 tjinguru   =ya   **mayi-lampa**   kati-ku //   reserved statement
           maybe   3PL   food-our   bring-FUT
        'Maybe they'll bring food for us.'

(40)   // 5 **ngayulu**   tjinguru   ana-ma //   neutral offer
           1s   maybe   will go
        'I might go.'

The same low probability is expressed non-saliently by the clitic *–mpa*. In the conditional question in Example 41, *–mpa* is suffixed to both the temporal adverb *kuwari-mpa*, and to the β process *nyaku-la-mpa*. In the latter instantiation, its probability value functions as condition 'if ... '

(41)
// 4 ka =li   **kuwari=mpa**   putu nyakula=mpa   // 2 **yaaltjiring**-ku   =li //
and=1DU   now=PROB:LOW   can't see=PROB:LOW   what.do-FUT?   1DU
'OK, maybe, so if we probably now can't see them, then what will we do?'

6.6.3.2 Median   Median probability is expressed by the adjunct *manti* 'probably', which normally follows the process, a participant or circumstance, or by the clitic *–nti*, suffixed to the process, a participant or circumstance. In the relation in Example 42, *manti* follows the Attribute *ngurpa* 'ignorant'. Reserved tone (Tone 4) is typical in clauses including this item.

(42)   // 4 ngurpa   **manti** //   reserved statement
         ignorant   probably
         'He probably doesn't know.'

In the negative proposition in Example 43 median probability is expressed by the clitic *–nti*, which typically occurs at the end of a tone group, on the rise of Tone 4.

(43)   // 4 wati panyatja   pitja-ntja   **wiya =nti** //   reserved statement
         man ANAPH   come-NOM   NEG=PROB:LOW
         'That man probably won't come.'

6.6.3.3 High

High probability is expressed by the adjunct *mantu* 'certainly', which is least frequent in discourse, and like *manti* follows another element. As may be expected since it expresses certainty, its typical tone is Tone 1. Example 44 illustrates a typical occurrence in dialogue, as an acknowledgement realised by a minor clause.

(44)   K2   // 2 paluru   amata-ku   **a-nu** //   yes/no question
              3s   Amata-to   go-PST
              'Has he gone to Amata?'

         K1   // 1 uwa   **mantu** //   neutral acknowledgement
                yes   certainly
                'Yes, certainly.'

The exchange pair in Example 45 illustrates the expression of certainty with the clitic *–tu* in the context of dialogue, again spoken on the certain Tone 1.

(45)
K2 // 2 ka =n   tju **pukulpa**   =nti //   yes/no question
      and=2s   WB   happy   =PROB:MED
      'And mate, are you happy perhaps?'

K1 // 1 uwa   tju pukulpa-l   // 1 pukul   =tu
      yes   WB   happy-ANAPH   happy   =PROB:HIGH
      kuli-ni //   neutral statement
      hear-PRES
      'Yes, mate, I'm happy with that, I'm certainly happily hearing it, it's great.'

In addition, high negative probability is expressed by the clitic *–munu*, which is affixed to a process (Example 46) or participant, again spoken on falling tone.

(46) // 1 ngayulu palula-kutu   **anku-ntja**   =munu //   neutral statement
       1s   there-towards   go-NOM   =PROB;NEG
       'I'm certainly not going there.'

6.6.4 Ability

Like probability, expressions of (in)ability are restricted to indicative clauses. Positive ability is marked only by the habitual tense selection: for example, *palyal-pai* 'does make – that is, when a person does something continuously they are able to do so. This is extended to the names given to occupations, such as labelling a builder *wali palyal-pai*, literally 'makes houses' (*wali* 'house'), construing an occupation as habitual behaviour. On the other hand, when a person is unable to do something, it is marked by a modal adjunct.

6.6.4.1 Negative   Negative ability is realised by the adjunct *putu*, typically in the context of a durative process – that is, the process is construed as unsuccessfully ongoing. Tonic focus is typically on *putu*, since it is the inability that is newsworthy (47–49).

(47)
   // 1 tjana   **putu**   kunyu   waru   mantji-ningi //   neutral statement
      3PL   unable   REPORT   fire   get-PST:CONT
   'They were unable, it's said, to get the fire.'

(48)
   // 1 ka   =ya   palu-nya   **putu**   mantji-ra //   neutral statement
      and   =3PL   3S-ACC   unable   get-IPV
   'And they were unable to get it.'

(49)
   // 1 ngayulu   **putu**   anku-payi //   neutral statement
      1s   unable   go-HABIT
   'I can't walk.'

6.6.4.2 Positive   Positive ability is inherent in habitual processes – that is, if a person 'does' (something), then they implicitly 'can do' (it). The sense of positive ability is brought out in the exchange in Example 50, where knowledge of an activity (i.e. competence) is questioned, and replied to with habitual process.

(50)
   K2 // 2 nyuntu   nyantju-ku   **ninti** //   yes/no question
         2s   horse-GEN   knowledgeable
      'Do you know (how to ride) horses?'

K1 // 1 uwa   ngayulu   nyantju   **tatil-payi** //   neutral statement
       yes   1s   horse   mount-HABIT
'Yeah, I can ride horses.'

6.7 Interpersonal Metaphors

Imperative MOOD type is the 'congruent' mode of expression for proposals: it is certainly the most common form in which proposals are expressed and is the form first learned by children. However, there are also a range of resources for expressing proposals through MOOD choices other than imperative, including interrogatives and declaratives in which the speaker rather than addressee is Medium, as well as affective mental projections and relational enhancements. These realisations are metaphorical as their discourse-semantic and grammatical meanings are in tension. This feature of Pitjantjatjara is consistent with Halliday's (1994, p. 342) observation that:

Metaphorical modes of expression are characteristic of all adult discourse. There is a great deal of variation among different registers in the degree and kind of metaphor that is encountered; but none will be found entirely without it.

Although metaphor is less a feature of Pitjantjatjara than of written registers in other languages, there is still considerable interpersonal metaphor used in certain registers, particularly when speakers wish to express deference or avoid direct demands. Children tend to learn these metaphorical expressions as they approach adolescence and their social circle and roles widen to include relationships that demand respect and circumspection.

A common type of interpersonal metaphor in Pitjantjatjara are proposals realised as mental projections, in which subjective modulation is realised as a projecting mental process. In Example 51, the mental process is a primary finite clause and the desired activity is non-finite projection.

(51)   // 1 β ngayulu **anku**-ntjikitja α muku-ri-nganyi //
              1s   go-PF:SAME   desire-INCEPT-PRES
       'I want to go.'

The mental projection (52) is a metaphor for an indirect command, 'our executives should build a *tawarra* school'. In this case the projecting clause α is itself a proposal, an optative clause modulated with high modulation *uti*, and oblique orientation *kulin-ma*.

(52)
α   // 1 uti   nganampa AP-nguru executive tjuta-ngku   **kulin-ma** //
         clearly   our executives from AP   think-IMP:OBL
     'Our executives from AP should consider.'

6 Interpersonal Grammar of Pitjantjatjara

'β   // 1 schoola nganampa **tawarra** palya-ntjikitja //
      school our   tawarra   make-PF:SAME
    'to set up our own school as a tawarra.'[5]

Modulation may be effaced by realising proposals in indicative MOOD type. An instance is Example 53, from Example 4, responding to the question 'where shall (we) go hunting?' The MOOD type is indicative on Tone 1, apparently realising a statement 'yonder (someone) is giving hunting', but implicitly a suggestion 'let's give hunting a go over there'.

(53)   // 3+ **tju** // 1 nyara   ungku-la   **nyakukati**-nyi //
               mate   yonder   give-IPF   look.out-PRES
      'Mate, (let's) give hunting a go over yonder.'

Proposals can by objectified by realising the obligated activity as a perfective verb enhancing a finite relational verb. This strategy construes the proposal as giving information and effaces others' responsibility. The action demanded in Example 54 is realised as *anku-ntjaku* 'to do', enhancing the relational verb *ngara-nyi* 'standing'. This translates literally as 'you are standing to do'.

(54)   // 1 nyuntu kunyu **anku-ntjaku** ngara-ngi //
            2s   REPORT go-PV:SWITCH   stand-PST:CONT
      'Apparently, you were expected to go.'

In Example 55, a mother addresses other adult family members to negotiate a plan to gather *tjala* 'honey ants'. In the initial A2 suggestion, she uses five different strategies for softening her proposal, in order to avoid any implication of power over the others:

- A suggestion is realised in indicative MOOD type, effacing the obligation with a metaphor of giving information rather than demanding compliance.
- Certainty is diminished with the low probability clitic=*nti* 'maybe'.
- Force is diminished with mild Tone 1.
- Future tense *ura-lku* 'will gather' is less certain than present tense.
- The tag question *mulapa* 'really?' leaves it open to agree or not.

One family member responds with a compliant minor clause, and the mother follows up by repeating the suggestion, with more certain present tense *ura-ni* 'are gathering', implicitly increasing the obligation.

---

[5] AP is the Anangu Pitjantjatjara regional land council. The *tawarra* was the traditional separate camp for adolescent male initiates, in which they lived and learnt the adult men's arts and knowledge.

(55)

A2	// 1 kuwari	=nti	=la	mungawinki	tjala	ura-lku	// 2 mulapa //	suggestion
	now	maybe	1PL	morning	tjala	gather-FUT	really	

'Perhaps in the morning we can gather honey ants, really?'

A1 // 1- uwa   mulapa //   compliance
      yes   really
'Yes, definitely!'

A2f // 1 kalala kuwari mungawinki ura-ni //   suggestion
       tomorrow now morning   gather-PRS
'Tomorrow morning in the daylight, we'll go gathering.'

The tension between the discourse-semantic and grammatical interpretation of interpersonal metaphors is illustrated in Example 56, in which the mood metaphor is misread. A mother requests a spare blanket of her son (A2), in indicative mood on Tone 2. The son misreads the metaphor as a yes/no question, replying with a K1 statement, 'yes, it's over there'. His father then reinitiates with an explicit command 'give me!', which the son tracks with 'sorry' on Tone 2 – that is, 'what do you mean?' (tr). The mother responds by trying to repair the misunderstanding, refusing the father's command 'no, it's your blanket, I'll ask again' (rtr).

(56)

A2	// 5 katja	// 2 nyuntu	blanketa kutjupa	**kanyi**-ni //	request
	son	2s	another blanket	have-PRES?	

'Son, do you have another blanket?'

K1	// 5 uwa	ngari-nyi	**nyara** //	statement
	yes	lie-PRES	yonder	

'Yes, it's over there.'

A2	// 5 **uwa**	=**ni** //	command
	give:IMP	1S:ACC	

'Give it to me!'

tr // 2 **munta** //   tracking
     sorry?
'Sorry?'

rtr	// 5 wiya	**nyuntu**-mpa //			refusal
	no	yours			
	// 1+ nyanga-ngka	=na	**tjapi**-ni	piruku //	offer
	this-LOC	1s	ask-PRES	again	

'No, it's yours. I'll ask here again.'

6.8 APPRAISAL

This section explores the contributions of grammar and phonology to realising the APPRAISAL systems of ENGAGEMENT and FORCE (Martin & White, 2005;

Martin & Rose, 2007). It begins by outlining the system of lexicogrammatical items termed MODAL ASSESSMENT (after Matthiessen 1995, Rose 2001). It then surveys the contributions of MOOD, MODAL ASSESSMENT and TONE to realising ENGAGEMENT and FORCE and concludes with a dialogue that illustrates these functions in dialogue.

6.8.1 MODAL ASSESSMENT

The system of MODAL ASSESSMENT includes modal items realising frequency, degree, intensity, continuity, responsibility, deference and desire. Options in MODAL ASSESSMENT are set out in Table 6.4; most are realised as modal Adjuncts, but a couple are available as clitics. Some of these options are gradable; others are not. All, however, enable speakers to exchange evaluations on their relationship and on the commodities they are exchanging.

Table 6.4 MODAL ASSESSMENT *systems in Pitjantjatjara*

system	feature		realisation
DEGREE	nearly		*Nguwanpa*
	utterly	positive	*Alatjitu*
		negative	*Wiyatu*
REALITY[6]	positive	only	*kutju*
		just	*unytju*
		really	*mulapa*
	negative	perception	*palku*
		other	*ngunti*
CONTINUITY	low		*unytju*
	high		*rawa;* =*tu*
FREQUENCY	occasionally		*kutjupara*
	sometimes		*kutjupara kutjupara*
	frequently		*tjuta ara*
	continually		*titutjara*
RESPONSIBILITY	indirect		*kunyu*
DEFERENCE	deferent		*wanyu*
DESIRE	addressee		*puta*
	other		=*wi*

---

[6] Options in REALITY assess an event or relation as more or less real or unreal.

6.8.2 ENGAGEMENT and FORCE

As we have seen for NEGOTIATION, strategies for realising APPRAISAL options are distributed across various grammatical and phonological systems. Martin and White (2005, p. 96) define ENGAGEMENT as construing 'a heteroglossic backdrop of prior utterances, alternative viewpoints and anticipated responses'. Its most general alternatives are to expand or contract options for anticipated responses. Grammatical and phonological systems that realise these general options are set out in Table 6.5.

Table 6.5 *Grammatical and phonological systems realising* ENGAGEMENT

			expand	contract
MOOD	IMPERATIVE	ORIENTATION	oblique	–
		MODULATION	low	high
	INDICATIVE	TAGGING	tagged	–
		PROBABILITY	all	–
		ABILITY	–	unable
MODAL ASSESSMENT		DEGREE	nearly	utterly
		REALITY	–	all
		CONTINUITY	–	all
		FREQUENCY	others	continually
		RESPONSIBILITY	indirect	–
		DEFERENCE	deferent	–
		DESIRE	all	–
TONE			uncommitted reserved inquiring solidary	committed

Other resources may also be deployed to realise ENGAGEMENT, such as conjunctions *palu* 'but', *palulanguru* 'therefore' and mental projection 'I/you think/like'.

FORCE is part of the system of GRADUATION concerned with grading the force of propositions and proposals. Gradability is a characteristic of many options in ENGAGEMENT, such as the low/median/high options for PROBABILITY. Similarly, values in COMMITMENT are graded by choices in TONE, as reserved [Tone 4], neutral [1] or committed [1+]. Choices in TONE are also deployed to grade the force of propositions and proposals, as mild, neutral, strong or insistent. In addition, force can be amplified through iteration of one or more of these resources. Table 6.6 gives some examples of the grading potential of these resources.

6 Interpersonal Grammar of Pitjantjatjara 187

Table 6.6 *Lexicogrammatical and phonological resources for* GRADUATION

		value	
resource	low	median	high
MOOD (obligation)	*tjinguru-n ma-pitja-ma* maybe-2s away-go-OBLIG	*uti-n ma-pitja-ma* clearly-2s away-go-OBLIG	*ma-pitja-ø* away-go-IMP
MODAL ASSESSMENT (probability)	*a-nu tjinguru* go-PST maybe	*a-nu manti* go-PST probably	*a-nu mantu* go-PST certainly
ITERATION (degree)	*Wala* quick	*wala winki* quick all	*wala winki alatjitu* quick all utterly
TONE (force) statement element question proposal	mild [1] mild [1]	neutral [1] neutral [5] neutral [5]	strong [1+] strong [1+] strong [1+]	interest [5+] insistent [5+]

The dialogue in Example 57 exemplifies the unfolding social functions of these resources in discourse. For each move, values are given for choices in SPEECH FUNCTION and TONE, MODAL ASSESSMENT, ENGAGEMENT and GRADUATION. Extracts from this text have already been used in this chapter to illustrate various features. Globally, it is a macro-proposal, negotiating the action of the two sisters going to see the huge python. However, this proposal must also be negotiated around the status difference between the sisters, as it is the deferent younger sister who demands the action of her dominant elder (see Rose 2001, 2008, 2018, for discussion of status and contact in the Pitjantjatjara kinship system).

Hence, while YS's initial insistent command contracts negotiability, this is neutralised with the deferent *wanyu*, and reversed in her next move with a yes/no question and deferent vocative *kangkuru*. Although the question move positions, the elder sister with authority to answer yes or no, lexically YS is positioned as delayed primary knower, with knowledge to 'tell'. In response, ES asserts her status, contracting negotiability with a series of strong demands for information that are amplified by iteration, and the urgent quality *walangku*.

YS then repeats her command far more deferentially, with Tone 1– and addressee desire *puta* 'if you please', expanding negotiability. Lexically, she invites her sister to 'come and see' for herself. She then supports this proposal with a series of committed statements that are amplified with high degree *pulka alatjitu* 'utterly big' and high reality *pulka mulapa* 'really big', contracting negotiability. The outcome of this subtle negotiation of status, using deference and intriguing evidence, is that both sisters then go to see the python.

(57)

YS	A2	// 1+ **wanyu paka**-ra pitja // defer arise-IPFV come:IMP 'Please get up and come!'	insistent command deferent *wanyu*	contract expand
	Dk1	// 1 **kangkuru** // 2 watja-lku =**na** =**nta** // elder.sister tell-FUT =1SG =2SG.ACC 'Elder sister, shall I tell you?'	yes/no question deferent *kangkuru*	expand expand
ES	K2	// 5 **nyaa** =n nya-ngu // 1+ **nyaa** // 1+ **nyaa** // what=2SG see-PST what what 'What did you see? What? What?'	neutral and strong element questions iterated	contract amplify
	=K2	// 5 **wala**-ngku watja-la // quickly tell-IMP 'Tell me quickly!'	neutral command urgent *walangku*	contract amplify
	=K2	// 1+ **nyaa** =n wangka-nyi // what =2SG say-PRS 'What are you saying?'	strong element question iterated	contract amplify
YS	A2	// 1- **wanyu puta** // 1 pitja-la **nya**-wa // defer desire come-IPFV look-IMP 'If you please, come and see!'	deferent command deferent *wanyu* desire *puta*	contract expand
	K1	// 1+ kuniya **pulk' alatjitu** tjarpa-ngu // python huge utterly enter-PST 'A huge python crawled into a burrow!'	committed statement high degree *pulk' alatjitu*	contract contract
	=K1	// 1+ piti-ngka =ni nguwanpa **tjarpatju**-nu // burrow-LOC =1S:ACC nearly put.in-PST 'It nearly dragged me in.'	committed statement	contract contract
	=K1	// 1+ pulka **mulapa** // big really 'It's really huge.'	committed statement high reality *pulka mulapa*	contract contract
	A1	[the two sisters go to look]		

6.9 Conclusion

This chapter has outlined resources for interpersonal meanings in Pitjantjatjara, focusing on imperative and indicative MOOD systems, in relation to phonological and discourse-semantic systems of TONE, NEGOTIATION, SPEECH FUNCTION, ENGAGEMENT and GRADUATION. Examples have illustrated social functions of these linguistic resources for enacting variations in social contact and status, but the focus here has been on the resources themselves, in order to contribute to this volume's orientation to functional language typology. A complementary perspective is provided in Rose (2001 and 2018), which explore social functions of these resources in the kinship-structured community of Pitjantjatjara speakers. While this type of egalitarian small-scale society differs in many ways from the stratified mass societies in which 'world languages' such as modern English, Spanish or Chinese have evolved, the interpersonal meaning potential of Pitjantjatjara is comparable to that of other languages described in this volume. This commensurability across such cultural differences and millennia of separate evolution points to deep-rooted stable relations between social functions and the functionality of the language systems described here (Rose, 2006). It also suggests that the kinds of social relations enacted by these interpersonal resources are not as remote as they are often painted in colonial imaginations.

References

Caffarel, A, Martin, J. R. & Matthiessen, C. M. I. M., eds., (2004). *Language Typology: A Functional Perspective*. Amsterdam: John Benjamins.
Halliday, M. A. K. (1967). *Intonation and Grammar in British English*. The Hague: Mouton.
Halliday, M. A. K. (1984). Language as Code and Language as Behaviour: A Systemic-Functional Interpretation of the Nature and Ontogenesis of Dialogue. In R. P. Fawcett, M. A. K. Halliday, S. M. Lamb and A. Makkai, eds., *Language as Social Semiotic*. Vol. 1 of *The Semiotics of Language and Culture*. London: Pinter, pp. 3–35.
Halliday, M. A. K. (1994). *An Introduction to Functional Grammar*, 2nd ed., London: Routledge.
Halliday, M. A. K. & Greaves, W. (2008). *Intonation in the Grammar of English*. London: Equinox.
Halliday, M. A. K. & Matthiessen, C. M. I. M. (2014). *Halliday's Introduction to Functional Grammar*. London: Routledge.
Martin, J. R. (1992). *English Text: System and Structure*. Amsterdam: John Benjamins.
Martin, J. R. (2008). Tenderness: Realisation and Instantiation in a Botswanan Town. In N. Norgaard, ed., *Systemic Functional Linguistics in Use*. Odense: Odense Working Papers in Language and Communication, vol. 29, pp. 30–62.
Martin, J. R. (2018). Introduction. *Functions of Language* (Special Issue on Interpersonal Meaning: Systemic Functional Linguistics Perspectives), 25(1), 2–19. https://doi.org/10.1075/fol.17018.mar
Martin, J. R. & Cruz, P. (2018). Interpersonal Grammar of Tagalog: A Systemic Functional Perspective. *Functions of Language* (Special Issue on Interpersonal Meaning: Systemic Functional Linguistics Perspectives), 25(1), 54–96. https://doi.org/10.1075/fol.17016.mar
Martin, J. R. & Rose, D. (2007). *Working with Discourse: Meaning beyond the Clause*, 2nd ed., London: Continuum.
Martin, J. R. & White, P. (2005). *The Language of Evaluation: Appraisal in English*. London: Palgrave.

Martin, J. R., Zappavigna, M., Dwyer, P. & Cleirigh, C. (2013). Users in Uses of Language: Embodied Identity in Youth Justice Conferencing. *Text and Talk*, *33*(4/5), 467–96.

Matthiessen, C. M. I. M. (1995). *Lexicogrammatical Cartography: English Systems*. Tokyo: International Language Sciences Publishers.

Rose, D. (2001). *The Western Desert Code: An Australian Cryptogrammar*. Pacific Linguistics.

Rose, D. (2006). A Systemic Functional Approach to Language Evolution. *Cambridge Archaeological Journal*, *16* (1), 73–96. https://doi.org/10.1017/S0959774306000059

Rose, D. (2008). Negotiating Kinship: The Language of Intersubjectivity in an Australian Culture. *Word*, *59* (1–2), 189–215. https://doi.org/10.1080/00437956.2008.11432586

Rose, D. (2018). Sister, Shall I Tell You? Enacting Social Relations in a Kinship Community. *Functions of Language* (Special Issue on Interpersonal Meaning: Systemic Functional Linguistics Perspectives), *25* (1), 97–134. https://doi.org/10.1075/fol.17015.ros

7 Interpersonal Grammar in Brazilian Portuguese

Giacomo Figueredo

7.1 Introduction

The rationale motivating our chapter rests on the premise that like all languages Brazilian Portuguese (henceforth BP) has evolved resources to enact social relations (Caffarel et al., 2004; Teruya et al., 2007). Linguistically, this means exchanging knowledge or facilitating the exchange of actions through a set of discourse-semantic and grammatical resources (see Martin & Rose, 2007, p. 219–23).

The fact that this semiotic labour is divided between discourse semantics and grammar raises the problem of establishing precisely how meanings are managed on each stratum and within each stratum how systems interact (see Martin et al., 2013, p. 75–93). It also impacts on the description of the relationship between systems in different strata (or different ranks within the same stratum) in relation to grammatical metaphor (Halliday, 1994; Martin, 1992; Halliday & Matthiessen, 1999; among others). Addressing these problems is crucial for any description that involves axial reasoning (see Fawcett, 1988, p. 4), is text-based and approaches grammar 'from above' (see Halliday, 2002, p. 408–9). Our primary goals are (i) to explore the boundary between discourse semantics and grammar within the interpersonal realm (see Martin, 1992, p. 33) and (ii) to derive a description of MOOD that explicates the relation of discourse semantics and lexicogrammar in BP – specifically, in the contributions MOOD has to offer to the exchange structure of dialogue.

The data analysed in this chapter is retrieved from spontaneous use, as compiled in the corpus CALIBRA (the Catalogue of Language in Brazil). CALIBRA is a 1 million-token corpus with 803 texts of naturally occurring BP, distributed across registers of spoken and written modes (Figueredo, 2014). For the present description, dialogic texts (both spoken and written) were analysed – roughly 8,000 major clauses from 120 texts (Figueredo, 2011, 2015).

In Section 7.2 we will focus on the discourse-semantics stratum (see Halliday, 1977, p. 176–7). More specifically, we will look at how exchange structure is organised by NEGOTIATION and SPEECH FUNCTION (see Martin, 1992, p. 46–50). We will then approach MOOD 'from above' by describing how BP exchanges and moves are realised grammatically. We will show how each MOOD selection realises a move and how MOOD ultimately contributes to an organised sequence of moves realising an exchange.

In Section 7.3 we will approach MOOD 'from below' and 'from round about', examining group elements operating as functions in the interpersonal structure of the clause and deriving systems from the descriptive work on agnate structures (see Gleason, 1965, p. 202–4). We will relate MOOD subsystems and explain how they work together in order to make interpersonal meaning. As a result of this trinocular view, we will generalise MOOD as a system network.

7.2 Enacting Exchange: MOOD from Above

The exchange structure of BP is similar to that of other languages (cf. Rose, 2005; Zhang, 2020; Wang, 2020; Martin & Quiroz, 2020). Let us start by presenting an excerpt from a dialogue.

Text 1 is a conversation between mother and daughter as they make a chocolate sponge cake for dessert. Its purpose is to enable people to organise their activities as well as negotiate their part in preparing the dessert. In the original recording, this procedure happened on Christmas Eve, as people were preparing Christmas dinner. The house was full of family members and so naturally the procedure was interrupted by other speakers coming into the kitchen and engaging in casual conversation. Only the procedural discourse was kept for this analysis. As with all the text samples in this chapter, the CALIBRA corpus is the source of the data.

Major clauses are numbered. A translation of Text 1 into English is also provided. This translation has been formulated to facilitate the reading by non-BP speakers. Punctuation indicates the transcription of phonological pauses (,), Tone 1 (.), Tone 2 (?), Tone 3 (...).

Text 1 [FAZ_FD_01]

Mother	(1)	Ana, traz chocolate granulado lá.
Daughter	(2)	Onde?
Mother	(3)	Lá dentro do bufê, filha.
Daughter	(4)	*(a filha pega o chocolate granulado)*
Daughter	(5)	Mãe, vai caber ali?
Mother	(6)	Vai, vai não?
Daughter	(7)	Não ué.
Daughter	(8)	Divide ele no meio pra pôr naqueles ali. *(apontando para duas bandejas)*
Mother	(9)	É.
Mother	(10)	Me dá uma faca aí.

7 Interpersonal Grammar in Brazilian Portuguese   193

(cont.)

Daughter	(11)	*(a filha dá a faca)*
Mother	(12)	Tira lá pra mim que sua mão tá mais limpa.
Daughter	(13)	*(a filha pega as bandejas)*
Mother	(14)	Parte no meio, né, Ana?
Daughter	(15)	Ah é.
Mother	(16)	Tá bom assim? *(transferindo para as bandejas)*
Daughter	(17)	Tá.
Mother	(18)	*(a mãe parte no meio 'assim')*
Daughter	(19)	Aí...
Daughter	(20)	Esse negócio é bom demais
Daughter	(21)	ninguém vai reparar nada [que o bolo está feio porque foi cortado]

Text 2 [English]

Mother	(1)	Ana, bring me some chipped chocolate, please.
Daughter	(2)	Where is it?
Mother	(3)	It's in the cupboard, darling.
Daughter	(4)	*(daughter brings the chipped chocolate)*
Daughter	(5)	Mom, will the cake fit here?
Mother	(6)	It will, won't it?
Daughter	(7)	Obviously not.
Daughter	(8)	Let's cut it in half so we can fit it on those. *(pointing to two trays)*
Mother	(9)	All right.
Mother	(10)	Hand me that knife, please.
Daughter	(11)	*(daughter hands over the knife)*
Mother	(12)	Get that for me please because your hands are cleaner.
Daughter	(13)	*(daughter gets the trays)*
Mother	(14)	Cut in half, right, Ana?
Daughter	(15)	Exactly.
Mother	(16)	Like so? *(moving the cake halves to the trays)*
Daughter	(17)	Yes.
Mother	(18)	*(mother cuts the cake 'like so')*
Daughter	(19)	There we go...
Daughter	(20)	This is so good
Daughter	(21)	no one will notice. [that the cake is not as pretty because it's been cut]

Text 1 is a dialogue. As such, people engage with language to do something for them (cf. Halliday, 1978), either 'to know something' (as in Example 1) or 'to get things done' (as in Example 2):

(1)   to know something:
      Onde? [*Where is it?*]

(2)   to direct action:
      Ana, traz chocolate granulado lá. [*Ana, bring me some chipped chocolate, please.*]

These negotiations are successful when one of the interlocutors either provides knowledge sought (see Example 3) or the service that is required (see Example 4):

(3)   give knowledge:
        Lá dentro do bufê, filha. *[It's in the cupboard, darling.]*

(4)   give what is required:
        (a filha pega o chocolate granulado). [daughter brings the chipped chocolate]

The speaker who performs the role of bringing the negotiation to a successful conclusion is the primary interlocutor (represented by '1'). In the exchange, this interlocutor is 'semioticised' as a function, either the primary knower – K1 in Example 3 – or the primary actor – A1 in Example 4.

Without primary interlocutors there is no complete negotiation; thus primary knowers and actors enact obligatory elements in the exchange structure of BP. Complete exchanges may consist simply of these roles (Example 5):

(5)   exchange with only a primary knower:
        K1 – Esse negócio é bom demais ninguém vai reparar nada. *[This is so good no one will notice.]*

Sometimes, the '1' move is not realised through verbal language; but it is always there. If the exchange is negotiating activity, then the non-verbal action is the A1 move (Example 6); if it is negotiating knowledge, non-verbal action can be treated as enacting a K1 move in cases where it invokes information sought or reacted to (Example 7):

(6)   A1 as non-verbal action:
        (daughter gets the trays)

(7)   K1 as non-verbal understanding:
        Dk1 – Tá bom assim? *[Like so?]*
        K2 – Tá. *[Yes.]*
        K1 – *non-verbal* *(mother cuts the cake 'like so')*
        K1f – Aí ... *[There we go ...]*

Most exchanges in BP have more than one element, because negotiations also realise the needs of interlocutors in addition to the primary knower and actor. In Text 1, the daughter needs to know things (*Mom, will the cake fit here?*); and the mother needs action (*Bring me some chipped chocolate*). In these situations there are secondary interlocutors (represented by '2'). They can request knowledge (represented by K2) or action (represented by A2). In the system of NEGOTIATION, the first system consequently distinguishes between

7 Interpersonal Grammar in Brazilian Portuguese   195

a self-contained 1 – which can be the end of negotiation (Example 5) – and a complex of 1 that is followed by a 2 (Figure 7.1).

In addition, there can be other non-obligatory elements in the exchange. BP can have a primary interlocutor anticipating a secondary interlocutor's request for knowledge or action (Example 8); the anticipation move is represented as 'D1' (Figure 7.2):

(8)   anticipating knowledge
      Dk1 – Parte no meio, né, Ana? [*Cut it in half, right, Ana?*]

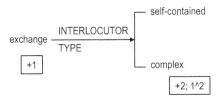

Figure 7.1 INTERLOCUTOR TYPE

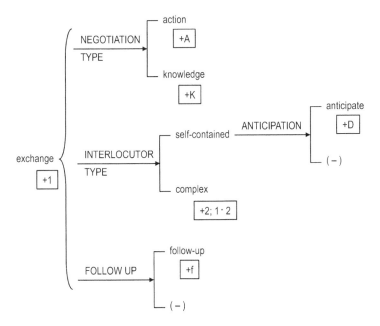

Figure 7.2 Basic options for the system of NEGOTIATION in BP

After knowledge is given or action is performed, there can also be some additional optional moves which conclude the negotiation; these are referred to as follow-up elements or 'f' or tracking 'tr' and challenge 'ch' (Example 9):

(9) A1 – [*Mother cuts the cake like so.*]
     A2 f – Aí .... [*There we go ...*]

Text 1 is analysed below for NEGOTIATION in Table 7.1. There are nine exchanges (numbered on the table from 1 to 9). The first, for example, is about the mother requesting an action from the daughter; it involves moves 1 (A2) and 4 (A1).

Table 7.1 *Exchange structure and* NEGOTIATION *functions in Text 1*

Move number			NEGOTIATION features	NEGOTIATION function structure	Exchange number
M	(1)	Ana, traz chocolate granulado lá. Ana, bring me some chipped chocolate, please.	action and secondary	A2	1
D	(2)	Onde? Where is it?	knowledge and secondary	tr	2
M	(3)	Lá dentro do bufê, filha. It's in the cupboard, darling.	knowledge and primary	rtr	
D	(4)	*(daughter brings the chipped chocolate)*	action and primary	A1	1
D	(5)	Mãe, vai caber ali? Mom, will the cake fit here?	knowledge and secondary	K2	3
M	(6)	Vai, vai não? It will, won't it?	knowledge and primary	K1	
D	(7)	Não ué. Obviously not.	knowledge and secondary and follow	Ch	
D	(8)	Divide ele no meio pra pôr naqueles ali. Let's cut it in half so we can fit it on those.	action and secondary	A2	4
M	(9)	É. Alright.	action and primary	A1	
M	(10)	Me dá uma faca aí. Hand me that knife, please.	action and secondary	A2	5
D	(11)	*(daughter hands over the knife)*	action and primary	A1	
M	(12)	Tira lá pra mim que sua mão tá mais limpa. Get that for me please because your hands are cleaner.	action and secondary	A2	6

7 Interpersonal Grammar in Brazilian Portuguese

Table 7.1 (cont.)

Move number			NEGOTIATION features	NEGOTIATION function structure	Exchange number
D	(13)	*(daughter gets the trays)*	action and primary	A1	
M	(14)	Parte no meio, né, Ana? Cut in half, right, Ana?	knowledge and primary and anticipate	Dk1	7
D	(15)	Ah é. Exactly.	knowledge and secondary	K2	
M	(16)	Tá bom assim? Like so? *(moving the cake halves to the trays)*	knowledge and primary and anticipate	tr	8
D	(17)	Tá. Yes.	knowledge and secondary	rtr	
M	(18)	*(mother cuts the cake 'like so')*	action and primary	A1	
D	(19)	Aí... There we go...	action and primary and follow	A2 f	
D	(20)	Esse negócio é bom demais This is so good	knowledge and primary	K1	9
D	(21)	ninguém vai reparar nada no one will notice.			

From the point of view of discourse, the labour of enacting interpersonal meanings is shared by systems derived from two different units. The unit of exchange is the entry condition for the system of NEGOTIATION and is responsible for the structure of an exchange, including functions for requesting (2), providing (1), knowledge (K), action (A), anticipating (D) and following-up (f). In discourse, these form the exchange structure. The unit of move is the entry condition for the system of SPEECH FUNCTION and is responsible for the meaning of each individual element in the structure of exchange. It includes the system of SPEECH ROLE (give or demand) and COMMODITY (information or goods-and-services).

The units of exchange and move are arranged in a hierarchy of composition (cf. Halliday, 1961; Martin, 1992). NEGOTIATION options are realised by the functions such K2 and Da1. These functions preselect options in the system of SPEECH FUNCTION. And SPEECH FUNCTION functions – such as give and demand (see Halliday & Matthiessen, 2014, p. 134) – preselect features of MOOD in the grammar. Figure 7.3 illustrates the interpersonal semantic rank scale with reference to the exchange structure of Text 1.

198   *Giacomo Figueredo*

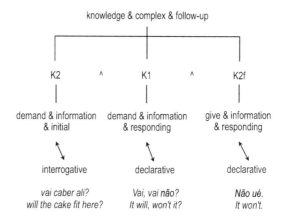

Figure 7.3 The structure of exchange 3 from Text 1

BP realisations of SPEECH FUNCTION options are illustrated in the examples below (see also Figure 7.4). Examples 10–13 are examples of information being given or demanded:

(10)   give information:
       Lá dentro do bufê, filha. [*It's in the cupboard, darling*]

(11)   demand information:
       Onde? [*Where is it?*]

Goods-and-services can be requested or offered.

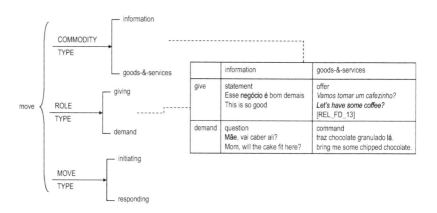

Figure 7.4 Basic SPEECH FUNCTION options in BP

7 Interpersonal Grammar in Brazilian Portuguese

(12) demand goods:
Tira lá pra mim *[Get those for me, please]*

(13) offer service [COM_FD_11]:
Quer que eu fale com ela? *[Would you like me to talk to her?]*

We now turn to the task of formulating the classes of clause that realise SPEECH FUNCTION. Let's have another look at Text 1 (Table 7.2), but now we'll examine it considering move and clause classes as well.

Table 7.2 NEGOTIATION, SPEECH FUNCTION *and* MOOD *in Text 1*

			NEGOTIATION :move	SPEECH FUNCTION :clause	MOOD
M	(1)	Ana, traz chocolate granulado lá, please. Ana, bring me some chipped chocolate.	action; secondary A2	initiating; demand; g-s	imperative
D	(2)	Onde? Where is it?	knowledge; secondary; tracking	initiating; demand; info	interrogative
M	(3)	Lá dentro do bufê, filha. It's in the cupboard, darling.	knowledge; primary; rtr	responding; demand; info	declarative
D	(4)	*(daughter brings the chipped chocolate)*	action; primary A1	responding; demand; g-s	–
D	(5)	Mãe, vai caber ali? Mom, will the cake fit here?	knowledge; secondary K2	initiating; demand; info	interrogative
M	(6)	Vai, vai não? It will, won't it?	knowledge; primary K1	responding; demand; info	declarative
D	(7)	Não ué. Obviously not.	knowledge; secondary; follow; challenge	responding; demand; info	declarative
D	(8)	Divide ele no meio pra pôr naqueles ali. Let's cut it in half so we can fit it on those.	action; secondary A2	initiating; demand; g-s	imperative
M	(9)	É. Alright.	action; primary A1	responding; give; info	declarative
M	(10)	Me dá uma faca aí. Hand me that knife, please.	action; secondary A2	initiating; demand; g-s	imperative
D	(11)	*(daughter hands over the knife)*	action; primary A1	responding; demand; g-s	–
M	(12)	Tira lá pra mim que sua mão tá mais limpa. Get that for me please because your hands are cleaner.	action; secondary A2	initiating; demand; g-s	imperative

200 *Giacomo Figueredo*

Table 7.2 (*cont.*)

			NEGOTIATION :move	SPEECH FUNCTION :clause	MOOD
D	(13)	*(daughter gets the trays)*	action; primary A1	responding; demand; g-s	–
M	(14)	Parte no meio, né, Ana? Cut in half, right, Ana?	knowledge; primary; anticipate	initiating; give; info	declarative
D	(15)	Ah é. Exactly.	knowledge; secondary K2	responding; give; info	declarative
M	(16)	Tá bom assim? Like so? *(moving the cake halves to the trays)*	knowledge; primary; anticipate; tracking DK1	initiating; demand; info	interrogative
D	(17)	Tá. Yes.	knowledge; secondary; rtracking K2	responding; give; info	declarative
D	(18)	*(mother cuts the cake 'like so')*	action; primary A1	responding; demand; goods-and-services	–
M	(19)	Aí... There we go...	action; secondary; follow A2 f	initiating; give; info	declarative
D	(20)	Esse negócio é bom demais This is so good.	knowledge; primary K1	initiating; give; info	declarative
D	(21)	ninguém vai reparar nada no one will notice.			declarative

Looked at from above (i.e. from the point of view of moves), the grammar of BP has developed distinctive resources to realise initial moves. There are classes for realising statements (give information), questions (demand information) and commands (demand goods-and-services), with no distinct class to realise offers. The major correlations are outlined here:
– initial give information: clause class 1.1 → MOOD: declarative
– initial demand information: clause class 1.2 → MOOD: interrogative
– initial demand goods-and-services: clause class 2.2. → MOOD: imperative
Looked at from below (i.e. from the point of view of grammatical and phonological constitution) there are some characteristic traits that separate classes of clause (Table 7.3).

Congruently, [give/information] (statements) are realised grammatically in BP by indicative declarative clauses selecting indicative VERBAL MOOD type (in

7 Interpersonal Grammar in Brazilian Portuguese   201

Table 7.3 *Congruent realisation of* SPEECH FUNCTION *in BP (full clauses)*

SPEECH FUNCTION (initiating)	Interpersonal prosody	VERBAL MOOD	TONE
Statement	Intonation	Indicative	falling
Question (elemental)	segment (Inquirer)	Indicative	rising-falling (mid-rising)
Question (polar)	Intonation	Indicative	rising
Command	segment (verb suffix)	Imperative	rising-falling; falling
Offer	Various	indicative; imperative	various

the verbal group) and a falling tone. In Example 14, '// 1' indicates a tone 1 (falling) group boundary; '/' indicates a salient syllable and '/**bold**' indicates the tonic syllable.

(14) // 1 Nin/guém | va-i | repa/rar | /**na**da //
           No one | will-IND.PRS.1SG notice | nothing
                    | verbal group
       'No one will notice.'

For [demand/information], elemental questions demand information with respect to some missing element. Elemental questions are realised segmentally by the function of Inquirer, realised by an adverbial group of the interrogative class (also known as 'qu–' adverbials): que [*what*], quando [*when*], qual [*which*], quem [*who*], etc.). Prosodically there is a Tone 5 or Tone +5, i.e. a rising-falling-(mid-rising) speech contour (Example 15).

(15) // +5 ⌢ O /**que** / você / faz //
             What   you   do
             Inquirer
       'What would you do?'

The information demanded can alternatively target the polarity of a proposition, in which case polar questions are deployed. Polar questions are realised in BP with indicative VERBAL MOOD type and prosodically by a rising tone – see Example 16.

(16) // 2 / Poss-o   fa/z-er   a per/**gun**ta //
            Can-IND.PRS.1SG make   the question
       'Can I ask the question?'

For demand; goods-and-services, commands are realised in BP by imperative MOOD. Grammatically, the element selecting for imperative VERBAL MOOD type is generally placed on the first position (Examples 17 and 18).

(17) Ana   traz   chocolate granulado   lá
      Ana bring.IMP.2SG chocolate chipped   ATTENUATE
      'Ana, bring me some chipped chocolate, please.'

(18) Tira   lá   pra mim
      get.IMP.2SG   ATTENUATE for me
      'Get that for me, please.'

For give; goods-and-services, offers can be realised by modalised interrogatives, declaratives or imperatives (with a rise-fall and slight rise again intonation contour); Example 19 shows offers realised by imperative and interrogative clauses.

(19) | Entr-a | sent-a. | Quer um cafezinho? | Uma água? |
     | Enter.IMP.2SG | sit.IMP.2SG | Want.IND.2SG a coffee | A water |

'Come on in; have a seat. Would you like a coffee? Some water?'

As a follow-up to initiating SPEECH FUNCTION types, responding moves vary according to function and to the willingness of the listener to respond. As a general rule, we can sum up the most typical realisations of responding moves to SPEECH FUNCTION types in BP as follows:

Statements can be acknowledged by means of a responding statement of agreement or by the Positioner function, realised by a modal particle with a rising tone. A contradiction is typically the Polarity function, realised by the negative adjunct 'não' followed by a statement contradicting the initiating move.

- The responding moves to elemental questions provide the missing information. A disclaimer for elemental questions would involve a declarative clause stating that the speaker does not have, or does not want to give, the missing information.
- Polar questions are typically responded by the Finite function, realised by a verbal group for an expected positive reply, or the Finite realised by a verbal group and the Polarity realised by negative adjunct 'não' for an expected negative reply. 'Não' alone is deployed when the response is discretionary, in effect: 'I don't want to answer.'
- Commands and offers can be compliantly responded to non-verbally. In addition, a verbal response can be present. Compliance with a command typically replays the clause, switching imperative MOOD type to declarative MOOD type. So, the imperative *Apanh-e [catch-.IMP.2SG]* has as compliance: *Apanh-o [catch-IND-PRS-1SG]*. A refusal is realised by adding 'não' to the declarative clause: *Não apanh-o [NEG catch-IND.PRS.1SG]*.
- Compliance with offers is realised by minor clauses; for non-compliance 'não' is added to these minor clauses. Alternatively, if an offer is realised by a polar question, then the responses can be the same as those to polar questions.

7.3 The System of MOOD TYPE

We begin this section with an overall presentation of MOOD TYPE in BP. We will discuss congruent realisations (see Halliday & Matthiessen, 1999, pp. 227–32) in this section (no metaphorical relations will be considered at this time). The basic characteristic of a major clause in BP is the presence of the function Predicator. This function is fundamental for the interpersonal configuration of the clause, as it enables the clause to realise an initial (give or demand) move. The Predicator is the function a verbal group element plays in the clause. There can be no major MOOD TYPE in BP without a Predicator. Responding moves often do not have a Predicator, as it is not commonly picked up in negotiation.

The basic major MOOD distinction in BP is between [imperative] and [indicative], the features that are preselected by options in SPEECH FUNCTION. Imperative clauses realise demand; goods-and-services (commands). Indicative mood clauses realise statements and questions and include both declarative and interrogative clauses. In turn, [declarative] agnates with [interrogative: polar] with respect to tone (declaratives falling; polar rising). [interrogative: elemental] is realised segmentally by the Inquirer pre-selecting an interrogative adjunct.

Indicative clauses negotiate information – that is, semiosis. As such, indicatives also need the insertion of a Finite function. The Finite anchors the clause relative to the 'here and now' of the speech event. It preselects a verbal group element and it also carries TENSE and MODALITY. The Subject is also a function of the clause. It is part of the structure of more delicate clause options, both for imperative and indicative clauses. The Subject is inserted in clauses where responsibility needs to be negotiated. Finally, the Positioner function realises features of the systems of ASSESSMENT. It is realised by a modal particle and negotiates the relationship between speakers in terms of their status and contact, values and feelings.

The functions involved in indicative clauses are Subject, Finite and Positioner. Imperatives involve Subject, Predicator and Positioner functions – but not Finite, since imperatives are effectively irrealis as far as temporality is concerned. It is the interplay of these functions that enables dialogue in BP.

Taken together these sets of functions form the core of interpersonal grammatical meanings in the BP clause – collectively speaking, they form a Negotiator element of structure. Typologically speaking, the Negotiator in BP is the functional equivalent of the Mood Element in English and German, and the Negotiator in French, Spanish and Tagalog (cf. Halliday & Matthiessen, 2014; Caffarel, 2006; Quiroz, 2015, 2018; Martin & Cruz, 2018). Figure 7.5 models the redundancy between units and systems of NEGOTIATION (exchange rank in discourse semantics), SPEECH FUNCTION (move rank in discourse semantics) and MOOD (clause rank in grammar) including the main MOOD types.

For the remainder of the chapter, we will look at MOOD 'from below' – describing in more detail the functions that constitute the interpersonal

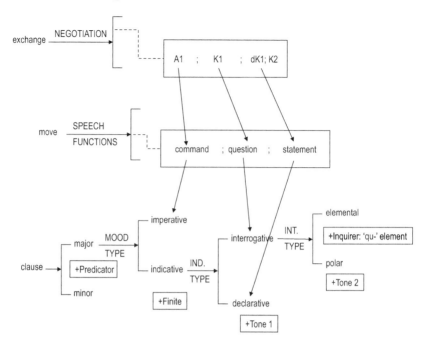

Figure 7.5 Initiating MOOD TYPE from above in BP with congruent realisations

structure of the clause and how they realise MOOD features. We describe imperative MOOD type in Section 7.3.1, talking briefly about the functions of Predicator and Subject in imperative clauses. The system of FORCE is introduced, since intonation co-selects imperative MOOD type to form more delicate options. Indicative MOOD type is described in Section 7.3.2 and the functions of Finite and Subject are discussed in more detail. In Section 7.3.3, we describe ASSESSMENT and the Positioner. All MOOD functions are typically realised at group rank. The Predicator is realised by an element of the verbal group, the Subject by a nominal group, the Finite by an element of the verbal group, and the Positioner by a particle group. In addition, looking at MOOD from below includes taking into account its realisation by words and morphemes, which will be specified when needed. We note in passing that other interpersonal clause systems such as POLARITY and MODALITY are also part of the interpersonal grammar of the clause; but they lie beyond the scope of this chapter.

7.3.1   IMPERATIVE MOOD and the Predicator

The main function structure for imperative clauses in BP is the Predicator. Looked at from below, the Predicator in imperative clauses is realised by

7 Interpersonal Grammar in Brazilian Portuguese

a verbal group (or sometimes a verbal group complex). The verb realising the Event in the verbal group is inflected for imperative VERBAL MOOD and for MOOD PERSON – either second person singular or plural, or first person plural (Table 7.4). Person is a function in the verbal group and is related to the function A1 in an exchange, as well as to [demand/goods-and-services] in moves illustrated in Example 20.

Table 7.4 *Imperative verbal morphology for regular verbs*

inflection	MOOD PERSON	Affirmative	Negative
-ar	2SG	-a, -e	-es, -e
	1PL	-emos	-emos
	2PL	-ai, -em	-eis, -em
-er, -ir	2SG	-e, -a	-as, -a
	1PL	-amos	-amos
	2PL	-ei (-er), -i (-ir), -am	-ais, -am

(20) Ana   *traz*   chocolate granulado lá
     Ana   **bring.IMP.2SG** chocolate chipped   ATTENUATE
     Vocative   **Predicator**   Positioner
     'Ana, bring me some chipped chocolate, please.'

Negative polarity imperative is realised through the Polarity Adjunct '*não*'. Negation may also affect the affixes realising imperative VERBAL MOOD type (Example 20a).

(20a) Ana   *não*   *traga*   chocolate granulado lá   *não*
      Ana   **not**   **bring-IMP.NEG.2SG** chocolate chipped   ATTENUATE   **not**
      Vocative   **Polar-** **Predicator**   Positioner **-ity**
      'Ana, don't bring me any chipped chocolate, please.'

The typical structure of an imperative clause has the Predicator placed in first position. It is worth noting that ideational or textual functions can also be found in clause initial position as in Example 21 (Beneficiary/Theme). However, interpersonally speaking, the Predicator is the first interpersonal function in structure.

(21) Me   *dá*   uma faca aí
     Me   **give-IMP.2SG**   a knife   ATTENUATE
                  Predicator   Positioner
     Beneficiary
     Theme
     'Hand me that knife, please.'

In an exchange, action and INTERLOCUTOR TYPE are realised by the function A1. This function can enact either the addressee or the speaker and addressee of an interaction. A1 is realised by a demand; goods-and-services (command) at move rank, which in turn preselects [imperative] in the system of MOOD. In turn, [imperative] is realised by the Predicator: verbal group.

There are two features of imperative. The [jussive] involves an addressee, and the [hortative] involves both the speaker and addressee. The morphology of the verb functioning as Event in the verbal group marks a distinction in the grammar between addressee and speaker-and-addressee (Table 7.4). In the case of hortative clauses, the verb *v-amos* (go-IMP.PL) can be added to the group, forming an extending verbal group complex (see Halliday & Matthiessen, 2014, p. 562). Examples 20 and 21 illustrate the [jussive] option. Examples 22 and 22a show instances of [hortative].

(22) hortative:
Próximo passo: *abr-amos*   *o documento*
Next step   open-IMP.1PL   the file
      Predicator
'Next step: let's open the file.'

(22a) hortative with verbal group complex extension:
Próximo passo: *v-amos abrir*   *o documento*
Next step   go-IMP.1PL open.INF   the file
      Predicator
'Next step: let's open the file.'

Sometimes in an exchange, interlocutors are in disagreement or misunderstand one another, giving rise to challenging and tracking moves. One possible challenge might be negotiation of which interlocutor should perform an action – in other words, who is the person to enact the addressee and function as A1, as recipient of a command. This kind of negotiation impacts on the grammar of imperative clauses, triggering more delicate options for the [jussive] type.

In these options, the Predicator forms a structure with another function, the Subject. In imperative clauses, the Subject is a function realising the addressee in the challenging and tracking of A1 moves and the recipient of a command – this is, in broad terms, the meaning of 'responsibility'. The Subject of imperative clauses is realised by a nominal group with the Thing preselecting second person from word system SPEECH PERSON. There are two cases where a Subject is inserted in the interpersonal clause structure:

(i) when the speaker makes precise the recipient of a command by singling out that addressee. In this case, the Subject is sequenced before the Predicator. This structure realises the delicate feature [jussive: singled-out], as in Example 23.

(23) singled-out:
Você   *fic-a*   *quieto*   *rapaz*
You   be-IMP.2SG   quiet   mate
Subject   Predicator   Vocative
'You be quiet, mate.'

(ii) when the responsibility for undertaking the command is being actively negotiated among interlocutors. In this case, the Subject follows the Predicator in structure. This structure realises the delicate feature [jussive: negotiated], as in Example 24.

(24) negotiated:
(A) Ney,   abr-e   a porta   Ney!
    Ney   open-IMP.2SG   the door   Ney
    Vocative   Predicator   Vocative
    'Ney, answer the door!'

(B) Abr-e   você!
    open-IMP.2SG   you
    Predicator   Subject
    'You answer the door!'

Other than these options, BP can manage still further distinctions for imperatives – in terms of requesting, pleading and forcing orders (Figure 7.6). These, however, are not solely organised in the grammar. Rather, they involve a co-selection of MOOD features and intonation (cf. Rose, Chapter 6, this volume, for a detailed account of grammar and intonation in interaction). BP has five basic tones, with the unmarked tonic syllable being the last salient syllable of the tone group (for a comprehensive description of intonation, including tones and scales, cf. Cagliari, 1981). For the purposes of this description, two of them are relevant: Tone 1 (falling) and Tone 5 (rising-falling).

A neutral imperative has a Predicator and Tone 1 (Example 25). The [singled-out] feature is structured as Subject ^ Predicator and Tone 1, with the tonic syllable mapping onto the Subject (25a). An [order], or a strong, forceful imperative, has the structure of Subject ^ Predicator and Tone 1, but here the tonic syllable maps onto the Predicator (25b). A [request], or a polite imperative, has a Predicator and Tone 1 (25c). Finally, a [pleading], or an imploring imperative, has the structure of Subject ^ Predicator, with the tonic syllable mapping onto the Predicator and Tone 5 (25d). Both [request] and [pleading] are frequently used to realise give; goods-and-services (offers) (Table 7.5).

Table 7.5 MOOD *and* TONE *for imperative*

	Tone 1	Tone 5
jussive: Predicator	neutral	request
jussive: Subject^Predicator	singled-out (tonic syllable/Subject)	
jussive: Subject^Predicator	order (tonic syllable/Predicator)	pleading

208   *Giacomo Figueredo*

(25) neutral:

// 1 *Peg-a*   *pra /mim* *lá*   *o ne/gócio* //
     get-IMP.2SG   for me   ATTENUATE that thing
     Predicator   Positioner
     'Get that thing for me, please.'

(25a) singled-out:

// 1 ∧ vo/**cê** *peg-a*   *pra /mim* *lá*   *o ne/gócio* //
                  get-IMP.2SG   for me   ATTENUATE that thing
       Subject   Predicator   Positioner
       'Get that thing for me, please.'

(25b) order:

// 1 ∧ você   /***peg-a***   *pra /mim* *lá*   *o ne/gócio* //
              get-IMP.2SG   for me   ATTENUATE that thing
       Subject   Predicator   Positioner
       'Get that thing for me, please.'

(25c) request:

// 5 ***Peg-a***   *pra /mim* *lá*   *o ne/**gó**cio* //
     get-IMP.2SG   for me   ATTENUATE that thing
     Predicator   Positioner
     'Get that thing for me, please.'

(25d) pleading:

// 5 ∧ você   /***peg-a***   *pra /mim* *lá*   *o ne/**gó**cio* //
              get-IMP.2SG   for me   ATTENUATE that thing
       Subject   Predicator   Positioner
       'Get that thing for me, please.'

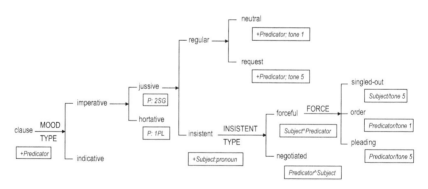

Figure 7.6 The system of IMPERATIVE TYPE in BP

7.3.2 INDICATIVE MOOD and the Finite

The key function realising indicative clauses in BP is the Finite. The presence or absence of the Finite is the most important distinction between an indicative and an imperative clause. Indicative clauses can be subdivided into declaratives and interrogatives. Interrogatives, in turn, are of the polar and elemental types.

In BP, there is no grammatical difference between a declarative and a polar interrogative. The difference is realised directly by intonation in phonology. However, since this agnation is crucial to account for move and exchange patterns, we will treat intonation as a form of interpersonal prosody realising grammar systems, similarly to the system of FORCE for imperative delicate features (see Halliday and Greaves, 2008, for an extensive account of intonation in grammar, and Rose, Chapter 6, this volume). The difference between polar and elemental interrogatives is the insertion of an Inquirer function (cf. Zhang, Chapter 3, and Wang, Chapter 4, this volume), which realises elemental interrogatives.

We will start by accounting for the Finite 'from below'. In BP, transitory elements (semantically, 'occurrences') are realised by verbal groups at group rank (Halliday & Matthiessen, 1999; Hao, 2020). A verbal group may include one or more words. One function in the verbal group, the Event, realises the experiential content of the Process. Interpersonally speaking, this element of the verbal group is an infinitive verb that is preselected by the Predicator from the system of EVENT TYPE. The other element of the verbal group is a finite verb preselected by the Finite from the system of TENSE. The structure of a finite verb involves two crucial morphemes, one for TENSE and another for PERSON (though sometimes they may be fused). Also, it is relevant to mention that Predicator and Finite can be conflated into one single structure when there is only one verb in the group (Example 26).

(26) | Ninguém | va-i | repar-ar | nada |
	No one	will-IND.PRS.1SG	notice-INF	nothing
	Subject	Finite	Predicator	
		verbal group		
		Tense	Event	
		finite verb	infinitive verb	

'No one will notice.'

The Finite provides indicative clauses with their anchoring in temporality as moves in exchange; thus, the most important grammatical job of the Finite is to position a proposition in relation to a moment of dialogic interaction (Figure 7.7). The Finite also carries TENSE and MODALITY. TENSE locates every proposition somewhere in time in relation to the 'now' of a move, circumscribing a proposition either in present, past or future, and in terms of

210 Giacomo Figueredo

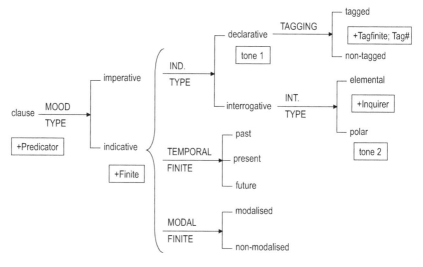

Figure 7.7 The system of INDICATIVE TYPE in BP

a speaker's assessment to what's being said – that is, in terms of MODALITY, since modal assessment is also part of enacting an exchange. Examples can be found in Table 7.6.

Table 7.6 *Finite 'from below' in relation to tense and verbal modality*

		Finite		Predicator	
		Tense		event	
non-modalised		present	está be-IND.PRS.3SG	abrindo open-GER	is opening
		past	estava be-IND.PST. IMPFV.3SG	abrindo open-GER	was opening
			tinha have-IND.PST. IMPFV.3SG	aberto open- PTCP	had opened
		future	vai will-IND.FUT.3SG	abrir open-INF	will open
modalised	modalisation	present	pode can-IND.PRS.3SG	abrir open-INF	can open (now)
	modulation		deve must-IND.PRS.3SG	abrir open-INF	must open (now)
	modalisation	past	pôde can-IND.PST.3SG	abrir open-INF	could open

Table 7.6 (cont.)

		Finite	Predicator	
		Tense	event	
modulation		devia must-IND.PST. IMPFV.3SG	ter aberto have-INF open-PTCP	must have opened
modalisation	future	poderá can-IND.FUT.3SG	abrir open-INF	can open (in the future)
modulation		deverá must-IND.FUT.3SG	abrir open-INF	must open (in the future)

We move now to an account of the Finite 'from above', relating it to discourse through the notions of validity, tags and responding moves.

A dialogue involving an exchange of information can be viewed as a negotiated process converting interactants' personal opinions into interpersonal 'shared knowledge'. That is, interlocutors 1 and 2 negotiate knowledge in their exchanges. In general terms, this negotiation preselects [proposition] from SPEECH FUNCTION and is organised by the grammar through resources such as MOOD, MODALISATION and ASSESSMENT. The types of exchange and their redundancies in moves and grammar are shaped so as to increase the chances for a speaker to enact their opinions, positions, values and feelings as shared by interlocutors. In this sense, the concept of 'validity' is interpersonal, since 'valid or not-valid' is an outcome of negotiation (cf. Halliday & Matthiessen, 2014, p. 138; Martin & Cruz, Chapter 5, this volume).

One of the resources used in BP to increase 'validity' through negotiation of a proposition is the system of TAGGING. The function of Tagfinite in BP is to nuance propositions (specifically of statements) – increasing their chance of being accepted. In BP, the Tagfinite copies at the end of the clause the features realised by the Finite function, except for polarity, which is inverted (Example 27).

(27) DAUGHTER Mãe   ø   vai   cab-er   ali?
              Mom   (the cake)   will-IND.PRS.3SG fit-INF   here
                     Subject   Finite   Predicator
              ng   ng   vg   adv.g
              'Mom, will the cake fit here?'

     MOTHER   Vai,   **não vai?**
              will-IND.FUT.3SG **not will-IND.FUT.3SG**
              Finite   **Tagfinite**
              vg
              'It will, won't it?'

The Finite performs another job in dialogue. When there is an exchange pattern of K2 realised by a question, realised in turn by a polar interrogative followed by

K1 realised by an answer realised in turn by a declarative, the Finite works as the expected realisation of a responding move. This could be seen in Example 27, where the Finite is picked up as the mother's answer to the daughter's question. In Example 28 we see another instance of the Finite being picked up as answer.

(28) (K2) Você não ia transfer-ir essa reunião?
You not would-IND-PST.IMPFV.3S postpone-INF this meeting
Subject Finite Predicator
ng adv.g vg ng
'Wouldn't you postpone this meeting?'

(K1) Eu ia
I would-IND-PST.IMPFV.3S
Subject Finite
ng vg
'I would.'

Note that the Subject is also picked up in Example 28. The Subject is also an interpersonal clause function. It is generated by the system of MODAL RESPONSIBILITY and it is important for more delicate options of indicative clauses as it cross-classifies with [indicative]. The Subject will be discussed in the next section.

7.3.2.1 MODAL RESPONSIBILITY *and the Subject* MOOD functions manage in broad terms 'a proposition about someone/something' or 'a proposal that must be carried out by someone'. The Subject realises the 'someone' or 'something' noted in these characterisations. In SFL, the general glossing for the meaning of Subject, in interpersonal terms, is 'modal responsibility'. Modal responsibility implies 'something by reference to which the proposition can be affirmed or denied' (Halliday & Matthiessen, 2014, p. 138) and the proposition can be (or not be) carried out.

When the perspective 'from above' is taken into account, the notion of responsibility starts at the unit of exchange, where speaker and addressee enact interlocutor types in discourse. These types are realised by the functions 1 and 2 and preselect SPEECH FUNCTION options, specifically the features [role: giving] and [role: demanding]. Different languages develop a range of strategies to manage these meanings (cf. all the other chapters in this volume and Martin, 2018). In the case of BP, these relationships are grammaticalised. So, the meanings of modal responsibility comprise a set of grammatical features organised as the system of MODAL RESPONSIBILITY.

In the previous section, we introduced the Subject in imperative clauses as the function realising modal responsibility in grammar. For imperative clauses, the Subject has the job of grammaticalising the roles of giving or demanding and the performance of an action. Indicative clauses need to insert a Subject for similar reasons. However, responsibility can be assigned to knowledge and information other than interlocutors and roles, since indicatives negotiate not only 'who is doing an action' but also the validity of certain information.

The Subject in BP is not a simple function when examined from round about. Rather it comprises co-selections of choices. There are structural differences between types of Subject, as well as more delicate options. Realisations vary depending on the degree of responsibility that is being enacted. MODAL RESPONSIBILITY has four subsystems and cross-classifies MOOD TYPE (which explains how the same function can realise both [imperative] and [declarative]).

Not all indicative clauses need a Subject. When an exchange involves only the anchoring of a proposition with reference to a move, the Finite alone realises [indicative]. Only more delicate options which require negotiation of responsibility need a Subject. This suggests that the least delicate terms for the system of MODAL RESPONSIBILITY are [+responsibility] and [-responsibility] realised by the insertion of a Subject or not.

The feature [-responsibility] is manifested in two situations. The first is the so-called meteorological clause (Example 29).

(29)   *Choveu*   *89.500 milímetros de água*
       rain-IND.PST.3SG   89,500 millimeters of water
       Finite/Predicator
       'It rained 89,500 millimetres.'

In Example 29, there is only a Finite (conflated with a Predicator) and no function grammaticalising responsibility for the raining. In this case, it is impossible in BP to assign any responsibility by inserting a Subject to this clause.

The second case, where there is no Subject in BP, is when there could be responsibility assigned (in other words, a Subject could have been inserted), but it was not because speakers might have considered responsibility irrelevant (as with MODALITY and ASSESSMENT, the system of MODAL RESPONSIBILITY is optional). For example, back in Text 1, there is an occurrence of [-responsibility] of this non-responsible type. In move 14 of Text 1, repeated here in Example 30, the mother asks:

(30)   Part-e   no meio   né   Ana
       cut-IND.PRS.3S in half   ASSENT   Ana
       Finite/Predicator   Positioner Vocative
       vg   ng   part.g   ng
       'Cut it in half, right, Ana?'

In Example 30, the mother is the person responsible for cutting the cake in half. In fact, she is holding a knife to the cake as she asks the question. However, this is enacted in language as if there is no responsibility assigned. Note that there is a K2 move realised by a question, realised in turn by an interrogative realised by a Finite, but there is no interpersonal element responsible for the proposition. In addition, the realisation 'from below' is a verbal group with a finite Event verb (*parte* 'cut-IND.PRS.3SG'). The verb is third person singular (she or it or he cuts); not first person (I cut). This configuration of discourse and grammar makes the meaning of 'she is not responsible for cutting', but that 'cutting the cake must happen'.

We will discuss another instance of [–responsibility] from Text 2. Text 2 is an excerpt extracted from an anecdote (here an oral monologue). The speaker is telling a story of how he and his brother became street vendors.

Text 2 [REC_FM_04]

(1) E nós chegamos lá por volta de 4 h da tarde.
(2) Abrimos a lona da caminhonete lá aí
(3) e começou a vender.
(4) E vendeu metade da carga até 8 h da noite

Text 2 [English]

(1) And we arrived there around 4 p.m.
(2) We set up the back of our truck
(3) and the selling happened.
(4) And the selling of half of our product happened by 8 p.m.

Clauses 1 and 2 have selected [responsible], realised by Subject realised in turn by a direct pronoun 'nós *(we)*' in clause 1 and Subject ellipsis in clause 2. In both cases there is finite verb agreement from the verbal group 'cheg-amos (arrive-IND.PST.1PL)' for clause 1 and 'abr-imos (open-IND.PST.1PL)' for clause 2. Responsibility can be traced back to the speaker and his brother – specifically, to how they got to the street market and set up their goods in the back of their truck (Examples 31 and 32).

(31) clause 1:
E   nós   cheg-amos   lá   por volta de 4 da tarde
And   1PL-DIRECT   arrive-IND.PST.1PL   there   around 4PM
           Subject: Responsible   Finite/Predicator
conj.g   ng   vg   adv.g   prep.phr
'And we arrived there at 4 p.m.'

(32) clause 2
Ø   abr-imos   a lona da caminhonete   lá
(we)-1PL-DIRECT   open-IND.PST.1PL   the canvas of.the truck there
(Subject: Responsible)
ng   vg   ng   adv.g
'We set up the back of our truck.'

7 Interpersonal Grammar in Brazilian Portuguese   215

Clauses 3 and 4 (Example 33) are different. There is no Subject, as shown in structure by the finite verb on the verbal groups '*começ-ou* (start-IND.PST.3SG)' and '*vend-eu* (sell-IND.PST.3S)' – third person singular instead of first person plural.

(33) clause 3
       e   começou a vender
       And
            start-IND-PST-3s to sell
            Finite/Predicator
       conj.g   vg complex
       'and the selling happened.'

(34) clause 4
       e   vendeu   metade da carga   até 8 h da noite
       And   half of.the product   until 8PM
            sell-IND-PST-3s
            Finite/Predicator
       conj.g   vg   ng   prep.phr
       'and the selling half of our product happened by 8 p.m.'

The system of MODAL RESPONSIBILITY has two basic features: [responsible] and [impersonal] at the next level of delicacy (see also Figure 7.8). The feature [responsible] is realised by a Subject that is responsible for the proposition or proposal (Example 35). Although this is a more delicate feature, it is by far the most frequent feature of BP.

(35) [responsible]:
       O seu pai   *com-e*   *muitas frituras*
       the your father   eat-IND.PRS.3SG   many fried.foods
       Subject Responsible   Finite/Predicator
       ng   vg   ng
       'Your father eats a lot of fried food.'

The last feature on the system is [impersonal] (Example 36). It is realised by an impersonal Subject, which in turn preselects indefinite, undetermined or

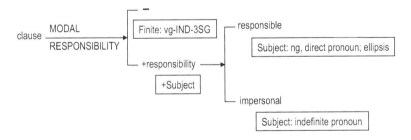

Figure 7.8 The system of MODAL RESPONSIBILITY in BP

general pronouns in the nominal group. Impersonal means the modal responsibility is assigned to a whole class.

(36)   [impersonal]: [REL_FM_44]
A gente	prefer-e	ir de carro pro trabalho do que andar a pé
We	prefer-IND.PRS.3SG	go by car to work then walk
Subject: Impersonal	Finite/Predicator	
ng	vg	ng

'We (everybody) prefer to drive than walk to work.'11

Along with MODAL RESPONSIBILITY there are other three subsystems realised by the Subject. They are PRESUMPTION, PERSON and POLITENESS. The entity realised through the Subject sometimes has to be recovered from the co-text or non-verbal context. Recoverability can be of two kinds: [explicit], when the identity of a Subject happens through reference; or [implicit], when its identity is understood through ellipsis.

In addition, the system of PERSON has two main options: [interactant] and [non-interactant]. These are related to the people who are enacting the exchanges as opposed to those who are not. The feature [interactant] opens two co-selective systems, INTERACTANT PERSON and POLITENESS, which have options for the speaker and the addressee as Subject. POLITENESS is only open for interactants since a speaker can be polite to the addressee, but not to non-interactants. The speaker can be polite to the addressee in two ways: 'playing up' the addressee, or 'playing down' the speaker.

A speaker 'plays up' the addressee when referring to them by using respectful (higher social status) nominal groups to realise Subject. In the system of POLITENESS, this selection is [polite: addressee]. It co-selects with [responsible] – see Example 37.

(37)   [COM_FD_01]
Esse dinheiro aqui	a senhora	compr-ou	alguma coisa	pra eles dois lá?
This money here	POLITE.FEM.2SG	buy-IND.PST.2SG	something	for they two there
	Subject	Finite/Predicator		
ng	ng	vg	ng	prep.phr

'As for this money here, did you buy something for those two people there?'

Here, the neutral second person pronoun '*você* (you)', the regular pronoun for addressee, is replaced by '*a senhora* (literally 'the owner')' – a politeness second person pronoun that assigns respect (higher social status) to the addressee, thus 'playing them up'.

Alternatively, a speaker may 'play themselves down' by taking away some of the speaker's responsibility as Subject for a proposition for which full responsibility might sound arrogant or self-promoting. The selection is [polite: speaker] and it co-selects with [non-responsible]. It is thus realised by elliptical first person speaker followed by a verbal group with a third person finite verb ⊘(1P)^vg-3SG.

(38)   [REC_ED_05]:
Sosõ	ø	**pod-e**	peg-ar	mais um Martini?
Sosõ	(I)	**can-IND.PRS.3SG**	get-INF	more one Martini
	Subject	**Finite**	Predicator	
ng	ng	**vg**	ng	prep.phr

'Sosõ, can I have another Martini?'

The way Subject is realised in Example 38 is a polite realisation of unequal status; the person asking for the drink deploys a [polite: speaker], realised by (I) ∅^pode-3SG. The meaning can be glossed next to literally as 'Sosõ, can another Martini be had?' (Figure 7.9).

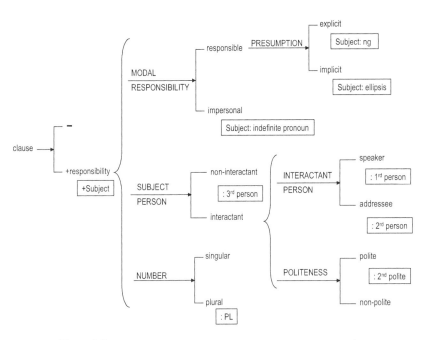

Figure 7.9 MODAL RESPONSIBILITY, PRESUMPTION, PERSON and POLITENESS

7.3.3   ASSESSMENT *and the Positioner: Modal Particles*

The system of ASSESSMENT is realised by the Positioner. A Positioner is the clause function preselecting modal particles at group rank; it enacts two complementary interpersonal roles in the clause: (i) it indicates how the clause should be exchanged in terms of agreement, assent, exhortation, etc.; and (ii) it is picked up by the addressee as a means of reaching consensus in exchanges. On many occasions the Positioner alone constitutes a responding move.

218 *Giacomo Figueredo*

Structurally, the Positioner tends to appear at the end of the clause. However, it is not unusual to find it in other places in the clause, often immediately following another element of structure (Subject, Predicator, etc.), which the speaker wants to negotiate more specifically. In phonological terms, it typically comes as a post-tonic tail. Features in the ASSESSMENT system cross-classify MOOD TYPE. Since it is negotiating consensus, it also takes into account three types of move: initial, responding expected and responding discretionary (Table 7.7) (cf. Figueredo, 2015).

Explanations and examples of classes realising Positioner are shown in this section, including indicative translations (this is a challenging area of study as far as rendering the meaning of BP in English is concerned; cf. Martin & Cruz, Chapter 5, this volume, on ASSESSMENT in Tagalog).

Figure 7.10 shows the system network for ASSESSMENT. The interdependencies with MOOD (as indicated in Table 7.7) are shown in Figure 7.11.

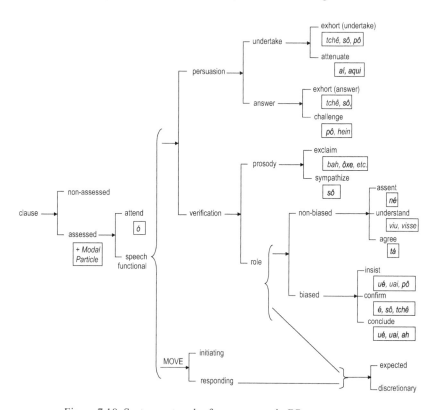

Figure 7.10 System network of ASSESSMENT in BP

Attend positions the listener to focus on a single move. This choice is the only one not constrained by MOOD choices and is available in both propositions or proposals (Example 39).

Table 7.7 Cross-classification of MOOD and ASSESSMENT in PB

MOOD type	ASSESSMENT type	Initial	Responding Expected	Responding Discretionary
declarative	attend	ó, ah (short)	tá	não
	assent	né, né não	é, ah é,	né não, né
	agree	tá	tá; ah tá	não; ah não
	insist	tchê, ué, sô, pô, né, uai	ah é; ah tá; tá	não sô; não ué; não tchê
	conclude	ué, uai, ah	é, é ué, é uai	ãh (short)
	understand	viu, visse	viu	não
	confirm	hein, é	tá (short), é	tá (long)
	sympathise	sô	—	—
	exclaim	bah, nó, uai, oxe, pô, tchê, ah (long) etc.	—	—
interrog. polar	confirm	é, sô, tchê	é	não
interrog. elemental	exhort	tchê, sô, pô, hein, né	answer	disclaim
	challenge			
imperative	exhort to undertake	sô, tchê, pô (order) tá, viu (request)	undertake	refuse
imperative or interrogative	attenuate to undertake	ai, aqui	undertake	refuse
	attenuate to accept	tchê, sô, ai, aqui	accept	reject

(39) Ó,   depois   eu   falo   com ele
    ATTEND   later   I   speak   with him
    Positioner   Subject Finite/Predicator
    '*Listen to me*, I'll talk to him later.'

Assent requires the listener to take the speaker's proposition as 'shared knowledge' (i.e. not negotiable) and allow the speaker to carry on (whether they agree with the speaker or not) – as in Example 40.

(40)   (A) Ele   me   falou   que ele tinha namorada
            He   me   told   that he had girlfriend
            Subject   Finite/Predicator
            'He told me that he had a girlfriend.'

       (B) Agora então par-a   de sair   com ele né?
            Now   so   stop-IMP.2SG   of going.out with he   ASSENT
                          Predicator   Positioner
            'So now you should stop going out with him, *eh*?'

Agree involves the speaker asking the listener to share knowledge and opinions – as in Example 41.

(41)   Esse bolo   não   vai   ficar   bonito igual o outro   tá?
       This cake   not   will   come.out   pretty as the other   AGREE
       Subject   Finite Predicator   Positioner
       'This cake won't come out as pretty as the other one, *don't you agree*?'

Insist places an onus on the listener to assess the proposition the same way the speaker does. It increases the chance of the listener letting the speaker retaining his speaking role (Example 42).

(42)   (A) Não   deve   ser   para ligar pra elas
            Not   should   be   to call to them
                   Finite   Predicator
            'We should not call them.'

       (B) Eu   acho   que é sim sô
            I   think   that is so INSIST
            Subject   Finite/Predicator   Positioner
            'I *really do* think we should.'

Conclude operates by encouraging the listener to arrive at the same conclusion as the listener about a proposition, but in terms of the speaker's values and knowledge. In other words, the speakers' values and knowledge about the proposition are considered true (interpersonally) and should not be questioned, building up to a conclusion (Example 43).

(43)   DAUGHTER Mãe   ø   vai   caber   alí?
                 Mom   (the cake)   will-IND-FUT-3s   fit   here
                        Subject   Finite   Predicator
                 'Mom, will the cake fit here?'

7 Interpersonal Grammar in Brazilian Portuguese 221

MOTHER	Vai,	não vai?
	will	not will
	Finite	Tagfinite
	'It will, won't it?'	
DAUGHTER	Não	ué
	Not	CONCLUDE
		Positioner
	'*Obviously* not.'	

Understand requires the listener to agree with the speaker. More particularly, the listener is required to understand the speaker's point of view about the proposition and assert they understood (Example 44).

(44)
(A) | Vocês | nunca mais | volt-am | pro lado de lá do rio | viu? |
|---|---|---|---|---|
| You | never more | go-IND.PRS.3PL | to.the other side of the river | UNDERSTAND |
| Subject | | Finite/Predicator | | Positioner |

'You don't ever go to the other side of the river, *do you understand*?'

(B) Viu
UNDERSTAND
Positioner
'*We understand*.'

Confirm is chosen when the speaker builds a proposition in such a way that the responding move is the expected option. It needs the listener to confirm the speaker's proposition (Example 45).

(45)
PROFESSOR	Você	grav-a	as minhas aulas	é?
	You	record-IND.PRS.2SG	the my lectures	CONFIRM
	Subject	Finite/Predicator		Positioner

'Do you record my lectures, *is this correct*?'

STUDENT	Grav-o
	record-IND.PRS.1SG
	Finite
	'I do.'

Sympathise is chosen when the speaker needs the listener to assess the speaker's emotional state in relation to the proposition. It increases the chances of an expected responding move that takes into account the emotions of the speaker (Example 46).

(46) | Hmm menino | aquilo | me | deix-ou | enfezado um tanto sô | |
|---|---|---|---|---|---|
| Oh boy | that | me | make-IND.PST.3SG | angry a lot | SYMPATHISE |
| | Subject | | Finite/Predicator | | Positioner |

'Oh boy, that made me really angry, *can you see how I feel*?'

Exclaim signals affect (Example 47).

(47)   Oxente   quem   tá   lig-ando   pra isso?
        EXCLAIM   who   be-IND-PRS-3S   care-GER   about this
        Positioner   Subject   Finite   Predicator
        '*Oh gosh!* Who cares about this?'

Exhort is selected when the speaker needs the listener to 'do something' (i.e. being the primary interlocutor of an exchange) by either undertaking a command or giving information (Example 48). It encourages the listener, so the chances of success of the negotiation are increased. It may also involve a challenge for the listener to give information when the speaker needs confirmation on some shared information or obvious answer (Example 49).

(48)   Exhort to undertake:
        Sob-e   logo   nesse carro   tchê
        Get-IMP.2SG   already   in.this car   EXHORT
        Predicator   Positioner
        '*C'mon just* get in this car *already.*'

(49)   Challenge:
        (A)   Teu trabalho   é   curar esses desgarrado
             Your job   be-IND-PRS-3S   to fix broken people
             Subject   Finite/Predicator
             'Your job is to fix broken people.'

        (B)   E   tu   ach-a   que eu to pronto   tchê?
             And   you   think-IND-PRS-2S   that I am ready   CHALLENGE
             Subject   Finite/Predicator   Positioner
             'So you think I am ready, *do you now?*'

Attenuate mitigates commands, increasing the chance of an expected responding move (Example 50).

(50)   Attenuate to undertake
        Me   d-á   uma faca   aí
        Me   give-IMP.2SG   a knife   ATTENUATE
        Predicator   Positioner
        'Hand me that knife, *please.*'

In Figure 7.11 we present a general system network for MOOD in Brazilian Portuguese, including information on the conditioning of co-selections from MODAL RESPONSIBILITY, MOOD TYPE and ASSESSMENT.

7.4   Conclusion

Drawing on systemic functional linguistic theory and description (cf. Halliday, 1978; Martin, 1992; Eggins & Slade, 1997; Martin & Rose, 2007; Caffarel

7 Interpersonal Grammar in Brazilian Portuguese

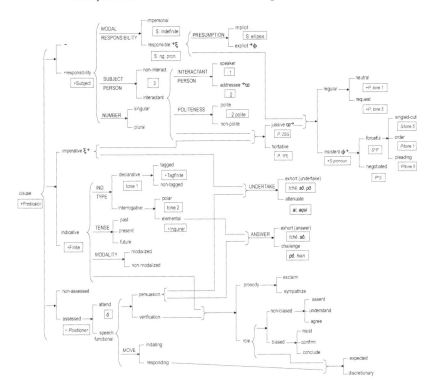

Figure 7.11 The system of MOOD in BP

et al., 2004; Teruya et al., 2007) of the role played by language in creating and maintaining relationships through the negotiation of interpersonal meanings, we have provided an interpretation of the grammatical resources responsible for realising exchanges in BP. We began 'from above', examining how speaker and addressee enact their social relations as these are encoded in language through NEGOTIATION and SPEECH FUNCTION. Then, we described how these discourse systems are grammatically realised by MOOD and ASSESSMENT.

The methodological framework for this volume was fundamental to the description. Approaching spontaneous language 'from above' enabled us to explain which meanings are at risk in exchange, and axial reasoning gave us the tools for describing how interpersonal grammar manages these meanings. Had we worked from an enclosed clause grammar perspective – without trinocularity or axial reasoning – we would not have been able to interpret how language makes meanings that might be generally glossed as 'responsibility', 'validity' or 'reaching consensus'; nor could they be accounted for in terms of their grammaticalisation.

The approach from 'round about' showed how speaker and addressee negotiate 'responsibility' by selections in the system of MODAL RESPONSIBILITY, which sets up options for the Subject – including the features [presumption], [person] and [politeness]. The meaning of 'validity' is related to the function of Finite, which carries primary tense and modality, circumscribing propositions in time related to the 'now' of the speech event; these are crucial to the system of MOOD TYPE. 'Reaching consensus' is the kind of meaning made by resources in the system of ASSESSMENT and its realisation as Positioner. The Positioner is deployed to position addressees to, in some sense, assent to the speaker's assessment of their initial role in a given a proposition or proposal – to confirm it, to be convinced by it, to agree with it, to understand it, to be exhorted by it and so on.

Together with other chapters in this volume (in particular, Zhang; Wang; Martin & Cruz; and Rose: Chapters 3, 4, 5 and 6, respectively), this description of BP suggests that languages have a far richer repertoire for enacting social relations than is afforded by the MOOD TYPE systems outlined in accounts of the grammar of many languages. A great deal of semiotic labour is accomplished by interpersonal systems in the grammar; however, it is only by integrating relations between strata that these can be observed and fully accounted for in a description. It is interstratal relations that enable us to explain the interpersonally charged workings of grammar.

References

Caffarel, A. (2006). *A Systemic Functional Grammar of French: From Grammar to Discourse*. London: Continuum.
Caffarel, A., Martin, J. R. & Matthiessen, C. M. I. M., eds., (2004), *Language Typology: A Functional Perspective*. Amsterdam/Philadelphia: John Benjamins.
Cagliari, L. C. (1981). *Elementos de Fonética do Português Brasileiro* [Elements of Phonetics in Brazilian Portuguese]. Unpublished PhD Thesis. Institute of Language Studies. State University of Campinas.
Eggins, S. & Slade, D. (1997). *Analysing Casual Conversation*. London: Cassell.
Fawcett, R. P. (1988). What Makes a 'Good' System Network Good? In J. D. Benson and W. S. Greaves, eds., *Systemic Perspectives on Discourse*. Norwood: Ablex, pp. 1–28.
Figueredo, G. (2011). *Introdução ao Perfil Metafuncional do Português Brasileiro: Contribuições para os Estudos Multilíngues* [Introduction to the Metafunctional Profile of Brazilian Portuguese: Contributions to Multilingual Studies]. Unpublished PhD Thesis, Faculdade de Letras, Universidade Federal de Minas Gerais, Belo Horizonte, Brazil.

Figueredo, G. (2014). Uma metodologia de perfilação gramatical sistêmica baseada em corpus [A Corpus-Based Methodolody for Systemic Grammar Profiling]. *Letras & Letras*, *30*(2), 17–45.
Figueredo, G. (2015). A Systemic Functional Description of Modal Particles in Brazilian Portuguese: The System of ASSESSMENT. *Alfa*, *59*(2), 275–302.
Gleason, H. A. (1965). *Linguistics and English Grammar*. New York: Holt, Rinehart & Winston.
Halliday, M. A. K. (1961). Categories of the Theory of Grammar, *Word*, 17(3),241–92.
Halliday, M. A. K. (1977). Text as a Semantic Choice in Social Contexts. In T. A. van Dijk and J. S. Petöfi, eds., *Grammars and Descriptions*. Berlin/New York: Walter de Gruyter, pp. 176–225.
Halliday, M. A. K. (1978). *Language as Social Semiotic: The Social Interpretation of Language and Meaning*. London: Edward Arnold.
Halliday, M. A. K. (1994). The Construction of Knowledge and Value in the Grammar of Scientific Discourse, with Reference to Charles Darwin's *The Origin of Species*. In M. Coulthard, ed., *Advances in Written Text Analysis*. London/New York: Routledge, pp. 136–56.
Halliday, M. A. K. (1996). On Grammar and Grammatics. In J. Webster, ed., (2002), *On Grammar, Vol. 1, The Collected Works of M. A. K. Halliday*. London: Continuum, pp. 384–417.
Halliday, M. A. K. & Greaves, W. S. (2008). *Intonation in the Grammar of English*. London: Equinox.
Halliday, M. A. K. & Matthiessen, C. M. I. M. (1999). *Construing Experience through Meaning: a Language-based Approach to Cognition*. London: Continuum.
Halliday, M. A. K. & Matthiessen, C. M. I. M. (2014). *Halliday's Introduction to Functional Grammar*. London: Edward Arnold.
Hao, J. (2020). *Analysing Scientific Discourse from a Systemic Functional Linguistic Perspective: A Framework for Exploring Knowledge Building in Biology*. London: Routledge.
Martin, J. R. (1992). *English Text: System and Structure*. Philadelphia/Amsterdam: John Benjamins.
Martin, J. R. (2018). Interpersonal Meaning: Systemic Functional Linguistics Perspective. *Functions of Language*, *25*(1), 2–19.
Martin, J. R. & Cruz, P. (2018). Interpersonal Grammar of Tagalog: A Systemic Functional Perspective. *Functions of Language*, *25*(1), 54–96.
Martin, J. R. & Quiroz, B. (2020). Functional Language Typology: A Discourse Semantic Perspective. In J. R. Martin, Y. Doran and G. Figueredo, eds., *Systemic Functional Language Description: Making Meaning Matter*. London: Routledge, 189–237.
Martin, J. R. & Rose, D. (2007). *Working with Discourse: Meaning beyond the Clause*, 2nd ed., London/New York: Continuum.
Martin, J. R., Wang, P. & Zhu, Y. (2013). *Systemic Functional Grammar: A Next Step into the Theory – Axial Relations*. Beijing: Higher Education Press.
Quiroz, B. (2013). *The Interpersonal and Experiential Grammar of Chilean Spanish: Towards a Principled Systemic-Functional Description Based on Axial Argumentation*. Unpublished PhD Dissertation, University of Sydney, Sydney, Australia.

Quiroz, B. (2015). La cláusula como movimiento interactivo: una perspectiva semántico-discursiva de la gramática interpersonal del español [The Clause as an Interactive Movement: A Discourse-Semantic Perspective to Spanish Interpersonal Grammar]. *Documentação de Estudios em Linguística Teorica e Aplicada – DELTA*, 31(1), 261–301. DOI: http://dx.doi.org/10.1590/0102-445023762456121953.

Quiroz, B. (2018). Negotiating Interpersonal Meanings: Reasoning about MOOD. *Functions of Language*, 25(1), 135–63. DOI: https://doi.org/10.1075/fol.17013.qui.

Rose, D. (2005). Narrative and the Origins of Discourse: Construing Experience in Stories around the World. *Australian Review of Applied Linguistics (Series S19)*, 151–73.

Teruya, K., Akerejola, E., Anderson, T., Caffarel, A., Lavid, J., Matthiessen, C., Petersen, U., Patpong, P. & Smedegaard, F. (2007). Typology of MOOD: A Text-Based and System-Based Functional view. In R. Hasan, C. M. I. M. Matthiessen and J. Webster, eds., *Continuing Discourse on Language: A Functional Perspective*, Vol. 2. London: Equinox, pp. 859–920.

Wang, P. (2020). Axial Argumentation and Cryptogrammar in Interpersonal Grammar: A Case Study of Classical Tibetan MOOD. In J. R. Martin, Y. Doran and G. Figueredo, eds., *Systemic Functional Language Description: Making Meaning Matter*. London: Routledge, 73–101.

Zhang, D. (2020). Axial Argumentation below the Clause: The Verbal Group in Khorchin Mongolian. In J.R. Martin, Y. J. Doran and Giacomo Figueredo, eds., *Systemic Functional Language Description: Making Meaning Matter*. New York/London: Routledge, pp. 35–72.

8 Interpersonal Grammar in British Sign Language

Luke A. Rudge

8.1 Introduction

The interpersonal metafunction has been studied in substantial typological depth from the perspective of SFL, as evidenced by the numerous publications covering this area (e.g. Caffarel et. al., 2004), including the various chapters presented in this volume. The present chapter extends the conversation on the interpersonal metafunction by adding another language to the current literature base – British Sign Language (BSL). Unlike the other chapters in this volume, BSL does not call on the use of written elements (although it may be glossed in an analytical fashion, as used in this chapter) or spoken elements (i.e. the oral-aural modality is not employed). Rather, BSL operates in the visual-spatial modality, relying primarily on the use of embodied articulators and space in order to communicate meaning. In spite of BSL being a natural language, its study – and indeed the study of other sign languages around the world – from systemic functional perspectives is fledgling (e.g. Johnson, 1996; Rudge, 2015, 2018).

This chapter begins by introducing BSL in terms of how meaning is produced, focusing specifically on the roles played by the hands, the upper body and the space in front of a signer. Put another way, the plane of expression in BSL is explored to a level that will permit readers who are unfamiliar with sign languages to understand basic tenets of signed communication. This is followed by a brief discussion on the distinction between the planes of expression and content in BSL, and the difficulties that ensue when trying to find a distinct division between these planes (i.e. the indeterminacy of associating productive components to the lexicogrammatical or phonological stratum).[1] The interpersonal systems of MOOD, POLARITY

---

[1] Terms such as 'phonology' and 'intonation' are used frequently in this work, and may appear to be misnomers when describing a language in the visual-spatial modality. As in other contemporary sign language research, these terms are intended in a modality-independent way. For instance, 'phonology' is understood as 'the level of grammatical analysis where primitive

and MODALITY are then exemplified through lexicogrammatical analyses of two dialogic BSL interactions, wherein a Predicator function is highlighted and argued for at various points. Following schematisations of these systems, a full interpersonal analysis of the dialogic interactions is provided, before finishing the chapter with a summary of where knowledge in this area currently stands and how it can develop in the future.

8.2 A Primer on BSL Production

British Sign Language is the main sign language used in the United Kingdom and one of nearly 150 recognised sign languages in use worldwide (Eberhard et al., 2019). It is a naturally evolving semiotic system and has been subject to developments from numerous forces for many centuries (Schembri et al., 2018; cf. 'designed' systems such as Makaton, and those that intertwine with and/or depend on elements of a spoken language such as Sign Supported English; see Rendel et al., 2018).

BSL differs from the other languages presented in this volume in two principal ways. Firstly, BSL engages the visual-spatial modality (Baker, 2016) in order to communicate meaning between its users. Understandably, given that BSL is used largely by the UK deaf community,[2] it calls on the use of embodied articulators that are visually salient (i.e. the upper body, hands and eyes) and the use of the area in front of a signer – the signing space – rather than employing the typical apparatus of a spoken language (i.e. vocal cords, ears, etc.). While other languages do often use the visual-spatial modality to produce gestures either alongside or in place of spoken expression (i.e. embodied paralanguage; see, e.g. Harrison, 2018; and Hao & Hood, 2019), languages such as BSL do not have recourse to the oral-aural modality. In other words, while a language such as English may choose to combine modalities, BSL is restricted in this regard.

Secondly, BSL has no written form of expression. While this has in no way impeded the use and transmission of BSL over time, a challenge arises regarding the recording of BSL in a format that suits typical methods of knowledge dissemination. Academic literature focusing on the phonological and/or phonetic components of signs, for instance, use written symbols to denote articulatory information. These symbol sets include Stokoe Notation, the Hamburg

---

structural units without meaning are combined to create an infinite number of meaningful utterances' (Brentari, 2002, p. 39), thereby removing a direct association with sound.

[2] Previous works have employed Woodward's (1975) 'D/d' distinction: 'Deaf' to represent those who identify as being part of a cultural, social and linguistic minority; and 'deaf' to represent a more clinical definition and those who do not see themselves as part of the Deaf community. However, these binary terms are not representative of the wide range of identities viewed from intersectional perspectives, such as those noted by Kusters et al. (2017). As such, the author follows the latter work by adopting 'deaf' as the primary term.

Notation System (HamNoSys) and, more recently, the Typannot Approach (Bianchini et al., 2018). However, these systems are rarely used in daily life by BSL users, and are not particularly suitable for use when focusing on higher linguistic strata (i.e. within the content plane). In these latter instances – as is the case for the present chapter – English glosses are used. This has its benefits (e.g. machine readability in digital/corpus analysis; see Johnston & Schembri, 2013 for discussion) and drawbacks (e.g. deciding how a sign should be split and then glossed into a language in a different modality; see Fenlon, Cormier & Schembri, 2015 for discussion) – often resulting in an impression akin to that noticed by Hole (2007), who suggests that 'the analysis and interpretation of [transcribed sign language is] as one might analyze and interpret a silhouette' (p. 703). Nevertheless, at the time of writing, English glossing is the most suitable method in this academic context and conventions for doing so are in active development (see Cormier et al., 2017).

Similarities also exist between spoken and sign languages. For instance, the production of meaning in BSL occurs in a linear sequence over time (i.e. logogenetically; see Matthiessen et al., 2010), and while sign languages may demonstrate a 'clear preference for simultaneous elements' (Johnston, 1996, p.3), this is not so different to what is found in spoken language production. Meaning in BSL can be made by concatenating manual configurations (i.e. as syllables are spoken one after another) and by simultaneous productions of various embodied articulators in different areas in front of or around the signer (i.e. not dissimilar to a combination of speech, co-speech gesture and intonation patterns). Sign languages, though, have the capability to produce more than one sign at a time, which may be argued as being analogous with being able to speak two distinct syllables clearly at any given moment. This latter kind of productive potential is due to the availability of multiple, separable embodied articulators (e.g. the use of two hands independently).

8.2.1   Articulating BSL

In terms of phonology (i.e. within Hjelmslev's expression plane), BSL production may be split into three broad categories: manual, non-manual and spatio-kinetic. The following is intended as an overview of these categories rather than an extensive insight into the productive capabilities of BSL. Further information can be found in introductory literature that focuses on sign linguistics (e.g. Baker et al., 2016) but what is presented here is sufficient in order for the remainder of the chapter to be understood.

Given that this chapter presents a written representation of a language in the visual-spatial modality which does not dispose of a writing system, conventions have been imported from sign language glossing used in sign linguistics (e.g. Cormier et al., 2017). In addition, the Systemic Functional glossing

conventions (2018) are currently such that the written representation of a language in the visual-spatial modality cannot yet be fully achieved. As such, a basic 'hybrid of conventions' is presented here:
- UPPERCASE words represent an English gloss of a BSL sign (with hyphens between uppercase words representing one sign that requires more than one English word to describe what is produced);
- 'CA:' represents constructed action, wherein the signer 'mimetically represent[s] a referent's actions, utterances or feelings' (Fenlon et al., 2018, p. 89);
- 'DC:' represents a depicting construction, wherein the signer uses a combination of articulators to represent entities, handling and interaction, among other things (see Cormier et al., 2012);[3]
- *Italic* words represent the non-manual and/or kinetic elements of a sign (with the accompanying underlined area identifying the scope of these elements across manual signs);
- 'PT:PRO' indicates a pointing sign that references:
  ○ '1' (the signer); '2' (an addressee); '3' (other);
  ○ 'SG' (singular); 'PL' (plural);
- Subscript words or letters represent a location in the signing space allocated to a referent. Hyphens between subscript and uppercase words represent signs that involve movement from a location (if the subscript word is before the uppercase word) and/or to a location (if the subscript word is after the uppercase word);
- '++' represents the repetition of a manual sign;
- Arrows represent a signer's eyebrow position (e.g. ↑ as 'raised').

8.2.1.1 Manual Components The hands play a core role in the production of BSL, but they do not operate alone. A signer's hands typically produce experiential meaning which is then accompanied by other embodied components of the production, discussed later in this chapter.

A manual sign can be split into four phonological parameters: *handshape*, *orientation*, *location* and *movement*. Each of the parameters is explained in this section, and a visual example of each is presented in Figure 8.1.

Handshape concerns the configuration of the fingers on each hand, taking into account which fingers are 'selected' (i.e. extended) and if these fingers are bent or curved at any joints (see Fenlon et al., 2018). For instance, a manual sign wherein the thumb is selected and extended without any bending or curvature (i.e. a typical 'thumbs up' configuration) can mean GOOD, and

---

[3] The glosses of depicting constructions in this chapter do not wholly follow the conventions provided in Cormier et al. (2017): the current glosses represent a contextualised translation rather than identifying specific primes or proforms. This was chosen for ease of reader understanding, but the author accepts that the glosses are not without issue.

8 Interpersonal Grammar in British Sign Language 231

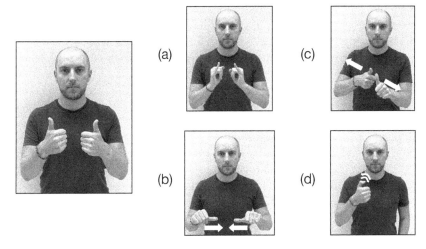

Figure 8.1 Differences in manual parameters creating variation from GOOD (left) to BAD (a), BRIEF (b), COMPANY (c) and ELEVEN (d)

a manual sign where only the pinkie finger is selected and extended without any bending or curvature can mean BAD.

Orientation concerns the direction in which the fingers and the palm are pointing. For example, variation in the orientation of GOOD to where the palms face towards the floor can produce BRIEF.

Location is the parameter regarding where the sign is produced relative to the signer's body, such as to the left or right of the face, near the neck, in front of the chest and so on. Using GOOD as a base sign again, a change in the location of the hands can produce FACTORY, as seen in Figure 8.1.

Finally, *movement* incorporates two subtypes: the movement path of the hand overall and movements that occur within the configuration of the hand (see van der Kooij & Crasborn, 2016). Path movement can be seen in BRIEF and FACTORY indicated by the arrows in Figure 8.1 (images [a] and [c]), and an internal movement within GOOD can produce ELEVEN.[4]

8.2.1.2 Non-manual Components As the four manual components combine to create experiential meaning, co-produced non-manual features serve to complement, expand and sometimes clarify these meanings. Non-manual components generally encompass facial articulators (e.g. the mouth, eyes,

---

[4] BSL is subject to substantial regional variation, particularly with numbers. ELEVEN as presented here is found in use around Bristol, although it is also noted to occur in other regions of the UK including Birmingham and Cardiff. Other regions will express ELEVEN in different ways (see Fenlon et al., 2014, and Stamp et al., 2014).

eyebrows, etc.) although other elements of the upper body are also included in this regard, such as the orientation and tilt of the head and torso (see Mapson, 2015). For brevity, an overview of the mouth as a non-manual component in BSL will be presented here, although further non-manual features will be called on and explained where necessary in later sections.

The mouth can be used in two manners in BSL: as *mouthing* and as *mouth gesture*. *Mouthing* can be used to accompany the four above-mentioned manual parameters of a sign to assist in the disambiguation of signs that realise different experiential meanings but have identical manual configurations (i.e. manual homonyms; cf. Giustolisi et al., 2017). This is performed by the signer mouthing the English word on the lips as the manual sign is produced. This helps, for instance, to distinguish between BATTERY and UNCLE (Woll, 2013). *Mouth gesture,* on the other hand, can assist in terms of adding gradations of lexical meaning (i.e. relating to APPRAISAL; see Martin & White, 2005). For example, an inflation of the cheeks accompanying BIG contributes to the sense of VAST; puckered lips (produced at the same time as lowered eyebrows and squinting eyes) while signing ANGRY contributes to the sense of FURIOUS; and WRITE accompanied by slightly protruding lips contributes to the sense of WRITE-WITH-EASE.

8.2.1.3 Spatio-Kinetic Components The production of manual and non-manual components occurs within the signing space: the area in front of the signer acting as the 'medium' in which meaning is expressed. These components relate to the manual phonological parameter of *movement* but differ with respect to what they realise. In general, spatio-kinetic components include the *speed* of BSL production, the *placement* of referents and the *interaction* between hands and referents.

Speed refers to the pace of the sign's production or a part of therein. An increase in the speed of production, for example, can alter aspects such as the abruptness of an action: if TAKE were produced with a faster articulation, it might instead be glossed as SNATCH.

Placement refers to the use of the signing space to identify and 'place' referents so that they may be referred to again later in the production. For example, a signer may sign CHURCH and then use a pointing sign to situate CHURCH somewhere in the signing space. The signer may then refer back to CHURCH by pointing to its ascribed location rather than having to sign CHURCH again.

Additionally, other signs can be linked with this placement: GO coupled with a path movement towards the area where CHURCH was placed would mean GO-TO-CHURCH. This latter example relates to the final spatio-kinetic component of *interaction*, or, how the hands and/or referents in the signing space are used together. An example of both hands interacting

8 Interpersonal Grammar in British Sign Language   233

Figure 8.2 Two depicting constructions in BSL – DC:PAPERS-SIDE-BY-SIDE (left) and DC:PILE-OF-PAPER (right)

in different ways to alter meaning can be seen in the use of a flat handshape to represent flat objects (i.e. classifier handshapes or 'proforms'; see Pfau, 2016) such as paper. If both hands – flat and with the palms towards the ground – are placed in front of the signer, this could indicate DC:PAPERS-SIDE-BY-SIDE. However, if either hand were to be placed on top of the other one, this could then change the meaning to DC:PILE-OF-PAPER (see Figure 8.2).

8.2.2   Expression versus Content Planes

Taking these three components into account, we can begin to look more closely at BSL production and, more specifically, the amount of semiotic labour that is realised within and across these components, including the division of this labour between the planes of expression and content. One way to investigate this is to consider what a lexicogrammatical rank scale for BSL may look like in terms of its structure and constitution (see Rudge, 2020, for further discussion on the rank scale of BSL).

The following demonstrates the lexicogrammatical rank scale of BSL with a simple clause which may be translated as 'The student is thinking hard': STUDENT PT:PRO3SG CA:THINK-HARD (see Figure 8.3).

234 Luke A. Rudge

Table 8.1 *An example of the lexicogrammatical rank scale of BSL*

clause		[STUDENT	PT:PRO3SG	CA:THINK-HARD]
group		[STUDENT	PT:PRO3SG]	[CA:THINK-HARD]
word		[STUDENT]	[PT:PRO3SG]	[CA:THINK-HARD]
morpheme	manual	STUDENT	PT:PRO	THINK
	non-manual	'Student'	–	furrowed brows; squinting eyes
	spatio-kinetic	–	3	repeated path movement

Figure 8.3 'The student is thinking hard' / STUDENT PT:PRO3SG CA: THINK-HARD

The clause can be split into two groups – a nominal group (STUDENT PT: PRO3SG) and a verbal group (CA:THINK-HARD) – thereby providing a group rank. In turn, these groups may be split into three signs – STUDENT, PT:PRO3SG and CA:THINK-HARD – thereby providing a word rank (with 'word' used in its systemic functional sense – a rank in grammar – rather than suggesting that sign languages use 'words'; see Matthiessen, Teruya and Lam, 2010). Rather than segmenting the gloss of a sign in a linear fashion, as is often seen in spoken language analysis, the embodied components that both form and accompany the manual production, thereby producing the full content of the sign, need to be considered. In this case: STUDENT is composed of the manual sign and the silent mouthing of the word 'student'; PT:PRO3SG is composed of a pointing sign and a location in the signing space; and CA:THINK-HARD is composed of a manual sign THINK and various non-manual and spatio-kinetic elements to represent the notion of 'thinking hard'.

For ease of written representation, the morpheme rank in Table 8.1 is split three ways to exemplify the composition of what is presented at word rank (rather than implying a hierarchical relationship within the morpheme rank). For example, the pointing sign PT:PRO3SG needs the manual component ('PT: PRO') to be combined with the spatial referent ('3'), otherwise the lexical content is not fully represented. Put another way, a pointing sign without a spatial referent would be paradoxical: it is not possible to point without the point having a target. The case is similar for the other two manual signs: if their non-manual or spatio-kinetic values were absent from the scale, then the rank scale would be incomplete as the content of the rank above is not fully accounted for in the rank below.

However, another facet of BSL production must also be considered. Looking again at Figure 8.3, there are embodied parts of the production that appear to be absent from the rank scale in Table 8.1. Specifically, the eyebrows are raised during the production of STUDENT and PT:PRO3SG but these non-manual components are not accounted for in the rank scale. The eyebrows are well-studied across sign languages (e.g. De Vos et al., 2009; Manrique, 2016; Salazar-García, 2018, inter alia) and their position (e.g. high, low or neutral/unmarked) when co-articulated with manual signs can realise various meanings. In the current example, the furrowed brows in CA:THINK-HARD add to the extent or intensity of the thought process (i.e. part of the ideational meaning). The raised eyebrows co-occurring with STUDENT and PT:PRO3SG, however, are argued to realise another kind of meaning in the clause, namely textual meaning (i.e. the Theme, see Rudge, 2018). Put another way, at the start of the clause the eyebrows function prosodically (i.e. in the phonological stratum) whereas during CA:THINK-HARD they realise experiential meaning (i.e. in the lexicogrammatical stratum). The eyebrows, therefore, are not restricted to one kind of semiosis and their form will not immediately relate to a specific function if viewed in isolation.

To briefly summarise, then, an initial distinction may be hypothesised. All manual signs (content) are produced by phonological components (expression) as discussed at the start of this section. If the non-manual and/or spatio-kinetic productions that co-occur with manual signs are integral to the experiential meaning of the sign, they operate on the plane of content and are thus represented in the lexicogrammatical rank scale. Otherwise, if non-manual and/or spatio-kinetic productions co-occur across a series of signs (i.e. prosodically) and realise meanings outside experiential concerns (i.e. textual, logical or interpersonal), the plane of expression is implicated. These parts of the production do not appear in the lexicogrammatical rank scale because they are situated in the phonological stratum.

A challenge therefore becomes apparent when trying to delineate non-manual and spatio-kinetic features such as the eyebrows into specific planes and strata. This will be revisited at various points in the remainder of this chapter as the focus now shifts to consider the interpersonal grammar of BSL.

8.3   Interpersonal Grammar of BSL

What is presented in this section follows Quiroz (2018) as far as the issue of using transfer comparison alone as the basis for analysis is concerned (Caffarel et al., 2004). In short, the analysis is presented in as glottocentric a manner as possible, avoiding 'a search for structural categories similar to those proposed in English' (Quiroz, 2018, p. 140). In fact, this work extends the suggestion in Rudge (2018) that descriptions of BSL should be visuocentric. It accordingly focuses on 'visual-spatial meaning-making resources as a point of departure' (p. 65) rather than relying solely on work on non-visual-spatial languages that may be understood as 'vococentric' or 'scriptocentric'.

This exploration of the interpersonal metafunction in BSL is based on two excerpts from an interaction between two signers, pseudonymised here as A and B. Both interlocutors are BSL users and have known each other for a number of years, permitting a level of familiarity in their interactions and suggesting a good amount of shared background knowledge. A and B were invited to take part in a data collection session, as part of a series in which various groups of language users were recorded during informal conversation and when performing language-based tasks. In this instance, A and B communicated with one another in a casual setting (a study lounge on a university campus) without constraints on topic or time, and one camera was used to record a front-facing perspective on the two signers. The two excerpts below were chosen from the full transcript as they demonstrate a number of fundamental aspects of an interpersonal grammar in BSL.

It must nonetheless be borne in mind that there are limitations with these excerpts. For instance, the glosses of non-manual or spatio-kinetic expression only display elements of BSL production that are relevant to interpersonal concerns (see Rudge, 2018, for further information on the metafunctional attribution of the different expressive components of BSL). Furthermore, these excerpts do not demonstrate the full extent of complexity in BSL and are not intended to be understood as such. Nonetheless, these excerpts provide a stable, initial and visuocentric description of BSL from which further work may develop.

Excerpt 1

A and B are signing about an upcoming party that has been organised by another person, K (who is known by both A and B). K has told other people about the party but has not told A, and B does not realise this.

A | K   PT:PRO3SG$_K$ TELL-$_{3PL}$
  | 'K told them.'

B | *headshake; eyebrows* ↑
  | BUT   PT:PRO3SG$_K$ TELL-$_{2SG}$
  | 'But K (did) not tell you?'

A | *headshake*
  | TELL-$_{1SG}$
  | '(K did) not tell me.'

8 Interpersonal Grammar in British Sign Language   237

(cont.)

B | <u>eyebrows ↓</u>
  | PARTY   PT:PRO2SG   KNOW   HOW
  | 'How (did) you know (about) the party?'

A | L   PT:PRO3SG$_L$ TELL-$_{1SG}$
  | 'L told me.'

A | SLY   PT:PRO3SG$_L$
  | 'L (is) sly.'

B | <u>headshake</u>
  | SLY   PT:PRO3SG$_L$
  | 'L (is) not sly.'

B | TALK++   PT:PRO3SG$_L$
  | 'L (is) a gossip.'

Excerpt 2

Later on in the conversation, A and B are discussing A's upcoming holiday. Upon questioning how A feels, A expresses animosity towards travelling in general with a short series of reasons.

B | <u>eyebrows ↑</u>
  | HOLIDAY   EXCITED   PT:PRO2SG
  | '(Are) you excited (for your) holiday?'

A | NERVOUS
  | '(I am) nervous.'

B | <u>eyebrows ↓</u>
  | WHY
  | 'Why?'

A | TRAVEL   HATE
  | '(I) hate travelling.'

B | DIFFICULT
  | '(It is) difficult.'

A | PEOPLE   DC:[MANY-PEOPLE-CROSS-PATHS-IN-FRONT-OF-1SG]
  | 'Lots of people getting in my way.'

A | STAFF   CA:[TALKING-TO-PRO1SG]
  | 'Staff talk to me.'

(cont.)

A	<u>head shake; command articulation</u> CA:[TALK PT:PRO1SG] 'Don't talk to me,'
A	<u>head nod; command articulation</u> CA:[SHOW PT:PRO1SG] 'show me!'
B	<u>eyebrows ↑</u> STAFF MAYBE HELP-$_{2SG}$ 'The staff might help you?'
A	SHOULD '(Staff) should (help me).'

8.3.1 SPEECH FUNCTION and MOOD

Using these texts as a base, it is possible to explore the interpersonal metafunction in BSL, beginning with an exploration of the moves made between the signers and relationships to SPEECH FUNCTION and MOOD. Following Halliday (1984), the system of MOOD is the lexicogrammatical realisation of the discourse-semantic system of SPEECH FUNCTION; it distinguishes different moves in dialogue (see Figure 8.4).

Quiroz (2018), p. 143) states that 'the conceptualisation of basic speech functions at discourse semantics is generally assumed as valid for human language overall [and] all languages are expected to grammaticalise primary speech functions as basic clause MOOD types specifically associated with them'. Given that BSL is a naturally occurring human language, it is therefore expected that lexicogrammatical realisations of SPEECH FUNCTION by MOOD will be observable (metaphorical realisations of SPEECH FUNCTION are also present, although the present chapter is concerned with congruent realisations; see Taverniers, 2018).

Beginning with the first half of the exchange in Excerpt 1, it can be seen that two statements are made by A, with B interposing between these statements – see Example 1:

(1)   A | K   PT:PRO3SG$_K$ TELL-$_{3PL}$
            'K told them.'

        B | <u>headshake; eyebrows ↑</u>
            BUT PT:PRO3SG$_K$ TELL-$_{2SG}$
            'But K (did) not tell you?'

8 Interpersonal Grammar in British Sign Language   239

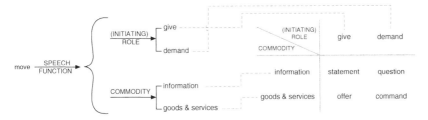

Figure 8.4 The system of SPEECH FUNCTION and congruent realisations

A | *headshake*
  | TELL-$_{1SG}$
  | '(K did) not tell me.'

Signer A begins by explaining the state of play as they understand it: K told a group of people about the party. B follows this move by interrogating A's statement, wishing to confirm if K also told A about the party. Signer A provides a response indicating that they were not told by K.

Example 1 demonstrates primary differences in giving and demanding information. Signer A gives information twice, and B demands information once. In comparing the three moves, the core sign involved in this distinction is TELL. In the first move, TELL is realised by a manual sign that indicates who was being told (3PL, or 'them'). In the second move, TELL co-occurs with B's eyebrows raising, and the third move shows A signing TELL again, although without a change in the position of the eyebrows. A headshake is also present in the second and third moves, although this may be attributed to the system of POLARITY (discussed further in this chapter).

An initial distinction may thus be made between a statement and a question via the use of the eyebrows. Further evidence for this is provided in Example 2 from Excerpt 2:

(2)   B | *eyebrows* ↑
        | HOLIDAY   EXCITED   PT:PRO2SG
        | '(Are) you excited (for your) holiday?'

      A | NERVOUS
        | '(I am) nervous.'

Similarly to Example 1, B queries how A feels about an upcoming holiday, wherein B's eyebrows are raised again to realise an interrogative move. Likewise, A's response is articulated without a change in the height of the eyebrows. Thus, the use of raised eyebrows appears to form a distinction between whether information is being given or demanded.

A further point of interpersonal concern may also be introduced at this point. In comparing the interactions in Examples 1 and 2, a distinction is visible in the element co-occurring with raised eyebrows: in 1, TELL (a verbal group) is repeated, whereas in 2 EXCITED PT:PRO2SG (a nominal group) is not repeated but instead substituted for NERVOUS (another nominal group). Observed lexicogrammatically, successful moves in dialogue can be achieved with or without a verbal group being realised (i.e. a nominal or adjectival group can suffice). Following other work on interpersonal descriptions (see, e.g. Martin & Cruz, 2018), it is thereby initially proposed that a Predicator function is present in the interpersonal grammar of BSL. This will be discussed and argued for further in the following sections.

Returning to Excerpt 1, it is possible to see the eyebrows being used in a different but similar fashion to the interrogating function suggested above. Example 3 presents two further moves in the first exchange.

(3) B | *eyebrows* ↓
  | PARTY PT:PRO2SG KNOW HOW
  | 'How (did) you know (about) the party?'

  A | L PT:PRO3SG$_L$ TELL-$_{1SG}$
  | 'L told me.'

Prior to this exchange, B had realised that A knew about the party without being told by K (see Example 1). This leads B to ask how A knew about the party, followed by A explaining that they were informed by someone else.

The previously observed difference in the non-manual elements between requesting information (i.e. changing eyebrow height) and giving information can now be expanded further. The function of B's move in Example 3 is to request further, *unknown* information from A, rather than seeking to confirm or challenge something, as in 1 and 2. When realised, the height of the eyebrows is lowered rather than raised.

A second instance of lowered eyebrows is presented in Example 4 from Excerpt 2:

(4) A | NERVOUS
  | '(I am) nervous.'

  B | *eyebrows* ↓
  | WHY
  | 'Why?'

Again, B asks for further information about why A is feeling nervous about travelling. As this information requires more than confirmation or denial, the request is accompanied by lowered eyebrows.

Two further points regarding interrogating moves should be noted before continuing. First, the instances of lowered eyebrows in Examples 3 and 4 co-occur with a specific set of signs: HOW and WHY (and, in other instances outside the current excerpts, WHEN, WHAT, WHICH, etc.). Lowered eyebrows thus occur with specific manual signs that realise an Inquirer function to allow for specificity in the request: HOW realises a request for the manner in which something is done; WHY for reasoning of an action or state; WHEN for a temporal location and so on. Secondly, while the exact scope of the change in eyebrow height may differ between moves, these changes are very often present near the end of the clause. In other words, interpersonal meaning appears to be most 'at risk' towards the end of a clause.

One final type of move is observed in the second half of Excerpt 2, wherein A is expressing dissatisfaction with people who attempt to communicate via talking rather than visual demonstration (Example 5).

(5) A | STAFF   CA:[TALKING-TO-PRO1SG]
        | 'Staff talk to me.'

     A | *head shake; command articulation*
        | CA:[TALK   PT:PRO1SG]
        | 'Don't talk to me,'

     A | *head nod; command articulation*
        | CA:[SHOW   PT:PRO1SG]
        | 'show me!'

In 5, Signer A uses a series of instances of constructed action, first taking on the role of a worker who is talking, and then returning to being themselves but as if being in conversation with the worker (i.e. a dialogue between A and an 'imaginary' worker). What is noticeable about these latter instances of constructed action is the shift in function from a statement to a command. This is glossed non-manually as 'command articulation' which consists of a number of non-manual and spatio-kinetic changes, including: a quicker pace of signing; a larger space used when signing; wide eyes; and more exaggerated body movements (e.g. the head nod in the final move of Example 5 is accompanied by a leaning forward of the upper body). If this 'command articulation' were absent, the function of stating information would be realised, similar to what is seen in previous examples.

We therefore arrive at a point where four different move realisations can be observed from these brief excerpts: declaratives (i.e. statement); polar interrogatives (i.e. question for confirmation or denial); elemental interrogatives (i.e. question for unknown information); and imperatives (i.e. command). The predominant factors that differentiate these moves paradigmatically from one another involve changes in non-manual and/or spatio-kinetic production, and requests for unknown information also require the inclusion of a manual sign to indicate the type of information being requested. These distinguishing factors co-occur with different functional elements (e.g. a Predicator or an Inquirer) and are usually found towards the end of the clause.

For ease of typological comparison, it will be assumed that the moves noted above fit into a low-delicacy system of MOOD that is often observed cross-linguistically (see Figure 8.5).

At this point, it is necessary to return to the previous discussion regarding the planes of content and expression, specifically the realisations of MOOD options and which strata of the linguistic system are called on for these realisations. The manual components of BSL are argued to be situated at the lexicogrammatical stratum, alongside various non-manual and spatio-kinetic components (see Table 8.1). However, these non-manual and spatio-kinetic components may act in a more prosodic way (i.e. phonological rather than lexicogrammatical) as is seen in the MOOD distinctions noted in Figure 8.5. Indeed, work in sign linguistics from other theoretical perspectives groups non-manual elements into the category of 'visual prosody' (see, e.g., Dachovsky & Sandler, 2009; Sandler, 2012).

With this in mind, it is argued that paradigmatic distinctions in BSL MOOD are predominantly realised by interactions with systems in the phonological stratum rather than the lexicogrammatical stratum alone (e.g. the distinction between [indicative: declarative] and [indicative: interrogative: polar] is realised by the height of a BSL user's eyebrows). Such a finding is not novel or unique to BSL: Halliday and Greaves (2008, p. 73) state that 'intonation functions in the grammar in a way that is consistent with ... other realizational resources', and parallels may be drawn with Quiroz's (2018) identification of rising and falling tone realising paradigmatic distinctions in declarative and polar interrogative clauses in Chilean Spanish. The only difference in these latter examples and BSL, of course, is the modality in which these distinctions are expressed.

Furthermore, it is suggested that the phonological stratum is pivotal in the realisation of [imperative] selections in BSL. However, successful realisation (at least concerning what is observed in Excerpt 2) requires more than just the eyebrows. Simultaneous selections of various non-manual and spatio-kinetic features are needed from systems that permit variation both in what features can be selected and the 'intensity' with which these are selected (e.g. smaller or larger use of space, smaller or larger eye aperture, etc.) to analogously reflect the variances in the 'force' of an imperative. Likewise, it is worthwhile to note that some imperatives in BSL may not be as 'forceful' as those observed in Excerpt 2. For instance, imperatives that recommend a group's course of action (e.g. if the people in that group are unacquainted) may express the Predicate with a slightly larger or quicker movement than what may be seen in an indicative realisation, but not to the extent seen in the current examples.

Figure 8.5 A system of MOOD in BSL

244 Luke A. Rudge

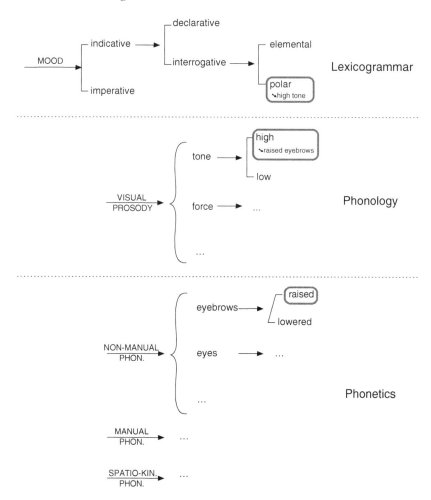

Figure 8.6 Interstratal relations and associated systems in BSL

To exemplify these interstratal relations concerning MOOD, a simplified diagram conjecturing the systems of VISUAL PROSODY (in the phonological stratum) and simultaneous systems in the phonetic stratum is posited in Figure 8.6 (although further development and elaboration of this area and of these systems is strongly encouraged).

To briefly summarise so far, examples drawn from the BSL excerpts demonstrate that SPEECH FUNCTION can be realised by lexicogrammatical realisations in MOOD. However, oppositions between features in MOOD are realised through phonological means, via the system of VISUAL PROSODY that operates

8   Interpersonal Grammar in British Sign Language   245

at the phonological stratum. An interpersonal Predicator function is also proposed for BSL, which will be discussed further as attention now turns to realisations of POLARITY within a clause.

8.3.2   Polarity

The grammatical polarity of a clause may be understood as the realisation of the validity of a statement or the performance of an action (see Matthiessen et al., 2010). Within Excerpt 1 in particular, a number of examples may be highlighted to interrogate the realisation of POLARITY in BSL, beginning with Example 6.

(6) A | K   PT:PRO3SG$_K$ TELL-$_{3PL}$
       | 'K told them.'

     B | _headshake; eyebrows ↑_
       | BUT   PT:PRO3SG$_K$ TELL-$_{2SG}$
       | 'But K (did) not tell you?'

     A | _headshake_
       | TELL-$_{1SG}$
       | '(K did) not tell me.'

Signer A begins by explaining a situation that they report to be correct or, in terms of POLARITY, is positive. B follows up with a [indicative: interrogative: polar] selection (indicated by the use of raised eyebrows) to confirm that K did not inform A of the event, to which A clarifies that they were not informed.

In the first move in Example 6, manual signs are produced without any co-occurring non-manual features. However, the second and third moves include the use of a headshake when TELL-$_{2SG}$ and TELL-$_{1SG}$ are produced. This addition of the headshake acts to change the grammatical polarity from positive to negative. If a headshake were to be used in the first move (i.e. co-occurring with TELL-$_{3PL}$), then this would also change from positive to negative (e.g. 'K did not tell them').

This opposition in the realisation of positive and negative is particularly clear in Example 7.

(7) A | SLY   PT:PRO3SG$_L$
       | 'L (is) sly.'

     B | _headshake_
       | SLY   PT:PRO3SG$_L$
       | 'L (is) not sly.'

In effect, B repeats the same manual signs produced by A. If the non-manual glossing tier were not visible in these examples, it would be assumed that B was providing a verbatim repetition. However, the headshake provides the point of distinction: B disagrees with A. Unlike Example 7, the scope of the headshake goes beyond the boundaries of one manual sign, but this does not result in a negative polarity for both of these signs (i.e. the resulting free translation would not be *'Not L (is) not sly.').

A final example of a headshake co-occurring with manual signs can be found in Example 8 from Excerpt 2.

(8)   A | *head shake; command articulation*
        | CA:[TALK   PT:PRO1SG]
        | 'Don't talk to me,'

      A | *head nod; command articulation*
        | CA:[SHOW   PT:PRO1SG]
        | 'show me!'

Again, the headshake in the first move of Example 8 serves to identify negative polarity, this time in a command. Immediately following is another command, but as there is an absence of the headshake, the polarity is positive. The moves therefore stand opposed to each other, with the first clause restricting what should be done and the second clause indicating the alternative action to take.

Examples 6, 7 and 8 demonstrate two aspects that align with current understandings in both SFL and sign linguistics. From the SFL perspective, positive clauses are typologically less marked than their negative counterparts, and BSL proves no exception to this pattern. From the perspective of sign linguistics, it is postulated that sign languages can be categorised into two groups regarding grammatical polarity: manual dominant (i.e. POLARITY realised via negative manual signs or particles) and non-manual dominant (i.e. POLARITY realised via other means). Pfau and Bos (2016) note that in the production of negative clauses in the latter category, 'the headshake is obligatory' (p.137). From the excerpts provided above, BSL appears to fall into this category.

This is not to say that the manual components of BSL play no part in POLARITY. Although the excerpts used in this chapter do not display it, current studies documenting BSL (e.g. Fenlon et al., 2014) note that a number of manual signs representing NO and/or NOT are in current usage (cf. Sutton-Spence & Woll, 1999),[5] and may be used alongside other signs to realise negation. There are also a small number of positive/negative sign pairs in which negation is expressed in the manual signs alongside the use of a headshake. For instance, LIKE is realised in BSL by a flat hand (palm towards the signer) tapping the chest once or twice, but NOT-LIKE is realised by the same handshape starting from the chest and moving

---

[5] At the time of writing, there are four different manual signs that may be used to represent NO. These may be viewed in the BSL SignBank: https://bslsignbank.ucl.ac.uk/dictionary/words/no-1.html.

a short distance up and away from the signer on an arcing path. The negation of the clause is thereby infused in the production of the manual sign itself, alongside the obligatory headshake. Other examples of this include: HAVE (an open hand with spread fingers, palm upwards, moving down and closing into a fist) and HAVE-NOT (a flat hand, palm towards the signer, sweeping in front of the face of the signer); and KNOW (a fist with the thumb extended, and the thumb tapping the signer's temple) and NOT-KNOW (both hands flat, palms facing the signer, with fingertips touching the temples and then both hands moving away in an arc).

Within an interpersonal system of POLARITY, then, similar realisations are seen to what was presented for MOOD. With a [positive] selection, there are no additional elements that require realisation, comparable to the realisation of a declarative clause. With a [negative] selection, a headshake must be included as a minimum. As this headshake may co-occur with multiple manual signs, VISUAL PROSODY in the phonological stratum is again called on, comparable to the realisation of [indicative: interrogative] and [imperative] selections discussed above.

In addition, the manual sign that co-occurs with the headshake (or one of the signs, should the headshake scope across a clause) can be argued again to realise a Predicator function. For instance, in Example 6, TELL is used in each of the three moves, and in the second and third moves it forms the convergence point for changes in MOOD and POLARITY. Furthermore, it may be argued that if heavy ellipsis were in place in Example 6, the only manual signs needed to progress the dialogue would be TELL and the associated spatial referent (written in subscript in the excerpts).

This discussion on POLARITY supports the argument that BSL can realise the binary poles of positive and negative through lexicogrammatical and phonological means. However, the excerpts also demonstrate evidence of clauses that do not fall at one of these two poles. The final subsection will address these instances.

8.3.3 Modality

Modality refers to 'expressions of indeterminacy between the positive and negative poles, which interpersonally construct the semantic region of uncertainty that lies between "yes" and "no"' (Matthiessen et al., 2010, p. 141). As noted in the previous section, the excerpts – in particular, the end of Excerpt 2 – demonstrate instances where this 'uncertainty' may be realised – see Example 9.

(9) B | <u>eyebrows ↑</u>
STAFF MAYBE HELP-$_{2SG}$
'The staff might help you?'

A | SHOULD
'(Staff) should (help me).'

At this stage of the interaction, signer A had just finished expressing dissatisfaction with travel, including experiences of staff at public transport locations tending to speak first rather than showing or demonstrating something. After a brief pause, B suggests that the staff that A will encounter during the holiday may be more helpful than what they have experienced before. Signer A replies somewhat abruptly and suggests that staff being helpful should be a given.

In both moves of Example 9, the signers produce manual signs that function to express gradation. In the first move, MAYBE expresses uncertainty in the actions of others in a future event: despite A's previous experiences, the next experience could be different. In the second move, SHOULD also expresses uncertainty in the actions of others, but also functions to indicate the implied obligation of the staff, whereas MAYBE does not do this. From an SFL perspective, it may be suggested that these two moves provide initial support for a system of MODALITY, and perhaps further systemic distinctions concerning probability (i.e. MODALISATION) and obligation (i.e. MODULATION). For the purposes of this chapter, two selections will be available within MODALITY: [−modality] and [+ modality].

While additional texts would require analysis in order to support and expand on this position, there are further points from within and beyond the excerpts to consider. First, there is a set of manual signs that appear to have a modalising and/or modulating function: SHOULD, MAYBE, CAN, MUST and WILL. These may be produced in sequence with other signs or, if the context is salient enough to permit ellipsis, produced on their own. These signs also realise different functions: CAN realises permission and ability; MUST realises obligation or necessity; and WILL realises certainty. Secondly, although MODALITY appears to be realised through manual signs, there are also visual prosodic elements that can add to this interpersonal domain, including the possibility that selections in systems of MODALITY may be realised without the need for a manual sign at all. Strong evidence for this is presented in Mapson (2015), who observes the visual prosodic features of BSL in interaction and investigates how combinations of non-manual and spatio-kinetic features impact perceived politeness between signers.

Mapson (2015) also notes that the multifunctionality of prosodic expression in BSL can lead to difficulties in analysis. This is interesting when considering B's polar interrogative in Example 9, wherein the signer's eyebrows are raised during the production of both MAYBE and HELP-$_{2SG}$ (i.e. the Predicator). In an earlier section, it was indicated that [indicative: interrogative: polar] is realised by the use of raised eyebrows co-occurring with the Predicator, and that this visual prosodic feature may extend across more than one manual sign (see Example 2). However, this then raises questions in B's selection of [indicative: interrogative: polar] in Example 9: what is the function of the raised eyebrows that co-occur with MAYBE? Was this produced in anticipation

8 Interpersonal Grammar in British Sign Language   249

of the question or to add to the perceived uncertainty realised by MAYBE? Are the raised eyebrows therefore multifunctional?

To reiterate, further texts need to be analysed in order to further support or challenge claims made for MODALITY in BSL. While it is certainly present, the complexity of the system(s) and interactions with other systems will be understood with further studies.

8.4   Applying Interpersonal Systems to Texts

Based on the above analysis of the two excerpts of BSL interaction, an interpersonal system network can be presented in Figure 8.7, demonstrating the simultaneous systems of MOOD, POLARITY and MODALITY, and (where appropriate and stable enough to do so) realisation statements.

Using this network, both excerpts can now have further information added to them regarding the feature selections made for each clause, allowing for a brief discourse analysis of each excerpt (Tables 8.2 and 8.3).

In this segment of the interaction (Table 8.2), B expressed greater variation in terms of the type of move used (one [indicative: interrogative: polar], one [indicative: interrogative: elemental] and two [indicative: declarative] selections),

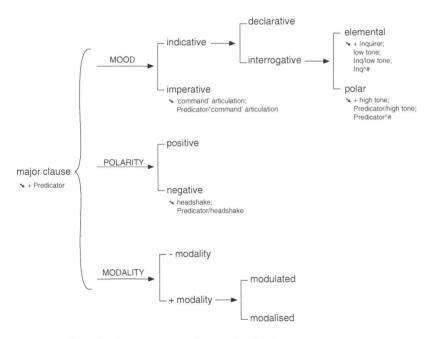

Figure 8.7 The interpersonal networks of BSL

Table 8.2 *Excerpt 1 analysed in interpersonal terms*

Excerpt 1		MOOD	POLARITY	MODALITY
A	K PT:PRO3SG_K TELL-3PL 'K told them.'	indicative: declarative	positive	– modality
B	*headshake;* *eyebrows* ↑ TELL-2SG	indicative: interrogative: polar	negative	– modality
	BUT PT:PRO3SG_K 'But K (did) not tell you?'			
A	*headshake* TELL-1SG '(K did) not tell me.'	indicative: declarative	negative	– modality
B	*eyebr:* ↓ PARTY PT:PRO2SG KNOW HOW 'How (did) you know (about) the party?'	indicative: interrogative: elemental	positive	– modality
A	L PT:PRO3SG_L TELL-1SG 'L told me.'	indicative: declarative	positive	– modality
A	SLY PT:PRO3SG_L 'L (is) sly.'	indicative: declarative	positive	– modality
B	*headshake* SLY PT:PRO3SG_L 'L (is) not sly.'	indicative: declarative	negative	– modality
B	TALK++ PT:PRO3SG_L 'L (is) a gossip.'	indicative: declarative	positive	– modality

Excerpt 2

		MOOD	POLARITY	MODALITY
B	_eyebrows_ ↑ HOLIDAY EXCITED PT:PRO2SG '(Are) you excited (for your) holiday?'	indicative: interrogative: polar	positive	– modality
A	NERVOUS '(I am) nervous.'	indicative: declarative	positive	– modality
B	_eyebrows_ ↓ WHY 'Why?'	indicative: interrogative: elemental	positive	– modality
A	TRAVEL HATE '(I) hate travelling.'	indicative: declarative	positive	– modality
B	DIFFICULT '(It is) difficult.'	indicative: declarative	positive	– modality
A	PEOPLE DC:[MANY-PEOPLE-...] 'Lots of people getting in my way.'	indicative: declarative	positive	– modality
A	STAFF CA:[TALKING-TO-PRO1SG] 'Staff talk to me.'	indicative: declarative	positive	– modality
A	_head shake; command articulation_ CA:[TALK PT:PRO1SG] 'Don't talk to me,'	imperative	negative	– modality
A	_head nod; command articulation_ CA:[SHOW PT:PRO1SG] 'show me!'	imperative	positive	– modality
B	_eyebrows_ ↑ STAFF MAYBE HELP-2SG 'The staff might help you?'	indicative: interrogative: polar	positive	+ modality: modalised
A	SHOULD '(Staff) should (help me).'	indicative: declarative	positive	+ modality: modulated

whereas A selected [indicative: declarative] only. As such, B was moving the interaction along by setting up requests for information, to which A responded either in the positive or the negative. After the fifth move, B did not continue the question-response pattern. Instead, A used another statement that expanded on the previous statement (i.e. in the sense of 'this is who told me' and 'this is *why* they told me,' possibly representing a textual shift in Theme). At that point, B interjects and refutes the statement by repeating A's clause, and by changing its polarity from positive to negative, realising another move in the dialogue. A final move is made via another [indicative: declarative] selection, offering an alternative perspective on A's judgement.

Moves in Excerpt 1 are thus enacted by question-answer sequences (i.e. via changes in MOOD) and by offering (and refuting) opinions and alternative interpretations (i.e. via changes in POLARITY). In terms of MODALITY, [− modality] is always selected (i.e. all moves are made with either positive and negative grammatical selections, and no instances of obligation or permission are present).

The sequencing observed in Excerpt 2 (Table 8.3) appears to be similar to that of Excerpt 1 with alternations in selections in MOOD between [indicative: declarative] and [indicative: interrogative], wherein B is again the predominant requester or information (unlike Excerpt 1, however, selections in POLARITY are almost all positive). Halfway through the interaction, A uses instances of depicting constructions and constructed action in a manner similar to recounting a story. Following this, A uses constructed action to signify a hypothetical interaction between themselves and a staff member (rather than keeping the interaction between A and B, as in previous moves), wherein A tells the staff member what to do, hence the imperative selection in MOOD. B then attempts to offer reassurance by conjecturing that A's next experience may not be as bad (via an [indicative: interrogative] selection), to which A replies that, ideally, it should not be as bad. These final two moves select [+ modality: modalised] and [+ modality: modulated], enabling a degree of possibility and a degree of obligation respectively, rather than indicating a firm positive/negative binary.

In sum, aside from demonstrating the range of interpersonal systems and selections made for the dialogue to be successful, the two excerpts reveal that signer B was perhaps the more inquisitive in the interaction in asking for both unknown information and clarity on other aspects. Signer A, conversely, was more of an information giver, both in direct response to enquiry from B and in indirect manners through discourse devices such as constructed action. Of course, the full transcript of this interaction may reveal other aspects, but these short instances of dialogic communication suffice to show the various selections within interpersonal systems of BSL.

8.5 Conclusion and Future Investigations

The use of the visual-spatial modality in social semiosis remains a largely understudied area from the perspective of systemic functional linguistics. This chapter has provided insight into one such language that operates in this modality – BSL – by analysing dialogic interaction between users and then presenting its systems of MOOD, POLARITY and MODALITY. When viewed from a glottocentric (and indeed visuocentric) perspective, it can be seen that interpersonal meaning can be successfully identified within BSL. This relies on *interactions and combinations* of three productive resources operating at lexicogrammatical and phonological strata: manual components, non-manual components and spatio-kinetic components.

The systems presented in this chapter offer an exciting foundation upon which a vast and fruitful area of study can grow. While other points of interest from the interpersonal perspective are ready to be explored in greater detail (e.g. networks for NEGOTIATION and APPRAISAL; see Berry, 1981; Ventola, 1987; Martin & Rose, 2007), both the ideational and textual metafunctions present new areas of investigation, alongside further theoretical questions and applications to real world concerns. These include but are certainly not limited to: the intersection of BSL and gesture from the perspectives of SFL and beyond; defining the planes of content and expression in greater detail; exploring pedagogical contexts when sign languages are the primary mode of communication; and how the wider field of sign linguistics may interpret lexicogrammatical structure beyond the syntagmatic and into the paradigmatic. Similarly, this research feeds back into ensuring that SFL operates as a theory that can encapsulate human communication holistically, thus including communication in the visual-spatial modality as typologically legitimate, analysable and describable.

As such, it is hoped that this chapter will spark further interest in such a fertile area of study, which incorporates the potential for real world impact, and encourages partnerships between linguists, signers and deaf communities to enable an authentic co-creation of knowledge within and beyond these domains.

References

Baker, A. (2016). Sign Languages as Natural Languages. In A. Baker, B. van den Bogaerde, R. Pfau and T. Schermer, eds., *The Linguistics of Sign Languages: An Introduction*. Amsterdam: John Benjamins, pp. 1–24.

Baker, A., van den Bogaerde, B., Pfau, R. & Schermer, T., eds., (2016). *The Linguistics of Sign Languages: An introduction*. Amsterdam: John Benjamins.

Barberà, G. (2014). Use and Functions of Spatial Planes in Catalan Sign Language (LSC) Discourse. *Sign Language Studies, 14*(2), 147–74.

Berry, M. (1981). Towards Layers of Exchange Structure for Directive Exchanges. *Network*, 2, 23–32.
Bianchini, C. S., Chèvrefils, L., Danet, C., Doan, P., Rébulard, M., Contesse A. & Boutet, D. (2018). Coding Movement in Sign Languages. In *Proceedings of the 5th International Conference on Movement and Computing (MOCO'18)*. New York, NY: ACM, pp. 1–8.
Brentari, D. (2002). Modality Differences in Sign Language Phonology and Morphophonemics. In R. P. Meier, K. Cormier and D. Quinto-Pozos, eds., *Modality and Structure in Signed and Spoken Languages*. Cambridge: Cambridge University Press, pp. 35–64
Caffarel, A., Martin, J. R. & Matthiessen, C. M. I. M., eds., (2004). *Language Typology: A Functional Perspective*. Amsterdam: John Benjamins.
Cormier, K., Fenlon, J. & Schembri, A. (2015). Indicating Verbs in British Sign Language Favour Motivated Use of Space. *Open Linguistics*, *1*, 684–707.
Cormier, K., Fenlon, J., Gulamani, S. & Smith, S. (2017). *BSL Corpus Annotation Conventions (Version 3.0)*. London: Deafness Cognition and Language (DCAL) Research Centre, UCL.
Cormier, K., Quinto-Pozos, D., Sevcikova, Z. & Schembri, A. (2012). Lexicalisation and De-Lexicalisation Processes in Sign Languages: Comparing Depicting Constructions and Viewpoint Gestures. *Language and Communication*, *32*(4), 329–48.
Cormier, K., Smith, S. & Zwets, M. (2013). Framing Constructed Action in British Sign Language Narratives. *Journal of Pragmatics*, *55*, 119–39.
Dachovsky, S. & Sandler, W. (2009). Visual Intonation in the Prosody of a Sign Language. *Language and Speech*, *52*(2/3), 287–314.
Davidse, K. (1997). The Subject-Object versus the Agent-Patient Asymmetry. *Leuven Contributions in Linguistics and Philology*, *86*(4), 413–31.
De Vos, C., van der Kooij, E. & Crasborn, O. (2009). Mixed Signals: Combining Linguistic and Affective Functions of Eyebrows in Questions in Sign Language of the Netherlands. *Language and Speech*, *52*(2–3), 315–39.
Eberhard, D. M., Simons, G. F. & Fennig, C. D., eds. (2019). *Ethnologue: Languages of the World*, 22nd ed., Dallas, Texas: SIL International.
Fenlon, J., Cormier, K. & Brentari, D. (2018). The Phonology of Sign Languages. In S. J. Hannahs and A. R. K. Bosch, eds., *The Routledge Handbook of Phonological Theory*. London: Routledge, pp. 453–75
Fenlon, J., Cormier, K., Rentelis, R., Schembri, A., Rowley, K., Adam, R & Woll, B. (2014). *BSL SignBank: A Lexical Database of British Sign Language*, 1st ed., London: Deafness, Cognition and Language Research Centre, University College London.
Fenlon, J., Cormier, K. & Schembri, A. (2015). Building BSL SignBank: The Lemma Dilemma Revisited. *International Journal of Lexicography*, *28*(2), 169–206.
Fenlon, J., Schembri, A. & Cormier, K. Modification of Indicating Verbs in British Sign Language: A Corpus-Based Study. *Language*, *94* (1), 84–118.
Giustolisi, B., Mereghetti E. & Cecchetto, C. (2017). Phonological Blending or Code Mixing? Why Mouthing Is Not a Core Component of Sign Language Grammar. *Natural Language and Linguistic Theory*, *35*, 347–65.
Halliday, M. A. K. (1984). Language as Code and Language as Behaviour: A Systemic-Functional Interpretation of the Nature and Ontogenesis of Dialogue. In R. P. Fawcett, M. A. K. Halliday, S. M. Lamb and A. Makkai, eds., *Language as Social Semiotic*. Vol. 1 of *The Semiotics of Language and Culture*. London: Pinter, pp. 3–35.

Halliday, M. A. K. & Matthiessen, C. M. I. M. (2014). *Halliday's Introduction to Functional Grammar*. London: Routledge.
Halliday, M. A. K. & Greaves, W. S. (2008). *Intonation in the Grammar of English*. London: Equinox.
Hao, J. & Hood, S. (2019). Valuing Science: The Role of Language and Body Language in a Health Science Lecture. *Journal of Pragmatics*, *139*, 200–15.
Harrison, S. (2018). *The Impulse to Gesture*. Cambridge: Cambridge University Press.
Hole, R. (2007). Working Between Languages and Cultures Issues of Representation, Voice, and Authority Intensified. *Qualitative Inquiry*, *13*(5), 696–710.
Hosemann, J. (2011). Eye Gaze and Verb Agreement in German Sign Language: A First Glance. *Sign Language and Linguistics*, *14*(1), 76–93.
Johnston, T. (1996). Function and Medium in the Forms of Linguistic Expression Found in a Sign Language. In W. H. Edmondson and R. B. Wilbur, eds., *International Review of Sign Linguistics (Vol. 1)*. Mahwah, New Jersey: Lawrence Erlbaum, pp. 57–94.
Johnston, T. & Schembri, A. (2013). Corpus Analysis of Sign Languages. In C. A. Chapelle, ed., *Encyclopedia of Applied Linguistics*. Hoboken, New Jersey: Wiley, pp. 1312–19.
Kusters, A., De Meulder, M. & O'Brien, D. (2017). Innovations in Deaf Studies: Critically Mapping the Field. In A. Kusters, M. De Meulder and D. O'Brien, eds., *Innovations in Deaf Studies: The Role of Deaf Scholars*. Oxford: Oxford University Press, pp. 1–56.
Manrique, E. (2016). Other-Initiated Repair in Argentine Sign Language. *Open Linguistics*, 2(1),1–34.
Mapson, R. P. (2015). *Interpreting Linguistic Politeness from British Sign Language to English*. Unpublished PhD thesis, University of Bristol, Bristol, UK.
Martin, J. R. & Cruz, P. (2018). Interpersonal Grammar of Tagalog: A Systemic Functional Linguistics Perspective. *Functions of Language*, *25*(1), 54–96.
Martin, J. R. & Rose, D. (2007). *Working with Discourse: Meaning beyond the Clause*, 2nd ed., London: Continuum.
Martin, J. R. & White, P. R. R. (2005). *The Language of Evaluation: Appraisal in English*. London: Palgrave.
Matthiessen, C. M. I. M., Teruya, K. & Lam, M. (2010). *Key Terms in Systemic Functional Linguistics*. London: Continuum.
Müller, C. (2018). Gesture and Sign: Cataclysmic Break or Dynamic Relations? *Frontiers in Psychology*, 9(SEP), 1–20.
Pfau, R. (2016). Morphology. In A. Baker, B. van den Bogaerde, R. Pfau and T. Schermer, eds., *The Linguistics of Sign Languages: An Introduction*. Amsterdam: John Benjamins, pp. 197–228.
Pfau, R., & Bos, H. (2016). Syntax: Simple Sentences. In A. Baker, B. van den Bogaerde, R. Pfau and T. Schermer, eds., *The Linguistics of Sign Languages: An Introduction*. Amsterdam: John Benjamins, pp. 117–48.
Quiroz, B. (2008). Towards a Systemic Profile of the Spanish MOOD. *Linguistics and the Human Sciences*, *4*(1), 31–65.
Quiroz, B. (2018). Negotiating Interpersonal Meanings: Reasoning about MOOD. *Functions of Language*, *25*(1), 135–63.
Rendel, K., Bargones, J., Blake, B., Luetke, B. & Stryker, D. S. (2018). Signing Exact English: A Simultaneously Spoken and Signed Communication Option in Deaf Education. *The Journal of Early Hearing Detection and Intervention*, *3*(2), 18–29.

Rudge, L. A. (2015). Towards an Understanding of Contextual Features That Influence the Linguistic Formality of British Sign Language Users. *Functional Linguistics*, 2 (11), 1–17.

Rudge, L. A. (2018). *Analysing British Sign Language through the Lens of Systemic Functional Linguistics*. Unpublished PhD thesis, University of the West of England, Bristol, UK.

Rudge, L. A. (2020) Situating Simultaneity: An Initial Schematisation of the Lexicogrammatical Rank Scale of British Sign Language. *Word*, *66*(2), 98–118.

Salazar-García, V. (2018). Modality in Spanish Sign Language (LSE) Revisited: A Functional Account. *Open Linguistics*, 4(1), 391–417.

Sandler, W. (2012). Visual Prosody. In R. Pfau, M. Steinbach and B. Woll, eds., *Sign Language: An International Handbook*. Berlin: De Gruyter Mouton, pp. 55–76.

Schembri, A., Stamp, R., Fenlon, J. & Cormier, K. (2018). Variation and Change in Varieties of British Sign Language in England. In N. Braber and S. Jansen, eds., *Sociolinguistics in England*. London: Palgrave Macmillan, pp. 165–88.

Stamp, R., Schembri, A., Fenlon, J., Rentelis, R., Woll, B. & Cormier, K. (2014). Lexical Variation and Change in British Sign Language. *PLoS ONE*, *9*(4), 811–24.

Sutton-Spence, R. & Woll, B. (1999). *The Linguistics of British Sign Language: An introduction*. Cambridge: Cambridge University Press.

Systemic Functional Glossing Conventions. (2018). Retrieved from: https://systemiclangua gemodelling.files.wordpress.com/2018/09/systemic-functional-glossing-conventions-version-september-2018.pdf (last accessed 10 November 2020).

Taverniers, M. (2018). Grammatical Metaphor and Grammaticalization: The Case of Metaphors of Modality. *Functions of Language*, *25*(1), 164–204.

Teruya, K., Akerejola, E., Andersen, T. H., Caffarel, A., Lavid, J., Matthiessen, C. M. I. M., Petersen, U. H., Patpong, P. & Smedgaard, F. (2007). Typology of MOOD: A Text-Based and System-Based Functional View. In R. Hasan, C. M. I. M. Matthiessen and J. J. Webster, eds., *Continuing Discourse on Language: A Functional Perspective*, vol. 2. London: Equinox, pp. 859–920.

Van der Kooij, E. & Crasborn, O. (2016). Phonology. In A. Baker, B. van den Bogaerde, R. Pfau and T. Schermer, eds., *The Linguistics of Sign Languages: An Introduction*. Amsterdam: John Benjamins, 251–78.

Ventola, E. (1987). *The Structure of Social Interaction: A Systemic Approach to the Semiotics of Service Encounters*. London: Pinter.

Wakeland, E., Austen, S. & Rose, J. (2018). What is the Prevalence of Abuse in the Deaf/Hard of Hearing Population? *The Journal of Forensic Psychiatry and Psychology*, *29*(3), 434–54.

Woodward, J. C. (1975). *How You Gonna Get to Heaven if You Can't Talk with Jesus: The Educational Establishment vs. the Deaf Community*. Paper presented at the 34th Annual Meeting of the Society for Applied Anthropology. Amsterdam.

Woll, B. (2013). The History of Sign Language Linguistics. In K. Allen, ed., *The Oxford Handbook of the History of Linguistics*. Oxford: Oxford University Press, pp. 91–104.

Zeshan, U. (2000). *Sign Language in Indo-Pakistan: A Description of a Signed Language*. Amsterdam: John Benjamins.

9 Interpersonal Grammar in Scottish Gaelic

Tom Bartlett

9.1 Introduction

In this chapter I use a text-based approach to grammatical description in order to explore the interpersonal grammar of Scottish Gaelic and to provide a partial network for the lexicogrammatical system of MOOD.[1] In order to do this I will analyse three extracts from two Scottish Gaelic novels (MacLean 2009; MacLeòid 2005) from the perspectives of the semantic systems of NEGOTIATION (Martin & Rose, 2007, chapter 7) and ENGAGEMENT (Martin & White, 2005, chapter 3) and correlate distinctions in these systems with function structures at the lexicogrammatical stratum. Working along these lines, I build up a profile of lexicogrammatical elements and function structures at clause rank, with contrasting structures systematised in the most economical way in terms of markedness and inheritance features (Halliday & Matthiessen, 1999, p. 326; Jakobson & Waugh, 1979, pp. 90–1), and labelled according to their distinctive usages in discourse – what Halliday (1984) refers to as the 'ineffability of grammatical categories'. On the basis of this analysis, I will suggest that Scottish Gaelic does not have a [declarative] versus [interrogative] opposition in MOOD, redounding with the system of NEGOTIATION at the semantic stratum, but rather an [assertive] versus [non-assertive] opposition, redounding with the system of ENGAGEMENT at the semantic stratum. This is, of course, not to say that the semantics of NEGOTIATION are not realised through the lexicogrammar of Scottish Gaelic, but that they are indirectly encoded through a combination of lexicogrammatical systems such as MOOD and KEY.

The structure of the chapter roughly follows Martin and Cruz's (2018) paper on Tagalog in the Special Issue of *Functions of Language* dedicated to interpersonal grammar across languages (Martin, 2018). However, where Martin and Cruz provided an introductory metafunctional profile of Tagalog clause

---

[1] Thanks to Ed McDonald for comments on various versions of this and other papers – Mòran taing, a' charaid! Thanks also to the editors for their patience and helpful suggestions.

grammar, followed by a discourse-semantic analysis which exemplified these functional structures in use, for Scottish Gaelic this is not possible. Apart from questions of space, there is only a scant literature on Gaelic from a functional perspective on which to draw (Mackenzie, 2009; Bartlett, 2016; Bartlett & O'Grady, 2019; McDonald, 2008; Byrne, 2002). Instead, therefore, I will provide a discourse-semantic analysis of Scottish Gaelic texts from the perspective of NEGOTIATION and ENGAGEMENT, and from there I will select relevant moves for further analysis in terms of interpersonal elements and function structures at the lexicogrammatical stratum. Both of these latter stages will draw on the systemic principle of agnation in order to distinguish between and categorise individual features and, from here, to build up a network of systemic contrasts within the interpersonal grammar of Scottish Gaelic. This will occasionally involve the use of examples from other sources and even, in the extreme case, invented examples. I will finish with some reflections on economy and the labelling of terms in systems networks, the process of 'shunting' (Halliday, 1961) between strata in developing linguistic representations and the potential implications of such an approach for the cross-linguistic validity of systems at the semantic stratum.

In the remainder of the paper I will refer to Scottish Gaelic simply as Gaelic. While the term Gaelic may also be used to refer to Irish Gaelic, it is customary to refer to Scottish Gaelic simply as Gaelic and Irish Gaelic simply as Irish.

9.2 Negotiating the Exchange of Knowledge

In this section I present and analyse a short extract from a Gaelic novel, *Na Klondykers* (MacLeòid, 2005). The book is set in a small town in the Highlands of Scotland and portrays the effects of industrial-scale fishing and the presence of Russian fishermen (the eponymous Klondykers) on the local community. The extract begins with one of the central characters, Iain (I), being questioned by his mother (M) about his friends, Donald (Dòmhnall) and Leanne, a couple who are on the point of breaking up.

The extract has been annotated following the schema for information exchange developed by Berry (1981), Ventola (1987) and Martin (1992), and a move-by-move translation is provided. In Section 9.3 I analyse a different extract in terms of action exchanges. These analyses provide a description of the text in terms of the discourse work performed by the individual moves with regard to the system of NEGOTIATION. Drawing on these analyses I consider what functional structures are used to perform this work in terms of the options at clause rank and the elements that comprise and distinguish between these structural choices. The analyses thus follow Halliday's (Halliday & Matthiessen, 2004, p. 31) trinocular approach in identifying functions of elements in terms of their relation to elements above, around and below them: discourse-semantic structures are analysed in terms of their contribution to the text as a whole, their systemic relations to each other and the clausal structures that realise them. Similarly, function structures at clause rank are analysed in terms of the discourse functions they realise, their relation to other options at clause rank and in terms of the functional elements that comprise them.

(For exchange structure notation, see Martin et al., Chapter 1, this volume; *** is used to separate exchanges in Text 1.)

Text 1

A mhàthair a' cur cheistean.
'His mother asking questions.'

***

M	K2	Am faca tu Dòmhnall?	
		'Did you see Donald?'	

***

	K2	Tha e a tighinn, nach eil?
		'He's coming, isn't he?'

***

	K1	Cha do fhreagair e am fòn.
		'He didn't answer the phone.'

***

	K2	An tuirt thu ris a thighinn?
		'Did you tell him to come?'

I	K1	Thubhairt.
		'Yes'

	K1f	Thuirt e gum biodh e an seo.
		'He said he would be here.'

M	cf	Airson diathad?
		'For lunch?'

	=cf	Tha e dol a ghabhail biadh?
		'He's going to have something to eat?'

I	rcf	Tha mi smaoineachadh gu bheil.
		'I think so.'

M	K2f	Glè mhath.
		'Very good.'

***

	K2	A bheil Leanne a' tighinn còmhla ris?
		'Is Leanne coming with him?'

I	ch	Chan eil fhios'am.
		'I don't know.'

***

M	K2	Nach fhaca tu i?
		Did you not see her?

I	K1	Chan fhaca.
		No.

```
                ***
    Cha robh Iain airson innse dhi;
    'Iain wasn't in the mood for talking to her;'
    cha robh e ach air èirigh.
    'he had just got up.'
    Rudeigin selfish, 's mathaid.
    'A bit selfish, maybe.'
    Ach b'fheàrr leis na ceistean fhàgail aig Dòmhnall.
    'But he would prefer to leave the questions to Donald.'
                ***
    I     K2    Cearc a tha an diugh?
                'Chicken today?'

    M     K1    Ròst,
                'Roast,'

    thubhairt a mhàthair.
    said his mother.'

    I     K2f   O. Math.
                'Oh. Good.'
                ***
    Bha glainne beag fìon aice fhad 'sa bha i a' còcaireachd, ag èisteachd ris an rèidio.
    'She had a small glass of wine while she was cooking and listening to the radio.'
                ***
    M     K2    An cuala tu mu dheidhinn Johana?
                'Did you hear about Johana?'
    Cionnas a bha fios aice cho luath?
    'How did she know so soon?'

    I     K1    Chuala.
                'Yes.'

    M     K2f   Uabhasach, nach eil.
                'Terrible, isn't it?'
                ***
    M     K1    Tha e gu bhith all right, ge-tà, tha iad ag ràdh.
                'He'll be ok anyhow, so they say.'

    I     K2f   A bheil?
                'Will he?'
                'S math sin.
                'That's good.'
                ***
    M     K1    Tha i ann an staid, ge-tà.
                She's in a state anyhow.'
                ***
    M     Dk1   Bheil fhios agad dè thachair?
                'Do you know what happened?'
```

9 Interpersonal Grammar in Scottish Gaelic

I	K2	Chan eil.
		'No.'
M	K1	Bha i ann am fight.
		'She was in a fight.'
	+K1	Cha bu chòir dhi ...
		'She shouldn't be.'
	=K1	cha bu chòir dhi bhith dol faisg air na Ruiseanaich ud.
		'She shouldn't be going near those Russians.'
	xK1	Bha sabaid aig an talla a-raoir, cuideachd, chuala mi.
		'There was a fight at the hall last night too, I heard.'
	***	
M	K2	Am faca tu i?
		'Did you see it?'
I	ch	Cha robh mi ann aig an am.
		'I wasn't there at the time.'
	***	
	K1	Cha robh ann ach scrap bheag, tha mi smaointinn.
		'It was only a wee scrap, I think.'
	***	

(MacLeòid 2005, p. 143–4)

Having seen how the whole extract unfolds as a phase of discourse, we can now analyse individual moves and exchanges to identify the lexicogrammatical means by which Gaelic lexicogrammar encodes the negotiation of information. I start with the opening move of the mother and son's dialogue sequence (Example 1), which is a K2 move, a request for information.

(1)
M	K2	am	faca	tu	Dòmhnall?
		INT	see.PST.DEP	2sg	Donald
		'Did you see Donald?'			

There is no response forthcoming to this question but, later in the text, we see a similar question (though in the negative) which is answered. This exchange, repeated as Example 2, represents a K2 ^ K1 sequence.

(2)   2.1
M	K2	nach	fhaca	tu	i?
		INT.NEG	see.PST.DEP	2sg	3sg.f
		'Did you not see her?'			

2.2

I	K1	chan	fhaca
		NEG	see.PST.DEP
		'No'	

There are several points to note here. First, there are the enclitic particles (or clitics), *an*, *cha(n)* and *nach*, which alter the exchange function of the clause or, in Martin and Cruz's (2018) terms, 'develop the negotiability of a move'. These can be *provisionally* classified as interrogative, negative and interrogative negative, respectively, and I will therefore refer to this set of features as 'mood clitics'.[2] I will use the labels INT, NEG and INT.NEG in the glossing for these clitics. Given that a central aim of this chapter is to challenge the relevance of the features declarative and interrogative in describing the MOOD system in Gaelic, it is important to stress that these labels, which are based on traditional analyses, are serving at this point simply as necessary placeholders, pending alternative analyses presented below.

We can compare the exchange in Example 2 with Example 3, in which Iain's mother asks Iain if he has heard about Johana (3.1) and, once Iain has responded with an affirmative K1 move (3.2), provides an evaluation as a follow-up (3.3).

(3)   3.1

M	K2	an	cuala	tu	mu dheidhinn	Johana?
		INT	hear.PST.DEP	2sg	about	Johana
		'Did you hear about Johana?'				

3.2

I	K1	chuala.
		hear.PST
		'Yes.'

3.3

M	K2f	uabhasach	nach	eil
		terrible	INT.NEG	be.DEP
		'Terrible, isn't it?'		

Here we see that Iain's positive K1 move in 3.2 has no mood clitic. And, though not apparent in this example, there is in many cases also a distinction in the

---

[2] I analyse these as clitics as they would appear, for various reasons too complex to discuss in the present paper, to operate at group rank. However, as there is no research into group structure in Gaelic, this analysis is open to revision.

form the verb takes in clauses with or without mood clitics. If we substitute a positive K1 response for the negative K1 response in Example 1, this becomes clear.

(4)   4.1

M	K2	am	faca	tu	Dòmhnall?
		INT	see.PST.DEP	2sg	Donald
		Did you see Donald?			

4.2

I	K1	chunnaic
		see.PST
		'Yes'

These different forms are traditionally labelled 'independent' (with no mood clitic) and 'dependent' (following a mood clitic). Although these names are unsatisfactory in many ways, I will maintain them for the remainder of the paper as it is not possible at this stage to provide more functionally appropriate labels.

The analysis of these exchanges has demonstrated the contribution of the different clitics to the clause as a whole within the ongoing negotiation, but we can also draw on these examples to identify the interpersonal functions of the individual elements within the clause. Accordingly, in Example 5 a line is added for the interpersonal structure of the clause. These include the Mood (realised by the mood clitics) and the Finite ('F'), along with the Predicator ('P')[3] and its associated Complements ('C1' and 'C2', discussed further below).

(5)

M	K2	am	faca	tu	Dòmhnall?
		INT	see.PST.DEP	2sg	Donald
		Mood	F/P	C1	C2
		'Did you see Donald?'			

We can recognise the Finite – the function that grounds the clause in time or hypotheticality (Halliday & Matthiessen, 2004, p. 111) – by comparing the functional structure for past reference (as shown in Example 5) with the functional structures for future reference and obligation in Examples 6 and 7 respectively. In Examples 5 and 6 the alternation between *faca* for past reference and *faic* for future reference indicates that the Finite element is conflated with the Predicator in the case of simple tenses (past and future), while Example 7 shows an alternation with a modal functioning as Finite.

---

[3] The Predicator is partially defined as specifying the process that is predicate to the Subject of the clause (Halliday, 1994, p. 79). As I am suggesting that there is no Subject function in Scottish Gaelic, the use of this term is not without problems. Here I am provisionally using it to mean, roughly, the specification of the central process upon which the truth of the clause as a whole is predicated.

(6)

am	faic	tu	Dòmhnall?
INT	see.FUT.DEP	2sg	Donald
Mood	F/P	C1	C2

'Will you see Donald?'

(7)

am	feum	tu	Dòmhnall	fhaicinn?
INT	must.DEP	2sg	Donald	see.INF
Mood	F:modal	C1	C2	P

'Must you see Donald?'

As these examples show, the Finite and Predicator are not conflated for modalised clauses (as in Example 7), and this also holds true for complex tenses such as present (8) and perfect/past-in-the-present (9), both of which are formed with the verb *bith* (to be) as the Finite at the beginning of the clause, with the Predicator as a verbal noun (VN) following a preposition.[4]

(8)

tha	Dòmhnall	a'	tighinn
be.PRES	Donald	at	come.VN
F	C	P	

'Donald is coming'

(9)

tha	Dòmhnall	air	tighinn
be.PRES	Donald	after	come.VN
F	C1	P	

'Donald has come'

While Examples 1 and 2 provided analyses of what we can provisionally label the unmarked functional structures for positive and negative K2 moves, Example 10 illustrates an alternative possibility.

(10)

tha	e	a'	tighinn	nach	eil?
be.PRES	3sg.m	at	COME.VN	NEG.INT	be.PRES.DEP
F	C1	P		Mood	F

'Donald's coming, isn't he?'

This is an example of a 'tag question', a specific subtype of K2 move that serves to confirm assumed information (what Hasan, 1996, p. 123, labels a *reassure* move). Example 11 illustrates a similar variation of a K2 move which serves as a *check* (Hasan, 1996, p. 123) on previously presented or assumed information.

---

[4] There are good reasons for the analysis of both *a'* (a contracted form of *ag*) and *air* as prepositions, including the nominalisation of the following process and the potential conflation of *ag* with any attendant pronominals (a characteristic of prepositions in Celtic languages). However, the analysis is not without the usual problems encountered when trying to pin down diachronic shifts to meet the demands of synchronic description.

(11)

tha	e	a'	dol	a ghabhail	biadh?
be.PRES	3sg.m	at	go.VN	take.INF	food
F	C1	P			C2
'He's going to have something to eat?'					

Given the author's use of the question mark, we can assume that what resembles a K1 in terms of lexicogrammatical structure, in fact differs in that it is spoken with a rising intonation. Furthermore, we can see from the textual progression that, rather than either a straight K1 or K2 move, Example 11 represents a request for clarification in response to the son's earlier K1 move 'he said he would be here'. In other words, what is sought is a development of her son's answer in terms of a clarification of Donald's purpose in coming. In contrast to the previous example, then, where the structure functioned to confirm (or reassure) a piece of assumed knowledge, in 11 Iain's mother appears to be signalling that she is checking on the purpose of the visit, on the basis of conventional expectations rather than prior assumptions in this case.

As we have seen above, and as further illustrated in Examples 12 and 13, K1 responses to K2 moves and tags in reassure moves are realised through the same functional structure of (Mood) ^ Finite.

(12)   12.1

K2	nach	fhaca	tu	i?
	INT.NEG	see.PST.DEP	2sg	3sg.f
	Mood	F/P	C1	C2
'Did you not see her?'				

12.2

K1	chan	fhaca
	NEG	see.PST.DEP
	Mood	F/P
'No'		

12.3

K1	chunnaic
	see.PST
	F/P
'Yes'	

(13)

chunnaic	tu	i	nach	fhaca?
see.PST	2sg	3sg.f	NEG.INT	see.PST.DEP
F/P	C1	C2	Mood	F/P

This commonality of structure allows us to identify a Negotiator function, comprising those elements of interpersonal structure that are 'crucial both to the negotiation process ... and to the realization of indicative MOOD options' (Caffarel, 2004, p. 94). This is illustrated in Example 14. Note that, as illustrated further in this chapter, it is only the Finite and any attendant Mood clitic that comprise the Negotiator, though the Predicator will necessarily also be included when this is conflated with the Finite. This is reflected in the examples that follow by analytically separating the Finite and Predicator even when they are conflated in the grammar.

(14)   14.1

K2	nach	fhaca	tu	i?
	INT.NEG	see.PST.DEP	2sg	3sg.f
	Negotiator	Scope		
	Mood	F	P	C1	C2
	'Did you not see her?'

14.2

K1	chan	fhaca
	NEG	see.PST.DEP
	Negotiator	Scope
	Mood	F	P
	'No'

In Example 15 we see how a twin-Negotiator can function to simultaneously state an assumption and also to query that assumption, hence giving rise to the 'reassure' move.

(15)

K2	tha	e	a'	tighinn	nach	eil?
	be.PRES	3sg.m	at	COME.VN	NEG.INT	be.PRES.DEP
	Negotiator$_1$	Scope			Negotiator$_2$	
	F	C1	P		Mood	F
	'Donald's coming, isn't he?'

Note that the Negotiator in Scottish Gaelic does not include any nominal referent realising the interpersonal function of Subject as 'something by reference to which the proposition can be affirmed or denied' (Halliday, 1994, p. 76). In other work (e.g. Bartlett & O'Grady, 2019), I analyse a syndrome of interconnected features and functions to make the case that there is no interpersonal element Subject in Gaelic and that all the entities involved function as Complements of the Predicator in the interpersonal structure of the clause. As already noted, therefore, I have provisionally used the labels C1 and C2 for the purposes of this paper. One further feature of Scottish Gaelic (and other Celtic languages) that is relevant here is that there is no simple word for affirmation or negation in Gaelic (such as *yes* or *no* in English), but that it is the Negotiator that is used to this effect (as shown in Example 14).

So far we have looked at polar questions, where an affirmation or denial of a proposition is expected (though the response may be modalised as something in between). For elemental questions, as in Example 16, in which the proposition itself is not in doubt but for which the enquirer lacks a detail, the function structure is a rather different.

(16)	cionnas	a	bha	fios	aice	cho	luath
	how	REL	be.PST	knowledge	at.3SG.F	so	fast
	Inquirer		F/P	C1	C2	A	
	'How did she know so soon?'						

What we have here is an identifying process with a predicated Theme in which the Inquirer (wh-word) is the thematised Token and the remainder of the proposition is a relative clause functioning as the Value (cf. Martin & Cruz, 2018, on the use of identifying clauses for elemental interrogatives in Tagalog). Notice in passing that in this case there is no interrogative clitic and the Finite is not in the dependent form.[5] These are important points that I will develop below.

To summarise to this point: I have identified three modal clitics in Gaelic, provisionally labelled the interrogative, the negative and the interrogative negative. I have also identified a Finite element and shown how this interacts with the clitics in two separate related ways: the post-clitic Finite takes a distinct form from the bare Finite; and the clitic and Finite are the two essential elements of the Negotiator. These interactions are related in that the functions of each clitic individually and the Negotiator element as a whole are related to the development of negotiation of information between speakers. In terms of this relation, I aligned these function structures with knowledge exchange structures in the interaction between primary knowers (K1) and secondary knowers (K2). It was noted in this regard that, while the interrogative clitic has strong associations with K2 moves, there were exceptions to this in the function structures realising checks and reassurances and also in the structure of elemental questions functioning as K2 moves.

---

[5] The only exception to this is *càite/where?*, which is followed by the interrogative clitic and a dependent Finite. This is a result of the word's origins in a more complex structure (see Mackenzie, 2009).

As suggested, however, interaction between speakers is not confined to the exchange of information, and we must also consider how the exchange of actions is negotiated across texts. To do this, I will introduce another extract from *Na Klondykers*.

9.3 Negotiating the Exchange of Actions

In the following extract, from little later in the book, Donald (D) and Leanne (L) are arguing about Donald's previous bad behaviour, how this has been a factor in their break-up, and the arrangements for Donald to see their children in the future. I have analysed the extract for the exchange of both information and goods-and-services, but the focus of my analysis at this point will be on the latter and the various ways in which such moves are realised in the lexicogrammar.

Text 2
Bha Leanne sàmhach nuair a thuirt e sin.
'Leanne was silent when he said that.'
Dh'fairich i pian ag èisteachd ri na facail.
'She felt a pain listening to the words.'
Bha pàirt dhith ag iarraidh sin a dhèanamh.
'Part of her wanted to do it.'
Pàirt eile dhith a bha cho feargach ris an diabhal.
'Another part was as angry as the devil.'
  ***
D A2   Nach tig thu air ais?
         'Won't you come back?'
  ***
D A1   agus faodaidh sinn an uair sin ar tìde a ghabhail a' còmhradh air rudan.
         'and we can take our time then, discussing things.'
  ***
L K1   Bha dùil agam gu robh cùisean a' fàs na b' fheàrr,
         'I was hoping things were getting better,'
thuirt Leanne.
'said Leanne.'
D cf   Bha.
         'They were.'

   ch   Tha iad.
         'They are.'

L rch   Chan eil mi cho cinnteach.
         'I'm not so sure.'
  ***
Stad i.
'She stopped.'
Seo cho fad' 's a dheigheadh e.
'That's as far as she would go.'
  ***

L	A2	Feumaidh mi barrachd tìde, smaoineachadh air.
		'I need more time, to think about it.'
I	ch	Nach eil gu leòr tìde air a bhith agad?
		'Haven't you had enough time?'

***

	K2	Cò mu dheidhinn eile a dh'fheumas tu smaoineachadh?
		'What else do you need to think about?'
L	K1	A bheil sinn a' dol a dh'fhuireach còmhla neo nach eil.
		'Whether we are going to stay together or not.'

Dh'fhairich Dòmhnall snaidhm na stamag.
'Donald felt a knot in his stomach.'

***

D	A2	Na can sin, Leanne.
		'Don't say that, Leanne.'
L	ch	Carson?
		Why not?

***

	K2	Nach eil fhios agad mar a tha thu air mo ghoirteachadh?
		'Don't you know how you've hurt me?'
D	ch/	Ach chan e càil serious a bh'ann.
	K1	'It wasn't anything serious.'
L	ch	'S e!
		'It was!'
	=ch	'S e rud serious a bh'ann!
		'It was something serious!'

***

	K1	Cionnas a b'urrain dhut sin a dhèanamh orm?
		'How could you do that to me?'

Bha deòirean a' tòiseachadh na sùilean.
Tears were forming in her eyes.

D	K2f	Tha mi duilich.
		I'm sorry.
	=K2f	All right, Leanne. Tha mi duilich.
		All right, Leanne. I'm sorry.

Bha Leanne cho troimh-a-chèile 's nach b' urrainn dhi bruidhinn ceart.
Leanne was so upset that she couldn't speak properly.

***

D	A2	Am faod mi a' chlann fhaicinn co-dhiù?
		Can I see the children anyway?

dh'fhaighnich Dòmhnall.
'asked Donald'

L	A1	Faodaidh tu am faicinn turas neo dhà san t-seachdain an dèidh na sgoile.
		'You can see them once or twice a week after school'.

***

(MacLeòid, 2005, p. 155)

In Text 2 we see a direct A2 move when Donald asks Leanne not to talk about splitting up, reproduced as Example 17. In order to distinguish between the rather different function and structure of the negative element in information and action exchanges in Gaelic (see Section 9.5), I will use the function term Prohibitive and the glossing label PROHIB in the tables.

(17)

D	A2	na	can	sin	Leanne
		PROHIB	say.IMP.2SG	that	Leanne
		Prohibitive	P	C	Voc
		'Don't say that, Leanne'			

This function structure (*na* followed by imperative P), realising an informal negative directive in the singular, alternates with the positive structure (without *na*), as in Example 18, and the plural/respectful structure, with the morpheme *-(a)ibh* added to the Predicator, as in Examples 19 and 20.

(18)

can	sin	a' rithist	Leanne
say.IMP.2SG	that	again	Leanne
P	C	A	Voc
'Say that again, Leanne'			

(19)

na	canaibh	sin	Leanne
PROHIB	say.IMP.2PL/RESP	that	Leanne
Prohibitive	P	C	Voc
'Don't say that, Leanne'			

(20)

canaibh	sin	a' rithist	Leanne
say.IMP.2PL/RESP	that	again	Leanne
P	C	A	Voc
'Say that again, Leanne'			

Each of these examples includes a Vocative element (glossed as VOC). In Gaelic a Vocative is generally realised by leniting the initial consonant of the relevant name, though with certain phonological constraints. In contemporary practice, however, the Vocative function is often realised by an unlenited form.

There is also a cohortative first person plural imperative form, which is one of only a small number that mark person distinctions morphologically. Once again the positive and negative alternation is realised by means of the absence or presence of the clitic *na*, as in Examples 21 and 22.

(21)

canamaid	sin
say:IMP.1PL	
P	C
'Let's say that'	

(22)

na	canamaid	sin
PROHIB	say:IMP.1PL	
Prohibitive	P	C
'Let's not say that'		

We can also note alternative lexicogrammatical structures functioning as A2 moves, as in 23, where Donald is trying to persuade Leanne to return to him.

(23)

D	A2	nach	tig	thu	air ais?
		NEG.INT	come.DEP	2SG	back
		Mood	F/P	C1	A
		'Won't you come back?'			

In terms of function structure, this is an example of the future tense with what we can provisionally label negative interrogative marking. The move functions, however, to mitigate the force of the A2 move through opening it up to some degree of negotiation. At the same time, note here that Gaelic has no everyday word functioning as an Entreaty (cf. *please* in English) and that the example could, in other contexts, have been translated as *Come back, please*.

Example 24, from the end of the extract, is a further A2 ^ A1 exchange in which Donald makes a request (A2) to which Leanne agrees (A1). In these examples the exchange of action is negotiated by means of a modal Finite rather than an imperative.

(24) 24.1

D	A2	am	faod	mi	a'	chlann	fhaicinn	co-dhiù?
		INT	might. FUT.DEP	1SG	DEF	children	see.INF	anyway
		Mood	F	C1	C2		P	A
		'Can I see the children anyway?'						

24.2

L	A1	faodaidh	tu	am	faicinn	turas neo dhà san t-seachdain an dèidh na sgoile.
		might. FUT	2SG	3PL. POSS	see.INF	once or twice a week after school
		F	C1	C2	P	A
		'You can see them once or twice a week after school.'				

With regard to the Negotiator element in action exchanges, we can say that for imperatives,[6] this comprises the Predicator and any attendant prohibitive particle, as in Example 25 (derived from 19).

---

[6] Caffarel's definition was limited to indicative clauses, but the extension to imperatives seems justified.

(25)   25.1

na	canaibh	sin	Leanne
PROHIB	say.IMP.2PL/RESP	that	Leanne
Negotiator		Scope	
Prohibitive	P	C	Voc
'Don't say that, Leanne'			

25.2

cha	chan
NEG	say.FUT.DEP
Negotiator	
Mood	F/P
'I won't'	

Imperatives tend not to get tagged in Gaelic, with the negative interrogative used to fulfil a similar function in opening up the action to some degree of negotiation, as noted for Example 23.

For action exchanges realised through modal forms, it is the modal and any associated mood clitics that comprise the Negotiator elements. This is shown in Example 26, which is derived from 24. Example 26.2 is a potential affirmative response and 26.3 a potential negative one.

(26)   26.1

am	faod	mi	a'	chlann	fhaicinn	co-dhiù?
INT	might.FUT.DEP	1SG	DEF	children	see.INF	anyway
Negotiator		Scope				
Mood	F	C1	C2		P	A
'Can I see the children anyway?'						

26.2

faodaidh
might.FUT
Negotiator
P
'Yes'

9   Interpersonal Grammar in Scottish Gaelic   273

26.3

chan	fhaod
NEG	might.FUT.DEP
Negotiator	
Mood	F/P
'No'	

This section leads us on to a more general discussion of modality, and also gives rise to a later discussion on the distribution of work between NEGOTIATION and exchange structure, on the one hand, and the system of ENGAGEMENT and the distinction between monoglossic and heteroglossic utterances (Martin and White 2005, pp. 99–100), on the other.

9.4   ENGAGEMENT and MODALITY

In the previous section we saw how modality can be used to temper the force of A2 moves. This is because the use of modality renders a move heteroglossic, with alternative possibilities to the action in question implicitly entertained (Martin & White, 2005, p. 117). Within the system of ENGAGEMENT, [heterogloss] stands in systemic contrast to [monogloss], in which alternatives are not entertained. In this section I will explore further the connection between ENGAGEMENT and MODALITY.

As illustrated in Example 24, modal verbs function as the Finite element and, as with other Finites, the form they take depends on the presence or absence of a mood clitic. An immediate point of interest here is that modal Finites inflect in the same way as non-modal Finites indicating future reference: both take the suffix *–(a)idh* in their non-dependent forms and the root alone in the dependent forms following mood clitics. This similarity, which can be seen in comparing Examples 24 and 27, would seem to reflect the inherent shared property of uncertainty encoded in modality and futurity.

(27)   27.1

nach	till	thu?
INT.NEG	return.DEP	2SG
Mood	F/P	C1
'won't you come back?'		

27.2

tillidh	mi
return.FUT	1SG
F/P	C1
'I'll come back'	

There is an important distinction to be made, however, between modulation (in action moves) and modalisation (for knowledge moves) (Halliday and Matthiessen 2004, p. 618). For modulation, as shown in Example 24, the modal Finite is followed by the modulated process in the infinitive form. For modalisation, however, there is a clause complex, with the modal Finite in the main clause 'projecting' the modalised event in the dependent form, as in 28 (cf. Martin & Cruz, 2018, and Martin, 1995, on Tagalog). The element introducing the projected clause is labelled a Projection linker and glossed as PROJ.

(28)

feumaidh	gu'	n	robh	an	t-acras	oirre	a-nochd
must.FUT	PROJ	INT	be.PST.DEP	DEF	hunger	on.3SG.F	last night
α	β						
F			Mood	F/P	C1	C2	A
'she must have been hungry last night'							

More often than modal Finites, however, Gaelic uses a range of function structures containing modal adjectives and nominals to express heteroglossic engagement. These take various forms, one of the most common being the placement of a noun or adjective with modal force as predicated Theme, as in Example 29, taken from Text 1. For present purposes, therefore, I will provisionally analyse the thematised modal element of such clauses as a Modal Theme.

(29)

cha	bu	chòir	dhi	bhith	dol	faisg air na Ruiseanaich ud
NEG	COP.PST	right	to.3SG.F	be.INF	go.VN	near those Russians
Modal Theme				P		A
'she shouldn't be going near those Russians'						

As expected from the previous discussion, and as 29 demonstrates, for action moves the Modal Theme is followed by an infinitive form. For knowledge moves, in contrast, a finite projection is used, as in Example 30.

(30)

is	dòcha	gu'	m	bi	na	croitearn	a'	cur	buntata
COP.PRES	likely	PROJ	INT	be.FUT.DEP	DET.PL	crofters	at	put.VN	potatoes
α		β							
Modal Theme				Mood	F	C1		P	C2
'the crofters will probably be planting potatoes'									

Notice that in 30 the Finite is in the dependent form after what I have been unproblematically referring to as the interrogative clitic, a point I will be returning to. This is not the case when the modal element appears after the main clause as an afterthought, and therefore as an Adjunct in the main clause. This is illustrated in Example 31, which is a modified version of a clause from Text 1.

9 Interpersonal Grammar in Scottish Gaelic 275

(31)

[b'	e]	rudeigin	selfish	's	mathaid
COP.PST	3sg	a bit	selfish	COP.PRES	possible
F	C1	C2		Modal Adjunct	
'it was a bit selfish perhaps'					

This pattern is repeated for other kinds of heteroglossia, such as attributing and entertaining, as well as propositions based on the evidence of the senses. In Example 32 we see a finite dependent form in an idea projected by a mental process.

(32)

bha	dùil	agam	gu	[n]	robh	cùisean	a'	fàs	na b' fheàrr
be.PST	expectation	at.1SG	PROJ	INT	be.PST.DEP	matters	at	grow.VN	better
α			'β						
F/P	C1	C2		Mood	F	C1	P		C2
'I was hoping things were getting better'									

In contrast, in Example 33, where the mental process appears after the proposition, the verb is in the independent form.

(33)

cha	robh	ann	ach	scrap	beag	tha	mi	a'	smaointinn
NEG	be.PST.DEP	PRO.EXIST	but	Scrap	little	be.PRES	1SG	at	think.VN
'1						2			
Mood	F/P	A	C1			F	C1	P	
'it was only a wee scrap, I think'									

Examples 34 and 35 show the same patterning for attributions realised by verbal processes.

(34)

thuirt	e	gu'	m	biodh	e	an seo
say.PST	3sg.M	PROJ	INT	be.COND.DEP	3SG	here
α		"β				
F	C1			Mood	F/P	C1	C2
'he said he would be here'						

(35)

tha	e	gu	bhith	all right	ge-tà	tha	iad	ag	ràdh
be.PRES	3SG.M	FUT	be.INF	all right	anyhow	be.PRES	3PL	at	say.VN
"1						2			
F	C1	P	C2	A		F	C1	P	
'he'll be ok anyhow, so they say'									

In this section I have illustrated the use of modality in Gaelic and its realisation through modal auxiliaries, modal Themes and modal Adjuncts.

I noted that the modal auxiliaries and the future tense in Gaelic share similar properties, reflecting their shared semantics of uncertainty, and I illustrated distinctions between the realisation of modulated and modalised clauses following modal Finites. I then showed how the characteristics described for modality were also relevant for other forms of heteroglossia within the discourse system of ENGAGEMENT and alluded to the fact that what I have so far been unproblematically referring to as the interrogative clitic is involved in the lexicogrammatical realisation of all these heteroglossic forms. On the basis of these examples, in the following section I will make the case that there is, in fact, no interrogative functional structure in the lexicogrammar of Scottish Gaelic and present an alternative system for MOOD that better reflects the systemic contrasts encoded in the language itself. In the concluding section, I will consider how the implications of such a move reflect back upon on the systems at the discourse-semantic stratum that were instrumental in producing this alternative representation of the lexicogrammar.

9.5 The Case against the Declarative/Interrogative System in Gaelic

In Sections 9.2 and 9.3 we looked at knowledge and action exchanges within the system of NEGOTIATION and saw how Gaelic grammar realises distinctions in interpersonal meaning through the use of mood clitics. These comprise a paradigm including what I have been calling the interrogative, the negative and the interrogative negative clitics. In all cases, the Finite verb takes a distinct dependent form after mood clitics. However, we have also seen that the presence of mood clitics is not limited to distinctions in exchange structure and the system of NEGOTIATION, but also to both entertain and attribute options in the system of ENGAGEMENT. Conversely, we have also seen that for elemental questions there is no mood clitic, with the verb in the independent form – a phenomenon that can be explained on the grounds that in such cases the proposition itself is not in doubt.

On this basis, I would argue that for indicative clauses in the lexicogrammar of Gaelic the primary paradigmatic choice is not a [declarative] versus [interrogative] opposition redounding with the system of NEGOTIATION at the semantic stratum, but a choice between the features [assertive] and [non-assertive], realised by the independent and dependent form of the verb respectively, and redounding with the semantic system of ENGAGEMENT. As we have seen, and in line with such an analysis, the dependent form of the verb and its attendant mood clitics all function to render propositions open to alternatives, whether this be through questioning, attributing or entertaining other possibilities. In contrast, independent forms without mood clitics realise the monogloss semantics of unmodalised K1 moves and of K2 moves eliciting specific details in an uncontested proposition. The labels [assertive] and [non-assertive] have

9 Interpersonal Grammar in Scottish Gaelic

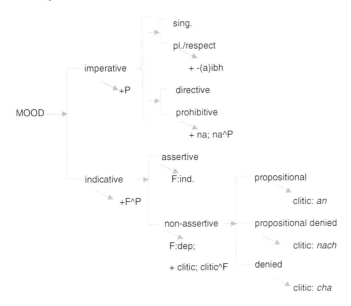

Figure 9.1 Provisional MOOD network for Gaelic, redounding with ENGAGEMENT

therefore been chosen to capture the essence of this distinction. This interpretation is outlined in the system network in Figure 9.1.

It is worth taking the time to talk through the distinctions captured in this representation. On entering the system of MOOD, the first option is between [imperative] and [indicative]. Imperatives are realised by the Predicator in its base form with no overt Finite element. The choice of [imperative] leads to further simultaneous choices: (i) between an unmarked [singular] and a marked form for [plural/respect]; and (ii) between [directive] and [prohibitive], with the latter realised by the presence of the clitic *na*. In contrast to imperatives, indicatives have an overt Finite element, which obligatorily precedes the Predicator (or is conflated with it in simple tenses). The choice of [indicative] leads to a further choice between [assertive] and [non-assertive]. For [assertive], the Finite element is realised by the independent form, while for [non-assertive] the Finite is realised by the dependent form and an obligatory mood clitic is introduced. Within [non-assertive] there are three options: [propositional], marked by the mood clitic *an;* [denied], marked by the mood clitic *cha*; and [propositional denied], marked by the mood clitic *nach*.

Figure 9.1, therefore, captures the *natural economy* of Gaelic grammar, representing the oppositions that are in play at different points in the system of MOOD on the basis of their distinctive realisations, without repetition or

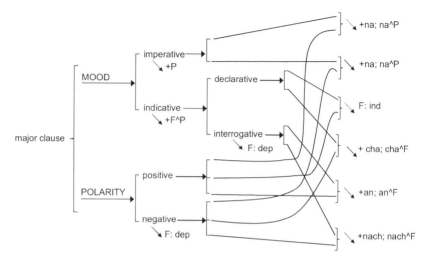

Figure 9.2 Rejected MOOD network for Gaelic, redounding with NEGOTIATION

redundancy. This contrasts with Figure 9.2, an alternative representation based on a [declarative] versus [interrogative] opposition in the system of MOOD and a simultaneous opposition between [positive] and [negative] in the system of POLARITY. Figure 9.2 omits the [singular] versus [plural/respect] opposition within the imperative for the sake of clarity.

As can be seen from the complexity and redundancy in Figure 9.2, such a representation fails to capture the natural economy of Gaelic grammar. In contrast with Figure 9.1, the independent form cannot be introduced until [declarative] and [positive] are chosen simultaneously, while the dependent form has to be introduced and motivated separately for [interrogative] in the MOOD system and for [negative] in the polarity system. This representation, therefore, fails to capture the idea of a single but ineffable meaning for the dependent form. And, by extension, the systemic connection between the three particles *an*, *cha* and *nach*, which comprise a single system of oppositions in Figure 9.1, is lost in Figure 9.2.

Following this logic, Figure 9.2 might seem to be more economical in representing [negative] and [positive] as options within a single system of POLARITY. This contrasts with Figure 9.1, which introduces a 'negative' option twice: once for imperatives, as [prohibition]; and once for indicatives, as [denied]. However, the introduction of separate systems for MOOD and POLARITY would be a false economy for several reasons. Most obviously, the particle used to realise 'negativity' is different for the indicative and imperative systems (*na* versus *cha*), so introducing a layer of complexity into the representation. And, as noted above, such a division would mean that the dependent form would have to be separately motivated within the two systems. These differences alone would rule out the need for a system of POLARITY on the grounds of economy. However, there is more at play here than formal distinctions in realisation, in that the denial of a proposition and the prohibition of an action are distinct concepts. And while there may be underlying similarities between the two, the evidence presented in Sections 9.2 and 9.3 suggests that the lexicogrammar of Gaelic encodes the distinction rather than the similarity. To elaborate on this point a little further: within the Gaelic imperative system, there is an immediate choice between [directive] and [prohibitive]. There is, therefore, a systemic opposition between the positive and negative features these choices index, with each defined in opposition to the other. Within the indicative system, however, the opposition is between [denied] and [propositional] as alternative but non-discrete sub-categories of [non-assertive], which is in turn defined in opposition to [assertive]. The concept of 'negativity', therefore, has a distinctive systemic value in the two systems, and it is this distinction that motivates the differences in realisation.

To back up this analysis of MOOD in Gaelic, let us turn to one last text. This time the text does not take the form of an exchange between two interactants but represents the interior monologue of a soldier preparing for battle and considering whether he is truly prepared or not. As can be seen, the text is structured in terms of an alternation between monoglossic and heteroglossic moves of different kinds, realised by precisely the lexicogrammatical distinctions captured in the system in Figure 9.1, as the soldier first persuades himself that he is indeed ready for battle and then entertains one last lingering doubt. In previous literature direct and indirect questions have not generally been analysed within the system of ENGAGEMENT but, in line with the general argument in this paper, I have done so here. I have provisionally chosen to label the first move [entertain] as it suggests the questioner is open to alternative possibilities.

Text 3

[entertain] Dh'fhainneachd e an robh mi deiseil ...
'He asked if I was ready.'
[attribute] Thuirt mi gu robh,
'I said I was.'
[monogloss] Agus tha.
'And I am.'
[entertain] Uill, tha mi a' smaoineachadh gu bheil.
'Well, I think I am.'

(MacLean, 2009, p. 18–19)

Example 36 provides a full analysis of the moves in this inner dialogue. In more formal Gaelic, the clitic AN/AM would be included before the Finite in the dependent form in the two projected statements in 36.2 and 36.4. In less formal use, however, the clitic is dropped for the present and past of the verb *bith*, but not other verbs.

(36)   36.1

dh'fhainneachd	e	an	robh	mi	deiseil
ask.PST	3sg.M	INT	be.PST.DEP	1sg	ready
α		"β			
		Negotiator		Scope	
F/P	C1	Mood	F	C1	C:At
'He asked if I was ready.'						

36.2

thuirt	mi	gu	robh
say.PST	1SG	PROJ	be.PST.DEP
α		"β	
		Negotiator	
F/P	C1	F/P	
'I said I was.'			

36.3

agus	tha
and	be.PRES
	Negotiator
	F/P
'And I am.'	

36.4

uill	tha	mi	a'	smaoineachadh	gu	bheil
well	be.PRES	1SG	at	think.VN	PROJ	be.PRES.DEP
α					"β	
					Negotiator	
A	F	C1	P			F
'Well, I think I am.'						

With regard to the notation, in 36.1 I have simply labelled the Negotiator of the projected clauses, on the basis that these, rather than the Negotiators in the projecting verbal process, represent the element that is picked up and negotiated throughout the extract.

9 Interpersonal Grammar in Scottish Gaelic

The moves in this example nicely illustrate the crucial distinction between the MOOD systems of English and Gaelic and their relation to the wider characterologies of the two languages. In the English version, we see that all the negotiated elements appear in declarative MOOD type, with the heteroglossia of the discourse semantics being indexed through the semantics of the Predicator in the projecting clause. In the Gaelic, however, we see that for all the heteroglossic moves the Finite is in the dependent form that realises non-assertive MOOD type. In contrast, for the single monogloss move the Finite is in the independent form that realises the assertive MOOD type. The evidence here, and in the extracts in this chapter, therefore, strongly favours an analysis of the lexicogrammar of Gaelic as redounding primarily with the semantics of ENGAGEMENT rather than NEGOTIATION, with the converse being the case for English.

As stated in the introduction, this is not say that distinctions in NEGOTIATION are not marked in Gaelic. Rather it suggests that these distinctions are not directly encoded at the lexicogrammatical stratum. They are realised, instead, through a combination of selections from lexicogrammatical systems such as MOOD and KEY (Halliday & Matthiessen, 2004, p. 142) and through the lexical semantics of Predicators. Gaelic and English, or indeed any pair of languages, differ in terms of the nature of the work done by each of these lexicogrammatical systems and the distribution of labour between them in realising distinctions in the semantics. And it is this differential distribution of labour across the system that defines the characterology of each language.

9.6 Conclusion

In this chapter I took a text-led approach to the description of some of the central features of the interpersonal lexicogrammar of Scottish Gaelic. To this end I provided a semantic analysis of three texts in terms of the systems of NEGOTIATION and ENGAGEMENT. At each point, I related the options in the semantic systems to the function structures realising them at the stratum of the lexicogrammar and, on this basis, I provided a partial systems network for MOOD in Scottish Gaelic, in which the primary options for [indicative] were seen to correspond to the semantics of ENGAGEMENT rather than NEGOTIATION. Shunting back and forth between the semantic and lexicogrammatical strata enabled me to present a systems network which: (i) was economical in accounting for the systemic oppositions within the grammar; and (ii) distinguished the terms of these systems in accordance with the meaning of the sum of their uses in discourse. For both aspects, the analytical method employed represented an antidote to the imposition of categories from English or any other language. And on this basis I argued that the MOOD system in Gaelic is not based on a [declarative] versus [interrogative] opposition, but on an [assertive] versus [non-assertive] opposition, with [propositional], [denied] and [propositional denied] as subcategories of [non-assertive].

The text-led approach therefore has certain advantages over an exclusive focus on lexicogrammar. There is a caveat, however, in that any recalibration of systems at the lexicogrammatical stratum will have repercussions when we shunt back up to the semantic stratum. If the meaning of individual elements in the lexicogrammar is reanalysed, then we would also expect their 'meaning in articulation' to be different, and this means that the semantic categories that were the starting point of the text analysis may need to be reconsidered. So, while we may expect a greater degree of equivalence between languages in terms of functions at the discourse-semantic stratum, it should not be expected that these can ever be exact equivalents in that they are the product of distinctive features from the lexicogrammatical inventory of each language. From the perspective of this chapter, this suggests that discourse roles such as primary and secondary knower may not be universal categories that can be treated as a neutral starting point for text-led descriptions. Zhang (2020), for example, discusses the use of modal particles in Khorchin Mongolian and the differences in *expectations of consensus* that these index. The systemic oppositions he suggests are similar to the distinctions in *response anticipation* suggested in O'Grady (in press) for the intonation system of English. Between them the two articles point to the possibility of systemic organisation at the semantic stratum which is based not on the traditional discourse moves of question, statement and so on, but on response anticipation and epistemic rights (Muntigl, 2009). From the analyst's point of view, such a possibility entails a continual shunting backwards and forwards between strata and cyclically recalibrating the description of each in terms of recalibrations in the other.

References

Bartlett, T. & O'Grady G. (2019). Language Characterology and Textual Dynamics: A Crosslinguistic Exploration in English and Scottish Gaelic. *Acta Linguistica Hafniensia*, 51(2), 124–59. DOI: https://doi.org/10.1080/03740463.2019.1650607.
Bartlett, T. (2016). Phasal Dynamism and the Unfolding of Meaning as Text. *English Text Construction*, 9(1), 143–64. DOI: https://doi.org/10.1075/etc.9.1.08bar.
Berry, M. (1981). Systemic Linguistics and Discourse Analysis: A Multi-layered Approach to Exchange Structure. In M. Coulthard and M. Montgomery, eds., *Studies in Discourse Analysis*. London: Routledge & Kegan Paul.
Byrne, M. (2002). *Gràmar na Gàidhlig* [A Grammar of Gaelic]. Stornoway: Stòrlann-Acair.
Caffarel, A. (2004). Metafunctional Profile of the Grammar of French. In A. Caffarel, J. R. Martin and C. M. I. M. Matthiessen, eds., *Language Typology: A Functional Perspective*. Amsterdam: John Benjamins

Caffarel, A., Martin, J. R. & Matthiessen, C. M. I. M., eds., (2004). *Language Typology: A Functional Perspective*. Amsterdam: John Benjamins.

Halliday, M. A. K. (1996). On Grammar and Grammatics. In R. Hasan, C. Cloran and D. Butt, eds., *Functional Descriptions: Theory in Practice*. Amsterdam: John Benjamins, pp. 1–38.

Halliday, M. A. K. (1994). *An Introduction to Functional Grammar*, 2nd ed., London: Arnold.

Halliday, M. A. K. (1984). On the Ineffability of Grammatical Categories. In A. Manning, P. Martin and K. McCalla, eds., *The Tenth LACUS Forum*. Columbia: Hornbeam Press pp.13–18.

Halliday, M. A. K. (1978). *Language as Social Semiotic: The Social Interpretation of Language and Meaning*. Maryland.University Park Press.

Halliday, M. A. K. (1961). Categories of the Theory of Grammar. *Word, 17*(3), 242–92.

Halliday, M. A. K. & Matthiessen, C. M. I. M. (2004). *An Introduction to Functional Grammar*, 3rd ed., London: Hodder Arnold.

Halliday, M. A. K. & Matthiessen, C. M. I. M. (1999). *Construing Experience through Meaning: A Language-Based Approach to Cognition*. London/New York: Continuum.

Hasan, R. (1996). Semantic Networks as a Tool for the Analysis of Meaning. In C. Cloran, D. Butt and G. Williams, eds., *Ways of Saying: Ways of Meaning. Selected Papers of Ruqaiya Hasan*. London/New York: Cassell, pp. 104–31

Jakobson, R. & Waugh, L. R. (1979). *The Sound Shape of Language*. Bloomington: Indiana University Press.

MacLean, I. (2009). *Cogadh Ruairidh* [Roddy's War]. Dingwall: Sandstone Press.

MacLeòid, I. (2005). *Na Klondykers* [The Klondykers]. Inbhir Nis: Clàr.

McDonald, E. (2008). *Meaningful Arrangements: Exploring the Syntactic Description of Texts*. Sheffield: Equinox.

Mackenzie, J. L. (2009). Aspects of the Interpersonal Grammar of Scottish Gaelic. *Linguistics 47*(4), 885–911.

Martin, J. R. (2018). Interpersonal Meaning: Systemic Functional Perspectives. *Functions of Language, 25*(1), 2–19.

Martin, J. R. (1995). Logical Meaning, Interdependency and the Linking Particle {-ng/ na} in Tagalog. *Functions of Language, 2*(2), 189–228.

Martin, J. R. (1992). *English Text: System and Structure*. Amsterdam: John Benjamins.

Martin, J. R. & Cruz, P. (2018). Interpersonal Grammar of Tagalog: A Systemic Functional Linguistic Perspective. *Functions of Language, 25*(1), 53–91.

Martin, J.R. & Rose, D. (2007). *Working with Discourse: Meaning beyond the Clause*, 2nd ed., London, Oxford, New York, New Delhi and Sydney: Bloomsbury.

Martin, J. R. & White, P. R. R. (2005). *The Language of Evaluation: Appraisal in English*. Basingstoke: Palgrave Macmillan.

Mathesius, V. (1964). On Linguistic Characterology with Illustrations from Modern English. In J. Vachek, ed., *A Prague School Reader in Linguistics*. Bloomington IN: Indiana University Press.

Muntigl, P. (2009). Knowledge Moves in Conversational Exchanges: Revisiting the Concept of Primary vs. Secondary Knowers. *Functions of Language, 16*(2), 225–63. DOI: https://doi.org/10.1075/fol.16.2.03mun

O'Grady, G. (in press) Intonation and Exchange: A Dynamic and Metafunctional View. *Lingua*. https://doi.org/10.1016/j.lingua.2020.102794

Ventola, E. (1987). *The Structure of Social Interaction: A Systemic Approach to the Semiotics of Service Encounters*. London: Pinter

Zhang, D. (2020). Towards a Discourse Semantic Characterisation of the Modal Particles in Khorchin Mongolian: A Case Study of an Interaction. *Journal of Pragmatics*, *158*, 13–32. DOI: https://doi.org/10.1016/j.pragma.2019.12.013.

Index

Adjunct, 162
  Comment, 19
  Modal, 104
agnation, 4, 5, 6, 73, 96, 106, 258
  agnate, 192
  enation, 4, 5, 106
APPRAISAL, 13, 19, 99, 160, 165
arguability, 37, 39
ASSESSMENT, 130, 160, 185
ATTITUDE, 19
axis, 2, 15, 67
  axial, 3, 191
  axial reasoning, 3, 5, 191
  paradigm, 2, 5, 15, 164, 242, 253
  syntagm, 3, 5, 15, 56, 74, 164, 253
  system and structure, 2, 96

Bakhtin, M., 147
Benveniste, É., 34
Brazilian Portuguese, 43, 146
British Sign Language, 228

challenging, 16
Classical Tibetan, 125
clitic, 51, 106, 179
  assessment clitics, 133
  enclitic particles, 130
  mood clitic, 262
  pre-enclitic, 131, 134, 150
  pronominal clitic, 48, 132
cohortative, 270
constructed action, 241
context, 21, 24, 86, 98, 145, 216, 229
  genre, 21, 149
  register, 21, 98, 149
    field, 21, 98, 149
    mode, 21, 98
    tenor, 21, 24, 98, 149
Conversation Analysis, 19, 26, 98, 159
co-text, 23, 87, 136, 216

cryptotype, 5, 107, 122
  phenotype, 107
  reactance, 4, 107

deaf, 228

echo question, 17
ENGAGEMENT, 19, 99, 130, 147, 160, 165, 184, 274
English, 4, 35, 171, 189, 203, 281
exchange
  action
    Da1, 15, 17, 75, 99, 166, 268
    immediate compliance, 73
    primary actor, 14, 98, 104, 194
    prospective compliance, 73
    secondary actor, 14, 99
  challenging (ch), 13, 16, 98, 166, 206
  confirmation request (cf), 17
  knowledge, 70, 75, 99, 236
    Dk1, 71, 99, 167
    primary knower, 14, 70, 99, 161, 194, 267
    secondary knower, 14, 70, 99, 161, 267
    secondary knower initiation, 71
  response to confirmation request (rcf), 17
  tracking (tr), 13, 98, 196, 206
eyebrows, 235

Finite, 39, 40, 52, 53, 209, 211, 263
  Tagfinite, 211
finiteness, 56, 57
PERSON, 48, 75, 99, 171, 174, 205, 209
POLARITY, 48
TENSE, 26, 48, 75, 161, 162, 209
FORCE, 166, 209
French, 41, 131

Gleason, H. A., 4, 192

Halliday, M. A. K., 18, 35
head nod, 241
headshake, 246

285

imperative, 74, 84, 91, 104, 160, 173
  hortative, 171, 206
  interactant
    speaker exclusive, 85
    speaker inclusive, 85
  jussive, 108, 172, 206
    request, 261
  non-interactant, 88, 91
  optative, 108, 171, 182
indicative, 74, 160
  addressee-oriented, 113
  declarative, 137, 165
  interrogative
    elemental, 78, 165, 267
      solicit circumstance, 81
      solicit participant, 81
      solicit process, 81
    polar interrogative, 79, 165
    verbal predication, 77
Inquirer, 79, 81, 112, 201, 209, 241, 267
intonation, 3, 5, 51, 164, 207, 229, 265
  rhythm, 5

Khorchin Mongolian, 64, 125, 282
Korean, 8, 9

langue, 34

Mandarin, 79, 80, 189
manual, 229
  non-manual, 229
manual sign, 230
metafunction, 11, 13, 22, 81, 164
  ideational
    experiential, 19, 79, 230
  interpersonal, 10, 35, 43, 236
  textual, 253
MODAL RESPONSIBILITY, 39, 40, 171, 175
  modally responsible, 48, 85
MODALITY, 3, 75, 229
Moderator, 107, 109
MOOD
  assertive, 276
  non-assertive, 276

negotiability, 42, 173, 187
NEGOTIATION, 3, 13, 96, 98, 194, 258
Negotiator, 42, 43, 51, 54, 266, 267
negotiatory structure, 40
non-manual, 229

particle, 75, 108, 109, 202
POLARITY, 48, 75
POLITENESS, 216, 248
pose, 122

Positioner, 78, 202, 217
Predicator, 39, 51, 53, 76, 84, 104, 105, 106,
    109, 204, 240, 263, 270
Priscian (Priscianus Caesariensis), 57
Prohibitive, 270
proposal, 37
  command, 163, 166, 187
  offer, 15, 154, 163, 166, 179
proposals, 14
proposition, 37, 115
  question, 163
  statement, 163
propositions, 14

rank, 6, 13, 21, 98, 104,
    164, 259
RELATIVE TENSE, 75
Remainder, 42

shunting, 21, 258
sign, 228, 229
Spanish, 10, 75, 131, 189, 203, 242
spatio-kinetic, 229, 232
SPEECH FUNCTION, 3, 15, 18, 36, 98, 160
  COMMODITY, 18, 36, 163
    goods-and-services, 18, 98, 163
    information, 3, 14, 18, 36, 70, 75, 98, 99,
      101, 163, 258
  ROLE, 36, 56, 71, 166
    demanding, 18, 36, 98, 163
    giving, 15, 18, 36, 98, 163
  tender, 122
tenor, 21, 24, 98, 149
stratification, 12
Subject, 39, 40, 109, 206, 213
syntagm, 3
system of MOOD, 37, 64, 98, 99, 242

Tagalog, 10, 203
TAGGING, 143, 211
  tag, 111, 183, 264
  Tagfinite, 211
Theme, 109, 132, 205, 235, 252, 267, 274
TONE, 160, 161, 186
  tone group, 161, 207
Tracking, 16
trinocular perspective
  from above, 3, 21, 23, 35, 38, 43, 68, 96,
    191, 200
  from below, 5, 21, 96, 112, 192, 200
  from roundabout, 4, 23, 96, 192
typology, 10, 26, 35, 37, 41, 225

verbal group
  elaborated, 75

finite, 48, 169
first person, 205
restricted, 75, 84
second person, 75, 104, 205
third person, 105

Vietnamese, 125
visual prosody, 242
visual-spatial modality, 228, 229

Whorf, B. L., 3, 4, 107

CPSIA information can be obtained
at www.ICGtesting.com
Printed in the USA
LVHW080920030821
694401LV00004B/314